# THE
# MARINER'S CATALOG

*A Book of Information for those Concerned with Boats and the Sea*

PUBLISHED JOINTLY BY NATIONAL FISHERMAN
AND INTERNATIONAL MARINE PUBLISHING CO.
CAMDEN, MAINE

DISTRIBUTED BY FUNK AND WAGNALLS PUBLISHING COMPANY
666 FIFTH AVENUE
NEW YORK, N.Y.

# Introduction

By David R. Getchell

This book is an experiment; not an untried one, but an experiment nevertheless. While we call it a catalog, which it is in a sense, we believe it can be described best as a book of information. The subject matter is specifically collected for the mariner, both pleasure and commercial, and for others who are interested in the sea and the activities connected with it. Boats, gear, fish and the special methods associated with them are the bread and butter of our pages.

The difference from other books — the experiment, so to speak — is the personal involvement of the reader. "The Mariner's Catalog" is basically a book of experiences: those of its contributors, those of the authors of the many fascinating books described and, hopefully, those of you who are reading this book. This catalog is for people who want to draw the most from their experience with the sea, who are looking for the right way to do things, the best way to buy, and the right place to find what they need.

But "The Mariner's Catalog" is not a buyer's guide, for its listings are in no way complete. In fact, many of the

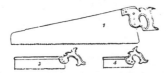

items described here simply won't be found in any guide because the demand for their special qualities is so small there is little economic sense in listing them. After all, in our world of plastic-packed tools and fittings, who needs a ship's carpenter's adze, an oil-drum stove, a wood rowboat or a one-lunger engine? Who needs to know how to make tallow, salt-down beef, make a greenheart deadeye or splice a half-inch cable? Not many people do, but some need these things. And they will find out about them in the pages that follow.

The beginnings of "The Mariner's Catalog" go back a year or more to the intentional ending of the spectacularly successful "Whole Earth Catalog," a big soft-cover book loaded with information and sources of tools and materials of use to individuals hopeful of making their way along other than "Establishment" roads. The WEC's principal claim was as an "Access to Tools" and it was this theme which generated the original spark for "The

Mariner's Catalog." But where WEC's aim was general, ours is specific — a service for mariners.

During the past 25 years, the marine scene in the United States has changed from what was a relatively small world of interest for a group of people who either made their living from the water or enjoyed being on it in an infinite variety of pleasure craft, to what is today a far larger marine world dominated by big boat manufacturers, by increasingly powerful regulatory agencies and by advertising people with little or no understanding of maritime history or tradition. Many view this changing marine world as progressive; we view it with considerable skepticism, seeing some gains but an equal or greater number of losses.

Superficially, we can see the degeneration of the language: "boaters" used to be straw hats, but are now boatmen; "salons" used to be beauty parlors, but are now the main cabins of yachts, instead of saloons; "flybridge" has replaced the beautiful term, flying bridge, and so on. More deeply, the American automobile mentality has become dominant in the marine field, in design, love of speed for speed's sake, in plastic isolation from one's immediate environment and even in traffic patterns. Sailing is thought of first in terms of racing, a perfectly acceptable pastime, except that advertising has fostered the belief that every boat must have a low racing handicap. In the commercial fields of fishing and workboats, there is a steady drift toward corporate operations, and the little guy is given short shrift both in regulatory planning and the market place. In brief, the marine experience, whether by design or ignorance — it makes no difference — is being taken from the hands of the individual to be carefully planned instead in board rooms far removed from salt spray.

But no world or organization is perfect; all have gaps and hiatuses. Within the maritime world is a hard core of traditionalists who remain that way not out of stubbornness but because of an awareness that much of what was learned and developed in the past had good purpose and has not been improved upon. High among

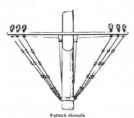

Futtock-shrouds.

these traditions is that of independence, based on a desire for freedom that only the sea, deserts, deep jungles, and high mountains can engender. And this hard core of independents is growing as more and more people pause to ask themselves if present directions are, in truth, "progressive."

A mark of these individuals is their desire to be able to go it alone — to ponder, plan, and build their own lives and means of satisfaction. "The Mariner's Catalog" is meant to be their book, an access to sources of information and tools they can find nowhere else. Our editors and contributors believe as do these independents, and our major purpose in preparing this catalog is to create a means of sharing what has heretofore been an almost impossibly scattered fund of valuable information.

This first catalog (and we hope there will be more, but

## The Mariner's Catalog

A book of information for those concerned with boats and the sea.

Editorial staff: Editor, David R. Getchell; Associate Editors, Peter H. Spectre and George Putz.

Published by International Marine Publishing Co. and National Fisherman, Camden, Me. 04843.

Address all correspondence to The Mariner's Catalog, Camden, Me. 04843.

Copyright© 1973 by International Marine Publishing Co.

Library of Congress Catalog Card No. 73-88647
International Standard Book No. 0-87742-038-6
Fifth Printing, 1976

that future depends entirely upon your response to this one) is primarily the work of three persons. The bulk of the material is the direct result of the efforts of Associate Editors George Putz and Peter Spectre. George is a competent anthropologist "retired" to an operating salt water farm on the magnificent island of Vinalhaven at the mouth of Maine's Penobscot Bay. George did much of the research into sources and a good deal of the writing in the catalog. You will see his byline and "GP" throughout the book. Pete Spectre organized the book review sections of the catalog and his "PHS" after many of the reviews assures you of an honest appraisal. Pete's business is books, since he is an editor with International Marine Publishing Co., co-publisher of this catalog. General collation and organization of the catalog itself was done by the writer, Dave Getchell ("DRG"), who has edited the marine newspaper "National Fisherman" since 1959. The three of us are ardent small boat men.

Naturally, in our initial effort, we have drawn upon sources and contributors with which we are familiar. George has consulted his many marine friends and acquaintances for sources; Pete has drawn upon the extensive resources of International Marine and its many writers; while I have turned to long-time friends and contributors to the "National Fisherman," such as Technical Editor John Gardner, boatbuilder and designer Pete Culler, eminent maritime historian Howard Chapelle, writers Mark White, Frank Daignault, NF editors Nim Marsh and Burt Coffey, naval architect Ted Brewer, and many others.

With the publication of this first issue, we now look to and encourage contributions of sources and information from our readers. Items, articles, photos, sketches, pages from books and catalogs — we can use them all. Identification of material, with addresses, is an absolute necessity. Just send it to "The Mariner's Catalog," Camden, Me. 04843. We'll pay for everything used in future "Mariner's Catalogs" and attempt to acknowledge receipt of all material although the latter may take time. If you wish any material returned, postage and self-addressed envelope should be enclosed.

George Putz offers the following thoughts on the catalog:

This is only a beginning, not a final product.

(a) There are many holes. It must be added to.

(b) It is not perfect. It must be corrected and constantly reviewed.

(c) Participate, suggest, and evaluate not only things,

persons, and firms listed, but also the catalog's evaluations.

Remember that evaluations are written by individuals who vary in their abilities, standards of fairness, accuracy and style. One evaluation of a product or service, then, is not enough, even if it comes from a recognized or famous authority. If you have a bone to pick or promote, do it. This is a user's book, not a commercial sheet or ego-trip.

There is a lot of stuff in this catalog. Most all of it is fun to dream and think about, and some of it is nice to use and own. There are perhaps a dozen men in the western world who could, if they wanted to, get it all. We suggest, then, the power of restraint in sending inquiries to the people listed in this book. Not one firm or person listed here

### A Word on the Books

Books are the world's greatest source of information and thus many are listed in the catalog. International Marine Publishing Co. publishes or sells, or both, many of the titles reviewed. These are marked with a small circled star ⊛ and can be obtained directly from IM. Of course, we'll be happiest if you buy from us, but all books in print are available through your favorite book store or from the publishers. International Marine will send a free listing of its 400 marine books and 100 marine prints for the asking.

asked to be listed. They were chosen because the editors thought that their product, service or title belonged in the catalog. Quite a few of those listed are very small, specialized, or otherwise limited individuals or shops, and having to respond to a sudden ocean of idle inquiries would be both burdensome and expensive for them. We like what these people and firms are doing and we want them to continue doing their thing happily and presumably, profitably. So courtesy is important. Be sure to represent yourself accurately as to your intent and level of interest when making inquiries, and try not to balk at paying the prices of catalogs. If you are at all familiar with today's costs of printing, you know that industrial and merchandizing catalogs represent the best in-print deals going.

Up until the minute this catalog hit the sales stands it belonged to the editors. Now it belongs to you. In your head right now is something the rest of us don't know about. Somewhere near you is pencil and paper.

Cuttle-fish Bone.

3

## Table of Contents

# Commercial Fishing

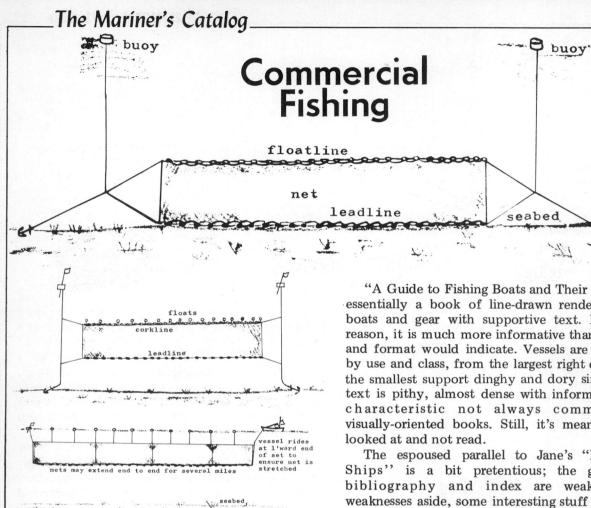

buoy

buoy

floatline

net

leadline

seabed

floats

corkline

leadline

vessel rides
at l'ward end
of set to
ensure net is
stretched

nets may extend end to end for several miles

seabed

"Top: bottom gillnets. Middle: midwater
gillnet. Bottom: Driftnet: from
"Commercial Fishing Methods""

4

* "Fish Catching Methods of the World" by A. von Brandt,
Fishing News (Books), London, $11.

* "A Guide to Fishing Boats and Their Gear"
by C.H. Hall and W.D. Ansel,
Cornell Maritime Press, Cambridge, Md. $5.

* "Commercial Fishing Methods" by J.C. Sainsbury,
Fishing News (Books), London, $10.95.

One man's reference is another man's coffee table, night stand or bathroom book. These three books are good examples of all three. Von Brandt's "Fish Catching Methods of the World" is an especially informative, broad-ranging and delightfully written work that literally covers the world's fishing methods from catching by hand through lining, spearing, blasting, lighting, making attractive sounds, all manner of netting (including spider webs!) to the most modern giant factoryship trawling. The general reader will probably turn to this one on his shelves more than other books on other subjects similarly covered. The fisherman is bound to get ideas from it and its appendixes, extensive bibliography, thorough index and geography make it a lasting solid value.

"A Guide to Fishing Boats and Their Gear" is essentially a book of line-drawn renderings of boats and gear with supportive text. For this reason, it is much more informative than its size and format would indicate. Vessels are covered by use and class, from the largest right down to the smallest support dinghy and dory sizes. The text is pithy, almost dense with information, a characteristic not always common to visually-oriented books. Still, it's meant to be looked at and not read.

The espoused parallel to Jane's "Fighting Ships" is a bit pretentious; the glossary, bibliography and index are weak. Such weaknesses aside, some interesting stuff emerges from this book. Did you know that there are Japanese purse seines 8500' long and 1000' deep? Wouldn't that be a handful from a dory! Did you know that Japan has more than 700 vessels with an average length of 175' cruising off the west coast of Canada and the U.S.?

Several times I have suggested to local fishermen that they could cut back their gear and reduce overhead by going back to sail. Naturally, this brings derision if not contempt. It turns out that China has the third-largest fishery in the world (after Peru and Japan), much of it based on sail and oars. Did you know that Peru has the world's largest fishery, based on anchovy and that they grind almost all of it up into fish meal used mostly for cattle food? Ah well, the big fish eat the little fish (?).

"Commercial Fishing Methods" has more or less the same subject and organization as the former book, but is much more technical, precise, expanded and useful. It is a book for the professional fisherman and others who really need to know how things work. It favors detailed diagrams and photographs over drawn renderings and is altogether a better book. Systematically organized, it takes the reader through towed and dragged gear, encircling gear,

*Contd. on next page*

Netherlands
Mussel
Dredge

_Contd. from preceding page_

From "A Guide to Fishing Boats
and Their Gear"

static set gear and mobil gear (harpoons, rod &
line, etc.). Each method is reviewed for its target
fish, waters, vessels, operations, crew
requirements, equipment, efficiency and
comparative advantages. As a new reader in the
fisheries field, I have found a few books more
interesting than this one, but none so generally
informative.

—GP

Codfish, p. 247.

⊛ "Inshore Fishing" by S. Judd,
Fishing News (Books), London, $7.95.
⊛ "Seafood Fishing" by R.C. O'Farrell,
Fishing News (Books), London, $7.95.

Books written by and for an industry and
which assume that you want to know something
about it and that it knows what is best about
itself are, naturally, very deductive in nature.
They place principles, rules, procedures and the
like well ahead of experiences. In the case of
fishing industry books, the fisherman himself is
seen and treated as a piece of the gear required,
an important piece, but just a piece nevertheless.

It is pleasant, therefore, to find a couple of
inductive books in the industry which place real
live experiences over the principles. Many
professionals would argue that such an approach
makes a work less valuable because a man's
individual experience is too unique to be of
universal value, that an experiential book is OK
for the pleasure fisherman but not the pro. This
is a common feeling in all professions among
professionals.

The foolishness of this position is that there
is no such thing as a general case in real life. One
is either here or there in this boat or that, with
specific pieces of gear in highly local conditions.

For this reason it is refreshing to get hold of a
fishing book that not only comes out of
experience, but is about experiences as a
fisherman. The results are not provincial at all.
Indeed, the inductive approach yields details
that are far more clearly described than any of
the general handbooks or "how-to" works, and
you get stories and anecdotes too.

These two books are like that, very
informative but also with flesh and blood. They
are autobiographical works by fishermen; how
they got into it, why, their early teachers and
foibles, their lives, ending in solid assuring
conclusions. The reader begins with a story and
ends with cohesive, clear lessons in how you and
I could actually get off our duffs and go fishing
for a living or, at least, a life. I don't care how
"professional" your standards are, you cannot
do better than that!

These two books are very similar in approach.
They differ to the extent that the men differ.
Judd is pragmatic, likes finfish more than
crustaceans and so spends more time on lines
and nets than on traps and pots. O'Farrell is
more experimental, primarily a lobsterman and
likes to travel and do research on alternative
methods of the trade and he takes an
investigative journey up the west coast of
Ireland. Judd is strong on the people end of it;
marketing, disputes that arise among fishermen
and the advantages of and blocks to the
development of cooperatives among fishermen.
O'Farrell likes the gear and fish themselves,
studies their life-cycles, baits, special problems
and is much more detailed about how fisheries
differ one from another. Judd has a section on
net repair that is better than books exclusively
about netting that I have seen. O'Farrell has a
guaranteed recipe for Irish Whiskey. Both books
would make good gifts to fishermen.

—GP

5

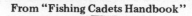

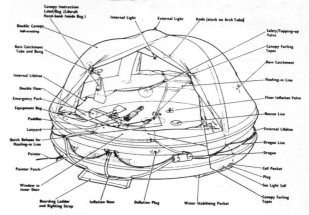

Ichthyosaurus.

● "The Fishing Cadet's Handbook" by A. Hodson, Fishing News (Books), London, $4.95.
● "Trawlermen's Handbook," Hull Steam Trawler's Mutual Insurance and Protecting Co. Ltd., Fishing News (Books), $7.

Show me a country's (blank) and I'll tell you much of the rest of it. All kinds of things can fill the blank, depending on who is saying it. It goes, therefore, to show much of the person who's asking. Tell a country what blank you wish to see and it will tell much of the rest of you. Show me a country's handbooks.

These are two English handbooks about fishing. They are excellent, clearly-written and solidly grounded in decades of modern fisheries practice and are highly recommended to the bigboat fishermen of any country.

They are English. Hodson is an old Grimsby skipper and his book possesses that certain patriarchal quality of good faith among working men who know who they are, what is to be done and how. It is essentially a list of what things are, why and how they are used. Unlike many handbooks from other countries, including ours, it is not a negative book, a list of "don'ts." It begins, not ends, with an illustrated glossary and the tone from beginning to end is more like a sports manual for enthusiasts rather than a handbook for beginners in a complicated and dangerous working occupation.

Different seine and trawl types, techniques and procedures are compared and illustrated with the cadet (beginner) in mind. The description of how fish are handled after they are caught, both above and below decks, is interesting and points up the value of handbooks over "information" books because so many of the latter pass over this subject for some reason. There is a unique section on the boiling of fish livers for their oil. There is a good safety chapter, of course, but an especially interesting one for its description of how to work with helicopters in sea rescue operations. Signals, gear repairs, clothing, sea law, weather and eating habits are also discussed.

The "Trawlermen's Handbook" is an advanced Hodson. The same subjects are covered but in much more detail and, in addition, pilotage, navigation and aids-to-navigation, electronic gear, ship-loading and stability theory, weight and strength of cables, ropes and lines,

A Razor-clam (Ensis americana).

6

Fig. 22. Detailed drawing of an RFD inflatable life-raft.

steering characteristics of ships and rules of salvage are covered. The most interesting instructions as to how to find your way about the shores of Iceland in case of stranding will perhaps be less valuable to the English trawlerman if Iceland's recent 50-mile limit declaration is made to stick. I cannot imagine a discussion of modern liferaft operation and conduct being more comprehensive than the one here.

The tone of these two books is different enough to justify owning both. But obviously the "Trawlermen's Handbook" is the kingspoke and, I would guess, one of the most important works in the field anywhere in print. —GP

From "Trawlermen's Handbook"

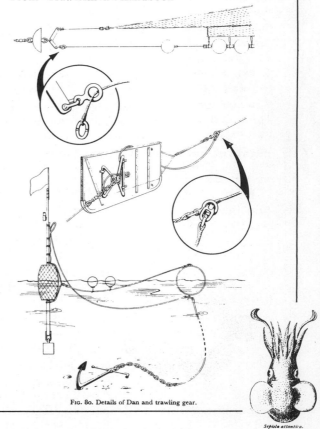

Fig. 80. Details of Dan and trawling gear.

Sepiola atlantica.

### Professional Fisherman Supply Houses

If it is your impression that the cost-inflation of pleasure boating equipment and work boat equipment is much greater than that for the rest of the economy generally you are correct, very correct. Yachtsmen aren't the only ones being exploited. The small isolated professional fisherman is getting it just as badly as the amateur.

It was February when I received several of these pro supply house catalogs, a time of year when fishing is slack here on the coast of Maine and a lot of the men are broke. Some fishermen dropped by one Sunday afternoon to jaw and bend an elbow. I passed around the catalogs to get their reactions and they couldn't believe it. They had thought they were getting a good price from local chandlers because it was half what the summer crowd was paying. When they saw what was available elsewhere and for what prices, they were "some pissed!"

To be sure, as an amateur or small operator you won't want 10,000 No. 6 Mustad hooks (for $4.03/1000!) or 600 fathoms of seine twine or 1000 floats and 5,000 leads, but I bet that PVC-lined knee boots for $3.99 a pair or men's insulated chest waders for $12.69 a set or a complete storm suit for $1.89 will get to you! You want netting to decorate the partyroom or cottage in any of a dozen different weaves? Landing nets? Wire baskets? Line and rope at rock-bottom prices?

It is important not to close these valuable sources off by poor communications and nickel-diming these people. They are used to working in bulk-orders and it is bulk-ordering that makes these prices possible. When you can, get together with others (clubs, etc.) on your orders and be sure that all is clear and correct so that you don't have to bug these companies the way you might your local over-the-counter house.

—GP

Nylon Net Company
7 Vance Ave.
P.O. Box 592
Memphis, Tenn. 38101

## EGG SINKERS
### Packaged 5 lbs. to cloth bag

Smooth oval shape with hole through center for line.

| SIZE | PRICE PER 5 LB. BAG |
|---|---|
| 1/8 oz. 1/4 oz. 1/2-3/4-1-1 1/2 oz. 2-3-4-6-8 oz. | $3.65 |

## BANK SINKERS
### Packaged 5 lbs. to cloth bag

The most universally used style sinker. Complete range of sizes for fresh water casting, up to deep-sea bottom fishing.

| SIZE | PRICE PER 5 LB. BAG |
|---|---|
| 1/2-3/4-1-1 1/2 oz. 2-3-4-6-8 oz. | $3.70 |

## DIPSEY
### SWIVEL SINKERS

STOCK SIZES

| STOCK # | PRICE PER BOX OF 36 |
|---|---|
| DS-10 | 73¢ Box |
| DS-9 | 87¢ Box |
| DS-8 | 99¢ Box |
| DS-7 | $1.16 Box |
| DS-5 | $1.68 Box |
| DS-4 | $2.36 Box |
| DS-2 | $4.45 Box |
| DS-1 | $1.70 Box of 12 |

## PINCH-ON
### SINKERS

STOCK SIZES

| STOCK # | PRICE PER GROSS |
|---|---|
| PO-0 | $1.16 Gross |
| PO-1 | $1.28 Gross |
| PO-2 | $1.46 Gross |
| PO-3 | $1.79 Gross |
| PO-4 | $2.11 Gross |
| PO-5 | $2.72 Gross |
| PO-7 | $4.18 Gross |
| PO-8 | $4.62 Gross |

## REMOVABLE SPLIT SHOT

BB  3/0  7  5  4  3

STOCK SIZES

SQUEEZES ON WITH YOUR FINGERS NO TOOLS NEEDED

| SIZE | SHOT IN EACH BOX | PRICE |
|---|---|---|
| BSS BB | 15 | |
| BSS 3/0 | 10 | |
| BSS 7 | 8 | $1.43 Per Carton (Of a Size) PACKED 12 BOXES PER CARTON |
| BSS 5 | 6 | |
| BSS 4 | 5 | |
| BSS 3 | 4 | |

**NYLON NET COMPANY**

### A Word For The Fish

"The importance of salmon and steelheads in our outdoor life as well as in commerce is so important that there certainly comes a time when their destruction might necessitate a halt in so-called 'improvement' or 'development' of waterways."

—Justice William O. Douglas

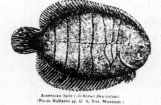

American Sole (*Achirus fasciatus*).
(From Bulletin 47, U. S. Nat. Museum.)

Rock-crab (*Cancer irroratus*).

7

# SMALL MESH NYLON READY MADE SEINES

Commercial fishing and fish farming supplies in wide variety and at relatively low prices are available from Sterling Marine Products. Fyke nets, gill nets, seines, trawls of all kinds, traps, umbrella nets, turtle nets and custom experimental trawls are only some of the products of this firm. Excellent catalog is free.

—DRG

**Sterling Marine Products**
**7 Oak Place**
**Montclair, N.J. 07042**

Complete Hand Hung Seines, complete with floats, float line, leads and lead line, ready to fish, ideal for minnows, catfish, crayfish, karp, etc.

| Material Style | Square Mesh | Price Per Running Foot | | | |
|---|---|---|---|---|---|
| | | 4 Ft. Deep | 6 Ft. Deep | 8 Ft. Deep | 10 Ft. Deep |
| REGENT | 1/8" | $1.04 | $1.44 | $1.84 | $2.24 |
| | 3/16" | .93 | 1.30 | 1.60 | 1.90 |
| | 1/4" | .74 | .99 | 1.23 | 1.47 |
| GEE BEE | 1/32" | 1.33 | 1.79 | 2.15 | 2.48 |
| ACE | 1/16" | 1.29 | 1.71 | 2.09 | 2.42 |
| | 1/8" | 1.04 | 1.44 | 1.81 | 2.21 |
| | 3/16" | .88 | 1.14 | 1.45 | 1.75 |
| | 1/4" | .79 | 1.00 | 1.14 | 1.28 |
| DELTA | 1/8" | 1.28 | 1.74 | 2.21 | 2.75 |
| | 3/16" | 1.01 | 1.36 | 1.72 | 2.08 |
| | 1/4" | .91 | 1.14 | 1.45 | 1.74 |
| | 5/16" | .88 | 1.07 | 1.37 | 1.66 |
| ATLAS | 3/16" | 1.21 | 1.56 | 1.94 | 2.30 |
| | 1/4" | .99 | 1.21 | 1.52 | 1.81 |
| | 5/16" | .94 | 1.14 | 1.49 | 1.79 |

**Tarred Seines:** Add 10%
**Tapered Seines:** Add 10% — state measurements required.
**Less Than 10 Feet:** Add 15%
Seines are complete with top and bottom lines, leads, floats — ready to fish — top and bottom lines — 460 lb. test nylon rope.
**Heavier Ropes** are recommended for seins over 50 feet and are available at the following upcharges.     (600 lb. test rope: Add .04¢ per foot)
(1000 lb. test rope: Add .07¢ per foot) (1750 lb. test rope: Add .10¢ per foot)

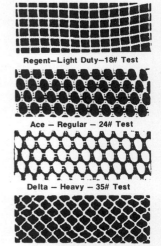

Regent—Light Duty—18# Test

Ace — Regular — 24# Test

Delta — Heavy — 35# Test

Atlas—Extra Heavy—48# Test

Ordering Procedure
1. Material Style
2. Square Mesh Size
3. Length x Depth
4. Special Requirements

From Sterling catalog

---

**From "Fishermen's Knots and Nets"**

On the rod set up a row of half meshes, using the mesh stick to regulate size and attaching with clove hitches or cow hitches (Fig. 8). Although the meshes on the rod are shown spread out, and this is advisable for practice, it is more usual in production to have them quite close. As the work proceeds, allow the meshes to pass along the gauge (Fig. 9A). A dozen will be enough for the practice net. Have the net with the working end on the left. Put the mesh stick against the bottom of the first mesh and take

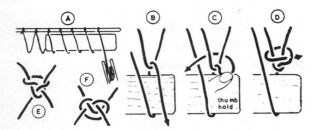

FIG. 9.—Steps in forming a mesh

the needle of line behind the mesh stick, through the loop and downwards (Fig. 9B). Hold with the left thumb and pass the needle behind the mesh (Fig. 9c). Bring it across the front and under the earlier part of the line (Fig. 9D). Pull the knot tight without distorting it (Fig. 9E) and the end will be in position to make the next mesh. If the knot is allowed to fall out of shape as it is tightened it will slide on the upper mesh and is useless (Fig. 9F).

☸ **"Fishermen's Knots and Nets,"** by R. Graumont and E. Wenstrom,
Cornell Maritime Press, Cambridge, Md. $4.
☸ **"Netmaking,"** by P.W. Blandford, Brown, Son and Ferguson,
Glasgow, Scotland, $2.25.

There has been a bushel of knot and net books over the years. For some reason, old ones are not reprinted. New ones come out and they are not any better than older out-of-print titles and, sometimes, they are considerably worse. Basically, there are two kinds; the this-is-how-you-do-it books that use **diagrams** and the this-is-the-way-it-is-supposed-to-look books that use **photographs**; the old inductive-deductive bit. These books are fair values, I suppose, especially the Blandford piece because of its uniqueness in a currently netbookless market. Next to Cornell's old "Encyclopedia of Knots and Fancy Rope Work," the giant inspiration of "Fisherman's Knots and Nets," the latter does not hold a candle. This is not to say that it is bad. In fact, it's good and real handy, but how many books on knots are you going to buy?

About fishing books generally, it seems to me that what applies to nautical book collections generally, applies specifically to fishing books. That is, just because one or two books can save you trouble and time, there is very little evidence that lots of books will do it for you altogether.

—GP

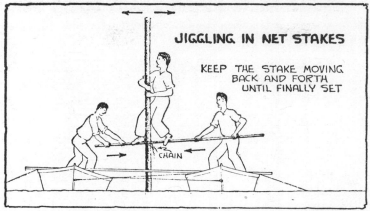

JIGGLING IN NET STAKES

KEEP THE STAKE MOVING
BACK AND FORTH
UNTIL FINALLY SET

CHAIN

This Tidewater Virginia method of getting in net stakes is simple; yet, quite heavy stakes and even light pound poles are driven in this way.

The two skiffs should be lashed together but held apart by a couple of planks secured across their gunwales. Then the positioning of the rig controlled with a couple of light anchors.

The steadying pole is secured well up on the upended stake by a loop of chain clamped or knotted there with the one end of the pole held well up. Lowering it then pulls the loop tight. The heaviest man of the three mounts the pole while the other two use it to steady the stake.

It is a matter of "jiggling" the pole back and forth while the man aloft jumps up and down and otherwise uses his weight to best effect. The trick seems to be not to stop the jiggling so long as the stake is still going down.

—Jim Emmett

Salmon *(Salmo salar)*.

The Sea Grant program, by which federal funding is used to support marine-oriented studies in colleges and universities similar in concept to the Land Grant program that has meant so much to U. S. agriculture, is beginning to produce many practical results for fishermen and boatmen along with a new flood of scientific data. Information on gear and methods development of interest to fishermen and seafood processors is available in a number of Sea Grant publications which are usually available from the institutions where the original work was done. An 8-page monthly leaflet on the latest news and publications in the Sea Grant field can be had by writing to Sea Grant College Program, Texas A&M University, College Station, Tex. 77843, and asking to be placed on the mailing list of "Sea Grant 70s."

Some of the Sea Grant schools have their own publications prepared especially for commercial fishing readers. Especially good are the "URI Commercial Fisheries Newsletter," published by the University of Rhode Island at Kingston 02881; "Texas Trawler," published by Texas A & M and available from: Ranzell Nickelson II, Seafood Technology Specialist, Faculty Mail Service Box 155, College Station, Tex. 77843; and the periodic Sea Grant newsletter from the University of Oregon at Corvallis.

—DRG

The 10 best books of the sea as determined by poll at the National Marine Exposition in New York, 1920:

1. "Treasure Island," Stevenson
2. "Two Years before the Mast," Dana
3. "The Sea Wolf," London
4. "Captains Courageous," Kipling
5. "Twenty Thousand Leagues Under The Sea," Verne
6. "Cruise of the Cachalot," Bullen
7. "Under Sail," Riesenberg
8. "Mr. Midshipman Easy," Marryat
9. "Lord Jim," Conrad
10. "The Nigger of the Narcissus," Conrad

You might (probably do) disagree. Send in your top ten, and if the response is good enough we will publish the results in a later issue of the Catalog. Here's how we'll keep score: Your number 1 choice will be awarded 10 points, your number 2 will get 9 points, your number 3 will get 8 points, etc. The book with the most total points will then make the top of the top ten, the runner-up will be number 2, etc.

—PHS

9

DUD SINKER

"Heeeeey, one of those topless bathing suits, eh, Baby."

"The Mother Earth News"
P.O. Box 70
Hendersonville, N.C. 28739
One Year (6 issues)/$6; two years/$11.

With our emphasis on personal involvement and do-it-yourself skills, we would be remiss without a few good words for "The Mother Earth News," a bi-monthly "edited by, and for, today's turned-on people of all ages. . . Heavy emphasis is placed on alternative life styles, ecology, working with nature and doing more with less." That's how the magazine's purpose is defined and the policy is followed with little deviation.

Granted, "Mother's weight of editorial coverage leans on land-bound activities — homesteading, gardening, house-building, etc. — but there usually are one or more articles on tools, boats and other marine-related subjects. More importantly, the magazine sends one's thoughts off in fresh directions, encourages new reliance on self and fosters a feeling of community with others of like belief. That constitutes a sizable service for any one magazine — and "Mother" does it well.

—DRG

# THE MOTHER EARTH NEWS

- STEVE AND HOLLY BAER OF ZOMEWORKS
- HOW TO RAISE HOMESTEAD CAPITAL
- FARM VACATIONS: A CASH CROP
- THE GENTLE ART OF HUNKERING
- RAISE SQUABS AND GUINEAS
- HOW TO RECYCLE BARRELS
- BUILD A PRIMITIVE LOOM
- MOTHER'S ALMANAC
- A $6.00 DOME
- MINI-GARDENS
- ELDERBERRIES
- THE GOOD ACRE
- PERPETUAL MOTION
- GROW IT!: GOATS
- MAKE A SCARECROW
- A MINNESOTA HOMESTEAD
- AND MORE INSIDE!

No. 22  $1.35

A Chesapeake Bay Pungy.

# Boat Types

Spritsail-rigged Boat.

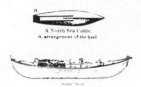

A North Sea Coble. a, arrangement of the keel.

Seine boat.

A Yawl (def 1).

A Randan-rig Thames Wherry.

A Bank-fisherman's Dory.

Umbrella-boat.

### By George Putz

*"Before you build a boat or have one built, you should own several, continue to study boats and read books . . . and keep a notebook."*

—David C. Forbes aboard
Prudence at sea, July, 1966

It begins with an idea. There are men who can go directly from an idea to a finished boat, but they are very few. Many try, of course, and add to man's great archive of minor tragedies. The conversational excerpt above is conservatism at its most appropriate and right-on best. First, YOU NEED TO OWN SEVERAL BOATS:

. . . AND CONTINUE TO STUDY BOATS: It is staggering to imagine the material that is available! Add up that accumulated from over 100 years of the boating press, journals and books, the archives of designers' estates, marine museums, the published books of plans by journals and designing firms and the plain reality of boats in commission, and you have . . . too much. We have here only the bare beginnings, a prolegomenon, as the teachers of those who invented yachting were wont to say, scratchings from corners we think interesting.

On the following pages we open a discussion of boat types; not an exclusive or exhaustive listing by any means, but a good sampling of boats owned or used by us and our correspondents. Again, we would like to hear from our readers as to their experiences with various types of small craft — both good and bad — with the hope that we can share this information in future issues of "The Mariner's Catalog."

Quite often when we have wanted specific study plans of historic yachts or working vessels we have located them through marine museums. William A. Baker, Curator of the F.R. Hart

Nautical Museum at M.I.T., sent us the following notice concerning this organization's archives:

Concerning our "comprehensive file" I can only wish that it really existed and say that, paraphrasing Mark Twain, reports concerning its extent and efficiency have been greatly overstated. The only true thing about it is that I have been clipping yachting and other marine magazines since 1923 and certain types of information seem to stick in my mind.

There is no catalogue of plans as they number over 20,000. If you will indicate your particular field of interest we will search the files and tell you what is available.

Prints from material in the museum's files are supplied at cost of reproduction (ozalid, photostat or photoprint) plus a handling charge which gives a figure of about $6 for one print, $8 for two prints, and so on. Prints are supplied subject to the following restrictions:

1. For personal study - no charge.
2. For publications in a scholarly work - no charge but we request a credit line.
3. For publication for profit - $5 per item upon publication plus a credit line.
4. For advertising - subject to negotiation.
5. For personal use in building a boat - a fee based on length overall of the boat.

The only plans that carry further restrictions are those for certain small Herreshoff-designed-and-built yachts for which the original drawings are owned by the Cape Cod Shipbuilding Co., Wareham, Mass.

Yacht designers represented in the museum's plan collections are: Arthur Binney, Edward Burgess, Clinton Crane (launches only), Nathanael Herreshoff, George Lawley & Son Corp., George Owen, and Frank Paine. The Clark Collection contains lines plans for about 50 British and American cutters, sloops and schooners of the 1850-1880 period.

William A. Baker, Curator.
Francis Russell Hart Nautical Museum
Room 5-329 M.I.T.
Cambridge, Mass. 02139

11

Dutch Galiot, with Lee-boards.

### Small Craft Types

**Canoes:**

*"Well, once again, the biggest is not the strongest."*
—Arlene Francis

There are fragments of a canoe discovered in a Swiss lake bog that are more than 23,000 years old. So long as the physical world continues to obey physical laws, a better, more practical watercraft will probably not be forthcoming. There are several small canoe and kayak companies about and we've noticed that they are not as long-lived as their boat type. Some of the more established or interesting firms are these:

The Old Town Canoe Co. has been at it for almost 100 years. They offer a very broad line of canoes and kayaks in glass or wood.

**Old Town Canoe Co.
Old Town, Maine 04468**

*18 ft.*

—Ideal for heavy loads. Long, flat floor for minimum draft. Low ends lessen effect of crosswinds. Stable, rugged, and dependable.

SPECIFICATIONS: Wood-canvas. Available with reinforced plastic—$30 extra. Stock color—Dark Green.

| Length | Width | Hgt. Bow | Depth | Wt. | Price |
|--------|-------|----------|-------|-----|-------|
| 16' | 35" | 20½" | 12" | 70 lb. | $640.00 |
| 18' | 37" | 23" | 12" | 85 lb. | $680.00 |
| 20' | 39" | 23½" | 13¼" | 100 lb. | $760.00 |

**WOOD** —Selected ⁵⁄₁₆" by 2¼" white cedar ribs (¼" thick on Lightweight) are spaced only 1½" apart to provide maximum strength. Straight grained ⁵⁄₃₂" (⅛" on Lightweight) red cedar planking smooth-laid and clinch-nailed to ribs with copper and brass fastenings. Gunwales, spruce inside, mahogany outside, left open to wash out easier. Seamless canvas is used as outside skin (Dacron on Featherweight, reinforced plastic on Trapper). Canvas is made waterproof with hard drying, flint-like filler which removes all texture. Seats are framed in ash and cane-filled. Bow seat is dropped on 4" bolts, stern seat and thwarts are bolted close to gunwales. Ash thwarts are easily removed (no middle thwart on 16' canoes). A ⅞" keel extends the full length of bottom on all models for directional stability. Some white water canoeists prefer canoe with no keel (omitted if specified on special order). Straight grained ash decks (16") and stems. The famous Old Town finish is achieved with three coats of waterproof varnish on all exposed surfaces and special enamel applied to exterior. Custom hand-painted designs and decorations are available on special order. Aluminum stem bands add the finishing touches to this world-famous canoe.

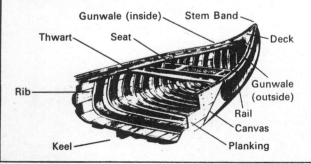

### All items from Old Town catalog.

**FIBERGLASS** —Sandwich construction begins in the mold with outside color layer. The Old Town F.G. Model is given final finish and shape at start of construction. The interior of this molded color is coated with flexible resin into which is embedded fiberglass cloth. A wooden filler piece fills molded keel depression making bottom area inside flat to receive layer of non-directional fiberglass mat. May be supplied without keel if specified with order. Over this mat is carefully placed end grain balsa core, fiberglass mat and a final inside liner of fiberglass woven roving. All layers are set in a clear resin, forming a high strength sandwich. Separate deck unit is molded which includes rails, decks and seats. Hull and deck are married with fiberglass joint. Polyurethane foam is expanded under gunwales and decks and locked in place with fiberglass cap. Attachment of chrome painter straps on decks completes your F.G. Model, a fine watercraft of great strength.

Kayak hulls are laminated of fiberglass cloth and woven polypropylene for extra strength. Decks are all fiberglass cloth. Balsa core construction is used in hulls of surfer and covered canoes. Carleton Model is constructed as the F.G., but with rigid extruded vinyl rails; acrylic/ABS decks, seats.

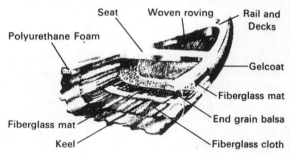

**ABS**—The most modern material for small boat construction, Old Town's special laminate of vinyl, acrylonitrile-butadiene-styrene, and foam offers ruggedness under the most adverse boating conditions, plus providing its own flotation. The raw material is produced to Old Town's rigid specifications, with the laminate components specifically located and layered to provide additional strength in the craft's hull where needed. The sheet material is heated in ovens, then placed on a vacuum-molding platform. (As sheet is heated, the core of expandable foam enlarges and will form flotation within the hull or deck of the craft itself.) The canoe or kayak is literally sucked into shape by vacuum. When cooled and removed from the mold, the excess is trimmed. Rigid vinyl rails and acrylic/ABS decks and seats form the finished craft. ABS resists corrosion. It will not flake or rust. It merely dents when hit with hard objects. Since its foamed core is closed-cellular, it will not absorb water and will float indefinitely. It has excellent sound and heat insulating qualities.

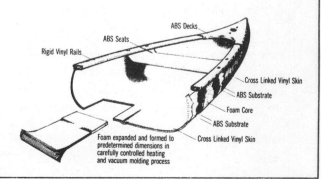

**Grumman Boats
Grumman Allied Industries Inc.
Marathon, N.Y. 13803**

"You can have your damn tin boat!" the purist said, as he again thunked the side of my little Grumman 15' Standard. As the pair of just-flushed black ducks veered over the treetops lining the river without even a parting shot being fired in their direction, I allowed as how a man had to be careful when stalking ducks in a "can," but that there were offsetting advantages. Those who have lived with aluminum canoes almost invariably come to adjust to their peculiarities, quickly learn to admire their toughness and — maybe — even come to love them.

**From the Grumman catalog.**

**CANOE GUNWALE.** Solid extrusion specially designed to accept the complete line of Grumman engineered accessories, e.g. sail rigs, motor bracket, rowing attachment, pontoons, gunwale covers. (See pages 10 and 11.) Gunwales are factory drilled to accept mast thwart of sail rig.

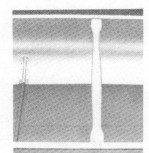

**THWART-TO-GUNWALE CONSTRUCTION.** The heavy-duty, heat-treated Grumman Canoe thwarts are fastened by stainless steel bolts to the extruded aluminum gunwales to absorb stress and shock. Close precision riveting of gunwales and location of thwarts are more reasons for Grumman's lifetime maintenance-free canoe enjoyment.

There is much to be said for a well-built boat, in any material, and the owner of a Grumman aluminum canoe soon realizes he has something special. I've used my 15-footer for just about everything but ocean voyaging — on lakes, rivers, streams, bays, tidal inlets, brooks and flooded backyards. It has carried my wife and me and a full load of camping gear down a river that was nothing more than a rushing brook in the middle of a rock pile, thanks to a tightly closed dam above. Two days and six inches of rain later, on another river, it carried my comfort-loving brother-in-law and me through heavy white water so noisy he couldn't hear my yells. We struck a boulder he never saw nearly broadside, bounced off and continued on with nothing more than a small dent.

Easily handled by one man, light enough to carry for considerable distances (a "launching ramp" can be the nearest town float), as close to maintenance free as a boat can be, this canoe may be the ultimate answer for the one-boat man. Grummans usually cost a few dollars more than other aluminum canoes, but — you're talking water-logged peanuts if you quibble. They should last at least two lifetimes.

—DRG

13

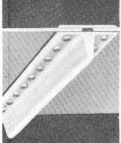

**STANDARD KEEL.** Heavy extrusion, heat-treated, full-length keel with keelson sandwich-type construction. Neoprene seal with close-spaced rivets on ⅝" centers. Built-in clips for mast step of Grumman sail rig accessory and floorboards. Construction allows quick and easy installation of accessories and maintains positive watertight seal.

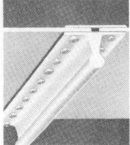

**BULB "T" KEEL.** 30% heavier than a standard keel. Specially designed for larger Grummans — 19' square stern, Sportcanoe, 20' double-end and Peace canoes. Keel is a single marine aluminum alloy extrusion which helps provide strength and rigidity for the longer length canoe and heavier loads.

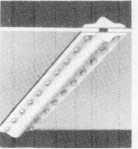

**SHALLOW-DRAFT KEEL** —sometimes called shoe keel— was designed for use in white water and for maximum maneuverability under all conditions. The ⅜" keel is made doubly strong by using the same extruded keel stock for an inner keelson. Extra ribs are added for increased strength. Available on 15', 17' and 18' standard weight canoes only.

**EXTRA RIBS IN WHITE WATER MODELS.** Two extra in the 15' model; four extra in the 17' and 18' models. Add this extra construction to a full strength standard weight Grumman with the heavy shallow-draft keel and you know why white water canoeists choose Grumman first. Extra ribs go into all square sterns and lightweight models.

From Trailcraft catalog.

Trailcraft
Box 606
Concordia, Kans. 66901

Kits for wood, fiberglass and canvas canoes seem to be rare at present. Trailcraft of Concordia, Kansas, offers six kits in four sizes, 12' to 16'. Prices seem very reasonable!

—GP

| Length | Weight | Amidship Depth | Width | Load Capacity | Cost |
|---|---|---|---|---|---|
| 12' CROSSBREED | 80 lbs. | 15" | 40" | 650 lbs. | $124.00 |
| 13½' ONE MAN KAYAK | 50 lbs. | 10" | 25" | 250 lbs. | $ 89.00 |
| 14' *TF or *TP | 70 lbs. | 12" | 32" | 750 lbs. | $134.00 |
| 16' TF or TP | 75 lbs. | 12" | 36" | 850 lbs. | $139.00 |
| 17'SS **TF or **TP | 80 lbs. | 12" | 36" | 900 lbs. | $144.00 |
| 18' TF or TP | 85 lbs. | 12" | 36" | 950 lbs. | $149.00 |

*TF refers to the TRAILFINDER with Fiberglass trim. *TP refers to the TRAILPACER with mahogany trim. **The 17' models are square sterns.

**EASIER** THAN YOU THINK TO JOIN THE FRONT & REAR SECTIONS, WITH THE WOODEN VICE GRIPS, FIG. 1. TO KEEP HULL ALIGNED WHILE YOU APPLY 3 LAYERS OF GLASS MAT TO INTERIOR SEAM. OUTSIDE SEAM IS FILLED WITH COLORED GLASS TO GIVE YOU A SEAMLESS APPEARANCE AND A **STRONG** MIDSECTION SEAM. FOUR MEN WEIGH IN EXCESS OF 750 LBS.

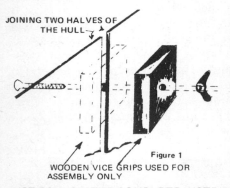

JOINING TWO HALVES OF THE HULL

Figure 1

WOODEN VICE GRIPS USED FOR ASSEMBLY ONLY

JUST FOLLOW THE COMPLETE INSTRUCTIONS WITH EACH KIT. SHIPPING CANOE KIT IN TWO NESTED HALVES SAVES OVER $100.00 IN FREIGHT COST AS COMPARED TO FULL LENGTH ONE PIECE HULLS. FULL LENGTH ONE PIECE HULLS MAY BE PICKED UP BY THE CUSTOMER AT THE FACTORY. SEE INFORMATION BELOW.

## Opposite Views

"... Western man viewed the sea as an enemy to be fought against; to be ventured upon with ships heavy and strong enough to withstand its perils. Eastern man, on the other hand, looked upon the sea without fear and skimmed on her surface in light craft ... Hence we Westerners have to reconsider altogether our feelings of what makes for safety when we go to sea in an Eastern style craft."

—Robert B. Harris in "Racing and Cruising Trimarans"

The Great Harry.

Proa.

14

From "Rushton and His Times . . ."

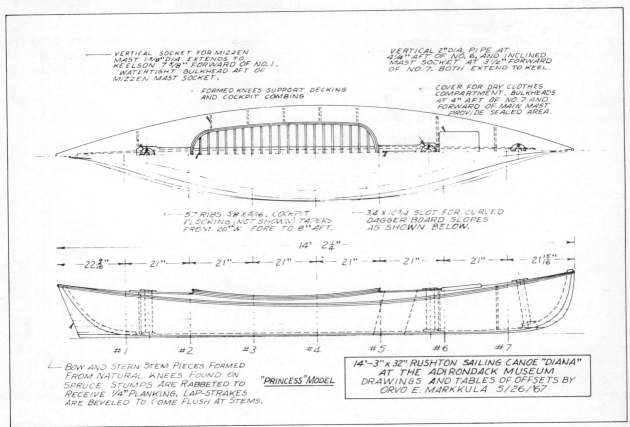

VERTICAL SOCKET FOR MIZZEN MAST 1⅜" DIA. EXTENDS TO KEELSON 7⅝" FORWARD OF NO. 1. WATERTIGHT BULKHEAD AFT OF MIZZEN MAST SOCKET.

VERTICAL 2" DIA. PIPE AT 4¼" AFT OF NO. 6, AND INCLINED MAST SOCKET AT 3½" FORWARD OF NO. 7. BOTH EXTEND TO KEEL.

FORMED KNEES SUPPORT DECKING AND COCKPIT COMBING

COVER FOR DRY CLOTHES COMPARTMENT. BULKHEADS AT 4" AFT OF NO. 7 AND FORWARD OF MAIN MAST PROVIDE SEALED AREA.

57 RIBS ⅝ X 5/16. COCKPIT FLOORING (NOT SHOWN) TAPERS FROM 20"W. FORE TO 8"AFT.

¾ X 10¾ SLOT FOR CURVED DAGGER BOARD SLOPES AS SHOWN BELOW.

14' 2¼"

—22⅝"— —21"— —21"— —21"— —21"— —21"— —21"— —21 15/16"—

#1    #2    #3    #4    #5    #6    #7

BOW AND STERN STEM PIECES FORMED FROM NATURAL KNEES FOUND ON SPRUCE STUMPS ARE RABBETED TO RECEIVE ¼" PLANKING. LAP-STRAKES ARE BEVELED TO COME FLUSH AT STEMS.

"PRINCESS" MODEL

14'-3" x 32" RUSHTON SAILING CANOE "DIANA" AT THE ADIRONDACK MUSEUM DRAWINGS AND TABLES OF OFFSETS BY ORVO E. MARKKULA 5/26/'67

---

⊙"Rushton and His Times in American Canoeing" by Atwood Manley.
Syracuse University Press, Syracuse, N.Y.
1968, 203 pp., illustrated, index, $14.

I never had much interest in canoes until I read this book. It's the type of book that is so well designed and put together that you want to look through it no matter what it's about. Then, after you read for awhile, Rushton and his expert craftmanship win you over.

At the turn of the century, Rushton was the Rolls-Royce of canoe builders. His designs and quality of workmanship played a large part in the developing interest in canoeing as a sport. This book gives you the flavor of "Rushton and his times" in a way that gives you scads of detail without boredom. The photographs and plans are excellent.

I gather from this book that canoeing in the late 1800s and early 1900s was quite a bit different from these days. The emphasis then was on cruising, both on salt and fresh water. Sailing canoes were taken seriously, and many of the real vagabonds slept aboard. Rushton during this time was to canoeing what Herreshoff was to yachting. Some of his most famous designs are spoken of with reverence by traditional canoeists: Stella Maris, Saranac Laker (an

Adirondack guideboat), Indian Girl, Arkansas Traveler, American Beauty, Rob Roy and Sairy Gamp.

Manley gives quite a few details on Rushton's building methods, which attained near-perfection. There are five appendixes with a lot of building information and line drawings for six canoes — Diana, Sairy Gamp, Nomad, Wee Lassie, Ugo and Wanderer — and one rowing boat — Saranac Laker.

—PHS

15

---

## A DIFFERENT DRUM

"It is a strange thing that, though the alphabet is taught us at a tender age, still few of us learn to read until we reach forty. At school and college he is counted best scholar who names the words 'most rapid.' Like an express train rushing down the track, the end of the run — the last page — is the object. But he who went on foot, so to say, and bathed his feet in the cool stream under the railroad bridge and sat with the haymakers at their noonday meal beside the swamp oak at the edge of the thicket, might take longer on the trip, but at the end of the book or journey he will have absorbed some lasting good from that junket."

—L. Francis Herreshoff in "How to Build H-28"

## A Real Birch Canoe!

The nostalgic reader may well be wondering whether somewhere, someone isn't still making bark canoes. We found one such craftsman in the "Whole Earth Catalog," wrote to him and sure enough, he makes them — and they are gorgeous!

Henry Vaillancourt of Greenville, New Hampshire, makes canoes by hand in the old Indian manner. He uses an axe and a crooked knife — no power tools at all — and his canoes are of two Malecite Indian styles, the "flare" and "tumblehome," as described in Adney. Woodwork for the canoes is split from white cedar or white ash logs and shaved with the crooked knife. Ribs and planking are white cedar and gunnels are cedar and ash, as are the crosspieces. The skin is white birchbark sewn with pine root. Framework is all pegged.

Were this not enough, he makes the paddles too. Again in Malecite Indian styles, made by hand in the old way, the paddle to the right in illustration has incised line decoration on the blade. The paddle grip to the immediate left of the snowshoes has bone-inlayed decoration. The snowshoes? Yup! these too are made by hand, webbed with deerskin and fine-webbed in the ancient Indian fashion.

Henry Vaillancourt is a rare breed of craftsman. Demand for his work is such that at present there is a one-year wait for your order. Not too long really. Just think, if you had ordered just a year ago, you'd be in yours now.

—GP

**16**

**Bark Canoes**
10' — $400
12' — $450
14' — $500
16' — $550
18' — $600

**25' Fur Trapper Type — $1,500**
**36' Fur Trapper type — $3,000**

**Henry Vaillancourt**
**Mill St. Box 199,**
**Greenville, N.H.**

**Paddles**

Hardwood — $40
Cedar — $25
Inlay — $15 extra

**Snowshoes**

$100

Those looking for a lightweight glass kayak or duck-boat pattern for hunting will find a good one at Hauthaway Kayaks.

Hauthaway Kayaks
640 Boston Post Rd.
Weston, Mass. 02193

**Items from Hauthaway catalog.**

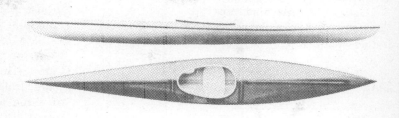

**DOWNRIVER TOURING KAYAK**  14' 8" x 24" x 11"  34 lbs.  $280.00

Large volume Swedeform hull, a fast and good tracking kayak but with some rocker for ease in maneuverability. Run between strokes makes this boat an excellent choice for extended touring, extra volume makes it a great heavy water boat. Equipped with molded seat and leg braces, five position foot brace, grab loops.

# Double Bladed Paddles

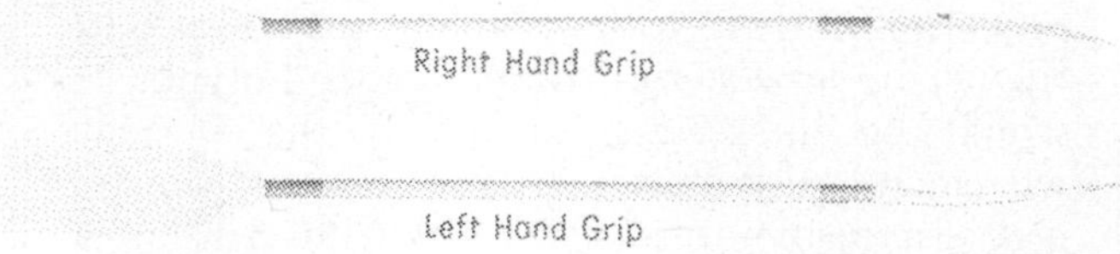

Right Hand Grip

Left Hand Grip

17

Pressure molded, white fiberglass blades, feathered at 90 degrees, with red trim at throat. One piece fir shafts, selected for grain and spline, finished with three coats of urethane varnish, hand rubbed and waxed. Blades set at 45 degrees to the grain. Spooned blades available in either right or left hand grip. Unless otherwise specified, we will supply left hand grip, if for no other reason than that is what we use ourselves.

| | Blade Area | Shaft Diam. | Weight | Lengths | Price |
|---|---|---|---|---|---|
| A. Spoon Blade | 7¾ x 19" | 1¼" | 3 lbs. | 80, 82, 84" | $29.50 |
| B. MiniSpoon Blade | 7½ x 17½" | 1³⁄₁₆" | 2¾ lbs. | 80, 82, 84" | $29.50 |
| (MiniSpoon Double Blade for Canoes) | 7½ x 17½" | 1³⁄₁₆" | 3¼ lbs. | 96, 98, 100" | $32.50 |
| C. Junior Spoon Blade | 7½ x 16½" | 1³⁄₁₆" | 2½ lbs. | 74, 76, 78" | $27.50 |
| D. Flat Blade | 9 x 19" | 1¼" | 3 lbs. | 80, 82, 84" | $28.00 |
| (Flat Double Blade for Canoes) | 9 x 19" | 1¼" | 3¼ lbs. | 96, 98, 100" | $32.50 |
| E. Junior Flat Blade | 8½ x 16½" | 1³⁄₁₆" | 2½ lbs. | 74, 76, 78" | $26.00 |

Recommended for use with 1½-2 H.P. outboard motors, but handles beautifully under oars.

Length: 9'  Beam: 40"

Weight: 55 lbs.

Colors: Duck Boat Green, White

Price: $345.00

Duck Boat

# FOLDING BOATS

Folbot Corp.
Stark Industrial Park
P.O. Box 7097
Charleston, S.C.
50-page catalog

Hans Klepper Corp.
35 Union Square West
New York, N.Y. 10003

Folding portable boats have been with us since at least the 1890s. They never really caught on for several reasons. The early golden days of, canoeing, from about 1860 to about 1925, were quite gentlemanly and one could always keep one's rigid model at the club. Later, during the early attempts at a plywood technology, the boats would simply fall apart or not go because they were designed by lubberly inventors and not boatmen.

But materials and design have improved enormously and they do catch-on locally, once one person or family gets one. They are terrific!

Two brand-name models are best-known; the domestic Folbot and the German import Klepper. Folbots are strong, good-looking and inexpensive. Kleppers are strong, elegant and more expensive. Folbot offers many models in many sizes of folding, prefab and factory-built rigid kayaks and boats. They also offer a full line of gear, outboard brackets, two sailing rigs and custom models for serious explorers. Own a VW and want to avoid a thousand miles of extra car-top windage? Take your boat in a bag.

Late in the summer of 1970 I spent a few weeks on an archaeological excavation at Innish Caltra (Holy Island) in the Shannon of County Clare, Ireland. The 43-acre island held the bones of three abbeys, five churches, an anti-Viking round tower and 22 sheep. Out of thin air a Teutonic voice said, "Excuse me please. . . " A young fellow stood there inquisitively, wondering what we were about. We asked how he had gotten out to the island, there being no available boats nearby. He pointed to his Klepper, pulled-up on the riverbank. He was spending the summer touring Ireland. He had come from Germany. Yup. Folbot has been in business for 30 years and Klepper for 70 years! Folbot's design is the design originally used by Klepper. The Klepper design is, then, more advanced. Its greater expense is a reflection of this. Notice that Klepper still sells its original model at a price comparable to Folbot's. It would be interesting to see if the German workmanship is better on the original Klepper model and, therefore, the better deal. A Klepper has crossed the Atlantic Ocean!

The Klepper has rudder control in addition to the usual paddle control. This allows one to maintain rhythm and, therefore, is less tiring in the long hauls.

—GP

All items from
Folboat catalog.

## CAMP-Cruising

In Folbot you can navigate the intimate waterways in secluded areas, the shallow mountain streams and the beautiful spring runs of low lands, . . . away from billboards, 'blitzburger' shanties and away from motors, which can not operate in the realm of the float cruising folboter. In your Folbot you luxuriate amidst the last sections of unspoiled America in its prime natural splendor. The great impressions you gain, the observations and pictures you bring back or the better friendships made, are the great joys of folboting . . . not possible with any other mode of travel. C. F. G. California: "Just returned from ALASKA trip, used Folbot in marshes, lakes, rivers, ocean in B.C., Yukon Terr. & Alaska and feel bound to express my satisfaction with Folbot . . . hit snags and rocks WITHOUT trouble and RODE OUT STORMS without shipping a drop of water. You are to be congratulated on putting out a QUALITY PRODUCT, a rarity on todays' market."

18

## THE KLEPPER QUALITY RECIPE:

Give the best-suited modern materials to the traditional Foldaway craftsman, don't rush him, let him use half a century of experience and know-how.

The "Aerius" is made of the finest harmonious elements — carefully selected for every phase of its construction:

**Long Parts:** all Mountain Ash, a hard wood with long elastic fibers, air-dried for 3 years, chosen for straight grain, as resilient as good skis.

**Cross Ribs:** superb marine grade, 9 layer cross-laminated Finnish Birch. Light, strong, elastic, made to our specifications. Guaranteed against warping or opening.

**Snaplock Fittings** (patented): tough Dural alloy, cannot rust, will not corrode even in saltwater. Exact to 1/32nd of an inch. No screws, bolts, or loose parts at all.

**Decking:** toughest long hemp and longstaple cotton. Impregnated, waterproofed, tightest weave, still breathing. Deep blue.

**Lower Hull:** strong as a heavy-duty conveyor belt. Vulcanized 5 layers of Hypalon rubber and long hemp. Silver-grey. Often lasts 15 years in average use and care before a new hull replacement is needed.

**Patented Gunwales:** Klepper boats get their exceptional strength and firm shape from I-beam girder construction.

**Built-In Airsponsons:** long tubes in chambers along gunwales. Usually mouth-inflated, make boat unsinkable, unusually stable, allow extra-heavy loads, in some cases up to 1000 lbs.

**Kayak Shape:** most seaworthy shape for a small boat, fast, comfortable seat positions.

"Folding" (compact engineering) is what we are famous for: **all** parts of the "Aerius" fit into these packbags, in fact oval bag can fit inside rucksack also. Has there ever been a boat like it?

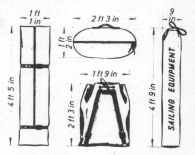

## GUARANTEED AGAINST SINKING

The "Aerius" has an exceptional safety factor built in: two large-volume sponsons in the best possible places. These, plus the inherent flotation of wood, make this Foldaway totally unsinkable. The "Aerius" cannot sink even when totally loaded with crew, plus baggage, and filled with water. A good thing to know for a family man.

19

_Items from the Klepper catalog._

### 'RUNABOUT'

| | |
|---|---|
| 14 foot 4 inches long | Space for 4 to 6 |
| 51 inches wide | Safe capacity: 910 lbs |
| 24 inches max. high | Cockpit size: |
| 15 inches side high | 114 inches long |
| 155 pounds net weight | 38 inches wide |

Three bags for Folding RUF measure:
26'' x 6'' x 38'' short
21'' x 10'' x 48'' medium
11'' x 11'' x 62'' long

If home storage and top-of-car transportation is assured, the thrill of a lifetime is yours with a Klepper rigid Single.

From our kayak background since 1907 comes the know-how to build such beauties, and to tailor them to size and need.

Klepper kayaks have a reputation for being stable, tough, carefully constructed. They are fitted with form-fitting contourseats and adjustable footbraces. Gracefully made of durable fiberglass or Diolen in racing models. As photos show, your need might be easy exercise, or a typical challenging riverrun with family or club, or your need might be extreme whitewater or advanced racing.

## Small Wood Boats For Oar and Sail

Of the billions of man-hours human beings have spent on the water since the Mesolithic Age (50,000 years ago), 99% of them were spent in wooden boats under 18' long. There is little prospect that this figure will significantly change. Who wants it to?

There are many small wood craft available in this country and abroad. We would like to see as many people as possible building their own, meeting not only their own needs for a small boat, but keeping alive the skills of small boat construction that give a personal sense of freedom and pride that few other activities can provide as well. Many persons have other things to do, of course, so we are interested in listing manufactured boats and craft that people **would** build themselves if they would or could.

—GP

---

Rana Boats are a good example. These sturdy seaboats are built in Rana Fiord on the northwest coast of Norway just below the Artic Circle. This area has been a boatbuilding center for more than 1,000 years. There are two distributors for them in this country, offering the same line at comparable prices, only slightly more on the West Coast.

In addition to the regular line, the Seattle firm offers the White Bear Skiff, as pretty a rowing craft as you'll find anywhere.

Above and below from   **The Old Boathouse**
**2770 Westlake N.**
**Seattle, Wash. 98109**

## LAPSTRAKE LTD.

20  **Quality boats for rowing and sailing**

The Rana boats are built by skilled craftsmen on the northwest coast of Norway at Rana Fiord, one of the oldest boat building centers of the world.

These sturdy lapstrake boats are constructed with spruce planks on oak frames. The planks and ribs are fastened with copper rivets and are varnished.

Included with every sailing model are dacron sails, spars, aluminum daggerboard, oars and rowlocks.

These seaworthy character boats are easy to handle and have a generous loading capacity. Their sturdy construction and classic design truly make them . . . quality boats for rowing and sailing.

**Lapstrake Ltd.**
**1422 Wisconsin Ave.**
**Washington, D.C. 20007**

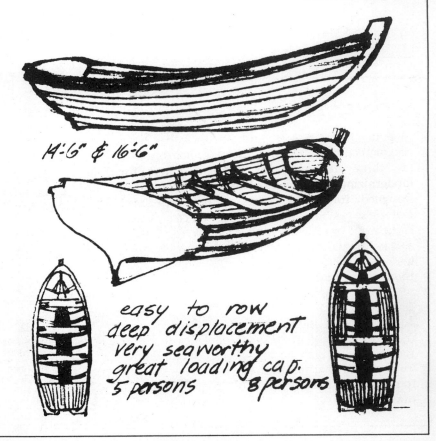

14'-6" & 16'-6"

easy to row
deep displacement
very seaworthy
great loading cap.
5 persons      8 persons

**Flat Bottom Boats:**

Most books about building boats suggest that you build the first one flat bottomed. Lots of boat users suggest that you don't need anything else, that it is a good place to stop. Either way, the Food and Agricultural Organization of the United Nations (FAO) has a wonderful paper on the subject: "Flat Bottom Boats," No. FIIV/T117 " . . . for distribution to boatbuilders and fishery officers in interested member countries."

**FOA**
**Fisheries Division**

**Via delle Terme di Caracalla Rome, Italy**

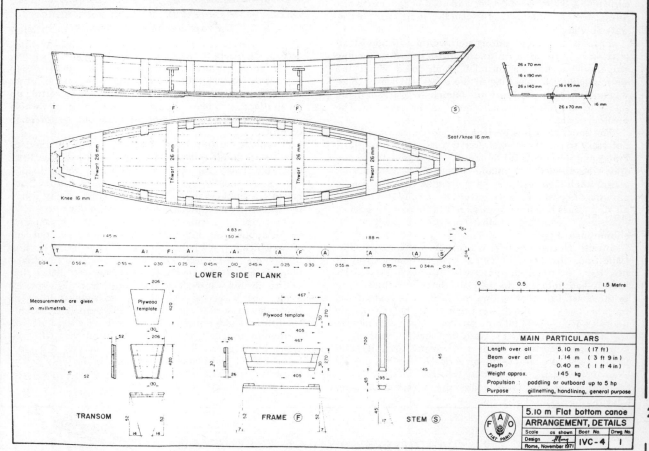

LOWER SIDE PLANK

Measurements are given in millimetres.

TRANSOM

FRAME (F)

STEM (S)

| MAIN PARTICULARS | |
|---|---|
| Length over all | 5.10 m (17 ft) |
| Beam over all | 1.14 m (3 ft 9 in) |
| Depth | 0.40 m (1 ft 4 in) |
| Weight approx. | 145 kg |
| Propulsion : | paddling or outboard up to 5 hp |
| Purpose | gillnetting, handlining, general purpose |

5.10 m Flat bottom canoe
ARRANGEMENT, DETAILS

| Scale | as shown | Boat No. | Drwg. No. |
|---|---|---|---|
| Design | | IVC-4 | I |
| Rome, November 1971 | | | |

**21**

## FAO PLANS

Boat plans worth looking into by both commercial fishermen and backyard boatbuilders are those drawn up by FAO designers for modernizing the fisheries of developing countries. Designed for simple construction from local materials, the boats range in size from those easily launched from an open beach to small trawlers and net boats. An example of the latter is shown here in a gillnetter of about 30' length, wood framed and planked with plywood, designed to replace the dugout canoes of the fishermen of Dahomey.

Information on plans of these boats is available from the Fishing Boats Section of the Food & Agricultural Organization (FAO), Rome, Italy. Further information on these boat types is to be found in the three volumes of "Fishing Boats of the World."

—DRG

## Cartopping
## Utility and Access

### By Frank Daignault

A fine greenhead mallard drifting belly up to the wrong side of a Connecticut creek was my first lesson in cartopping. Six miles of driving and hoofing taught me of a need for a small, easy-to-handle craft for better waterfowling.

Years later I stood among a crowd on a Rhode Island jetty waiting for my turn to cast into a school of feeding stripers. This spot was an inlet which doled bait to the waiting gamefish that hugged the other side where there was no one. My little "cartop," launched upstream in the safety of the estuary, would have put me into fish. The next day it did.

The small cartop is perfect for sportsmen who find it necessary to travel over sheltered water in pursuit of game. Prams and johnboats fill the needs of trappers, fishermen and waterfowlers in inland marshes. Larger, deeper aluminum-hulled utilities carry anglers to the fishing grounds of coastal bays and rivers. Here wind and tide can kick up a fuss but these sturdy craft offer yeomen service. In recent years our steady has been a shallow 14' aluminum utility.

In the North Truro/Provincelands section of Outer Cape Cod, "tin boats" such as these were once a way of life. Here, surfmen equipped with four-by-four vehicles took full advantage of the light surf that graces this section of the coast. Considering that the shallow 14 is about the most boat any man would want to heft, the hernia-reviving qualities of a deeper hull brought about the inevitable turn to trailering of larger, more seaworthy craft. Surf launching of "cartops" is not common; however, it serves as an excellent example of the scope of applications for these little vessels.

Not to be overlooked are the access advantages

Car-toppers on Cape Cod beach.

cartopping offers the sportsman. Fifty dollars for a pram, or a hundred for an aluminum johnboat, is a small price to pay for the seclusion that comes from being on the "other side." By simply crossing a river or inlet, or by setting up on an island, you leave the crowd behind opening a whole new vista of hard-to-reach hotspots shut out to sportsmen on foot.

The little cartopper is all but forgotten in the modern boating crush. Many is the late night we slipped our little craft by husky offshore fishermen and gadget-loaded "bass boats" neatly tied to their moorings; we, drifting our herring or bunkers in a snug estuary, took trophy fish — the kind many were preparing to steam for hours to get.

Cartopping, as with all our outdoor skills, is a sensitive art of application. For that reason I've worked out this chart which is intended to only generalize the application of each craft to a specific mission. Examine it in terms of your own outdoor needs remembering the places that you've always wanted to fish or shoot from. The smaller range of cartops should be considered only as conveyances, for they are usually too cramped or unstable for fishing and gunning. When selecting material, choose aluminum over plywood. Keep in mind that with the larger boats you will be lifting only one end at a time. Select a craft that you or partners can comfortably handle and travel with in safety; only a fool launches a johnboat in a foaming sea — never overreach.

## CARTOPPERS — WHERE THEY STAND

| Type | Best Use | Weight (approx.) | Recommended propulsion | Capacity |
|---|---|---|---|---|
| 8' pram (plywood) | marshes, beaver ponds small river crossings | 70 | oars | one man |
| 9' pram (alum.) | same | 73 | 3 horse | two men |
| 10' pram or johnboat | marshes, beaver ponds, small rivers | 81 | 5 horse | two men |
| 12' pram | same | 95 | 10 horse | two men |
| 12' alum. utility | lakes, bays, larger rivers | 130 | 10 horse | two men |
| shallow 14' alum. utility | up to open water; also limited surf launching | 144 | 25 horse | three men surf — two |

### The Cape Dory

By Roger C. Taylor

We have had a Cape Dory 14 footer for four years, rowing and sailing her in and around the harbor of Camden, Me. We forced ourselves to get a fiberglass boat to see if our longtime prejudice in favor of wood and against any other boatbuilding material would stand up in the face of actually using a boat built from some material other than wood. (The prejudice still exists, but we still have and enjoy the plastic boat.)

We chose the Cape Dory 14 footer because we thought she had the prettiest model of any fiberglass rowing and sailing boat on the market. We still feel that to be true.

The boat rows beautifully. She moves easily and is heavy enough to carry her way through a chop. She is low enough not to be stopped by a head wind, yet she is dry.

She sails extremely well in light and moderate going, footing fast off the wind and being an exceptionally good performer to windward. Her tall, sliding-gunter rig and narrow hull with the deep, heavy centerboard make her very close-winded indeed.

In a breeze of wind, the Cape Dory 14 is a handful. She is quite narrow, so that you can't get your weight out to windward very far, and when sailing single-handed, you can't make her stand up and drive to windward. Off a strong wind, she flies along, demanding plenty of attention to the helm.

One of the nice features of this boat for cold water sailing is that she has really excellent flotation. Swamped, she floats with the top of the centerboard trunk out of water.

The boat comes with aluminum spars. My reaction was, "I'll try them, and replace them after a season." But the tin sticks are still on the boat. They don't corrode; they are strong, light and limber.

There are nine small faults on this boat, as she is delivered from the Cape Dory people, eight of which can be easily corrected by the owner, and all of which could be even more easily corrected by the Cape Dory folks in the first place. Once at the New York Boat Show, I naively started down my list with a Cape Dory salesman, after carefully setting the stage, I thought, by complimenting him on his mighty fine little vessels. But after about the third nit-pick, he said, "Now we can put you in a 1971 Alberg Typhoon for less than you might think."

Well, anyway, Mr. Cape Dory, here is the complete gripe list for what it is worth.

The bottom of the boat amidships, where the floor is rather flat and thus gets no built-in rigidity through curvature, needs stiffening. She "oil cans" right under the midships thwart. There is foam flotation under this thwart, and it could easily be extended to the bottom of the boat to form a stiffening bulkhead. The bulkhead would be some 6" thick in the fore-and-aft direction to spread the load. The rest of the hull is perfectly stiff.

The first time I sailed the boat there was a pretty good breeze, and the plywood rudder cracked. Since the crack was at the narrow part of the blade, above the waterline, there was no harm in through-bolting a pair of thin oak pads on either side of the rudder over the crack. This satisfactory repair should have been done at the factory before delivery.

She needs a hiking stick on the tiller so you can steer while hiking out to windward.

The aluminum boom is too light. Off the wind in any kind of breeze at all, it wants to fold right up against the mast. My solution has been to rig a vang from a becket block on the forward end of the centerboard trunk up through a single block on the boom about 2½' abaft the

An interesting and much less expensive alternative to the justly popular outboard cetacean named after a prominent Northeastern metropolis is the Pickerell Boat line.

**Pickerell Boats
23 Highland Dr.
Centerport, N.Y. 11721**

From Pickerell brochure.

# IDEAL FISHING OR WORK BOAT

**All boats bronze fastened, fir plywood with 1 1/2" oak framing. All frames are sawn from one solid piece of oak. Ribbing and longitudinals are screwed and bolted in place. All boats have 1 1/2" transoms. V bottoms with flush decks are completely self bailing.**

gooseneck, back through the block on the centerboard trunk and aft to a cleat. It saves plenty of jibes.

The halyard should lead to a block on top of the stem and then aft to a cleat within reach of the helmsman. This way it doubles as a forestay when sailing.

The boat needs a topping lift from the end of the boom, through a single block at the masthead, down through a cheek block on the rail beside the mast, and aft to a cleat within reach of the helmsman. No sailboat should be without a topping lift, but especially on a combination rowing and sailing boat, you need a lift to hold the boom up out of the oarsman's way.

The wire traveller for the main sheet, as delivered from the factory, is really no traveller at all, for the sheet block is fixed to a swedged loop at the midpoint of the wire! I replaced the wire with a rope traveller so the sail will trim automatically to the lee quarter. If you trim the sail to a midship block, the boat won't go to windward very well.

The various dime store plastic fittings that hold the sail to the spars need to be replaced. I use laceline on the boom and gunter club and varnished mast hoops on the mast.

The sail needs two rows of reef points, so you can sail the boat in a wind. These should not be put in parallel to the foot of the sail, but rather with the reef deeper on the leach than it is on the luff because of the gunter club which rakes aft a bit when the sail is reefed.

That's the end of my list, and I am going to stay put in my nice 14' dinghy, thank you.

# MULTIHULLS

⬦ ⭐ **"Multihull Sailboats"** by Edward F. Cotter.
Crown Publishers, New York.
1971, 275 pp., illustrated, index, $6.95.

This book is good because Cotter doesn't have an axe to grind. Because multihull sailing is fairly new in the Western world, and many of the designs are experimental, books by proponents tend to be propagandistic. Controversy rages over outriggers, catamarans, trimarans, proas, asymmetrical hulls, symmetrical hulls, rigs and so forth.

Though he is obviously in favor of multihulls (his credentials are impressive), Cotter takes a relatively objective view of his subject. There are as many cons discussed as there are pros. The book is divided into five parts: Multihull Development, The Modern Multihull, Handling the Sailing Multihull, Multihull Cruising, Racing in Multihulls. As you can see, Cotter covers the territory.

The plans and photographs are especially good, and the chapter describing 46 one-design classes is an excellent guide to what is available.
—PHS

⬦ ⭐ **"Racing and Cruising Trimarans"** by Robert B. Harris.
Charles Scribner's Sons, New York.
1970, 216 pp., illustrated, bibliography, $7.95.

24

This is essentially a designer's view of trimarans. Harris is in the forefront of trimaran design and, to his credit, he discusses other designers and their products objectively. A good third of the book is devoted to the history of trimaran development; Harris' method is to present designers and their ideas as they appeared on the scene.

The rest of the book is an analysis of the trimaran itself. Subjects include choosing a design, habitability, hull forms, seaworthiness, construction, rigs and sails and power. Especially worthwhile is the chapter on construction. Harris doesn't tell you how to build trimarans, but does discuss the various construction methods in use today: molded veneer, strip planking, plywood, foam sandwich, balsa sandwich, fiberglass and aluminum. For someone contemplating building a tri but unsure about what method to use, this chapter serves as a good introduction.

—PHS

**"Searunner Construction"** by Jim Brown.
Jim Brown, Box 2627, Santa Cruz., Calif.,
310 pp., illustrated, $8.

This is the book that started out as a construction manual for Jim Brown-designed trimarans, and got out of hand. True, it serves its primary purpose admirably, but it also goes so much further that the title becomes misleading.

For instance, there is a complete dissertation on auxiliary power which covers every aspect of the subject from the question of whether or not through propellers. The same is true for sails and rigging, and even heads. At the other end of the spectrum are many little one line items of information and advice such as, " . . . beer spilt on deck (during building) inhibits the bonding of fiberglass, so sand off any stickyness before 'glass'."

The point is that this book is solid information. And it is extremely well written and organized. Where appropriate, the language is almost poetical, as in the explanation of the front cover; on the other hand, highly technical language is avoided, or fully explained.

This is the book you'll be tempted to try to read through at one sitting, but won't be able to because there is just too much to it, and yet you'll want to keep it forever as you know you'll want to refer to it many times in the future.

One more thing. This book is extremely well illustrated with both photos and drawings, and the illustrations are right where they belong in the text.

For anyone interested in building or just owning a trimaran, this is the best eight bucks worth you'll ever find.

—Paul Brown

The above review first appeared in the "TRImaraner" and is reprinted courtesy of Paul Brown, editor. "TRImaraner" is an excellent little quarterly devoted to trimarans (the only such publication in the world) and carries designs, commentary, building info, news of launchings and such. Subscriptions are $3 per year and can be obtained by writing to "Trimaraner," P.O. Box 884, Kaneohe, Hawaii 96744.

Getting back to Jim Brown, the trimaran designer, you might want to look at his other book, "Searunner Trimarans" ($4.), which is a book on his designs. Actually it is more than that, since Brown is giving you his design philosophy in narrative form, with, naturally, his trimarans as an example. There are loads of drawings and photographs, and some of the funniest cartoons you ever want to see.

—PHS

The Sirens and Ulysses.
(From an antique gem.)

# INFLATABLES

About five times a year, year in and year out, you get into landing situations where you really wish you had an inflatable. They don't row for beans, but they outboard well and they can take it no end. The British have shown the way on these craft and for British, read Avon, who offer 16 models.

**Avon Inflatable Boats**
**151 Mystic Avenue, Medford, Mass. 02155**
**79 East Jackson St., Wilkes-Barre, Pa. 18701**
**3107 Washington Blvd., Venice, Calif. 90291**

Another top-quality inflatable, much liked by a New England salvage firm we know of, is the French-made Zodiac. Note the semi-rigid bottom on this boat, a feature common to most inflatables designed for fast outboard use. The Zodiac Mark II shown here, a 13'10" model weighing 155 lbs., was tested by Mercury Marine using that manufacturer's 40 h.p. outboard. With one person aboard, the Zodiac was clocked over a measured course at 31.1 m.p.h.; with three aboard, it still managed 26.9 m.p.h. For such bulky looking craft, that's traveling.

—DRG

**Zodiac**
**11 Lee St.**
**Annapolis, Md. 21401**

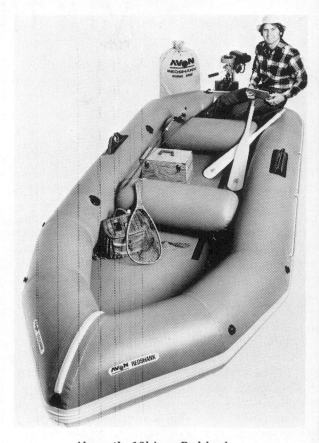

Above, the 12' Avon Redshank.

Below, the 13'10" Zodiac Mark II.

25

Remember the innertube? It is the original inflatable and in some ways the best. Well, the lily has been gilded and it is called the Flipperboat. An aircraft engineer from Seattle figured out a way to human-power that classic craft without resort to oars, sail or paddle — an honest four knots is claimed.

**Flipper-Boat Co.**
**16256 8th Ave. S.W.**
**Seattle, Wash. 98166**

⬤ "Inflatable Boats" by G.W.R. Nicholl.
Adlard Coles, London, England.
1969, 96 pp. illustrated, index, $3.95.

Probably the only book on the subject. Though the idea of relying on air-filled rubberized fabric to stay afloat makes me nervous, Nicholl does build a good case for the boats. Along with his presentation of the advantages and disadvantages of inflatable boats, the author discusses design, fabrics, construction, handling, and care and maintenance. He also includes a good buyer's checklist.

I guess if the Royal National Lifeboat Institution can use the boats for rescue craft, they couldn't be anywhere near as scary as my mind's eye makes them.

—PHS

Photo, text from "Inflatable Boats"

### Down the Urubamba
The value of the boat's unique characteristics is emphasised in another context by the remarkable exploit of two Bristol graduates, Mark Howell and Tony Morrison, during an expedition to South America in 1965. Teaming up with a United States explorer and his native guide, the four men (two on a balsa-log raft, two in a 9-foot Avon dinghy) made a descent of the entire Andes by water, a feat not previously accomplished and one which the native inhabitants had said would be suicidal.

Starting from Cuzco, 12,000 feet up in the Peruvian uplands, they descended to the headwaters of the Amazon down the tortuous Urubamba river in four and a half weeks of what must surely have been the severest trial any craft could be asked to face. Throughout that arduous period, which included an incredible succession of turbulent rapids and vicious whirlpools among other hazards, the inflatable gave no trouble whatever. It suffered no damage during the entire expedition, even withstanding needle-like thorns during portage through dense jungle at one stage (and Howell uses it still). What they had to attend to, however, was something that sea-level sailors are not obliged to cope with—re-inflation of the boat every five- or six-hundred feet of descent to compensate for the rising barometric pressure at the lower latitudes.

26

Avon dinghy at 12,000' on the more placid reaches of the upper Urubamba in the Peruvian Andes.

"Motors enable a boat to make headway against swift streams or gale winds, or to cover a long distance quickly, or to keep heavy loads moving reliably; they're not needed or efficient for short distances, light loads, and pleasant weather, and in particular they're not sensible when the thing sought is recreation for a given time, rather than arrival over a certain distance."

—Phil Bolger (N.A.) on rowing

The American Plywood Association, Tacoma, Wash., publishes plans for two-boat storage ports. There is a 24' permanent structure (ask for Form L500, $.25) and a 12' folding structure (Form M50, $.25). Either one allows you to use your garage for what it was built for — your car.

—PHS

Goramy (Osphromenus olfax).

## FIBERGLASS DORIES

There are a few lines of fiberglass dories of various models available in the Northeast and these are fairly well-advertised and known. A western firm with dories is the W.D. Schock Co. which offers two models; a 15' "New England" dory and a 20' Lifeguard model.

W.D. Schock Co.
3502 So. Greenville St.
Santa Ana, Calif. 92704

### SPECIFICATIONS
**20' Lifeguard Dory**

| | |
|---|---|
| LOA | 20'4" |
| Beam | 70" |
| Weight | 300 lbs. |

......based on traditional Georges and Grand Banks dory lines, but molded in rugged fiberglass to withstand abuse.

Scheel Yachts Inc., South Main St., Rockland, Me., a builder of luxury sailing yachts, has branched into fiberglass dories intended for commercial fishermen, but which also have pleasure use possibilities.

According to a spokesman for the firm, the mold was taken off a wooden working dory. Dimensions are: 25' l.o.a., 20' long on the bottom, 41" high transom and bow, 30" freeboard amidships, 6'10" max. beam and weight about 1,000 lbs. The length of the bottom inside is 17'5" if forward and aft ballast tanks are omitted; 14'6" if built-in tanks are included. The maximum width of the transom is 25". Rocker might be termed "moderate."

The firm has reportedly sold several to fishermen, particularly those involved in seining. Construction is rough and the hull is reinforced with fiberglass-covered plywood ribs.

Also, the gunwales have oak rub rails inside and out. The joiner work here is unnecessarily poor. One inboard rail on the dory we inspected was a continuous strip of oak from stem to stern. On the other side, two strips were used, meeting amidship and were only square-butted with a small space in between.

The price for the dory is $925 f.o.b. Rockland, somewhat higher than wooden models by other builders. However, it's a big low-upkeep boat for the money and it would seem that she'd have the same seakeeping abilities as her more traditionally-constructed cousins.

—Burt Coffey

**27**

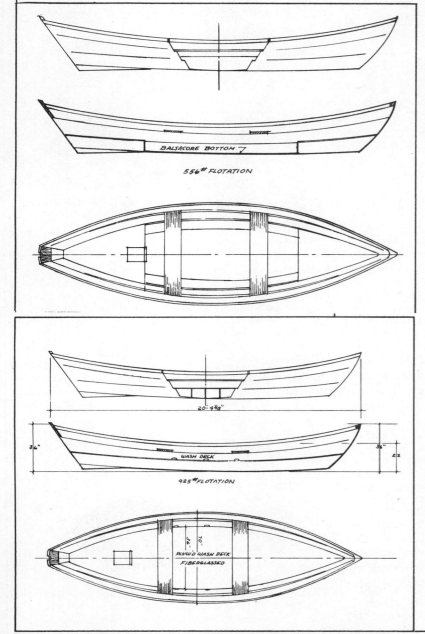

# A Seaworthy Workboat—*CHEAP!*

By David R. Getchell

Conventional seine dory and author's modified boat of the same type
show how easy it is to convert a simple net boat into a fine little workboat.

A good boat, capable of handling rough seas, hard use and a great variety of jobs, does not have to be expensive. A perfect example of this is the 25' l.o.a. dory shown here, a simple craft built for herring seining which we modified for fishing, island exploration and general pleasure use. Our total cost for this fine little ship, including an 18 h.p. outboard motor, was less than $400. And this in the inflationary days of 1972.

The dory itself was only a few years old, little used and one of several owned by a fisherman friend of ours who died. We bought the dory from his estate for $150. Like most such boats in Maine, the dory was Nova-Scotian built with pine planking and natural crook frames of hackmatack and with only a small amount of rocker in its 1¼" pine-planked bottom.

Having modified a slightly smaller dory a few years earlier, we knew pretty much what we wanted to do, our main aim being to keep things as simple as possible with lots of working room in the cockpit. The forward deck, extending back 7' from the stem, is ¼" plywood bent over 1" x 4" beams that are bolted to frames. A lengthwise 1" x 4" let into the cross beams adds stiffness while offering a solid backing for the big cleat made out of a piece of oak cut in our backyard. Heavy fiberglass woven roving assures tightness of this little deck.

A bulkhead with cuddy door was built one frame forward of the after end of the foredeck. This allows for tool and anchor/rope storage in the cuddy while at the same time giving a sizable protected area under the foredeck for day gear, clothing, etc. The cockpit deck is nothing more than a sheet of 3/8" exterior plywood well soaked with linseed oil and lightly tacked to the floor frames. It can be taken out or replaced in minutes. Seats are 2" x 8" spruce planks notched to fit over the side frames and thus be movable, and removable.

We bought the 18-horse long-shaft Evinrude used for

*Contd. on next page*

Modified seine dory in foreground now has long-shaft motor in well. Cleat and chock on foredeck are made of oak. Foredeck is fiberglassed for tightness and durability.

*Contd. from preceding page*

$100, figuring we needed more power than the short-shaft 9.8 h.p. Mercury we already owned. But in going on big waters, we're a firm believer in carrying a spare motor, so we were presented with somewhat of a problem as we contemplated the building of a motor well. We had two motors, but their shaft lengths differed by some 5". To solve this problem, we built the well box with 2" x 10" spruce planks, which gave us the proper transom height for the long-shaft motor. To accommodate the Merc, the top plank of the forward side of the well was made removable, to be replaced by a 2" x 4" piece that provided a 15" (appx.) transom. The replaceable transom pieces were held in with 3" screws and 1½"-wide galvanized strap iron bands with lag bolts — and they worked just fine, the switchover taking just a few minutes work with wrench and screwdriver. Details of a similar tilt-up well are shown in the sketch. By the way, we have found this well, with its hinged "planing board," a most effective compromise for this sort of installation; it is simple to make, very rugged since it is through-bolted into the bottom, and it lets you beach the dory without damage to the prop.

We should note here that twin skegs, about 18" apart and 8' long, made from ordinary 2" x 4"'s, are bolted to the bottom just forward of the well opening. These help hold the dory on course and also let her be beached without damaging the bottom paint. These, too, are easily replaced when worn out.

The space aft of the well is not wasted. There is just the right amount of room here for spare gasoline cans, the second outboard motor, clam hods and rakes and other bulky gear. The 10' oars, cut down from a pair of lifeboat oars, also extend back into this area — they're useful for around rocks and in the shallows, but we wouldn't want to have to push this big boat very far into a breeze.

What's a boat such as this like? Well, it will do its 6-7 m.p.h. equally well with the 10 or 18 h.p. motor; we prefer the small mill because it uses far less gas. Light,

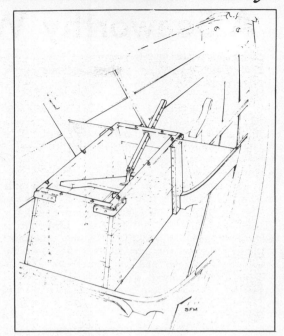

OUTBOARD WELL in this sketch is similar to one described here, although construction details differ somewhat since well in the article had to be modified for two different motors with long and short shafts. Most importantly, well should be ruggedly built and, preferable, be designed for a particular motor.

the boat is somewhat lively although heavy enough to give you a big-boat feeling. Loaded with gear or five or six people, she's quite comfortable, even in a sea. Of course, it's an open boat so spray comes aboard in a chop. One might want to install a couple of pipe bows and a canvas dodger for greater comfort and

*Contd. on next page*

## W. Lawrence Allen Dory Builders Ltd.

Post Office Box 1057
Lunenburg, Nova Scotia
Telephone 634-4861 (Area Code 902)

One of the largest dory builders on the East Coast is the W. Lawrence Allen firm in Lunenburg. They have been supplying fishermen of the Maritimes and New England with dories of all sizes for many years. They still do, although now they occasionally turn out some of mahogany for uncommon yachtsmen. The prices shown here are early 1973, so expect to pay a few more dollars.

—DRG

**DORY SPECIFICATIONS**

| | Bottom Length | Overall Length | Sheer | Rocker | Maximum Beam | Depth | |
|---|---|---|---|---|---|---|---|
| LITTLE SISTER | 8' | 11'3" | 8" | 2½" | 3'10" | 1'3" | $250. |
| ADMIRAL'S DORY | 10' | 13'7" | 10" | 4" | 4'3" | 1'4" | 217. |
| BLACK ROCKS DORY | 11' | 14'8" | 11" | 4" | 4'6" | 1'4½" | 234. |
| LUNENBURG DORY | 12' | 15'6" | 1' | 4" | 4'8" | 1'5¾" | 261. |
| HANDLINE DORY | 13' | 17' | 1'3" | 4½" | 4'11" | 1'7" | 286. |
| SINGLE DORY | 14' | 18'4" | 1'5" | 5" | 5'4" | 1'10½" | 306. |
| TRAWL DORY | 15' | 19'9" | 1'5" | 5½" | 5'5" | 2' | 338. |
| FISHMAKER'S DORY | 16' | 21'1" | 1'6½" | 6" | 6'1" | 2'1" | 376. |
| FORTUNE BAY DORY | 17' | 22'2" | 1'7½" | 6½" | 6'4½" | 2'2" | 430. |
| NEWFOUNDLAND DORY | 18' | 23'1" | 1'9" | 7" | 6'8" | 2'4" | 465. |
| SEINE DORY | 20' | 25'9" | 1'11½" | 8½" | 7'1" | 2'7" | 595. |

*Contd. from preceding page*

overnighting, although I like the room of the fully open boat. A dory, even this size, is easily beached and will sit level on her skegs until the tide returns. And remember, these boats are built of thick wood and thus can be banged around, loaded with driftwood, used for lobstering, or what-have-you, and still be easily repaired or touched up with paint. With motor well and deck, a simple seine dory becomes a highly versatile craft, slow, to be sure, but safe and sound.

Seine or banks dories with 16' — 22' bottoms (18' — 25' l.o.a.) are fairly common in the Northeast and, to a lesser extent, in the Pacific Northwest. Of course, dories are not the only low-priced workboats available. The flat-bottomed Weaver skiff has great possibilities as do the Rhode Island quahog skiffs and similar small craft from 15' to 25' l.o.a. common to all coastal areas. All one needs are sharp eyes and ears, a modicum of basic carpentry skill and common sense, and a willingness to compromise yacht speed and beauty for plainness and utility. Look around — the boat of your dreams may be just a cove away.

## Vaitses on Wells

The only man who needs a well is one who wants to use an outboard engine on a boat that calls for inboard power. Now, if it isn't talking too nearly in circles, a boat that calls for an inboard engine is one in which it would be best for various reasons if the engine were in the boat.

Double-enders, dories and innumerable sail or power boats with fine sterns or long overhangs fit this description. In such boats an outboard through a well might be preferred for one or more of the following reasons:

1. Lower first cost.
2. Easier maintenance. Take motor to repair shop, not vice versa.
3. Easier beaching, haulout or trailering. No permanent lower appendages necessary.
4. Less drag when rowing or sailing, provided bottom of well is closed over at such times.
5. Takes up less room in boat.
6. Very infrequent use, making all of the above more important.
7. The possibility, not often mentioned, of slipping a second or standby power plant down the same well.

*Contd. on next page*

30

## Conrad's Wisdom

"Of all the living creatures upon land and sea, it is ships alone that cannot be taken in by barren pretences, that will not put up with bad art from their masters."

—Joseph Conrad in
"Meretricious Glory"

A Bug-eye.

Weaver skiffs are built mainly for use in the Mississippi and Ohio valleys and are heavily-built boats with a long history. The two above are 18' and 16' rowing skiffs for towboat yawls. Reinforced gunnels and thole pins are standard for this type. At left is a 20-footer built to inboard power. Prices begin at $200 for the 16' skiff and range upward from $250 for the 20-footers.

—DRG

## Don't Spoil It

"So, Gentle Reader, please don't write in to me about the wonderful idea you have of spoiling Rozinante with a dog house for a galley, for if you like eating better than sailing, you should stay home and have a barbecue in the back yard."

—L. Francis Herreshoff in
"How to Build Rozinante"

Weaver Skiff Works
J.W. Weaver, Jr., Prop.
Racine, Ohio

*Contd. from preceding page*

It is true that many boats which will not take an outboard on the transom could have it mounted on a bracket on the stern or on the topsides. However, a well is superior on three counts:

1. The motor is inboard where it is easier to handle and repair.

2. The motor is not vulnerable to dunking by pitching, rolling or a cresting wave that slaps the hull.

3. On small sailboats, the motor will not interfere with the rudder or main sheet.

Before anyone is carried away by the advantages of an outboard well, we hasten to list some distinct disadvantages.

1. Distinct? Right! Dey stink, plenty, dose outborts; and dey neffer vas fixin dose stink so use couldt stand it for longer!

2. The sound and vibration frequencies of outboards are more tiring to the nervous system than those of most inboards. From this point of view, an outboard would be better mounted on a 40' outrigger than in a well. Or, after some hours, under the keel.

3. Outboards use more gas than inboards per h.p.

4. Few outboards are made with the right speeds and wheels for efficient propulsion of displacement boats.

5. Since outboards spit some of the exhaust out of a hole under the water level, steps must be taken when the wind is light to keep these fumes from rising around the motor and starving the air intake; also from adding to the pallor of the passengers.

6. In some boats, the well and motor will spoil too much valuable space; though there are few cases when an inboard would not be as bad or worse.

In the writer's opinion, the most important features of well design are the size of the opening in the bottom, the proper fairing of this opening to the rush of water past it, and the proper baffling against slop. For these reasons, I long ago ruled out wells in which the motor could be tipped up as it is on a transom as too crude for serious consideration. It is obviously unnecessary to have a hole through the bottom much wider than the diameter of the propeller, or much longer than the length of the lower unit.

In a boat with a rudder, a small box built around the motor dropped into a simple box well takes care of all of the fairing and slop problems. When the boat must be steered with the motor, a curved baffle in the after end of the bottom of the inner box over the propeller will force the water down and aft, and keep the propeller from paddling slop up into the well. An arc cut into the forward end of this baffle clearing the after edge of the vertical shaft housing will allow the motor to swing from side to side.

When the motor is too heavy to lift vertically out of such a well, the forward side of the well and inner box or motor mount can be radiused; and the motor actually lazy-susans right up and out of the same small opening in the bottom. The plans of this concentric well were published in MCF in January 1959.

Much can be done to improve on these basic wells. If half as much had been spent to perfect them as has been spent to develop inboard power plants that have built-on propulsion units made to project through the bottom or transom for some obscure reason, then we might see some really trim and useful, inexpensive and handy inboard-outboard installations.

—Boatbuilder Allan H. Vaitses of Mattapoisett, Mass., in a letter to the editor of the "Maine Coast Fisherman."

## Rhode Island Box

Several years ago I built a 16' outboard skiff, intended for low power playing about Hyannis Harbor and Lewis Bay. The boat was designed with the Seagull English outboard in mind and has proved to be most satisfactory. The makers of the Seagull stress common sense and simplicity and the boat was designed with the same ideas in mind.

After several seasons use I began to think about how often in the spring or fall there are fine days for boating except for a cold raw wind. After thinking about folding canvas dodgers and Arctic clothing and other related things, I chanced one cold November day to be down in Rhode Island and observed a large fleet of big quahog skiffs with outboards, each fitted out with what looked like a refrigerator crate with one side knocked out in which the quahogger could stand out of the wind on the way to and from the grounds.

On my return home I made some sketches and soon decided that on a 16' skiff a standup size house would be much too awkward looking. Finally I went to work with some laths and brads and mocked up a house just high enough to sit in. This was converted into ½" pine on a light frame, with a hinged top, so that I can steam around sitting down when making a passage across the bay and then on entering confined waters the after half of the house folds forward allowing me to stand for better visibility and maneuverability, it being pure accident that the top comes at perfect elbow leaning height when standing.

Some of my friends suggested all kinds of complicated steering gears but a spruce stick thrust into the tubular tiller of old Seagull does nicely.

The house is held fast to the sternsheets of the boat by two dime store C-clamps and during the warm months the whole business unclamps and goes ashore.

I find that to get in out of the cold wind and also out from under the raw drizzle which we are apt to have in the spring and fall adds about six weeks of enjoyment to each end of the yachting season.

Out of respect to the Rhode Islanders who gave me the inspiration, I call my contraption my "Rhode Island Box."

George B. Kelley
20 Lookout Lane
Hyannis, Mass.

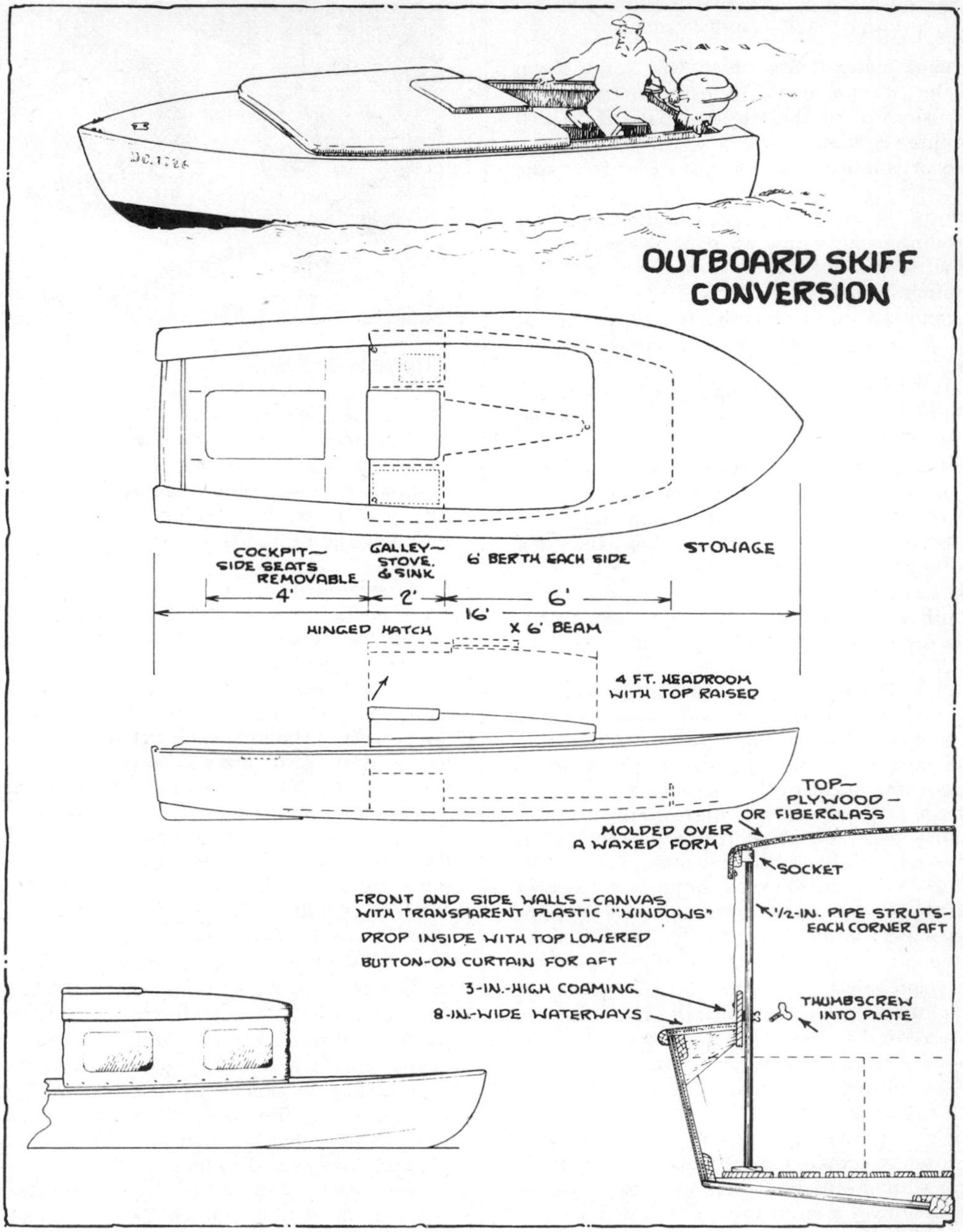

**OUTBOARD SKIFF CONVERSION**

COCKPIT—
SIDE SEATS
REMOVABLE
4'

GALLEY—
STOVE
& SINK
2'

6' BERTH EACH SIDE
6'

STOWAGE

HINGED HATCH

16' X 6' BEAM

4 FT. HEADROOM
WITH TOP RAISED

TOP—
PLYWOOD—
OR FIBERGLASS

MOLDED OVER
A WAXED FORM

SOCKET

½-IN. PIPE STRUTS—
EACH CORNER AFT

FRONT AND SIDE WALLS—CANVAS
WITH TRANSPARENT PLASTIC "WINDOWS"

DROP INSIDE WITH TOP LOWERED

BUTTON-ON CURTAIN FOR AFT

3-IN.-HIGH COAMING

8-IN.-WIDE WATERWAYS

THUMBSCREW
INTO PLATE

32

We passed this novel rig on our way south last fall to finally meet its owners, a young couple on a year's sabbatical leave from their government jobs in Washington. The boat had originally been a conventional 16' outboard skiff. Later, the waterways or side and forward decks had been put on and the boat used for overnight trips weekends with a camping outfit aboard. Finally, with the thought of making the trip south, the cabin arrangement was added and the interior accommodations built in.

The biggest job was to make the cabintop. A rough wood form was made to give the shape wanted, and its upper surfaces well waxed for building up the alternate layers of fiberglass cloth and roving to give a shell approximately 3/16" in thickness. Note that with the top down, as for running, its edges drop over the deck's low coamings, allowing the side and forward curtains to fold down inside. With the boat anchored or tied up to a dock for the night the top is raised and held up by three pipe

uprights, the pair at the after corners and another up forward.

The cabin's pair of bunks with air mattresses and sleeping bags provide comfortable sleeping. There's sitting-up headroom over them for lounging purposes, and with the hatch aft hinged open the cook can stand up to work. A canvas panel with a section of mosquito netting buttons in place for closing the after end of the cabin.

Jack and Jane explained that it makes for a big improvement over their formerly having to depend on a camping outfit. All clothing and gear can be kept in the dry. And particularly for cruising the southern tidewater country where suitable campsites are often scarce, they're virtually independent of the shore, except for occasionally putting in for fuel and supplies. What with overnight dockage becoming high priced, they figured what they were saving by anchoring out more than offset their fuel costs.

—Jim Emmett

Various forms of Ships' Blocks :
*a*, long-tackle block ; *b*, clew-line block ; *c*, double block

● "Small Craft Conversion" by John Lewis.
Adlard Coles, London, England.
1972, 288 pages, illustrated, glossary,
index, $15.

There probably isn't a sailor alive who hasn't looked at an old ship's lifeboat or derelict workboat and said: "Hey, with a little modification and paint here and there, that could become a nice cruising boat."

Quite a few go past the dreaming stage and give it a try. I've seen some beautiful conversions; one in particular was a lifeboat-turned-ketch moored in the harbor when I was a boy. I've also seen some incredible conversions, like the 50' cutter a friend of mine converted backwards. He bought the boat on the beach after a storm, plugged the holes, cut the mast away with an axe, sold everything that had anything to do with making her sail, towed her to a mooring in the harbor, and lived on her rent and mortgage free for years. He was my town's first hippie. He'd be sitting on the deck of the weirdest conversion of all time, soaking in the sun, his arms wrapped around a half-gallon of Thunderbird, and yachtsmen in shining white ducks and blue blazers would sail by and say: "You really ruined a fine craft, Boy," and he'd almost fall overboard from laughing so hard. Which just goes to show that a first-class conversion to one person is a complete waste of time to another.

John Lewis was bitten with the conversion bug and this book is the result of his experiences and research. There's plenty of general information on the hows and whys, but the strength of the book is the specific examples, like lifeboats, whaleboats, punts and workboats. For instance, there are 31 pages on transforming a 26' lifeboat to a ketch-rigged cruiser. Lewis has specifics on installing engines, sail rigs, centerboards, leeboards, cabins, accommodations, wheelhouses and more. He even discusses how to give a straight-stem lifeboat a raked stem by adding a false bow.

This book will do one of two things to you —you'll either run out to search the waterfront for a suitable hull for conversion, or you'll exclude all further thoughts of the matter from your mind. All of which means that Lewis will have served his purpose.

—PHS

33

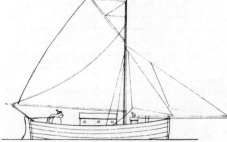

Fig. 1 Lifeboat conversions have a habit of looking like these:
'I believe in comfort'
'The importance of a high aspect ratio'
'She's a homey little boat'
'There's nothing like a gaff cutter'

"The Riddle of the Sands" by Erskine Childers.
First published 1903. Available in two editions:
Duttons, New York, $3.95.
and the Imprint Society, Barre, Mass., Barre Publishing, $35.

It is some measure of the stature of this book that there is a sort of informal, international "Riddle of the Sands" Society of its admirers. It is easy to identify the members of this group if you can overhear their conversation.

Say you are at the airport in Cairo. You notice a weatherbeaten chap with a sea bag slung carelessly over his shoulder, swinging along through the crowd. He nearly collides with a gentleman in a derby of greenish tinge, the sort of fellow who seems used to giving orders in his own spacious pilothouse. The two eye each other cautiously at first, then their faces light up with a mysterious mutual recognition of kindred spirits.

He of the sea bag says excitedly, "When Carruthers had been put ashore from the dinghy by Davies at Memmert to spy on Dollmann and his friends, what was the name shouted through the fog, the name Carruthers had to repeat as if relaying the call, lest he be made out to be an intruder?"

You can tell by the beaming countenance under the derby that its owner has heard this one before. "Karl Schicker," he bubbles gleefully, glad to be able to demonstrate a close knowledge of the "Riddle" to a fellow member of its admiration society.

Then, closing one eye and cocking his head, Derby tests Sea Bag with, "On that first night when the Dulcibella was grounded out on the sands, the night the intruder came aboard, you remember Carruthers grabbed the intruder's leg but the man's boot came off in his hand and the fellow got away; well, which boot was it, the right or the left?"

You can tell this one stumps Sea Bag by his look of mortification. He needn't feel too badly though. The derby-hatted one has given him a trick question, for Childers didn't specify which boot.

That's the way "Riddle" fans are.

"The Riddle of the Sands" is a cruising yarn and spy thriller rolled into one. Imagine the authors of "The Compleat Cruiser" and "The Spy Who Came In From The Cold" somehow combined into one person and you have Erskine Childers, for "The Riddle" reads as if it might have been written by L. Francis Herreshoff and John Le Carre working as a team.

From this it may be presumed that Erskine Childers was an interesting man. He was, indeed, and "Riddle" readers everywhere are indebted to Brigadier E.F. Parker for his article about Childers, "Life and Death of a Yachtsman," published in "Skipper" magazine, and reprinted in the book, "Tales from the Skipper."

Childers was born and raised in Ireland and was familiar with the shallow, sandy waters of Arcklow, Wicklow, Dublin Bay and Kingstown. While a clerk to the English House of Commons in 1895, he explored during vacations the shallow coast of Northern Europe in a 30' shoal-draft cruising sloop, the Vixen. Sometimes he sailed with a companion and sometimes he sailed alone, and he became an expert pilot among the estuaries, creeks and sands of the North Sea coasts of Germany and Holland and of the Baltic coasts of Germany and Denmark.

Childers fought in the Boer War and returned home in 1901 firmly opposed to Britain's colonial policies. He began a lifelong struggle for an independent Ireland, first against the British and later against his own countrymen. At the same time, he resumed his North Sea cruising in a 40-footer, the Sunbeam.

After his first season in the Sunbeam, he wrote "The Riddle of the Sands." He presented the tale as a true story with the subtitle, "A Record of Secret Service Recently Achieved," and his byline read, "Edited by Erskine Childers."

The story tells of a playboy Englishman who joins a casual acquaintance for a cruise in the latter's "yacht." The yacht turns out to be a shoal-draft converted lifeboat, the acquaintance is bent on solving a sinister and internationally important riddle, and the cruise takes them among the sands and channels of the Frisian Islands. The playboy turns out to have considerable common sense and courage.

To say too much about this story would spoil it for those who inexplicably may not yet have read it. (We "Riddle" fans have trouble coming to grips mentally with the simple statement of fact that there are still mariners who have not yet read "The Riddle.")

But at least let me throw out a tidbit of the story. There is a chapter called "Blindfold to Memmert" in which Davies and Carruthers row their dinghy 16 miles in thick fog over tide-swept sands to an objective and return in order to try to put one more piece into the puzzle. Just in this one little part of the story, Childers has conjured up one of the great small boat adventures.

Childers went on to an adventurous life on his own, cruising and running guns for Ireland in his 50' Colin Archer ketch Asgard, serving in Royal Navy intelligence in World War I, fighting as an Irish guerrilla and finally dying before an Irish Free State firing squad in 1922.

Brigadier Parker wrote, "In Ireland Childers is a legendary hero — one of the founders of the nation."

To boatmen, he is the author of one of the greatest pieces of small-boat fiction ever written.

—Roger C. Taylor

---

## A CATALOG OF CATALOGS

"Masterlog" is a remarkable little work, for it lists a fantastic number of firms and their catalogs, where to send, what they are about and how much. Only a fraction of the listings is of direct interest to marine fields, of course, but it certainly is a fun broth to spoon through.

—GP

Lumpsucker (*C. lumpus*).

One-masted Schooner. *A*, full sail; *B*, jib reefed.

"Masterlog"
Box 24413-CM
Oakland, California 94623

# Non-Western Craft

Jangada.

### By George Putz

Tucked away in obscure corners of museums throughout the Western World lie thousands of watercraft made and once used by any one or another of a thousand non-western cultures. Their titlecards say something like "native dugout," "bark canoe cleverly made by sewing the bark of the white birch and 'paying' the seams with pitch," or "unidentified proa-type canoe, probably from Micronesia."

Non-western craft have received incredibly short shrift by most museums, not only because information about them is generally lacking or hard to come by, but also because of their (our) ethnocentric tendency to see and interpret all things in terms of our own values. Even curators of marine museums are prone to this, deciding that the native craft shall be the one to be hung by ropes from the ceiling, set aside in storage or stacked together with other craft from all over the world.

These same curators would not think of letting the little Rob Roy canoe go-by or of categorizing it with their 1888 Yale racing shell or a Herreshoff dinghy. How is it, then, that a serious working craft with some thousand years of tradition behind it, often beautifully made and decorated and often utterly unique in aero- and hydro-dynamic characteristics, gets pushed aside to dry and check and rub shoulders forever with totally unrelated craft from other corners of the world?

Some craft have caught the West's imagination, of course. Sampans, junks, dhows, proas and a dozen others have been cited and one or two characteristics extracted from the whole and experimentally adapted to yachting's requirements. But this editing also falls in the shortshrift department, for all of these types vary enormously, contain touches of personal builder's genius and reveal their best features when integrated as originally conceived and built.

The point is sometimes made that heritage is a limiting thing, that ours is a tradition different from others and that it is quite enough to do to study it, that there is not time or resources or energy available to devote to traditions other than our own — let· those who descend from others study and preserve the others. This is a

luxurious sentiment at best! On every lake, river and sea-front since the Mesolithic period men have grappled with the problem of how to cross and live on water. Some few saw themselves as patients to the sea, timid intruders who beseeched the sea and whatever powers that be to let them pass across alive. Others saw themselves as agents, superior beings taming forces that could kill them if allowed that gall. Some developed a marine stoicism, others a fatalism, a sense of destiny and discovery and anon. In other words, non-western craft do not simply reflect a technical tradition or a particular array of tools or resources. They were vehicles of a way of life in more ways than one.

The problem is deeper still. Those who made these craft are dead, their legacy desecrated and their descendants either demoralized, westernized or both. Our infectious diseases, religion and technology brought irreparable havoc to these cultures and it would seem that the least we could do is preserve the remnants of their material culture, boats, in this case, and learn from them.

When asked about this, many curators say that, "well, you have to make choices. Our resources are limited and the job is too big to do it all. Yes, you are right, but there you are. . ." This being so, we can begin by bringing it to the attention of watermen. We need to extract a bibliography from anthropological sources and those wonderful eccentrics here and there who have made non-western craft their private study and thing. And we can, when we are there and it seems appropriate, mention to curatorial persons the role these craft could have in our growing understanding of things, water and people if they were given proper care, research and display.

Meanwhile, some of the bibliographical works mentioned in "The Mariner's Catalog" list books and papers on non-western craft. We need more. Our plan is to place notices in various professional journals and to solicit sources of information on non-western craft, probably by culture-area, and to construct a good core maritime anthropology resources bibliography on as many marine cultures, past and present, as we possibly can.

Some quick research on Oceanian (Melanesia,

35

*Contd. on next page*

Canoe with Outrigger.

Sampan.

A Polynesian Proa with Outrigger.

*Contd. from preceding page*

Micronesia and Polynesia) small craft, for example, produced the following most interesting books:

(1) "Vikings of the Pacific," by Peter Buck, U. of Chicago Books; chapters on Polynesian canoes, building techniques, importance of religion in building and use of small craft and a good bibliography.

(2) "People of the South Pacific," by Albert B. Lewis, Chicago Natural History Museum; several discussions about Melanesian canoes and an excellent, though dated, bibliography (to 1951) on the ethnology of every Melanesian island group.

(3) "Canoes of Oceania," by A.C. Haddon and J. Hornell, three volumes, The Bishop Musuem, Honolulu; 884 pp., of definitive work.

(4) ☸ "Polynesian Seafaring," by Edward Dodd, Dodd-Mead; a large beautifully illustrated, somewhat polemical work on the techniques of oceanic navigation, craft construction, rigging and seamanship with a bibliography that either hands you what you wish to know or tells you where to find it.

(5) ☸ "We, The Navigators," by David Lewis, U. of Hawii, Honolulu; a fantastically eclectic book on the navigation techniques of Oceanian peoples with an excellent bibliography and index.

Indian Catamaran.

36

This is only a small rudimentary beginning, of course, but at least a core from which a person interested in the craft of this culture-area can expand his studies and understanding.

Other areas that need covering are:
—Ancient Western Craft
—Mediterranian Craft from Middle ages to Present.
—Northern European Traditions.
—The Many North American Indian Traditions, including Eskimo.
—West Indian Traditions.
—South America, especially the Amazon Basin.
—N.W. Pacific.
—Japan and China.
—Circum-Indian Ocean Traditions.
—Afro-Riverine.
—Various Lacustrian and Riverine Traditions of Mid-Continental Areas.

If you know something; share it.

—GP

A Chinese Junk.

## An Unusual Camera

The Nikonos-11 is really an extraordinary camera that is constructed perfectly watertight, permitting use not only without an additional case under water down to the depth where a skin diver can endure the pressure of water, but also under severe conditions such as where the camera is likely to be exposed to water, rain, snow, sand,

mud, dust cloud (radioactive or not), a high degree of humidity, etc. It will satisfy the most exacting requirements of action-bound photographers in many conditions. The flash unit is specifically designed for underwater use with the Nikonos. The unit can also be used apart from the camera. Basic cost of the camera alone is about $250 and can be ordered from most camera stores. But special lens and other attachments can zoom the price to double and triple the base cost. It will pay you to dicker with your dealer.

—Vince Mecca

"Salt Water Aquarium"
Coral Reef Exhibits.
P.O. Box 1000 Belleview, Fla. 32620
One year (6 issues)/$4.50 in U.S., $5.50 foreign.

Do you prefer your fish live and swimming in a glass tank to fried and swimming in a wine sauce? Even if you like both, you'll have no trouble finding good cook books. But how to keep salt water fish in tanks is something else again.

Bob Straughan's little bi-monthly, "Salt - Water Aquarium," which he describes as "The International Magazine for Aquarists," is probably just what you need. Breezy, informative and pleasantly personalized by Straughan's contributions and comments, this magazine should prove useful to divers, collectors and underwater photographers as well as the little old lady with a school of truculent triggerfish.

—DRG

## USED BOOKS

The time will come when you will discover that a book you want is out of print, or the price of a new book is more than your pocket can bear. Bookstores that specialize in nautical books are rare; those that specialize in used nautical books are rarer still. There are quite a few mail-order, used nautical book dealers both here and in England who issue lists of their stock periodically. These lists are available on request and, presumably, later editions will be sent as they come out.

My experience has been, however, that your name will stay on their mailing lists as long as you place an order occasionally; if you do not, the lists will stop coming (you can't blame them, really; printing costs money and the booksellers are trying to make a living).

In general, you will find that the prices from mail-order dealers are on the high side. There are many reasons for this. For instance, the rarity of the book will be a factor, its condition (you pay a price for out-of-print books in excellent condition) will make a big difference, and, of course, the booksellers must make up the costs of postage and printing and distributing lists. Not the least is charging what the market will bear, but this is not anything new in any field of commerce. I would suggest that you exhaust all sources of used books in your area before you turn to a mail-order firm. You might find what you want at home at a much cheaper price.

### ENGLISH DEALERS

**Francis Edwards, Ltd.**
**83 Marylebone High St.**
**London, W1M 4A1, England**

A three-pronged catalog: maritime and naval history, military history and aeronautics. Strong on past editions of "Jane's Fighting Ships." Good descriptions of condition.

**Fisher Nautical**
**130 Hollingbury Park Ave.**
**Brighton, BN1 7JP, Sussex, England**

Has over 5000 titles in stock. Brief annotations and descriptions of condition.

**Navigator Bookstore**
**31 Newtown Road**
**Warsash, Southhampton, England**

Catalog broken down into categories, such as Dinghies, Model Ships, Voyaging and Cruising, etc. Brief annotations; condition of most books not indicated. They have a system of premiums whereby you get a free copy of a book with a minimum purchase (List 3/72 offers a copy of "Bristow's Book of Yachts" for a $5 order; "Reflections in the Sea" for a $10 order.)

**Michael Prior**
**29 Chestnut Grove**
**Isleworth, TW7 7HA, Middlesex, England**

Short annotations and brief descriptions of condition.

**Norman Kerr, Bookseller**
**Cartmel, Grange-Over-Sands**
**Lancashire, England**

Good catalog for Americans: prices are given in both British and American currency. Books listed by subject area. Good descriptions of condition. Will handle orders for new books on request, but requires full name of author, book and publisher.

### AMERICAN DEALERS

**John Roby**
**3703 Nassau Drive**
**San Diego, California 92115**

Carries both current and out-of-print books. Books are briefly annotated with an indication of their condition.

**Jack Clinton**
**High St.**
**Hope Valley, Rhode Island 02832**

Out-of-print, scarce and rare books. Books are annotated and there are good descriptions of their condition.

**Owen Davies, Bookseller**
**1214 North LaSalle St.**
**Chicago, Illinois 60610**

Catalog lists more new books than out-of-print ones. Good annotation.

**Caravan-Maritime Books**
**87-06 186th Place**
**Jamaica, New York 11432**

Good selection, good annotation, good description of condition.

**Alfred W. Paine**
**Wolfpits Road**
**Bethel, Conn. 06801**

Exceptional descriptions of each book in stock. Concentrates on rare books on voyages, maps and charts and nautical science.

—PHS

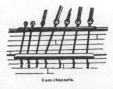

Fore-channels.

37

A Cutter Yacht.

# The Literature of
# Small Craft Design

Fin-shaped Keel of a Racing-yacht
("Smuggler," 1893).

Metacenter of a Vessel.
g, center of gravity; b, center of buoyancy when vessel is upright; b', center of buoyancy when she is listed as shown; m, metacenter for this particular list; for lists of less than 15° the position of m does not vary appreciably; m g, metacentric height; g s, righting-lever, or purchase of the force of buoyancy acting upward through b'.

### By E.S. Brewer, N.A.

There is no such thing as a complete book in small craft design for the simple reason that no one book could possibly begin to cover everything a designer needs to know.

Consider a few of the subjects which are a daily part of the small craft designer's work and you will see why it requires a fairly complete library to cover all of them: Hull design, including sail and power, mono and multihull; construction in wood, steel, aluminum, ferrocement and fiberglass (both custom and production); sail plans; engine installations; propellers; rudders; steering gears; spar and rig calculations; fishing gear; deck layouts; cabin arrangements; plumbing; electrical and electronic systems; tanks; fuel systems; rating rules; scantling rules; seaworthiness; tank testing, etc.—and these are just the highlights.

The complete design library must necessarily encompass a multitude of books on various subjects. But saying this, there is still the fact that modern advancements in technique and materials often render a book obsolescent before it leaves the publisher's hands.

There are a few volumes which are invaluable for reference, though, and deserving of a spot on the library shelves. However, before looking at these, let's clear up one point. No book, no matter how good, can teach a person to be a small craft designer. One publisher claims his offering contains "all the information one needs to design both sailing and power vessels." Even if this were true, the book could not give the reader the practical experience and background necessary to design a sound vessel. This can only come from several years of working under a leading designer, studying design and actual boats, sailing, racing and generally learning why one idea works where others don't, why some boats are handsome and others ugly, some fast and others slow. Such knowledge cannot be obtained from books but it can be added to, refined and updated by selective reading and study.

"Basic Naval Architecture" by K. C. Barnaby is an excellent book with which to begin our reviews as it provides all the basic calculations in one volume. The book is devoted to ships primarily but the methods of calculation are equally applicable to small craft. "Skene's Elements of Yacht Design," newly revised, by Francis S. Kinney, (Dodd, Mead, New York, 1973, 351 pp., $15.) is, without a doubt, the most complete one-volume work available on small craft design. The new version has a great deal of updated and added material compared to Kinney's original revision and is replete with many good illustrations of lines drawings, sail plans, layouts, etc., from leading designers. The accent of the work is on sail but there is some information on power boats, primarily planing hulls, and, of course, the basic calculations are applicable to both.

The standard hull calculations are gathered in one section at the back (stern?) of the book and are a useful reference. Spar and rigging strength calculations are covered in good detail in another chapter and this data

is particularly valuable as no other volume covers it quite so completely. Readers should note that there are some errors in the rigging calculation data though and obtain corrections from the publisher. This may be provided in an addenda in later issues of the book.

Scantling tables for wood hulls, both Nevins and Herreshoff, are given and are excellent reference data, hard to find elsewhere. However, metal, fiberglass and ferrocement construction are still treated lightly though in considerably more detail than the earlier edition. Despite a few shortcomings this is the best single volume available on small craft design and can be a nucleus about which a complete design library is built up.

"Yacht Designing and Planning" by Howard Chapelle, ( W. W. Norton, New York, 1971, 373 pp. $15.) has also been revised recently. It is quite dated, however, and the revisions are not as complete as is the Kinney work. The book is weak on calculations but strong on the practical aspects of design. Excellent sections on preliminary design work, appearance, seaworthiness and a particularly good description of the mechanics of drawing a set of lines are of value to the young designer.

The only construction discussed is wood and there are no scantling tables given, but there is a great deal of both general and detailed advice on wood construction. Rigs are reviewed in reasonable detail as well but the illustrations are of older types and the details very much dated.

Generally, this book will have more appeal to the man interested in traditional boats and cruisers than to the modern racing sailor. But it is a very readable, non-technical introduction to design and can be valuable to the beginner regardless of interest.

"Sailing Yacht Design" by D. Phillips-Birt (International Marine, Camden, Me., 1971, $12.50.) is another very complete volume but as the title implies, it is wholly concerned with sail. The book is somewhat dated, typically English in some of the author's views but still very worthwhile.

Birt's dissertations on hull shape including midsections, lateral plane, waterline shapes, displacement, etc., are more modern than in "Yacht Designing and Planning" and a bit more thorough than in "Skene's Elements of Yacht Design." The student designer will find this material informative provided he uses it as a stepping stone for further research and thought and does not accept all of the author's views blindly. Obviously, the same can be said for almost every book on small craft design as each author/designer has his own ideas and methods which he espouses.

Not to be confused with Birt's book is "Sailing Yacht Design" by Henry and Miller, (Cornell Maritime Press, Cambridge, Md. 1965, 139 pp, $5.) The book is concerned with American practice, primarily CCA type yachts prior to introduction of the IOR rule. The book does not attempt to teach design but discusses the state of the art as it existed in the early '60s. There are some useful discussions of proportion and

*Contd. on next page*

*Contd. from preceding page*

hull form along with reasonably complete spar and rigging calculation data. While much of the data contained can be found in more complete and/or updated form in Birt's or Kinney's books, "Sailing Yacht Design" is well written and a good addition to the design library.

We have discussed a number of books dealing primarily in sailing craft. There are fewer worthwhile design books on powerboats. "Naval Architecture of Planing Hulls" by Lindsay Lord (Cornell Maritime Press, Cambridge, Md. 1963. 319 pp, $6.) deals only with fast craft, as the name implies, but is even more limited in that it specifically is written about monohedron hulls, a type favored by Dr. Lord. There is an excellent section on calculations as well as data on powering, steering and similar topics of general interest. The material on construction deals only with wood and is somewhat limited in scope but it does touch on modern laminated composite construction techniques. The book will be of interest only to the designer of planing motorboats but it is one of the few deserving books available on the subject.

Another book on fast powerboats is John Teale's "High Speed Motor Boats." (Nautical Publishing, Lymington, Eng., 1969, 144 pp, $6.50). It is a slim volume but contains solid information on round-bilge, and deep-V hulls as well as stepped hulls and multihulls. There is also some data on construction, machinery, steering and related subjects. The book assumes that the reader has a sound knowledge of basic design and builds upon that.

Uffa Fox, the well known British designer and writer wrote "Seamanlike Sense in Powercraft," (Henry Regnery, Chicago, 1968, 257 pp. $15.) a thoroughly modern book about motorboats. Like Teale's, this is not a how-to book but is replete with drawings (including lines) and technical descriptions of a whole

range of craft from Venetian gondolas through German E boats to the deep-V ocean racers of the late '60s and even Hovercraft. There are sections on proportion, construction, propellers, drives, engines and rudders; all in all an extremely valuable and informative book that every powerboat designer should obtain. The accent is on fast boats but also on seaworthiness and like all of Fox's writing it is very enjoyable reading.

Another book that builds upon basic design knowledge is Phillips-Birt's "Naval Architecture of Small Craft." It contains much worthwhile information with particularly good chapters on resistance, high-speed craft and powering calculations. As well it is one of the few volumes which discusses displacement powerboats and fishing vessels to any extent. There are also meaty sections on course keeping, seaworthiness and stability, and discussions of sailing yachts and motor-sailers. All in all this is a valuable book and though now out of print, it deserves to be revised, updated and republished.

"The Sailing Yacht" by Juan Baader (W.W. Norton, New York, 1965, 336 pp. $15.) is another work that, like the foregoing, is a classic in its field. It does for sailing craft what Birt's book does for small craft in general, discussing the theory of sailing, aerodynamics, resistance, stability and similar topics in detail along with chapters on hull shapes and many other aspects of sailboat design and handling. I would consider it a must for the student of sailing yacht design.

The foregoing books have been those dealing with small craft design in general with emphasis on basic naval architecture, hull form, and powering. The naval architect must have detailed knowledge of many other phases of the art and one of the most important of these is construction.

There are several books dealing with wood construction — "Boatbuilding" by Howard Chapelle, (W.W. Norton, New York, 1969, 623 pp., $15.) "Boatbuilding

*Contd. on next page*

39

From "Yacht Design and Planning"

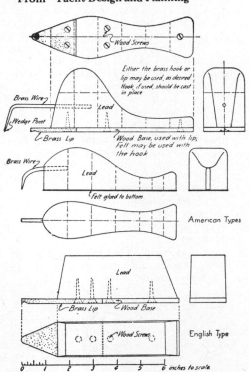

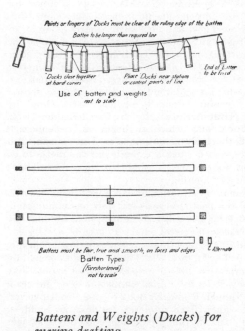

*Battens and Weights (Ducks) for marine drafting.*

*Contd. from preceding page*

Manual" by Robert Steward, (International Marine, Camden, Me. 1970, 220 pp., $9.50.). "Complete Amateur Boatbuilding" by Michael Verney, (Macmillan, New York, 1967, 160 pp., $7.95.) and "Yacht Construction" by K.H.C. Jurd. The first three books are aimed at the boat builder but all contain much valuable information for the designer of wood boats as well. Chapelle's book is far the most complete with numerous plans and almost 200 sketches of various details. Unfortunately, there is little data on modern building techniques such as longitudinal framing, cold molded construction or laminated timbers, but all the basic techniques are there and the book is still a must for the designer. "Boatbuilding Manual" is also in the "must" category. It is more concise than "Boatbuilding" and also more up to date and very well illustrated, altogether an excellent book. Verney's book is also very good but, being English, it varies from American practice in some ways.

"Yacht Construction" is a revision of "Practical Yacht Construction" by C.J. Watts and is addressed more to the designer than the builder. Although just issued, it is very British, very dated and quite useless. The rigging details shown would have been considered obsolete 25 years ago by U.S. standards.

Metal construction is detailed in only one book, "Small Steel Craft" by Ian Nicholson. (Adlard, Coles, London, 1971, 206 pp., $12.) Fortunately it is very good, with a wealth of information on design, construction and maintenance. Nothing equal has appeared on aluminum construction but many of the techniques described by Nicholson are applicable to aluminum craft as well. Some good books and pamphlets on aluminum boat construction can be obtained directly from the aluminum companies such as "Recommended Guide For Aluminum Crewboats" — Reynolds Metal Co.; "Aluminum Afloat" — Aluminum Co. of America; "Aluminum Boats" — Kaiser Aluminum and Chemical Co., and "Marine Aluminum Design and Construction" — The Aluminum Association.

Fiberglass construction is almost as poorly represented in print as aluminum. "Marine Design Manual for Fiberglass Reinforced Plastics" by Gibbs and Cox (McGraw, New York, $19.50.) is very thorough and very technical. It is a bit dated as well but is still needed by the designer working in fiberglass reinforced plastic. The methods described (longitudinal framed construction) are not common U.S. practice but the strength calculations, though tedious, are suitable to any construction method and are very useful. "Foam Sandwich Boatbuilding" by Peter Wynn (International Marine, Camden, Me. 1972, 128 pp., $9.95.) and "Amateur Fiberglass Boatbuilding" by Bruce Roberts-Goodwin are aimed at the amateur builder and are rather basic. Roberts' book appears to be more useful to the man desiring to learn more about one-off-fiberglass techniques.

Ferrocement construction has been written up in a rash of books in the past few years but few of them contain useful engineering data. "Ferro-Cement Boatbuilding" by Hartley, "Practical Ferro-Cement Boatbuilding" by Jay Benford and Herman Husen, (International Marine, Camden, 1971, 216 pp., $10.) and "Ferro-Cement" by Romack Marine are three examples. Benford's book is the best as it is written by a man who is a builder and naval architect, although Romack's book is good also. However, these books are written primarily for amateur builders, not designers, and the one good design book on the subject is "An Introduction To Design For Ferrocement Vessels," by Vessels and Engineering Division, Industrial Development Branch, Fisheries Service of Canada.

Essential references for designers on construction are the scantling rule books available from Lloyd's Register of Shipping. Individual books cover steel yachts, wood yachts, fiberglass yachts, ferrocement yachts, meter class yachts, fiberglass trawlers, etc. The steel scantling rules are applicable to aluminum by modifying plate and frame sizes by a certain percentage. Data on this change to aluminum is also available from Lloyd's Register of Shipping, 17 Battery Place, New York, N.Y., who should be contacted for information on price and availability of the various scantling rules.

Another essential reference is "Safety Standards for Small Craft" published by the American Boat and Yacht Council, 15 East 26th St. New York, N.Y. 10010. This large looseleaf volume contains a wealth of data on machinery, electrical, fire protection and dozens of similar installations. It is a must.

Most of the foregoing books are in the category of general design and construction. Many designers and students who wish to specialize in certain types of craft will require particular information to meet their needs. Works that will be of assistance in such cases are listed below. As you will see, the complete design library is a big one and the average designer is constantly adding to his library in an attempt to keep up to date on modern developments in all phases of the art.

—"Fishing Boats of the World" by J.O. Traung. (Fishing News Books, Ltd., London.) —Several volumes (Vol. I, 1969, 619 pp., $28.50; Vol. II, 1967, 619 pp., $28.50; Vol. III, 1971, 559 pp., $45.) published with valuable data on fishing boat design.

—"American Small Sailing Craft" by Howard Chapelle. (W.W. Norton, New York, 1951, 381 pp., $12.50.) Essential to the designer of small traditional sailboats.

—"Boatbuilding In Your Own Backyard" by S.S. Rabl (Cornell Maritime Press, Cambridge, Md. 1958, 233 pp., $10.) Simplified textbook on wood construction.

—"The Common Sense of Yacht Design" by L. Francis Herreshoff. Wonderfully readable treatise with many excellent pointers for the designer.

—"Sailing Theory and Practice" by C.A. Marchaj (Dodd, Mead, New York, $15.) Thorough technical work on the aerodynamics and hydrodynamics of sailing yachts.

—"Further Offshore" by John Illingworth (Quadrangle, Chicago, 1969, 336 pp., $20.) Very useful volume for the designer and owner of ocean racing yachts.

—"Racing and Cruising Trimarans" by R. Harris (Charles Scribner's Sons, New York, 1970, 216 pp., $7.95.) Interesting to the multihull designer.

—"Multihull Sailboats" by Edward Cotter (Crown Publishers, New York, 1971, 275 pp., $6.95.) Little information for a designer.

—"Cruising Under Sail" by Eric Hiscock (Oxford University Press, London, 1965, 408 pp., $15.95.) Many good points on design of cruising yachts.

—"The National Watercraft Collection" by Howard Chapelle (U.S. Govt. Printing Office, Washington, D.C.) Some data, drawings of interest to traditional boat designers.

—"Cruising Yachts" by T. Harrison Butler. How-to-design book on sailing yachts containing many dated ideas and methods.

Waterman's Knot.

# Where to get
# BOAT PLANS

### By Roger C. Taylor

This little essay is meant to answer the question, "Where do you get 'good' boat plans?" It is not meant to answer the question, "What are the characteristics of a 'good' boat?" Hopefully it will lead the interested reader to enough sources of boat plans that he can pick out some designs that he thinks will meet his requirements. For him, these will be "good" boats.

We are first tempted to answer the question about where we get our boat plans after the manner of the Boston ladies, who, when asked where they got their hats, drew themselves up and said, "We have them."

For we were lucky enough to be brought up in a household where there were years and years worth of boating magazines on various closet shelves, and the hundreds and hundreds of boat designs on all these pages were simply taken for granted. Their value is now better appreciated, and we can state categorically that the best source of boat plans is the back issues of boating magazines.

I would list "Yachting," "Rudder," "Motor Boating," and the "National Fisherman" as the best. Nor should one overlook foreign publications such as "Yachting Monthly" or "Le Yacht." Old issues of these and other marine periodicals should be obtained whenever possible, prized and hoarded, digested and indexed, and clipped. This last is difficult emotionally until one realizes that the only use of the designs in such magazines is just that, to be used. Slit your favorite designs right out with your knife, get them separated physically from the rest of the paraphernalia in the magazine and the boats you select for this treatment will begin to develop their true character in your mind. You will be able to visualize them at sea much better.

Another logical answer to the question of getting boat plans, and one that does not depend upon inheritance, is simply to look for them where you find them. Be alert to the possibilites.

Last winter while nursing a New York Boat Show headache, we wandered absentmindedly into one of those spiffy Manhattan bookstores where everything in the window has a page size of a couple of feet by three and costs upward of $47.50. "All right," we thought, "let's go look at how beautifully the Dutch can print gorgeous color photographs of rare Austrian porcelains in eight or nine colors." Boat plans were the furthest thing from our mind.

Back in a corner we sighted what appeared to be a nautical coffee table offering from Italy, called "Lo Yacht," by one Carlo Sciarrelli. Wearily did we lift the cover expecting to find the same old shopworn pictures of Britannia, Stormy Weather and Intrepid. Happily did we discover that Mr. Sciarrelli had put together easily the best collection of boat plans ever included within the boards of a book. We almost learned Italian to be able to read the text. We plan to sell this book in Italian at International Marine because of the great value of the plans it contains, and we hope someday to help make available an English language edition.

The copy of "Lo Yacht" in the store had obviously been there for some time, judging by the paw marks of the New York art set it displayed. That was nothing to the beating it's taken at our hands since. And to think that the clerk, with eyebrows raised and just a trace of a smile to indicate his recognition that we had

selected a mongrel from among his highly pedigreed stock, actually knocked a couple of bucks off the price for a somewhat damaged binding. We were glad he had no idea what we would have been willing to pay for the thing.

There are, of course, many fine books containing boat plans. To begin with the traditional, one of the best is Howard Chapelle's "American Small Sailing Craft." If you can supplement this with the out-of-print and hard-to-get "American Sailing Craft" by the same author, by all means do so. And, of course, Chapelle's new "The American Fishing Schooners" has plenty to offer.

Whenever boat plans are discussed, the Spray will command attention sooner or later. The best book

**41**

about her is "In the Wake of the Spray" by Kenneth Slack. It has plans and photos of a good many replicas as well as an extraordinary amount of detail on the Spray herself.

A great set of books for boat plans is the five titles by Uffa Fox: "Sailing, Seamanship and Yacht Construction," "Uffa Fox's Second Book," "Sail and Power," "Thoughts on Yachts and Yachting," and "Racing, Cruising and Design." These books have cruising, racing, and power craft, with all the plans redrawn for publication by the author, and among naval architects he was an outstanding draftsman. All these are, unfortunately, long out of print. Hopefully, Peter Davies in London can be prevailed upon to reprint all or some of them.

Two excellent books that show many modern boat plans are "The Proper Yacht" by Arthur Beiser, and "The Sailing Yacht" by Juan Baader. At present, the

*Contd. on next page*

*Contd. from preceding page*

former is available only through the Dolphin Book Club, which has reprinted its own edition.

A similar book from years back with plans of a good many of the older racing classes is "Sailing Craft" by Edwin J. Schoettle. This title is out of print, but does show up with some regularity on the secondhand market.

Two days before this writing, we were happy to have in hand the new reprinting of L. Francis Herreshoff's "The Common Sense of Yacht Design." This time the publisher went back to the original photographs, so that the reproduction of the photos is excellent in this printing. It is good to have this old friend available again, for it does contain some of the finest boat plans anywhere. It may be appropriate to add here that not long after the publication of the "Mariner's Catalog" International Marine will be publishing "Sensible Cruising Designs" by L. Francis Herreshoff, a book with 10 chapters of detailed plans and building instructions on 10 of Mr. Herreshoff's designs, with an appendix containing some 40 more of his designs for cruising boats.

The Seven Seas Press in New York has done a service by bringing out pamphlets of designs of certain designers, including John Hanna, Tom Colvin, Thomas Gillmer, A. Mason, and Winthrop L. Warner.

One standby for boat plans is the old "Motor Boating" publication, "Designs for 363 Boats You Can Build," now out of print. A number of designs are by one or the other of the Atkins, William or John, and this reminds us that their books, "The First Book of Boats" and "The Second Book of Boats" are also sources of interesting boat plans. The "Second Book of Boats" is still available, but the "First" is out of print.

If shallow draft interests you, by all means get a copy of "The Good Little Ship" by Vincent Gilpin if you can. This book has been in and out of print and is now out.

Moving to Europe for a bit, one of the best books is "Fore and Aft Craft" by E. Keble Chatterton, or in its later version, "Fore and Aft Sailing Craft" revised by Douglas Phillips-Birt. Both versions contain excellent boat plans. Both are out of print.

Maurice Griffiths, the retired editor of "Yachting Monthly" and a naval architect, has put together two fine books of boat plans, "Dream Ships," out of print, and "Little Ships and Shoal Waters," which has been reprinted. Then there is Claude Worth's "Yacht Crusing," which contains the plans of the boats he owned and sailed, and which has been reprinted.

If you have an interest in Dutch craft, "Dutch Yachts in the Future" is a must. This book is one of the best examples of how to publish boat plans in book form.

Some cruising books include the plans of the vessel whose voyage is described. Every cruising book should. There is great value in including the plans of a boat whose behavior and performance is discussed in detail. A couple of examples that come to mind are the plans of the excellent Redningskoite Norwegian ketch Gaucho in Ernesto Uriburu's book, "Sea Going Gaucho;" and the plans of the Starling Burgess-Francis Herreshoff designed cruising brigantine, Varua, in William A. Robinson's book, "To the Great Southern Sea."

Another source of boat plans is the study plan booklets provided by naval architects themselves. Some of these are excellent, such as those published by Jay Benford or Steve Seaton. Most leave a good deal to be desired as to presentation and usefulness. A couple of these booklets well worth writing for in our opinion

are those of Harold H. Payson, Pleasant Beach Road, South Thomaston, Maine 04858, for Texas Dories and other small craft; and of Arthur R. Wycoff, 23244 West Road, Cleveland, Ohio 44138, for some interesting cruising ketches and trawler-type yachts.

Perhaps it would not be out of place here to mention that International Marine has in preparation a large, hard-cover book presenting and describing the boat designs of John G. Alden, and also a similar book on the designs of Phil Bolger, the latter written by the designer himself. And we'd like to make something of a point of that last statement, because Phil Bolger happens to be one of the best writers we've had the privilege of working with, even though he is a boat designer.

Finally, the seeker of boat plans can of course go straight to the horse's mouth, that is he can seek out the original drawings of a naval architect. For example, the plans of Ralph Winslow are now collected at the Mystic Seaport. And if anyone wants to make a pilgrimage out of this sort of thing, we would urge him to travel to the Hart Nautical Museum at M. I. T. in Cambridge, Mass., where, if he can demonstrate a reasonable affinity for boats and the water to Curator William A. Baker, he will perhaps be allowed to climb to the very pinnacle of studying boat plans by carefully viewing the drawings of the Herreshoff Manufacturing Company, showing the boats designed by Nathanael Greene Herreshoff.

## It Would Be Nice

"Sea Sense" by Richard Henderson.
International Marine Publishing Co., Camden, Me.
1072, 307 pp., illustrated, index, $12.50.

If every boat owner in America took the time to read this book and followed its advice, nobody would ever get into trouble again on the waters. This is a far-fetched presumption only, mind you.

It would fail on two counts; (1) you couldn't make every "Joe Boat Owner" read this book, and (2) the sea is an unpredictable thing which can create a multitude of situations that can't be covered in any book.

However, Richard Henderson has covered the subject of safety afloat about as well as anybody can. This book contains a wealth of information and advice ranging from choosing a suitable boat to weathering severe storms offshore. He covers in detail many aspects of safety not found in other books. One that I found extremely informative was the section on fire prevention and control.

Just as important as all the information and advice is the feeling of respect for the sea that the author instills in the reader. This respect combined with knowledge is what I think the term "sea sense" is all about.

—Bruce White

## Drafting Tools

From Alvin & Co. catalog.

**COPENHAGEN SHIP CURVES**

**No. 1020** Set of 56 ship curves as illustrated below. Packed in clear lacquer finished solid walnut case with 3 compartments. (illustrated approx. 1/10 actual size)

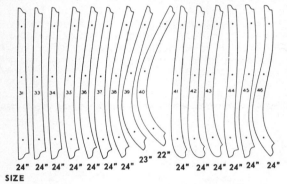

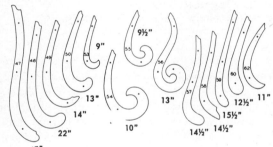

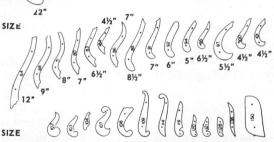

**No. 1021 SEPARATE ACRYLIC COPENHAGEN SHIP CURVES**

| Pattern | | Pattern | | Pattern | | Pattern | |
|---|---|---|---|---|---|---|---|
| 31 | 39 | 46 | 55 | 64 | 89 | 101 | 114 |
| 33 | 40 | 47 | 56 | 68 | 91 | 102 | 119 |
| 34 | 41 | 48 | 57 | 71 | 92 | 103 | 120 |
| 35 | 42 | 49 | 58 | 80 | 94 | 104 | 121 |
| 36 | 43 | 50 | 59 | 83 | 95 | 107 | 128 |
| 37 | 44 | 53 | 60 | 84 | 97 | 108 | 136 |
| 38 | 45 | 54 | 62 | 86 | 100 | 109 | 150 |

It must be grand to know how to draw. What an aid! Alas, some must trace and draft alone, trusting that other gifts will come in other lives. Talent or no, a notebook is crippled without some means of rendering ideas and thoughts and recording the gadgets and gilhickies of others. Furthermore, virtually every book on designing and boatbuilding begins with several pages on the proper tools for use in marine drafting. Where to get them?

Alvin and Company carries tools to meet every drawing, drafting and graphing need, including ship curves, splines and spline weights, all manner of templates, transfers, tapes, etc.

**Alvin and Company**
**Windsor, Conn. 06095**

Various Spicules from Glass sponges (*Hexactinellida*).
1, oxydiact; 2, echinate oxydiact; 3, echinate hexact; 4, amphidisk; 5, ancora; 6, tetract; 7, oxyhexact; 8, discohexaster; 9, triact.

Charrette is another organization which can meet every drawing need. It is an especially interesting firm to the marine notekeeper because of its wonderful array of drafting papers, mylars, tracing papers, specialized drawing instruments and very useful and, in some cases, unique modeling materials and equipment. Their catalog reveals some very classy shopping and, when your drawings are done, their reprographics services will print, blueprint, blow up or down most anything you want. Individuals and institutions engaged in oceanographic bottom or shoreline studies will be interested in the topographic three-dimensional map reproduction service. They'll give you a price estimate free of charge and claim that their costs are just equal to what it would cost to make the models in-house except that you won't have to tie up key people. In any case, Charrette should be an arrow in the quiver of anyone who's lief to put things down on paper.

—GP

**Charrette Cambridge**
**2000 Mass. Ave.**
**Cambridge, Mass. 02140**

**Charrette New York**
**139 East 47th St.**
**New York, N.Y. 10017**

Charrette items shown on next page.

Items from Charrette catalog. Topofoam Contour Models

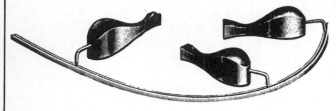

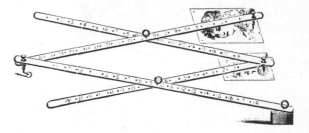

### Splines and Weights

Transparent plastic spline used with weights for drawing long, true curves. Weights are attached to track on spline to hold curve in position.

| | |
|---|---|
| 24″ | $1.45 • |
| 36″ | 2.25 |
| 48″ | 2.95 • |
| 60″ | 4.50 |

Spline Weights — lead, 4 pounds each. $7.50 •

### 1311 Compensating Planimeter

Same as No. 1310, but with adjustable pole arm that will extend to 13″. Especially suitable for measuring very large or very small surfaces. The constant can be adjusted to a round figure of 20,000. Comes with two tables of settings for English and Metric systems and testing rule. Packed in velvet lined case, with instruction book. $95.00

### 1290 Quick Change Pantograph

All aluminum pantograph for enlarging, reducing, reproducing. Slight pressure with finger permits micrometer setting to desired ratio. All bars accurately numbered. 26 and 32 given ratios, but can be set to any desired ratio. 21″ long metal bars, ¾″ wide x 3/16″ thick. Extra steel point for technical work. Comes assembled, with accessories and instructions. $12.65

1311

44

Adjustable curves have been a hot drawing item in the last few years. The trouble is that that is what they have been — a hot item. Everyone who needs to draw curves ever-so-wishes he could have one tool to do them all and not always have to pick through the pile trying this and that one until a fit is found. Unfortunately, the lead core ones are not really up to standard; they do work all right but visitors and friends somehow can't keep their hands off and, once they have put three or four hard bends in them, you have to fuss a lot to get them to fair again. In many cases, little time is saved in getting the curve right over picking out the right curve.

The Hoyle Engineering Co. has come up with a development in an Adjustable French Curve. This flexible curve has one edge flat for pencil and the other has a bead for a ruling pen. Each unit is made of 12 interlocking channels extruded from clear butyrate plastic. Looks interesting, and we would like a use-report from anyone who's tried it on their own board.

**Hoyle Engineering Co.**
**302 Orange Grove**
**Fillmore, Calif. 93015**

**From Hoyle catalog.**

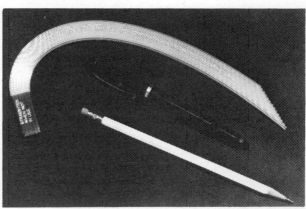

## Improve Your Clipping

Many boatmen are enthusiastic magazine boat plan clippers and there probably is not one of them who has not wished he could enlarge the plans to see them in a bigger scale. Edmund Scientific Co. has published a fine little pamphlet called "Optical Drawing Devices" and in it are plans for many drawing aids that you can build yourself using simple tools, plain wood and some few very low-cost optics that Edmund offers as well. The plans for drawing projectors are especially interesting, for they allow you to enlarge anything in print without having to clip them.

—GP

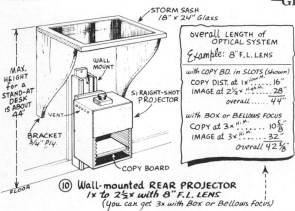

overall LENGTH of OPTICAL SYSTEM

*Example:* 8" F.L. LENS

with COPY BD. in SLOTS (shown)
COPY DIST. at 1x Low M. ... 16"
IMAGE at 2½x High M. ... 28"
overall ...... 44"

with BOX or BELLOWS FOCUS
COPY at 3x H.M. ... 10⅝"
IMAGE at 3x H.M. ... 32"
overall 42⅝"

**⑩ Wall-mounted REAR PROJECTOR**
1x to 2½x with 8" F.L. LENS
*(You can get 3x with Box or Bellows Focus)*

VERTICAL REAR PROJECTION. You use the same straight-shot box as before, except it is now pointing upward to the work surface, Fig. 10. It will be apparent that only a limited amount of vertical space is available, especially if you want a sit-down console. Fig. 10 is a stand-at desk, with the copy in slots. You can gain a little more M. in the same space by using box or bellows focus, as tabulated above.

For higher M. in the same or shorter space, you will need a shorter f.l. lens. If also you want a fair-size field of at least 6 x 6 inches, it means your lens must be a fairly expensive camera or enlarger objective. A typical choice would be a 6-3/8 in. Kodak anastigmat; the same lens is available at times in military surplus, being the objective of the K-20 Aerial Camera, Fig. 12. This lens and focal length is used for 4 x 5 inch or smaller cameras, but it will cover 6 x 6 in an opaque projector because you never use it at the infinity setting. For example, if your top M. is 4x, the copy distance will be 8 in., Fig. 11, and in this distance you get the needed spread of the light cone to cover 6 x 6 in. copy. At 2x, the lens will cover 9 in. copy.

Fig. 13 shows the construction of desk-mounted rear projector. Rough focusing is done by pushing the whole projector up or down, the instrument being counterbalanced to stay put at any position. The final focus is done with a sliding box carrying the K-20 aerial camera lens or similar. Focusing is a bit awkward in that you must squat down and look up at the image; rack-and-pinion focusing with remote control by flexible shaft would be an improvement. Do not try to make the sliding box a snug slide fit in the outer box—a loose, free-sliding fit is all you need.

**Edmund Scientific Co.**
**101 East Gloucester Pike**
**Barrington, N.J.**

Catalog is free; "Optical Drawing Instruments" is 50 cents.

All material below from Edmund catalog.

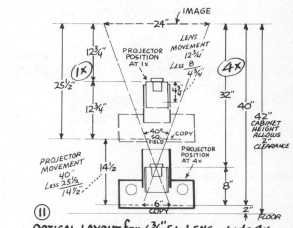

**⑪ OPTICAL LAYOUT for 6⅜" F.L. LENS - 1x to 4x**

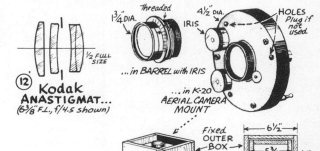

**⑫ Kodak ANASTIGMAT...**
(6⅜" F.L., f/4.5 shown)

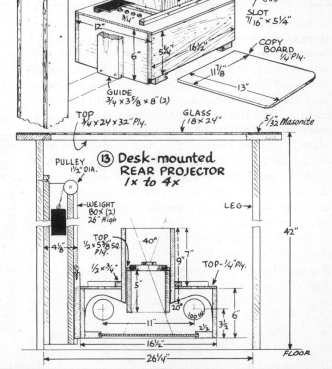

**⑬ Desk-mounted REAR PROJECTOR 1x to 4x**

45

# WOOD

I know people for whom wood has replaced sex, doing ill neither to the wood, nor to sex. Wood is the heart of the fetish for many boatmen and, once you begin to learn about it and to work it up, it is easy to understand why. It is an uncanny and wonderful substance. It can draw you, baffle and frustrate you, do anything you tell it to, or nothing. In any case, the study and use of woods is part and parcel of much of the serious small pleasure boat experience.

There are thousands of wood suppliers and if you have a good one locally who runs a conscientious business, you'd best share his name only with a few people you like. Every boat builder cultivates a private relationship with his wood supplier, for this man has his finger on the pulse. He can't see the forest for the trees and that is just the way you want it. Supplies are often short and expensive and the boatbuilder's requirements are often in the special favors department.

There are several really good discussions of woods appropriate to boatbuilding in books and some of these books are so fundamental to even a rudimentary library in the field (Chapelle, Steward, etc.), that I won't discuss them. The listings below are of large specialist firms whose business is to meet large-scale specialists' wood needs, including boat construction. We like to see people use local woods when possible. It is always less expensive and often very sensible in that the wood is geared to the local climate and micro-organisms and can be replaced easily. Too, it helps keep the pressure off of the rare-woods market. To be sure, it is very hard to beat a nice piece of teak or Honduras mahogany here and there, but if you are familiar with the politics surrounding the marketing of these woods, you probably would as soon pass up the luxury. In the case of redwood, if you know the ecological situation and the results of the lumbering methods for this species, you don't touch a toothpick made out of it, let alone put a piece of it in your boat.

So these firms are specialists, for your special needs or luxuries:

—GP

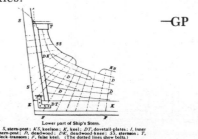

Lower part of Ship's Stern.

S, stern-post; A'S, keelson; K, keel; DT, dovetail-plates; I, inner
stern-post; D, deadwood; DK, deadwood-knee; SS, sternson; T,
deck-transom; F, false keel. (The dotted lines show bolts.)

A sculptor friend of mine mentioned to me that he had just purchased an entire 7' log of rosewood for $50. Fifty Bucks!? I had just paid $20 for a knife with a little tiny rosewood handle! He had a **log** of it! I asked where and he directed me to Monteath. This amazing organization sells wood in plywood, veneer, lumber, timber and log form. Note that the illustrated list begins, "A **few** of the. . ."

**J.H. Monteath Co.**
**Foreign and Domestic Woods**
**Logs, Lumber, Plywoods and Veneers**
**2500 Park Ave.**
**Bronx, N.Y. 10451**

A few of the many woods available from Monteath. Most of the woods can be furnished in either lumber, veneers or plywood.

| WOODS | COUNTRY OF ORIGIN | COLOR |
|---|---|---|
| AFRORMOSIA | Africa | Yellowish brown |
| ASH | United States | Cream to light brown |
| AVODIRE | Africa | White to gold |
| BALSAWOOD | Ecuador | White to pink-white |
| BENGE | Africa | Tan, black stripe |
| BIRCH | U.S. & Canada | Light brown, red tinge |
| BOXWOOD | Venezuela, Columbia | Yellowish-white |
| BUBINGA | Africa | Red, purple stripes |
| BUTTERNUT | United States | Pale brown |
| CARPATHIAN ELM | France | Brick red to tan |
| CEDARS | United States | Light red |
| CHERRY | United States | Light reddish brown |
| CHESTNUT | United States | Reddish brown |
| COCOBOLO | Nicaragua, Costa Rica | Yellowish brown |
| CYPRESS, PECKY | United States | Yellowish red |
| DEGAME | Central America | Creamy yellow |
| EBONY | Africa, Ceylon | Black |
| OLLA | Brazil | Dark brown, pink, |
| GREENHEART | Guyana | Light olive to black |
| GRENADILLA | Africa | Black |
| HICKORY | United States | White to cream |
| HOLLY (WHITE) | United States | White |
| IMBUYA | Brazil | Rich brown |
| KOA | Hawaii | Golden brown |
| LIGNUM VITAE | Cent. Amer., W. Indies | Olive brown to black |
| LIMBA | Africa | Pale yellow to light brown |
| MAHOGANY | Honduras, Africa, Philippines | Pink to redish brown |
| MAKORE | Africa | Pink-brown to red-brown |
| MAPLE | U.S. & Canada | Cream to light redish brown |
| OAK | United States | Light brown |
| PALDAO | Philippines, Indo China | Gray to reddish brown |
| PECAN | United States | Reddish brown |
| PERSIMMON | United States | Dark brown |
| POPLAR | United States | Pale yellow-green |
| PRIMA VERA | Guatamala | Yellow-white to Yellow-brown |
| PURPLEHEART | Guyana | Deep purple |
| RAMIN | Malaysia | Golden |
| ROSEWOOD | Brazil, Honduras, E.India, Africa | Dark brown to purple |
| SATINWOOD | Ceylon | Pale gold |
| SITKA SPRUCE | United States | Yellowish white |
| SNAKEWOOD | Dutch Guiana | Reddish brown |
| TEAKWOOD | Thailand, Burma | Tawny yellow to dark brown |
| TULIPWOOD | Brazil | Light, red & yellow streaks |
| WALNUT | America, Africa, France, England | Gray brown to purple brown |
| WENGE | Africa | Blackish brown |
| ZEBRA | Africa | Straw and dark brown |

Another source of fine rare woods, this one on the West Coast, is R.M. Albrecht of Northridge, Calif. Most of their stock is high-grade rough-sawn wood and, back-to-back with a line of very high-grade tools for carving, they should be a good one-source supplier for anyone's carving need. How would you like half of a 10" diameter log of avacado? No? Well, how about some 12" apricot? No? Well . . .

**Robert M. Albrecht**
**8635 Yolanda Ave.**
**Northridge, California 91324**

46

**Craftsman Wood Service Co.**
**2727 South Mary Street**
**Chicago, Ill. 60608**

Most of what Craftsman offers is in the trailboards and fiddleheads department; woods and tools for small carving, filigree, inlays, veneering and gilding. But for woodwork of this sort they are terrific. How about an inlayed chessboard in the cabin table? Inlayed banding around the bulkheads? Gilded fiddleheads? A walnut kingspoke for the ship's wheel? How about a three-string dulcimer kit for knee-to-knee music in the cockpit?

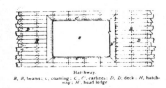

Hatchway.

_B, B, beams; C, coaming; C, C, carlines; D, D, deck; H, hatchway; H, head ledge_

**Material at right from Craftsman catalog.**

●"What Wood is That?" by Herbert L. Edlin.
**Viking Press, New York.**
**1969, 160 pp., illustrated, $7.95.**

The ability to identify types of wood is important for boatmen and boatbuilders, but how many have it? It takes time and experience to learn your wood. Those who have a teacher are lucky; those who do not, have to turn to books. But most books are inadequate because they don't give you concrete examples. This one does.

Along with the text is a fold-out section that has genuine samples of 40 different types of wood ranging from afrormosia to zebrawood and including ash, cedar, Douglas fir, iroko, mohagany (African and Honduras), oak, teak and walnut. The text describes each one of the 40 types as to origin, selection, characteristics, use, availability, etc. And, to help you identify these types by sight, feel and smell, the author has devised a system of 14 keys, which works whether the wood is new or old, finished or unfinished.

The system is based on the process of elimination and it works remarkably well. For a general understanding of wood, the author has written a section that lays bare the secrets of botany for the layman and describes the various ways of cutting wood to provide lumber and veneers. The book is a steal at the price.

—PHS

**Quote at right from "What Wood . . . "**

## MULTICOLORED INLAY BANDINGS

These beautiful Bandings are made of rare woods of different colors and the design goes through, making both sides the same. Are supplied in a multitude of designs and patterns, to harmonize with any and all classes of fine examples of woodwork. Illustrations are actual width and color. Thickness about 1/20th of an inch.

This material is sold in strips of 1 yard or 36 inches and the price quoted is for full length strips. To use, a suitable groove is routed in the work and the banding glued in place. Before applying filler and stain, the banding should be prevented against absorption of

**Liberal Discounts to Schools, Manufacturers, Quantity Users**

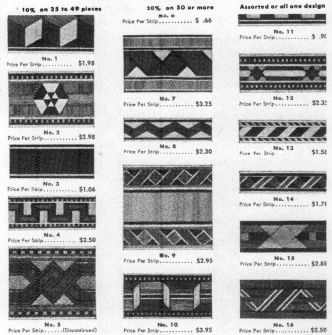

10% on 25 to 49 pieces

No. 1 — Price Per Strip........ $1.98
No. 2 — Price Per Strip........ $2.98
No. 3 — Price Per Strip........ $1.06
No. 4 — Price Per Strip........ $2.50
No. 5 — Price Per Strip......(Discontinued)

20% on 50 or more

No. 6 — Price Per Strip........ $ .66
No. 7 — Price Per Strip........ $3.25
No. 8 — Price Per Strip........ $2.30
No. 9 — Price Per Strip........ $2.95
No. 10 — Price Per Strip........ $3.95

Assorted or all one design

No. 11 — Price Per Strip........ $ .90
No. 12 — Price Per Strip........ $2.35
No. 13 — Price Per Strip........ $1.58
No. 14 — Price Per Strip........ $1.78
No. 15 — Price Per Strip........ $2.88
No. 16 — Price Per Strip........ $2.50

**18 Iroko** _Chlorophora excelsa_

FAMILY: Mulberry (Moraceae)     KEY: E6
SOURCE: West Africa

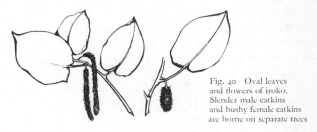

Fig. 40 Oval leaves and flowers of iroko. Slender male catkins and bushy female catkins are borne on separate trees

Iroko is a strong, mid-brown, durable timber that has a close resemblance to teak, indeed it is often marketed as African or Nigerian teak. It can readily be distinguished by its scattered pores, contrasting with the ring-porous structure of true teak. Yellow bands of soft tissue form a lively zigzag pattern on all surfaces, and this, too, contrasts with the uniform colour of teak. Iroko is fairly soft and easy to work, and the Africans use it for carving wooden platters and bowls, spoons and similar household utensils, and for sculpturing wooden figures and statues. Canoes are hollowed out of large trunks, and because of its natural durability it is used for fence posts and building construction.

Supplies are plentiful, and much iroko is exported as large logs or baulks. In America and Europe it is employed for much the same jobs as teak, including benches for workshops and laboratories, counters for shops, sturdy joinery, outdoor seats and tables, and in boat building.

Iroko grows wild as a tall savanna tree right across Africa from Sierra Leone through Ghana and Nigeria to Tanzania. Its bark is greyish white, wrinkled and scaly, and holds a sticky latex which oozes out from any wound and seals it off. The young twigs, purplish in colour, bear simple oval leaves that end in blunt points. The flowers are catkin-like, and droop downwards. Native names include 'odoum', 'mvule' and 'kampala'.

47

### The 'New' Balsa

I hadn't paid much attention to balsa since I was a kid. It was something that ship's liferafts were made of, and model airplanes. Generally, one thought of it as a cheap utilitarian or play substance and certainly not a serious wood. Then a friend showed me how strong balsa really was and how a strip-built model boat made of it could take anything made of pine on the pond and I looked into it. It turns out the stuff has been sitting around for years just waiting for modern materials to give it the nod.

Balsa Ecuador specializes in balsawood, especially as it applies to modern structural applications. Their Contourkore is particularly interesting to the boatbuilder. A field of end-grain balsa blocks is attached to an open-weave fiberglass scrim, making a blanket which can literally be laid over a mold for strong and light wood-fiberglass composite construction. They have a pamphlet call "Belcobalsa" and it gives even the hard-core materials reactionary pause for thought.

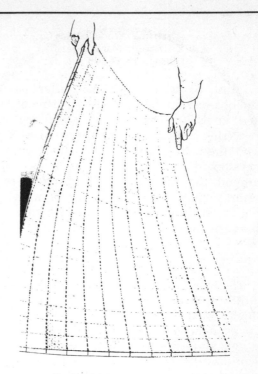

## MECHANICAL PROPERTIES
(Data For Pieces Averaging 12% Moisture Content)

| | Weight in pounds per cubic foot | 6 | 11 | 15½ |
|---|---|---|---|---|
| | Specific gravity | .0962 | .176 | .248 |
| | **COMPRESSIVE STRENGTH (pounds per sq. inch)** | | | |
| | **A)** Parallel to grain (end grain) | | | |
| | — Stress at proportional limit | 500 | 1,450 | 2,310 |
| | — Maximum crushing strength | 750 | 1,910 | 2,950 |
| | — Modulus of elasticity | 330,000 | 768,000 | 1,164,000 |
| | **B)** Perpendicular to grain (flat grain) | | | |
| | — Stress at proportional limit | | | |
| | high strength value | 84 | 144 | 198 |
| | low strength value | 50 | 100 | 145 |
| | — Modulus of elasticity | | | |
| | high strength value | 16,000 | 37,000 | 55,000 |
| | low strength value | 5,100 | 13,000 | 19,900 |
| | **BENDING STRENGTH (pounds per sq. inch)** | | | |
| | Static bending | | | |
| | — Stress at proportional limit | 825 | 1,725 | 2,535 |
| | — Modulus of rupture | 1,375 | 3,050 | 4,525 |
| | — Modulus of elasticity | 280,000 | 625,000 | 925,000 |
| | **TENSILE STRENGTH (pounds per sq. inch)** | | | |
| | **A)** Parallel to grain (end grain) | | | |
| | — Maximum | 1,375 | 3,050 | 4,525 |
| | **B)** Perpendicular to grain (flat grain) | | | |
| | — Maximum — high strength value | 112 | 170 | 223 |
| | — low strength value | 72 | 118 | 156 |
| | **TOUGHNESS (inch pound per specimen)** | | | |
| | — high strength value | 125 | 310 | 475 |
| | — low strength value | 120 | 267 | 400 |
| | **SHEAR (pounds per sq. inch)** | | | |
| | — high strength value | 180 | 360 | 522 |
| | — low strength value | 158 | 298 | 425 |
| | **HARDNESS (pounds)** | | | |
| | load required to embed a .444" ball to one half its diameter | | | |
| | **A)** Parallel to grain (end grain) | 102 | 250 | 386 |
| | **B)** Perpendicular to grain (flat grain) | | | |
| | — high strength value | 50 | 120 | 186 |
| | — low strength value | 47 | 103 | 151 |
| | **CLEAVAGE (pounds per inch of width)** | | | |
| | Load to cause splitting | | | |
| | — high strength value | 56 | 70 | 87 |
| | — low strength value | 37 | 63 | 86 |

**Contourkore**
Where construction requires the sandwich core to conform to contoured surfaces, such as a boat hull, CONTOURKORE is the answer—a blanket formed of end-grain BELCOBALSA blocks attached to an open-weave fiberglass scrim.

**Balsa Ecuador Lumber Corp.**
**10 Fairway Court**
**P.O. Box 220**
**Northvale, N.J. 07647**

Knockabout.

Raceabout.

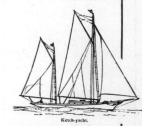
Ketch-yacht.

### Strength of BELCOBALSA as Compared with Light Weight Materials

| | Weight lbs./cu. ft. | Specific Gravity | Maximum Crushing Strength (Parallel to Grain) | Stress at Proportional Limit (Perpendicular to Grain) | Modulus of Elasticity Parallel to Grain | Modulus of Elasticity Perpendicular to Grain | TENSILE STRENGTH (psi) Maximum Parallel to Grain | TENSILE STRENGTH (psi) Maximum Perpendicular to Grain | BENDING STRENGTH Modulus of Rupture | BENDING STRENGTH Modulus of Elasticity |
|---|---|---|---|---|---|---|---|---|---|---|
| BELCOBALSA* | 6 | .0962 | 750 | 50-84 | 330,000 | 5,100-16,000 | 1,375 | 72-112 | 1,375 | 280,000 |
| BELCOBALSA* | 11 | .176 | 1,910 | 100-144 | 768,000 | 13,000-37,000 | 3,050 | 118-170 | 3,050 | 625,000 |
| BELCOBALSA* | 15½ | .248 | 2,950 | 145-198 | 1,164,000 | 19,900-55,000 | 4,525 | 155-223 | 4,525 | 925,000 |
| Polyvinyl Chloride** | 4 | .064 | 140 | | 6,400 | | not given | not given | not given | 7,000-8,500 |
| Polyvinyl Chloride** | 6 | .0962 | 230-320 | | 7,900-10,000 | | not given | not given | not given | 10,000-13,000 |
| Polyurethane Foam** | 2 | .032 | 16-43 | not given | 1,300 | 600 | 36 | 29 | not given | 600-1,300 |
| Polyurethane Foam** | 6 | .096 | 150 | not given | 5,600 | not given | 190 | not given | not given | 5,600 |

*At 12% m.c.
**At 70°F

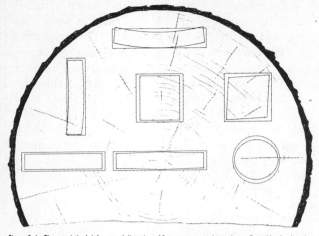

Figure 3-6. Characteristic shrinkage and distortion of flats, squares, and rounds as affected by the direction of the annual rings. Tangential shrinkage is about twice as great as radial.

The highly recommended three-volume work entitled "Wood: A Manual For Its Use As A Shipbuilding Material," published by the U.S. Government Printing Office (Navships 250-336) is now unfortunately out of print. The Public Documents Department recommended that anyone interested in consulting this excellent work look for it in any public library that is a repository for government publications.

—GP

"Wood: A Manual for its Use as a Shipbuilding Material," 3 vol. Bureau of Ships, Department of the Navy.
Available from Superintendent of Documents, Washington, D.C.
Paperbound. Vol. 1, $.45; Vol. 2, $.45; Vol. 3, $.60.

These booklets were prepared by the government to provide technical information on boat-building woods not usually found elsewhere. Volumes 1 and 2 are of interest in a general sense, giving details on types of wood, the use of wood in boats, cause of rot, prevention of rot, seasoning and storing wood, repairing and storing wooden boats. Volume 3 has more technical data concerning the boat and ship design aspects of wood — it has tables, formulas and diagrams to determine the strength and durability of boat-building woods. It also goes into detail beyond the ordinary on the strengths and characteristics of fastenings, joints and glues. A feature of all three volumes is the bibliographic material: each chapter has a list of primary sources where you can find more information.

—PHS

### Particleboard

Particleboard has some few uses around a boatshop. It is a product often made from wastes of other wood industries and its use is encouraged where its extra weight characteristics are not a disadvantage. It's very useful for shelves, benches, some bulkhead situations, galley counters and the like. It laminates and veneers well and its shaping properties are excellent. Most craftsmen who try a sheet of it look for ways to use it again. There are many sources. One is

**The Celotex Corp.**
**Tampa, Fla.**

Their Baraboard is excellent, especially because of its stability. Their biggest problem is that they harvest hardwood logs and chip them to make the product rather than use other's wastes. They produce 44,000,000 square feet of board annually and use 80,000 hardwood logs to do it.

The "National Fisherman" of February 1968 had the following remarks from Dr. Alan A. Marra of Michigan on the future of wood:

Dr. Alan A. Marra, professor of wood science and technology at the University Michigan, pointed out in an address here at State College of Forestry that:
—Wood does not corrode.
—Wood does not burn unless heated to 450 degrees F or more.
—It does not decay at moisture content below 18%.
—It is more heat-stable that metal or plastics.
—Weight for weight it is stronger than steel.
—Wood is long-lived. Japanese temples exist today which were built more than a thousand years ago.
Prof. Marra told members of a symposium on wood design and aesthetics, however, that wood does not have a good history of responding to technological change.
"Although there has been considerable mechanization and modifications or refinements of standard products and processes, with some shift toward more panelized or sheet products, total consumption of wood has remained fairly constant for many years," he said.
"This means a downward trend in per capita consumption and suggests that this old material requires new approaches in order to extract in the future the benefits for which wood is noted."
Marra discussed a number of concepts involved in the economical production of wood articles.
Performance attributes of wood must change, he explained, noting that current consumer demands include better paint holding, more fire resistance, more decay resistance, more dimension and shape stability, less splitting and grain raising, larger sizes and lower costs. These, he noted, will have to be provided with a timber resource which is declining in quality through an increasingly mechanized industrial system.
Much of today's U.S. forest resource, still recovering values after "the catastrophic harvesting of virgin timber

**49**

*Contd. on next page*

Contd. from preceding page

during the last century, is expected to serve multiple (and sometimes incompatible) purposes of watershed control, recreation, fish and wildlife habitat, grazing and climate control," the U-M authority explained. Pressures exist to harvest only the best trees.

"The new technologies, as a broad, far-reaching objective, should permit the utilization of any tree irrespective of its form, size, species or quantity," Marra said. "With such a capability, forests could produce a perpetual supply of low-cost woods even though managed for other purposes."

One means of using low-cost woods is to reduce them to flakes:

"While varying degrees of mechanization are applicable throughout the series of wood elements, automation begins with the flake," Marra declared.

"The flake also represents the point where wood begins to lose one of its most important characteristics: beauty of grain," he added. "From the flake on, aesthetic qualities must be conferred the same as for other materials."

—GP

"Guide to Plywood Grades" (Form Q390)
American Plywood Association
Tacoma, Wash.
Free for the asking.

If you're going to build in plywood, you've got to have this pamphlet. Tells you how to read all those code letters and numbers on plywood sheets and allows you to talk knowledgeably with your lumber yard man.

—PHS

An interesting aspect of the history of small craft is their regionalism, not only in form and use, but in their materials as well. An expanding marketplace and developments in transportation have blurred many of these regional uses beyond validity. Boatbuilding, especially of workboats, still finds cost differences enough to favor local woods over those that require long shipments. We wrote Stanley Horn, president of J.H. Baird Publishing Co., who publishes, "Southern Lumberman," and asked him about sources of boat lumber in the South. He sent us the following gracious note:

> Dear Mr. Getchell:
> Most of the wood boats now being built in the South use longleaf yellow pine for framing and timbers and white cedar or cypress for planking. The Gulf Lumber Co., P.O. Box 1663, Mobile, Ala. 36601, would be a good source of supply for longleaf timbers, for keels, etc., as they have the facilities for getting them out.
> Most of the white cedar is cut by small mills on a strictly custom basis and it is hard to give you a source of supply for this. However, I believe A.H. Johnson & Sons Lumber Co., P.O. Box 1553, Suffolk, Va. 23434, has some cedar timber and is cutting some. I am also writing the secretaries of some of the lumber manufacturers associations to see if they can give me a reliable source for this item. A good supplier of cypress would be Coastal Lumber Co., P.O. Box 829, Weldon, N.C.; 27890.
> Yours very truly,
> Stanley F. Horn, Jr.

**50**

### Typical Back-stamp

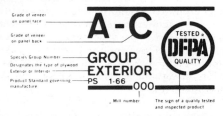

### Typical Edge-mark

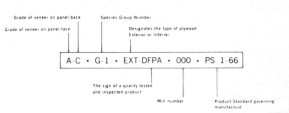

### Wood & Rot

Mention wood to one or another of our society's eager, earnest and meritocratic sorts and he'll condemn it on grounds of rot if not the sanding he might have to do. Off to the files of the "National Fisherman" again, where we find the following good exchange on the secrets of composite construction:

To the Technical Editor:
I have followed your articles on composite construction with great interest as I have been building a 45' ketch using this method. The question of dry rot started me on a bit of research, the results of which might be interesting.

First, as it is most generally known, "dry rot" needs moisture for the action to take place. Actually, for the process of dry rot decay to work on the wood, several conditions have to exist — the lack of any one will always prevent the decay process from starting.

1. The decay fungi must be present in the wood. The spores produced by fungus fruiting bodies are everywhere so it is well to conclude your lumber will contain them.

2. The conditions of moisture must be right. A moisture content of at least 35% must be present for rapid decay to take place. Decay never takes place if the moisture content remains below 20%.

3. Fungi must have air as well as water and common decay fungi are unable to work in wood that is completely waterlogged.

4. The temperature must be correct. Most decay fungi can make progress at any temperature between 40 degrees F. and 100 degrees F. with fastest decay in the neighborhood of 70 degrees to 85 degrees F.

Contd. on next page

_Contd. from preceding page_

It is also well to realize that periods of extreme cold only halt the action of the fungi temporarily for they become active again as soon as the temperature reaches a favorable level. On the other hand, kiln drying or steaming for bending will kill the fungi but this does not prevent the wood from being reinfected at a later date.

The question now is how best to construct a composite boat to minimize the possibility of dry rot. In my own case the first decision was the use of the proper wood. Sapwood is definitely more susceptible to the effects and action of the fungi than the heartwood. It is well worth a builder's effort to make sure that the lumber used in his boat is the heartwood.

It is also common knowledge that some woods are more prone to dry rot even if the most select of heartwoods are used. On the list of the native species of heartwood with high resistance to decay are:

### Softwoods

Bald cypress
Cedars
Redwood
Junipers

### Hardwoods

Black Walnut
Chestnut
Black Locust

Those woods of moderate resistance to decay are:
### Soft Woods

Honeylocust
Sweetgum
White Oak

Some of the low resistance woods are:
### Soft Woods

Firs, True
Hemlock
Pine, Ponderosa
(Pine, white)
(several species)
Spruces
Tamarack

### Hardwoods

Ashes
Beech
Birch
Cherry
Hickory
Oaks
Elms
Maples
Sycamore
Willow
Yellow Poplar

Certainly all the woods are more resistant to decay when they are treated with the standard preventative products on the market today. The problem is, are any of the products on the market compatible with the resins so that the wood may be treated prior to coating with fabric and resins? Personally, I don't know of any.

The wood I selected was edge-grained Douglas fir because of its moderate resistance to decay, its ready availability in the local lumber yard as edge-grained material and its clear grain. It also "takes" the resin well.

It is agreed by all that a good covering job will not have any surface breaks which will allow water to enter under the fabric and possibly start the decaying process.

The separation of the wood from the fabric is generally caused by the difference in expansion coefficients of the two materials. This effect can be minimized by using the

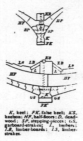

vertical grain of the wood at right angles to the fabric. By doing this the forces tending to separate the two materials are reduced and you are more likely to have a long lasting bond.

This means using rift-cut lumber for the strips. Plywood, because of its construction, has a minimum amount of working so is ideal in this respect.

Another point of interest on which your readers may be advised is the design of a boat for composite construction. Originally I thought that a standard design using strip planking was satisfactory and all that was required was to use the fabric inside and out and a satisfactory craft would result.

In discussions with Dr. Lindsay Lord, he hastened to advise that a boat of standard wood construction with floors, frames and beams would possibly require a dozen layers of fabric on the inside before it was stronger than the wood structure and thus not separate. For a good composite boat it requires sound designing and an understanding of the forces at play within the structure.

On the other hand, this does not preclude an owner from covering the outside of his standard strip-planked boat and benefitting from the advantages of a fabric covering. In the case where only the outside is covered, the debatable point of what to do with the inside arises. Some opinions say apply a wood preservative only, others a wood preservative and paint. Dr. Lord advises two coats of clear resin before painting. His advice is based on minimizing the shrinking and swelling of the wood.

As for covering my ketch, I will probably delay this operation until the last possible moment. When I started the boat, Dynel was considered to be superior to fiberglass, and then along came polypropylene. With improved resin formulations being introduced daily, it seems most prudent to wait.

I will definitely use epoxy as I believe the superior bonding properties justify the added cost over the polyester.

Burton A. Bromfield
72 Woodchester Drive
Weston, Mass.

51

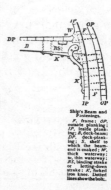

## METAL AND FABRICS

(Short-Shrift department)

We could hem and haw, cover our tracks, pad and so on. But we won't. WE DON'T HAVE ANY INFORMATION ON METALS AND FABRICS. There, that feels much better. Now that it is out of the way, we will mention that there are some sources of metal stock mentioned in the metal-working tools section and a note about canvas sources in the fittings section. But it isn't much and contributions on metal and fabrics are hereby invited and wanted very much.

For starters, Reynolds Metals offers a pamphlet called "Marine Guide for the Finishing of Aluminum Hulls."

Reynolds Metals Co.
6601 W. Broad St.
Richmond, Va. 23261

In Fabrics, The Canvas Products Asso. International offers an "Industrial Fabric Products Buyers Guide," a 128-page where-to-buy source guide for everything from air structures to windbreaks.

Canvas Products Asso. International
600 Endicott Building
St. Paul, Minn. 55001

52

All aluminum shrimp trawler, _Bill Angus_, has natural aluminum boom and outriggers.

## Breeches Buoy Notes: 1

There is an important symbol in the skin of a boat. No small part of the attraction of a boat is the fact that the hull is a thin, fabricated shell separating a world of wet awesome danger and another of warm, secure and personal confinement. Sigmund Freud and his followers have documented rather fully the symbolic array that surrounds our dreams, fixations and fears that come from the trauma of birth. Virginia Wolfe, and other writers too, have written at length about the symbolic draw of water and watery places; places that, beckon even while they horrify, simultaneously desirable and repelling.

Personality is made in such a nexus. The convergence of opposing forces is called a syndrome and it is in the resolution of syndromes that ego, self, is forged. It is called growing-up.

Literate yachtsmen and their wives often joke about the motives of their sport; of a long, slim, irrespressible form cutting through the water under a firm guiding hand, of the henpecked clerk suddenly become a captain to whom all others are crew. These jokes, not by accident, often end in divorce.

But there is this skin thing under it all. One does not have to experience it to know the Uncanny difference between "above" and "below" in heavy going. The unbelievable noise of even a moderate gale and the quiet though animated calm of a well laid-out cabin. The early joys of a secret hideout or a big appliance box are reawakened in boat fever and, newly bolstered by adult belligerence, they provide a key to the confusing urgencies that are part of suddenly wanting a boat.

Men who are otherwise sane, sensible, happy, educated and well-placed, suddenly begin to pore over old magazines, take short-notice weekend trips with friends, find ways to turn astounding thousands into easily-managed hundreds and to wonder at their former wretchedness. All of a sudden, a boat is so terribly important!

This boat thing seems to be some kind of relationship, a relationship that one can enter into literally and of which one becomes an integral part, an organ as it were. This relationship is not just internal. It is also inviolate, something that a relationship to a corporation, a club or lodge or a marriage is not and can never be. The violence of birth can never be undone. The fact of expendability at work can never be resolved. The core of loneliness in even the most satisfactory memberships

_Contd. on next page_

*Contd. from preceding page*

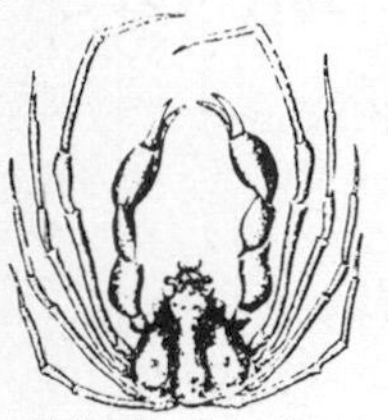

and marriages is never requited because, somehow another ego or other egos control a diverse and confusing helm.

But not in a boat. The feeling is that here at last is an absolute relationship that is identical to one's own sense of self and self-mastery. Here is a place where direction, state and process are simultaneously embodied in one's own self and not subject to rule, arbitration or the seven deadly sins of one's constant fellows. Dangers are real dangers, not man-made obstructionisms and success or failure is the sure black and white image of success and failure that we received in our youthful instruction.

In short, the sentiment often surrounding a yacht satisfies, in terms of classical psychology, a standard definition of infantile regression.

—GP

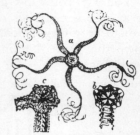

*a, Euryale Palmifera (Ophiuridæ), front view; b, disc and part of arm, front view; c, disc and part of arm, back view.*

# fasteners

Materials do you no good unless you can put them together. Adhesives are covered elsewhere in the catalog and the ordinary resources available to most of us are adequate for ordinary fastening. Here we have some items of special interest because of their rarity or virtual absence from ordinary retail outlets.

## BOAT NAILS
### Commercial Bronze
### Silicon Bronze
### Monel

Helix Thread           Fetter Ring Thread

| Penny | Length In. | Stub's Gauge | Deci. In. | Nails Per Lb. Approx. |
|---|---|---|---|---|
| | ⅝ | 16 | .065 | 1400 |
| | ¾ | 16 | .065 | 950 |
| | ⅞ | 16 | .065 | 825 |
| 2D | 1 | 12 | .109 | 350 |
| 3D | 1 ¼ | 12 | .109 | 280 |
| 3D | 1 ¼ | 10 | .134 | 155 |
| 4D | 1 ½ | 14 | .083 | 400 |
| 4D | 1 ½ | 12 | .109 | 230 |
| 4D | 1 ½ | 10 | .134 | 135 |
| 4D | 1 ½ | 8 | .165 | 95 |
| 5D | 1 ¾ | 10 | .134 | 120 |
| 5D | 1 ¾ | 8 | .165 | 83 |
| 6D | 2 | 10 | .134 | 105 |
| 6D | 2 | 8 | .165 | 75 |
| 7D | 2 ¼ | 10 | .134 | 94 |
| 7D | 2 ¼ | 8 | .165 | 64 |
| 8D | 2 ½ | 10 | .134 | 84 |
| 8D | 2 ½ | 8 | .165 | 58 |
| 9D | 2 ¾ | 8 | .165 | 53 |
| 10D | 3 | 8 | .165 | 48 |

**Many other sizes carried in stock for immediate shipment.**

*Monel and Bronze Boat Nails made to Commercial Specifications*

## Regular Cut Copper Nails

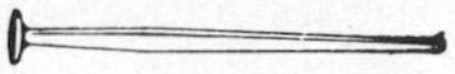

Clendenin cut copper nails are stamped from sheet metal, and are used where greater holding power is needed than that given by a wire nail. A cut nail is especially necessary where the wood is constantly expanding and contracting.

| LENGTH Inches | DWT | NUMBER to Pound (Approx.) | LENGTH Inches | DWT | NUMBER to Pound (Approx.) |
|---|---|---|---|---|---|
| ½ | ... | 1636 | 2 | 6d | 96 |
| ¾ | ... | 928 | 2½ | 8d | 58 |
| 1 | 2d | 512 | 3 | 10d | 38 |
| 1¼ | 3d | 240 | 3½ | 16d | 32 |
| 1½ | 4d | 176 | 4 | 20d | 24 |
| 1¾ | 5d | 128 | 4½ | 30d | 17 |

Above and left from Clendenin catalog.

Clendenin Bros., Inc.
4309 Erdman Ave.
Baltimore, Md. 21213

Screw-shank nails, aluminum nails, silicon bronze, Monel, stainless and copper, screws, both wire and cut nails, copper burrs, rivets of all kinds and materials, 14 sizes of copper and/or bronze hammers (½ lb. to 15 lbs.) and every kind of washer. Need we say more? Catalog is free.

We understand that the Vietnamese have a new growth industry; copper mining! Until these newly discovered supplies are available on the open market, some very little of the old supply is turned into boat fastenings. Use these matchless fasteners judiciously, with love and gratitude.

100% hard drawn boat nails and dished (the best) roves:

S.E. MacDonald
29 Hastings Rd.
Belmont, Mass. 02178/U.S.A.

53

### Forged Iron Boat Nails

You say you can't do things in the old way because the materials are no longer available; wrought iron forged boat nails, for example? Put down that box of bronze screws, friend, we've found one!

From Tremont Nail catalog.

# Tremont Nail Company History

Nails in their crudest form date back to 3000 B.C. The Romans hand-forged them and they have been found in excavations and sunken ships from the period 500 A.D.

When our ancestors first stepped from the Mayflower onto that soil that was to become Plymouth County, they discovered a soil which was essentially sandy and difficult to cultivate. As they plowed for their first crops, they noticed that the earth yielded small deposits of crude iron ore mixed with the ooze of the swampy regions. From this ore and with crude smelters, they separated the metal from the ore and began the fashioning of nails and metal tools they had left behind them when they sailed into the unknown.

Cooking utensils, shipfitters hardware, nails and wagon treads grew from this ore dug in the swamps where the cranberries grow today. As the Massachusetts Bay Colony grew, the residents of Wareham were able to supply newcomers with nails for their homes. The industry had been born.

The original factory was established by Issac and Jared Pratt in 1819 on the site of an old cotton mill which had been shelled and burned by the British in the War of 1812. Known originally as Parker Mills Nail Company, it later became known as the Tremont Nail Company. The first cut nail machines appeared during the late 1700's and the first machine to cut and head a nail in one operation was invented by Ezekiel Reed of Bridgewater, Mass.

The present nail factory has about 60 nail machines and was completed in 1848. Among those who managed the business in the early days are men whose names are famous throughout New England: John Avery Parker, William Rodman, Charles W. Morgan, Bartlett Murdock, Benjamin Fearing, William Caswell, Horace Pratt Tobey and William A. Leonard.

For a century-and-a-half the company has achieved a reputation for skilled nail cutting that has made its product readily saleable throughout the markets of the world. Through all the changes and the hurried pace of modern industry the same product is still being produced for customers who prefer the superior holding power and durability of this time-tested nail.

Tremont Nail Company originated hardened steel nails on this same furnace still in use today. Once heat-treated, nails can be driven through the same gauge steel from which manufactured.

Tremont Nail Co.
21 Elm St.
P.O. Box 111
Wareham, Mass. 02571

Really nice free brochure.

## BOAT

| Size | Length in Inches |
|------|------------------|
|      | ¾ |
|      | ⅞ |
| 2d   | 1 |
| 3d   | 1 ¼ |
| 4d   | 1 ½ |
| 5d   | 1 ¾ |
| 6d   | 2 |
| 7d   | 2 ¼ |
| 8d   | 2 ½ |
| 9d   | 2 ¾ |
| 10d  | 3 |
| 12d  | 3 ¼ |
| 16d  | 3 ½ |
|      | 3 ¾ |
| 20d  | 4 |
|      | 4 ¼ |
| 30d  | 4 ½ |
| 40d  | 5 |
| 50d  | 5 ½ |
| 60d  | 6 |

**Off-The-Shelf
Hard-To-Find: Boston**

Stone Hardware
P.O. Box 128
327 Belmont St.
Brockton, Mass. 02403

People in the Northeast will be interested to learn of Stone Hardware. They sent us the following note and several customers have confirmed that they mean it.

Dear Mr. Putz:

Replying to your letter, we do not put out a catalog as our offerings are always changing. We are always picking up job lots and the only thing that we stock all the time are copper rivets and all kinds of fasteners — brass, bronze, stainless steel, iron. Like our header says, When you can't find it anywhere, come to Stone Hardware. A trip to our store is an eye-opener.

Very truly yours,
Russel T. Stone

## Bolts And Fasteners

What could be more prosaic than bolts? They are terribly important in our lives all-over-the-place; but in the flesh few things are so mundane, so almost repulsively elemental as a bolt. If you've a backbone or keel to bolt up or a dock or wharf to tie together, you'll need **wrought iron bolts** and we found a company that sells not only wrought iron bolts of every size, shape and description, but boat and dock spikes and mooring post, bitt and bollard bolts as well. Jersey Bolt's catalog verges on the prurient for its precise and beautiful illustrations and clear use-descriptions and it comes from one of the last producers of wrought iron hardware in this country.                                    —GP

> Jersey Bolt
> 21 Humphreys Ave.
> Bayonne, N.J. 07002

Items below, right from Jersey catalog.

## DOCK SPIKES
### Up to 1″ square
### Available with flat head
### only and chisel point
Standard Theoretical Weights per 100 Pieces'

| LENGTH | 5⁄8″ | 3⁄4″ | 7⁄8″ | 1″ |
|---|---|---|---|---|
| 8″ | 93 | 134 | 183 | 238 |
| 9″ | 105 | 151 | 206 | 268 |
| 10″ | 116 | 167 | 228 | 298 |
| 11″ | 128 | 184 | 251 | 327 |
| 12″ | 140 | 201 | 274 | 357 |
| 13″ | 151 | 218 | 297 | 387 |
| 14″ | 163 | 234 | 320 | 417 |
| 15″ | 174 | 251 | 342 | 446 |
| 16″ | 186 | 268 | 365 | 476 |
| 17″ | 198 | 285 | 388 | 506 |
| 18″ | 209 | 301 | 411 | 536 |
| 19″ | 221 | 318 | 433 | 565 |
| 20″ | 233 | 335 | 456 | 595 |
| 22″ | 256 | 368 | 502 | 655 |
| 24″ | 279 | 402 | 547 | 714 |
| 26″ | 303 | 435 | 593 | 774 |
| 28″ | 326 | 469 | 638 | 833 |
| 30″ | 349 | 502 | 684 | 893 |

## Metric Fasteners

Slowly but surely the guy with the V.W. feels less lonely. No longer is he spoken of in low bitter tones as "that nut who don't fit our wrenches." It finally begins to look possible to get rid of the insane system of measuring we've enjoyed so badly since the Middle Ages, even on our boats. A nice catalog and good products are available from:

> Metrics International
> Oak Ridge, N.J. 07438

## BOAT SPIKES
### Up to ¾″ square
### Available with diamond shaped
### or flat heads and chisel point

Standard Theoretical Weights per 100 Pieces*

| LENGTH | ¼″ | 5⁄16″ | 3⁄8″ | 7⁄16″ | ½″ | ¾′ |
|---|---|---|---|---|---|---|
| 5″ | 11 lb. | 17 lb. | | | | |
| 6″ | 12 lb. | 19 lb. | 30 lb. | 38 lb. | 52 lb. | |
| 7″ | 13 lb. | 21 lb. | 34 lb. | 44 lb. | 59 lb. | |
| 8″ | | 23 lb. | 38 lb. | 49 lb. | 66 lb. | |
| 9″ | | | 42 lb. | 55 lb. | 73 lb. | |
| 10″ | | | 46 lb. | 60 lb. | 80 lb. | |
| 12″ | | | 54 lb. | 71 lb. | 94 lb. | 202 lb. |
| 14″ | | | | | 108 lb. | 235 lb. |
| 16″ | | | | | 122 lb. | 267 lb. |

*If Galvanized add 3% to the above weights

## Bolt Cutters

To those who have tried to hacksaw a rusty bolt on a pitching, heaving deck, a bolt cutter can be a real joy. H.K. Porter Inc., Somerville, Mass. 02143, makes a complete line of such handy implements and they seem to work well and easier than most.

I once thought a bolt cutter was a luxury that only cement contractors could afford. After having bought one I find it saves quite a bit of time and labor for hacking off rusted shackles, mending crab pots, cutting rod, bolts, chain, heavy wire, hose, tubing, pipe, etc. I bought a ½" capacity model and am sorry I didn't get a bigger one as the need to sever 5/8" and 3/4" material often comes up. One word of caution; stay away from steel cable, drill bits and very hard bolts. The cutter will take them, but only once. Then the jaws become badly nicked. The jaws can be sharpened and/or replaced and the cutters are adjustable to take up the slack after sharpening.

My ½" set cost me about $33 with shipping. A 4' long set with a 5/8" capacity should run about $40. Stay away from anything under 3' long as it won't do much.

—Mark White

Samples of variously formed Screws used in Carriage-making and Carpentry. a, b, c, d, e are special forms of wood-screws in common use.

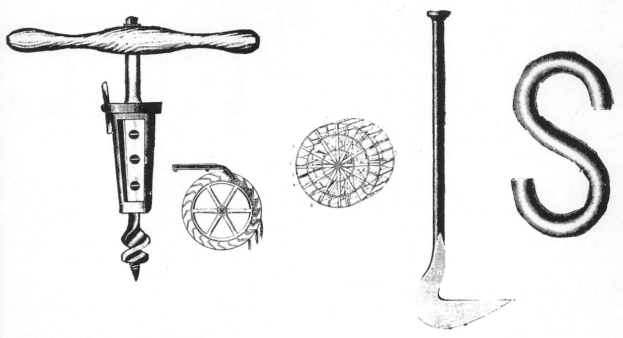

### By George Putz

And so to the heart of it, to tools. It is not simply to the heart of the catalog, it is to the heart of most of what we are as a sapient species who get that way through tools. For humans, life itself is a matter of tools. Our whole conception of what life is and is about is seen through the fabric of our ability to manipulate materials and so, in a profound sense, access to tools is much more than a privilege of the marketplace, it is a constitutional and probably a phenomenological right.

An enigmatic cluster of events in the recent past has come together to endanger this right in the experience of the individual craftsman. It is not simply enigmatic, it is ironic, for there are more tools and craftsmen now than ever before in history. But the nature of the tools and crafts has changed in a way that has taken control out of the individual's hands, both literally and figuratively. Control of number, types, styles and quality of tools has somehow escaped us. We takes our choice and pays our money. If we don't like the choice, well, there is always painting or cooking or rug-hooking, if we can find a decent brush, pot or hook.

The situation can perhaps be traced back to our original tools, our hands. There is one on the right and one on the left. We favor one and the other is then cast in the role of a life-time helpmate. One expresses our intention and follows commands with fair alacrity and competence. The other is not so good about commands given. Really, it has a kind-of life of its own, working best without much attention given to it. It is the ornery one, a mixture of creativity, awkwardness and quiet partnership. This business of being right or left-handed expresses our nature with respect to tools generally; some of them we use and see as being direct expressions of our intention. Others we use and see in an indirect manner, as being somehow beyond an expression of our individual will. When people grow to depend a great deal on institutions for their life and living, there is more and more a tendency to avoid the responsibility of intention, They tend to the "other" hand with a life of its own and for which they have less responsibility. Ergo, the preference for tools with a life of their own (power) and/or tools which are inferior and, therefore, excuse failure.

The problem has more obvious dimensions, of course. Very few American homes have a shop in which a child can learn manual skills or a parent can provide a child with an example of pride in personal manual achievement. Many schools have well-equipped shops, but their emphasis tends to be on the use of power tools and the manual arts curriculum tends to be geared to the academically weak child who is being pre-

_Contd. on next page_

56

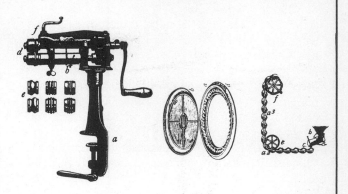

pared for the "realities of life" by throwing switches and mutilating a few hundred feet of number two pine over a year's time making ash trays and pipe racks.

The average hardware store does not carry industrial grade tools, the only ones with the tolerances and strength to withstand serious use. Instead, they carry "shopgrade" tools which, in the case of handtools, means poor design, cheap finish and grades of steel which take forever to sharpen and, in the event an edge is obtained will not hold it for more than a few strokes. In the case of power tools, it means too little power, weak mountings, sloppy specs and inevitable and early breakdown with parts soon unavailable because of model discontinuation. Once you are past your faith in hardware stores, you are reduced to very few (though some very good) mail-order houses whose prices tend to follow one another very closely (upwards) and which are in a position to ignore individual market demands and complaints. Beyond the mail-order outlets are the industrial outlets, out of reach to the average man without an institutional affiliation and its critical letterhead.

And those grab-bins full of bargain tools are an absolute disaster. With few exceptions, if you buy one of those tools to be that tool in your kit, it will accomplish one or all of the following: Do its job poorly, not do its job at all, break, teach your child that this type of tool does not work — that it's part of a trick the world plays on kids, so he or she is shown yet again to be incompetent and dependent upon daddy or the power company. Unless you take pleasure in turning your home into a giant charm bracelet, purchase a few really good tools rather than lots of poor ones.

The book problem is equally acute. There are scads of titles, to be sure, but most of them are about using your lousy tools on a cardtable building bird-houses. Perhaps 10% of the titles are really excellent and, of these, most are geared to some special craft; sculpting, violin-making, boatbuilding or whatever. There are no books currently in print that deal adequately with general shop theory and practice.

The American tool buyer automatically thinks of Stanley, Miller's Falls and Craftsman, the latter being an array of sub-contracted tools sold by Sears. From childhood, these brand names are synonymous with handtools and, lately, power tools as well. Generally, they are good tools at their prices and their top-grade lines are excellent. In recent years there has been some erosion of finish care on the tools, probably to keep prices down, but the grades of steel used in the better tools remain high and, in some cases,

have been considerably improved. Any problem with access to quality domestic tools is not the fault of the manufacturers. It is the fault of distributors and retail marketers.

Sometime, very soon after the Second World War, someone in the hardware industry read an economics textbook and discovered "consumer market analysis" which, among other things, told him that society is made up of different sub-groups, each with its own needs and market demands. To his shock and dismay, the hardware man realized he didn't have enough lines of cheap tools to meet the requirements, I suppose, of cheap tool users. Bins full of tool sets, multipurpose and general-purpose tools began to appear and, of course, because they were cheaper and "more useful," according to the packaging, they sold better than did the best grade tools. Because they sold better, hardware retail outlets ordered more of them, thus closing the vicious circle — and here we are. Unless you use a really large and conscientious retail outlet, you will ordinarily have to special-order the best of our domestic tools.

*Contd. on next page*

57

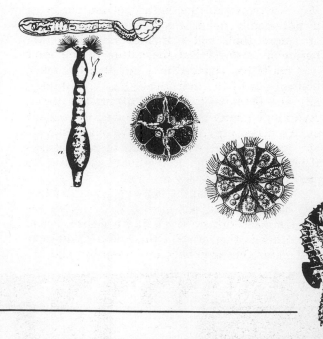

Stanley tools are a good example. They offer far more and usually much better tools than you usually find in the store. Their Broadline Catalog #34 is full of surprises. For example, in the plane department they continue to offer adjustable throat blockplanes, side-rabbet planes, bullnose planes, a good classical fillister plane and an open-throat hand routerplane, all of which you just "can't git anymore," in the opinion of many even experienced craftsmen. They still offer double-geared heavy-duty hand drills and a broad hatchet! Their rules, levels, hammers, saws, chisels, etc., are a mixed bag but, again, they offer more in each department than meets the retail-counter eye.

However, a look at the catalog cover is eloquent testimony to the heart of the problem, the chasm that exists in industry between production and promotional departments. Pictured on a softwood (!) workbench is a block of wood in which some "woodworker" is in the process of carving the word "Stanley." The endgrain of the wood block shows that it was sawn out with a power circular saw, irrelevant in a catalog of handtools. The block has been planed with a finish plane, a relevant product, but the planed face of the block and the type of shavings in the plane indicate that the plane is neither sharp nor set properly. The carving itself is shown to be done with a one-inch-wide butt-chisel hit with a roof-claw hammer, which is curious, and the whole thing was apparently laid out with a steel tape, also curious.

58

Stanley Tools
New Britain, Conn. 06050
Sold Through Distributors Only

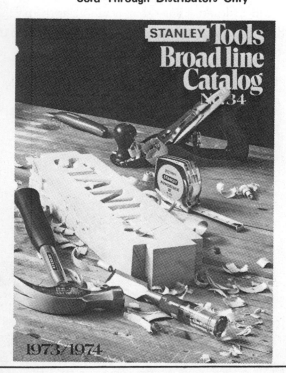

1973/1974

Items from Stanley catalog.

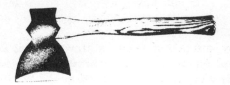

## BROAD HATCHET

| No. | EDP No. | Cut Inches | Overall Length | FLC No. |
|-----|---------|------------|----------------|---------|
| 59-145 | 59-145 | 4½ | 15 | 2472 |

## HEAVY DUTY

### 4″ Speed Gear ⅜″ Chuck

Die cast aluminum, parallel sided frame. Gear teeth and double pinions are machine cut. 8 drill points, sizes 1/16″ to 11/64″ furnished in hollow handle. 3 steel jaws, steel chuck. Handle has cordovan finish.

| No. | EDP No. | Chuck Capacity Inches | Length Inches | FLC No. |
|-----|---------|----------------------|---------------|---------|
| 624 | 03-624 | ⅜ | 13¾ | 2552 |

## RABBET PLANES

### For Regular and Bull Nose Work

This Plane has two seats for the cutter: one for regular work, and the other for bull nose work. It is fitted with a Spur, a removable depth gauge and adjustable fence. When used in the rear seat, the cutter is adjustable.

| No. | EDP No. | Length Inches | Cutter Width Inches | FLC No. |
|-----|---------|---------------|---------------------|---------|
| †78 | 13-078 | 8¼ | 1½ | 2510 |

## 100 PLUS® AUGER BITS IN SETS

Any discussion such as this requires some organization, a criterion by which some sort of sense can be made of it all. Here we've chosen the amateur and small shopman, an obvious "target group," I suppose, since much time and tide will be required before any other group would get so sincere a rap out of us. . .

## HANDTOOLS

You can tell, you know, that it was made by hand. Machine-made things give themselves away. The stylized angularities in the work they do accomplish does the job required just fine. But there is no "depth" to the work, no complex of micro-variation which, though not directly visible to the eye, gives hand work that quality of life and presence and ambience.

Few believe in handtools any longer. Our inept educators kept from us the information, skills and attitudes that make handtools work under our own hands. The emotional perversities of a generation escaping from the farm and depression and the hidden personal messages of wars in this century somehow gave handtools an obliquely bad symbolism. Indicative of this warped outlook is the sizable number of my contemporaries who really do not believe that a handplane can be made to work. They do not know how a plane works, how to select one or how to sharpen and set it, so of course their planes bark and clog and tear and veer and plain don't go.

In any case, the boatbuilder has all kinds of problems of his own, for many of his tools are domestically rare or not available and, often, when they are available, they must be purchased in quantity and either at inflated prices or by cajoling for special treatment from industrial suppliers.

The powers can be thanked that money, space, time and ability are limited, for it means that needs are limited too, at least with a modicum of realism cast on the problem. Some few are boatbuilders. Most are not, considering the activity as a vocation (from the Greek "to call") and not a profession. Rising from a dream of a boat, the motives mature into the acquisition of some discipline, skill, and, for many, therapy and even spiritual fulfillment. Of course, eventually you get a boat!

# NONFERROUS TOOLS

Ferrous tools and the marine environment have always been a frustrating combination. Not only do ferrous (iron and steel) tools rust, they also spark — creating extreme danger in and about bilges when fuel system damage complicates engine work — and they are magnetic. More than one bad course has been steered because the "mate" placed a ferrous screwdriver near the compass. Rusting, sparking and magnetism can all be overcome with nonferrous tools. They are expensive but, with care and luck, you'll only buy them once, something almost impossible to say of even the best seagoing ferrous tools.

Kawecki Berylco Industries of Reading, Pa., offers a complete line of nonferrous (beryllium copper) tools; not only the expectable hammers, pliers, screwdrivers, etc., but knives, hatchets, punches, brushes, clamps, chisels, and more. Most major marine hardware outlets carry at least some of their line.

**Berylco Safety Tools
Reading, Pa. 19603
Catalog**

59

**From Berylco catalog**

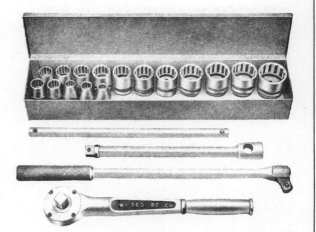

A complete set providing a wide range of socket sizes and the necessary attachments to get any job done . . . these well-designed sockets and accessories provide the highest margin of strength and utility available in non-ferrous tools. The safety metal case is 16¼" long, 4½" wide and 2" deep.

A Sharpie.

# Forged Tools

Two companies whose catalogs will send chills up your spine are the Manhattan Tool Manufacturing Co. and John Stortz and Son, Inc. They offer ship and boatbuilder's tools; forged tools!

Both companies offer caulking irons, making irons, reefing irons and hull and deck scrapers. Manhattan has, in addition, spike irons, horsing irons (!), marline spikes, forged grappling hooks, blacksmithing tools and a perfectly awesome array of hooks, punches, hammers, wedges, chisels, drills, etc.

Stortz, in addition to shipbuilder's tools, offers a full and unique line of cooperage tools, many of which have practical use in a boatbuilder's shop. Barrels, of course, have a noble place in maritime history and Stortz' interesting pamphlet, "The Wooden Barrel Manual," is a definitive gem.

Manhattan Tool Mfg. Co.
38 Van Buren St.
Newark, N.J. 07105
Catalog

John Stortz and Son, Inc.
210 Vine St.
Philadelphia, Pa; 19106
Catalog

60

**TOOL NO. 12830 HULL SCRAPERS**

| 2" blade | 18" | 1½ lb. | 6 |

**TOOL NO. 129000 HAWSING IRONS**

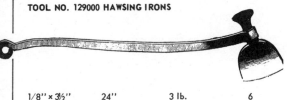

| 1/8" x 3½" | 24" | 3 lb. | 6 |

**TOOL NO. 12650 MARLIN SPIKES**
**(MANILA ROPE)**

**Tool No. 90 Scotch Screw Eyed Augers**

**TOOL NO. 11650 BOAT CALKING IRONS**
**(FORGED TOOL STEEL)**

| POINT THICK | WIDTH BLADE | LENGTH OVERALL | | PACKED EACH |
|---|---|---|---|---|
| 3/16" | 2" | 5-1/2" | 6 lb. | 6 |

(PRICE LIST PAGE NO. 13)

**TOOL NO. 11750 MAKING IRONS**
**TOOL STEEL – TWO CREASE**

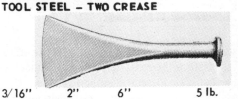

| 3/16" | 2" | 6" | 5 lb. | 6 |

(PRICE LIST PAGE NO. 13)

**TOOL NO. 11850 CALKING IRONS–OFFSET**
**(FORGED TOOL STEEL**

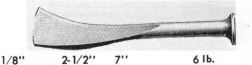

| 1/8" | 2-1/2" | 7" | 6 lb. | 6 |

(PRICE LIST PAGE NO. 13)

**TOOL NO. 11950 SHARP OR BUTT IRONS**
**FORGED TOOL STEEL**

| SHARP | 1-1/4" | 9" | 7 lb. | 6 |

(PRICE LIST PAGE NO. 13)

**TOOL NO. 12500 SPIKE IRONS**
**FORGED TOOL STEEL**

| 5/64" | 1/2" | 6-1/2" | 6 lb. | 6 |

(PRICE LIST PAGE NO. 13)

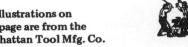

All illustrations on this page are from the Manhattan Tool Mfg. Co. catalog.

## CHAMFER KNIFE

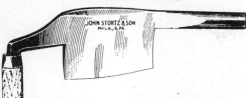

Right Hand knife is illustrated. Forged all in one piece, heavy enough and well rounded at back of knife to fit curve of barrel with angle to cutting blade, thus making an easy to use, good cutting tool. Blade fully and finely polished overall. Note at left hand side the heavy tang running through large size ferruled hardwood handle, firmly riveted at end; other handle end rounded forged steel. Blade is especially heat-treated to hold a keen long lasting tough cutting edge. STORTZ chamfer knives are made of STORTZALLOY, an extra quality deep hardening tool steel which will out-wear any ordinary carbon tool steel. In addition, blade may be repeatedly ground and resharpened without need of retempering and still keep a tough hard-wear resisting edge.

| ITEM NUMBERS | DESCRIPTION |
|---|---|
| 381-A...... | Complete Knife, REGULAR Wt. 6" cutting edge, 6" depth, ¾" thick at top, wood handle length 8". Wt. approximately 7 lbs. |
| 381-B...... | Complete Knife, HEAVIER Wt. 6" cutting edge, 6" depth, ¾" thick at top, extra length handle 13½". Wt. approximately 8-9 lbs. |
| 400-A.............. | Chamfer Knife, Handle Only 8" |
| 400-B.............. | Chamfer Knife, Handle Only 13½" |

For other sizes and weights made to your order, either RIGHT or LEFT hand, submit sketch with details or used sample, for quotation.

### _A HEAVY DUTY CUTTING KNIFE_

## COOPERS' ADZE

Blade forged of solid high quality carbon tool steel, with special curve, hardened and tempered to give best working results. Cutting blade and head end driving face are polished, hardened and tempered for extra toughness and best working results. Note hardwood handle with removable bolt and nut through center joining it firmly to adze head.

| ITEM NUMBER | DESCRIPTION |
|---|---|
| 387-A (Large size Adze) | For tight cooperage work, cutting edge 3" to 3¼". Wt. complete 3½ lbs. |
| 387-B (Small size Adze) | For slack cooperage work, cutting edge 2¼" to 2½". Wt. complete 2¼ lbs. |
| 389-A.............. | Handle Only for Large Size Adze |
| 389-B.............. | Handle Only for Small Size Adze |

### _USED FOR DRIVING, TRIMMING BUNGS, PLUGS, CHIMES AND GENERAL COOPERAGE REPAIR WORK_

61

## COMBINATION PAINT SCRAPER SETS

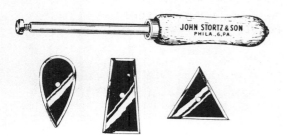

### ITEM NO. 422-A   Complete Set as Illustrated.
### Over All Length 9"

All items on this page from John Stortz catalog.

## DECK and DUMB IRON
### without crease

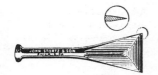

### ITEM NO. 86-3F

## REEFING IRON
### Without crease

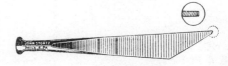

### ITEM NO. 86-9J

| WIDTH OF BLADES | LENGTH OVER ALL |
|---|---|
| 2" | 6½" |

| WIDTH OF BLADES | THICKNESS OF BLADES | LENGTH OVER ALL |
|---|---|---|
| 1¼" | 3/16" | 10½" |

The Woodcraft Supply Corporation is an extraordinary organization. Beginning several years ago in a cubbyhole shop in Boston, its management began to import quality hand woodworking tools from England and Germany and the professional cabinetmakers in the Northeast soon made the shop a byword. Today, Woodcraft does an astounding business out of its Woburn store and through an efficient mail-order service.

Their lines of Swiss and English carving tools and chisels, English planes, screwdrivers and saws, German planes and benches are absolutely first-rate — the best obtainable. They also have a good selection of books and, get this, a broadaxe, a boatbuilder's adze and a slick! We have found no other ready domestic source for most of these tools. Prices are very high, but so is the quality.

**Woodcraft Supply Corp.**
**313 Montvale Ave.**
**Woburn, Mass. 10801**
**Catalog is 25 cents**

## BROAD AXE

**15Q04-AW.** Broad Axe. A scaled down version of the frontiersman's broad axe, this smaller model is a true copy in design and purpose. Blade is 7" along cutting edge; overall length (front to back) 8". Head weighs approx. 3 lbs. The offset eye permits the handle to align entirely to one side of the cutting blade so that a flat, rather than a chopping stroke can be made. It was with the broad axe that timbers were hand-hewn from logs in Colonial Days. These axes are made

exclusively for Woodcraft in Europe. Supply is limited. Handles not furnished. NOT AVAILABLE UNTIL AFTER DECEMBER 1ST. $18.90 ppd.

## BROAD HATCHET

**15R09-AW.** The broad hatchet or "hewing hatchet" is very similar in physical characteristics to the broad axe, but on a smaller scale. Blade is 5¼" at cutting edge; overall length (front to back) 7". Head weighs 2 lbs. Handle not furnished. Made exclusively for Woodcraft. $13.70 ppd.

## ADZ HEADS

The following two adz heads are usually used with hatchet length handles. Sorry, but we cannot furnish handles to fit; they are for those who are willing to improvise their own handles.

**15S04-AW.** Straight Adz Head. Straight 3¼" blade. $9.45 ppd.

**15S03-AW.** Curved Adz Head. Curved gouge type, about 2¾ inches across. Its degree of arc is that of a 3 inch circle. $9.75 ppd.

All items are from Woodcraft Supply Catalog.

## SHIPBUILDER'S ADZ

**15Q03-AW.** Shipbuilder's Lipped Adz. The correct tool for squaring up a log or for creating the hand-hewn effect on already sawed timbers. Will hew timbers without its corners digging in. Cutting edge approximately 6 inches. Length to center of eye, approximately 7 inches. Unhandled. Made specially for Woodcraft. NOT AVAILABLE UNTIL AFTER DECEMBER 1ST.
$21.30 ppd.

**15A02-CA.** Hickory Handle. 36". Suggested for the **15Q03-AW** lipped adz. Must be fitted by the owner. NOT AVAILABLE UNTIL AFTER DECEMBER 1ST. $4.00 ppd.

## BOATBUILDER'S SOCKET SLICK

**14L02BS.** Slick. Rugged design; toughened for heavy timber construction. Blade forged from solid high carbon tool steel. Blade length 10"; width 3". Blade has ground face. Socket invisibly welded to the blade. Sturdy 14" hardwood handle. Made specially for Woodcraft. NOT AVAILABLE UNTIL AFTER DECEMBER 1ST. $24.50 ppd.

## SLEDGE

**09F02-I.** Sledge or Hand Drilling Hammer. Hardened and tempered, forged steel head. Face machine turned and polished. Hickory handle. Overall 10-¾". For heavy duty work. Please specify weight.

| | |
|---|---|
| 3 lb. | $7.45 ppd. |
| 4 lb. | $7.95 ppd. |

## TIMBER SCRIBER

**07M02-E.** Timber Scriber. Or "raise knife". Used to scribe the waterline of boats. Single blade. Closed 3½", open approx. 5 inches. Simulated stag handle. $5.95 ppd.

## GROMMET KIT

**06C01-BO.** Grommet Kit. Complete with anvil, die cutter, cutter block and 1 gross of brass grommets. Complete instructions tell how to repair or "do-it-yourself" for awnings, curtains, tarpaulins, etc. Please specify size of grommets wished.

| Size | Dia. of Grommet | Price |
|---|---|---|
| 0 | 1/4" | $5.50 ppd. |
| 1 | 9/32" | $5.60 ppd. |
| 2 | 3/8" | $5.90 ppd. |
| 3 | 7/16" | $6.10 ppd. |

62

### All You Have To Do Is. . .

How many times have you sat about with friends on a leisurely evening and yarned about some variation on a theme that usually begins, "Well, you know, we could make a million dollars. All we would have to do is. . . ." The dotted line more often than not is filled with some business notion to fill a blank you've discovered in the marketplace.

Well, some genius in New Hampshire got off his duff and did it. Brookstone Company specializes in the mail-order of hard-to-find, often unique tools for the shopman in wood, metal, models, gardening, etc. Their line is large and growing, high-quality and fantastically interesting. Their prices are fair and their service is FAST.

### A Shop In One

Most craftsmen find real pleasure in shopping for their shop, building it up slowly as needs are discovered and budgets allow. Some, though, feel moved or compelled to get it all in one whack. Craftool of Harbor City, California offers a complete quality woodworking shop with imported bench included. Their interesting catalog does not indicate whether their tools can be purchased one at a time. It does indicate by illustration, however, that their wares are marked up considerably over East Coast prices for the same tools and bench. Only a fraction of the catalog is devoted to woodworking, many other crafts being featured; Ceramics, graphics, weaving, lapidary, art-metal, etc.

**From the Craftool catalog.**

The 10575 is a self-contained shop. It has a 48" x 18" tilting compartment containing 51 of the finest tools available and of a quality equal to that of the work-bench. The large compartment pulls out and tilts down at a 45° angle to allow complete accessibility to these tools without interference of movement around the bench. Cabinet and saw rack below provide for an easy check-up. Listed at the right are the tools contained in this model.

**51 TOOL ASSORTMENT (10575)**

| | |
|---|---|
| 1—Fine Tooth Saw | 6—Assorted Wood Chisels |
| 1—Oil Stone for Sharpening | 1—Marking Gauge |
| 1—Pliers (for Pulling or Cutting off Nails) | 3—Spiral Drills |
| 1—Brace with Ratchet | 3—Squares—Different Sizes |
| 1—Medium Plane with 2 Blades | 1—Plane with Side Handles and Vernier |
| 1—Rabbitt Plane with 2 Blades | 1—Center Drill |
| 1—Triangular File | 1—Fine Scraper |
| 1—Ratchet Screw Driver | 1—Half Round Rasp |
| 3—Screw Driver Bits | 1—Claw Hammer |
| 2—Punches | 1—Mallet |
| 1—Very Fine Small Saw | 1—Big Counter Sink |
| 1—Mitre Square | 1—Keyhole Saw |
| 1—Folding Rule | 1—Fine Plane for Finishing |
| 1—Half Round File | 1—Joiner |
| 1—Very Fine Plane with Single Blade | 1—Rip Saw |
| 1—Frame Saw with Adjustable Blade Tension | 1—Sandpaper Block (Cork) |
| 1—Pick | 1—Rough Plane with 1 Knife |
| 1—Divider | 1—Pebble Square |
| | 1—Screw Driver |
| | 1—Rough Plane with Rounded Knife |
| | 1—Coping Saw |

Bench and 51 Tools with tilt tool compartment.

**No. 10575** . . . . . . . . . . . . . . . . . $895.00

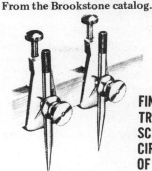

From the Brookstone catalog.

## FINE QUALITY TRAMMELS SCRIBE ARCS, CIRCLES OF ANY RADIUS

Mount these on a bar anywhere from 5/8" to 1-5/8" wide (use wood, aluminum, steel, etc.) and you can lay true arcs and circles limited in radius only by length of bar. Useful also to lay out distances between points.

Hardened, ground points are eccentric, permitting finest adjustment up to 5/16" merely by turning knurled end of point before final clamping.

Points can be set vertically or at 45 degrees, the latter to permit marking under a ledge or other obstruction. And ordinary pen or pencil will fit in place of either point.

Very nicely made. Ideal for pattern makers, builders, carpenters, sheet metal workers, boat builders, loftsmen, machinists.

**The Brookstone Company**
**Peterborough, N.H. 03458**
**Catalog is free**

**The Craftool Co.**
**1421 W. 240th St.**
**Harbor City, Calif. 90710**
**Catalog**

63

## 6" BENCH GRINDER WITH HONE

Built-in drill sharpening guides, shatterproof eye shields, water tray, fine and coarse wheels plus hone attachment for fine-edge sharpening. 8 amp. 110-120 Volt, 60 Hz, AC. Industrially rated. 3450 rpm grinder; 78 rpm hone. Die-cast aluminum housing. Self-lubricating bearings. 3-conductor power cord.

**110-715130E6440     $39.95**

**NEW!**

U.S. General Supply Corp.
100 General Place
Jericho, N.Y. 11753
Catalog

---

## DISCOUNT HOUSES:

Two remarkable sources of brandname tools of all sorts from poor to excellent, hand and powered, are the Silvo Hardware Company of Philadelphia and the U.S. General Supply Corp. of Jericho, New York. Their prices are, to our knowledge, the best you can do by mail order in the U. S.

Silvo seems to be more selective in its offerings and does carry some import items such as the superlative Record planes and vises made in England. U.S. General Supply carries a broader range of brandnames for each tool type and has the edge in the penny department. Mark White, up Alaska way, says of their Stickleback speed rasp:

**64**

## MALLEABLE IRON

### "C" CLAMPS

Made of specially heat-treated, heavy malleable iron. Screws are fitted with swivel heads and sliding cross bars.

| Stock No. | | Price Ea. |
|---|---|---|
| 205-141E90 (1" Throat) .........(N) | $ | .54 |
| 205-142E120 (2" Throat) ........(N) | | .72 |
| 205-142½E230 (2½" Throat) (N) | | 1.40 |
| 205-143E240 (3" Throat) ........(N) | | 1.46 |
| 205-144E400 (4" Throat) ........(N) | | 2.80 |
| 205-145E500 (5" Throat) ........(N) | | 3.46 |
| 205-146E570 (6" Throat) ........(N) | | 3.98 |
| 205-148E880 (8" Throat) ........(N) | | 6.08 |

---

### HANDY BAR CLAMP

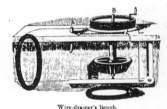

Clamp jaws are red finish wrought steel . . . open to 6". 1" bar and adjustment are polished steel. Quick-action type.

**200-157E220** (6" Capacity) Each (N) **$1.49**
**200-157E200** (Three or More) Each  1.35

Wire-drawer's Bench.

---

## STICKLEBACK SPEED RASPS

10" HAND RASP

4" DRILL RASP

Speed-Rasp for surface forming, enlarging holes, and making all kinds of irregular shaped holes in wood, plastic, plasterboard, masonite and plywood.
Hand Rasps have confortable, solid-wood handles for fast, easy shaping. Drill Rasps have ¼ shanks for use with any electric drill. They're made from the finest tool steel, hardened and tempered for extra service-life. A special feature is the patented Stickleback non-clogging tooth formation.

| 152-4604E320 | 10" Hand Rasp ......... | $2.40 |
|---|---|---|
| 152-4615E240 | 4" Drill Rasp .......... | 1.60 |

**SAVE MOST.**                                 63

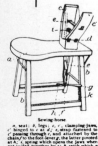

Sewing-horse.
_a_, seat; _b_, legs; _c, c_, clamping-jaws, _c'_ hinged to _c_ at _d_; _e_, strap fastened to _c'_ passing through _e_, and attached by the chain/to the foot-lever/, the latter pivoted at _h_, _i_, spring which opens the jaws when not pulled together by _e_; _k_, ratch which _g_ engages to hold the jaws together.

"This is one of the handiest tools available for an emergency modification or repair. It has a gimlet tip which screws a starting hole in wood or plywood, and many sharp raspy teeth which can enlarge that hole to any size wanted. Many local fisherman say it is the cutting tool that they would least like to have to do without. It is hand operated, takes muscle and does a fairly sloppy job; but it's a whole hell of a lot easier than a Boy Scout knife when a hole has to be bored or an opening has to be cut and the boat is at sea and away from electrical power. It is primarily a wood tool and will dull quickly on fiberglass or aluminum. It won't do very much at all on steel. Cheap if you ever need to use it. A piece of ¼ plastic tubing will slide over the blade and keep all those little teeth sharp."

## PLOUGH AND COMBINATION PLANES

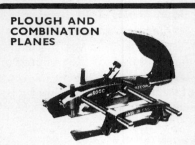

Silvo Hardware Co.
107-109 Walnut St.
Philadelphia, Pa. 19106
Catalog is 50 cents

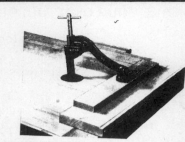

**Record**

**Record Combination Plane** — 18 Cutters — Rabbets, ploughs, grooves and cuts dados, beads, centre beads, fillisters and tongues. Cross grain spurs and positive locking depth gauge.
**050C-R10** P—3 lbs. 18 Cutters ...... **$33.98**

**Record Plough Plane** — (not illustrated) — same as 050C above but with **3 cutters** — cuts small rabbets and grooves. Adjustable depth gauge, double arm bridged fence. Cutter size: 1/8", 3/16" and 1/4".
**043-R10** P—2 lbs. 3 Cutters ........ **$10.50**

Items from Silvo catalog.

**Record H. D. Bench Vises** — Ridgid Base — Plain screw — castings guaranteed against breakage. Back anvil. Back bolted jaw plates with extra deep jaws. Massive base area gives complete rigidity. **No. 110P—4½" jaws**, opens to 5", net wt. 43 lbs. **No. 111P—5¼" jaws**, opens to 6", net wt. 52 lbs. **No. 112P—6" jaws**, opens to 7", net wt. 72 lbs. **No. 114P—8" jaws**, opens to 9", net. wt. 90 lbs.

| | | |
|---|---|---|
| **110P-R10** P—46 lbs. 4½" jaws | ...... | **$59.65** |
| **111P-R10** H—55 lbs. 5¼" jaws | ...... | **$68.50** |
| **112P-R10** H—76 lbs. 6" jaws | ...... | **$85.75** |
| **114P-R10** H—95 lbs. 8" jaws | ...... | **$119.98** |

**Record Bench Holdfast** — acts like a third hand holding difficult shapes flat to the bench. Speeds the whole job up! Quickly removed from its collar leaving the bench top free. With 2 collars (and screws) for alternative positions.
**No. 145 has** 5⅞" Reach (Max.) by 6⅞" opening (Max.), **No. 146 has** 7¹/₁₆" Reach (Max.) by 7⅝" opening (Max.).
**145-R10** P—5 lbs. .................. **$8.98**
**146-R10** P—6 lbs. .................. **$10.50**

**Record Side Rabbet Plane** — for side Rabbeting, cleaning grooves, freeing doors, cleaning grooves, freeing dados and trimming damaged mouldings. Nose removable for corner work. 9/16" cutter width.
**2506S-R10** P—1 lb. ................. **$8.95**

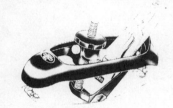

**Record Circular Plane** — 10" long — 1¾" cutter width — for convex and concave surfaces, flexible sole plate adjusts to suit contour of work.
**020C-R10** P—5 lbs. ............... **$24.98**

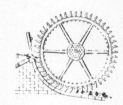

**Record Bench Stop** — fits to bench top and prevents end movements of work when planing — Lays flush when not in use.
**167-R10** P—1 lb. ................. **$1.98**

65

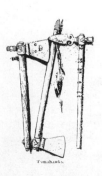

Tomahawks.

## POWER HANDTOOLS

What are you going to do? I'm a Rockwell man. Another very experienced contributor swears by Black and Decker. A contractor friend of ours has contempt for any man who comes onto the job with anything but Skil. And a whole flock (pod?) of boatbuilders we know at a well-known maritime history exhibit think that Milwaukee's the one.

Probably different companies make the best and most appropriate of the various tools that are desirable in a boatshop. We've got theories and arguments about it all, but would feel more secure with more. If you have a power handtool you swear by and can give a reasonable argument why it is better than competing tools, let us know and we will help a lot of people and get a lot of industry very esctatic and/or very uptight and, just maybe, better tools. Meanwhile, consider the next four pages or so to be missing, a cop-out of a very temporary nature only.

Ax of jadeite from New Ireland.

**MAKE YOUR OWN TOOLS DEPT.:**

### Machinist's tools:

The "Thomas Register of American Industry" contains a listing of more than 100,000 American Manufacturers. A major portion of these are involved in the tooling industry, meaning manufacturers of tools that make tools or whatever. Most of this activity has to do with machining and to get much involved with this morass is ridiculous. There are too many, and anyway, they are usually so far out of any individual's ability to acquire that there is no point.

There are exceptions, of course, and one is the Maximat V-10 and 7 machine lathes manufactured by American Edelstal, Inc. of Tenafly, N. J. They seem to us to be absolutely outstanding values. With a machine lathe/milling machine such as this, back to back with basic founding and forging equipment (discussed later), you can be on top of virtually any tooling requirement that is practically faced by the small shopman.

Some will recognize American Edelstal as the same firm which offers the fine little Unimat, one of the most versatile, useful and reasonably-priced power tools ever devised for people who do lots of benchwork, modeling, etc. The Maximats are Unimat's big brothers. Prices are currently between about $800 and $2000, depending on setup.

American Edelstal, Inc.
One Atwood Ave.
Tenafly, N.J. 07670

66

There is no point having machinery capable of close precision tolerances unless you can lay them out and measure them. One of the largest most reputable manufacturers of the required instruments is the L.S. Starrett Company of Athol, Mass. They manufacture more than 3,000 tools; gage blocks, optical measuring instruments, electronic gauges, inside and outside micrometers and rules of all kinds. Starrett will be a "sleeper" for many readers who will be surprised to find they offer fine domestic wood-handled screwdrivers, old-fashioned quality bench levels, a line of rugged vises and many, many others. Their products are available only through distributors, so you will have to order through one, the names of which they will supply on request.

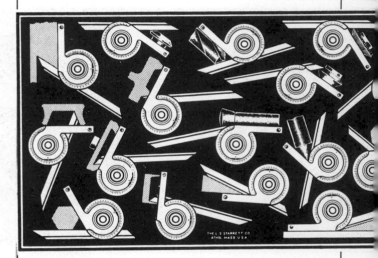

The L.S. Starrett Co.
Athol, Mass. 01331

# Maximat V10:

# One-Tool Machine Shop

## Specialty Houses

This again brings up the issue of distributors. We would like to know about the ones you like, those which keep prices down, are fast, well-stocked, courteous, etc. Specialty houses very often carry what you need in an area outside of their specialty. In precision tools, for example, specialty houses serving watch-repairers, display panel contractors, electronics firms, etc., may carry what you need. One interesting organization of this sort, and which carries General's line of precision tools, is the Alley Supply Co. of Gardenerville, Nevada. They supply gunsmiths and reloaders with their paraphernalia. About half their catalog has to do with tools and supplies for the general small shop machinist at good prices.

### VERSA-VISE

#### VISES

| | F.O.B. | Retail | Net |
|---|---|---|---|
| VERSA - VISE, Complete with Pipe Jaws and Standard Base, Shipping weight, 17-lbs----- | | $22.00 | $16.50 |
| Standard Base, for above----------------#31016 | | 2.50 | 1.88 |
| Clamp on Base, for above---------------#31014 | | 15.00 | 11.25 |
| Flush Base, for above------------------#31009 | | 10.30 | 7.72 |
| Tilt Adapter, for above---------------#31008 | | 4.30 | 3.22 |
| Drill Press Base, for above------------#31009 | | 10.00 | 7.50 |
| Saw Horse Base, for above--------------#31011 | | 5.98 | 4.48 |

**Items from Alley Supply catalog.**

**Alley Supply Co.**
**P.O. Box 848-A**
**Carson Valley Industrial Park**
**Gardenerville, Nev. 89410**
**Catalog is $1.00.**

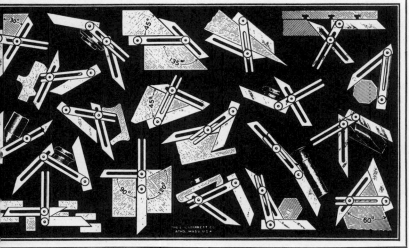

### NO. 55 HEAVY DUTY CIRCLE CUTTER

with ½" diameter Round Shank for Drill Press use. Adjustable for making 1¾" to 7½" holes in steel, brass, aluminum, plastics, wood, hardboards, and other materials. Complete with ¼" High Speed Steel Cutter Bit and ¼" Drill and Hex Wrench. Individually boxed. Weight 12 ounces.

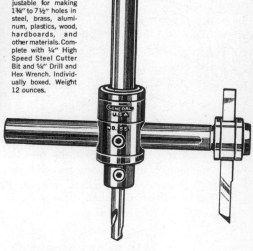

67

### SUPER METRIC SET WITH HEXAGON DIES No. 6312

### SUPER SET 614

| | Retail | Net |
|---|---|---|
| Gunsmith's Tap and Die Kit, includes 10 taps, 10 Dies, 10 Die Guides, Tap Handle, Die Stock and Case----------------------------- | $56.68 | $45.35 |
| Mechanic's SUPER SET #614 Tap & Die Kit, 39-Pc | 46.95 | 28.17 |
| Metric #9M Tap & Die Set, 21 piece set------- | 61.00 | 36.60 |
| Metric #6312 SUPER-Set 42-Pc Tap & Die Set--- | 65.00 | 39.00 |
| Model Makers Tap & Die Set #913, 23 piece set | 49.50 | 29.70 |

### NO. 11 WASHER & GASKET CUTTER

For cutting washers and gaskets of leather, rubber, cork, graphite and asbestos packing, copper and other similar soft materials. Made of steel with graduated beam or crossbar, with 2 adjustable blade holders and hardened tool steel blades, and center pilot pin. Combination round and square shank permits use with Bit Brace, Hand Drill or Drill Press. Adjustable from ½" to 6½" diameters. Individually boxed. Weight 7 ounces.

### 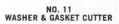 GENERAL® CIRCLE CUTTERS

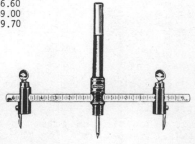

Carpenters' Boring-machine.

### Japanese Tools

Japanese woodworking tools are excellent — interesting, adaptable and very practical in many marine building applications. Their saws, for example, cut on the pullstroke, thus eliminating binding and crooked kerfs, especially in thin stock.

Tashiro Hardware Company in Seattle and the Japan Woodworker in Berkeley both offer standard lines of Japanese tools, the latter being particularly interesting for its slick (MK-308). Their advertised intention is soon to offer full lines of Japanese drawknives, planking saws, adzes, long jointer planes, etc.

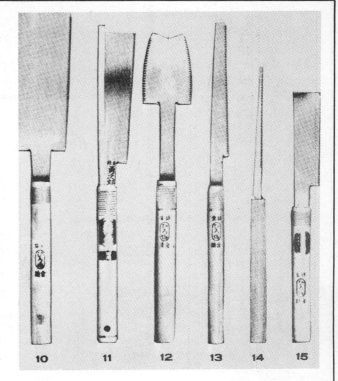

**Tashiro Hardware Co.**
**109 Prefontaine Place**
**Seattle, Wash. 98104**
**Catalog**

**The Japan Woodworker**
**1701 Grove St.**
**Berkeley, Calif. 94709**
**Catalog**

68

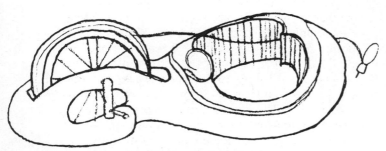

**MK-656 Snap Line:** Traditional Japanese carpenter's snap line. A work of art in itself, this snap line is excellent for 'snapping' or marking long straight lines on wood. Comes with charcoal, string, cotton and pins. 195mm in length. The snap-line body is made from wood.

Snapline from the Japan Woodworker catalog. Saws and cutting technique from Tashiro Hardware Company catalog.

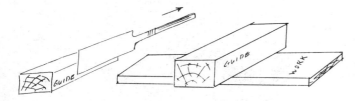

The fine pitch, light set and light weight of the tension saws, make them ideal for use with guide blocks to make precision cuts. Merely fix the guide block along the saw line with clamps, etc., and hold the saw flush against the guide block when sawing. Since the saw cuts parallel with the face of the guide block , end finish cuts are made by butting the work in the desired relationship with the guide block. Precise feathered cuts may be easily be made by this method. For oblique cuts, use angular guide blocks.

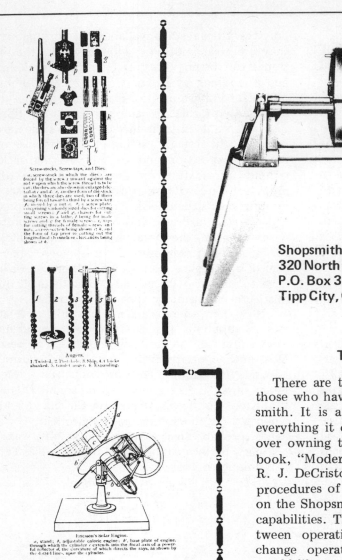

Screw-stocks, Screw-taps, and Dies

*a*, screw-stock in which the dies are forced by the screw *i* inward against the rod *e* upon which the screw thread is to be cut; the dies are also shown in enlarged detail at *e* and *d*; *z*, another form of die-stock in which three dies are used, two of them being forced toward a third by a screw-key *f*, moved by a nut *n*; *A*, a screw-plate comprising variously sized dies for cutting small screws; *f* and *g*, chasers for cutting screws in a lathe, *f* being for male screws and *g* for female screws; *i*, taps for cutting threads of female screws and nuts, a cross-section being shown at *k*, and the form of tap prior to cutting out the longitudinal channels or clearances being shown at *k*.

Augers.

1, Twisted; 2, Pod-lade; 3, Ship; 4, Cocks-shanked; 5, Gimlet auger; 6, Expanding.

Ericsson's Solar Engine.

*a*, stand; *b*, adjustable caloric engine; *b'*, base plate of engine, through which the cylinder *c* extends into the focal axis of a powerful reflector *d*, the curvature of which directs the rays, as shown by the dotted lines, upon the cylinder.

Shopsmith Inc.
320 North Second St.
P.O. Box 32
Tipp City, Ohio 45371

Shopsmith Mark V

**The All-In-One Tool:**

There are those who live it, swear by it and those who haven't the time of day for the Shopsmith. It is a well-made tool that really does everything it claims. It saves space and money over owning the individual tools. The 351-page book, "Modern Power Tool Woodworking," by R. J. DeCristoforo, devoted to technique and procedures of shop tool woodworking all done on the Shopsmith, is an impressive witness to its capabilities. The only hangup is setup time between operations and the common need to change operations from one to another. We would like to hear from users of the Shopsmith.

69

Somewhere someone must specialize in electric motors in big ways. Right? In the Northeast it's New England Electric Motor Service Corp. in Chelsea, Mass. Literally a warehouse jammed with motors of every type and power - thousands of them new and used. Who is it out your way?

**New England Electric Motor Service Corp.**
214 Arlington Street
Chelsea, Mass. 02150

## Casting Tools

Before you mill it, perhaps you want to cast it. Cast it? Yes, cast it. To be sure, you aren't going to be casting diesel engine blocks in your basement shop, but there is no reason why you cannot easily do your own patternmaking and founding of smaller fittings and tools at home at modest cost and greater satisfaction.

First, you need a pattern. A pattern is a model of what you wish to cast in metal. Traditionally, original patterns are made of either wax (cire perdu) or sugar pine, which is easily carved, takes a good finish under the blade and is light and stable. The plastics industry has opened the field wide and a host of materials for patternmaking is now available. They allow not only original patterns but also simple duplication of existing patterns, broken parts to be replaced and so on.

To make a good pattern one needs an understanding of the founding process and the characteristics of the metal being used, especially how much it expands at casting heat and shrinks on cooling. You also need to "see" how the metal needs to flow to fill the pattern mold in the casting sand. This often indicates the need for a pattern that comes apart in sections, calling for careful planning and toolwork.

Books and information on the subject currently in print are scandalously few. We found only two titles readily available and, fortunately, they are clear and good enough so that the intrepid can begin. One book is "Patternmaking and Founding" by Robert Smith, McKnight and McKnight Publishing Co., Bloomington, Ill. This is a highly informative pamphlet that most shopmen will want on their shelves whether they are interested in actually casting or not, because of its clear exposition and very interesting background information on the manipulation of metals. The other book, "The Foseco Foundryman's Handbook," Foseco International Ltd., Pergamon Press, New York, is an absolute necessity, giving the characteristics of most metals for most purposes in most circumstances — a real gem of a reference manual. For others, you will have to browse with us and others through the misty groves of the secondhand book trade.

Now then, there is a company which specializes in supplying the needs of patternmakers. They supply all the materials and tools you need. Most of their offerings, however, assume, naturally, that your requirements are industrial — huge fancy saws, surfacers, millers and so on. This is the Kindt-Collins Company of Cleveland and, when writing them, be sure to state clearly your needs, probably just their line of woods, waxes auxiliary pattern supplies and bench tools. This is a unique company.

The Kindt-Collins Co.
12651 Elmwood Ave.
Cleveland, Ohio 44111

70

From Kindt-Collins catalog.

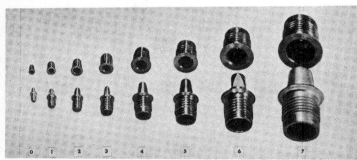

# MASTER BRASS DOWELS

Smelting-furnace.

*a*, fire-brick lining; *b*, masonry; *c*, opening in the side of the upper part of the furnace through which it is charged; *e*, boshes; *f*, throat; *g*, hearth or crucible; *h*, dam-stone; *t*, twyer. That part lying below the widest diameter, above the boshes, is called the *shaft*.

## For Wood Patterns and Core Boxes

Master Brass Dowels (broach type) are an exclusive patented development designed to meet the patternmaker's need for stronger holding power and easier insertion in both hard and soft wood patterns. These new improved Master Brass Dowels are a substantial improvement over our original Master "Square Head" type of brass dowels. They offer the following advantages:

1. Do not twist off in hard wood. Insertion is made easier and more positive by the distinctive design of the broached head of the male part.

2. A tighter hold especially in soft woods is attained by special type threads.

3. The pin of the male Master Brass Dowel is completely round (no squared surfaces) offering more bearing surface and assuring a more accurate draw.

4. Easily removed for replacement if desired.

5. Precision-made to very close tolerances.

### Quality Plus

Perhaps the most interesting product they offer is the incomparable patternmaker's vise! There is nothing in a shop so satisfying as a well-adjusted patternmaker's vise! Nothing! They are wonderful and only one company in the U. S. still makes them — Oliver Machinery Co. of Grand Rapids, Michigan. This is shocking, really, for their superiority and versatility over other vise types wherever any woodworking other than straight cutting and planing is involved is so obvious that their paucity can only be explained as a massive cultural forgetfulness — a mistake of some kind — for there used to be several makes available and the prices they command in second-hand tool outlets would be paid only by the strong in heart and stomach.

These vises swivel through 360 degrees, tilt through 90 degrees, clamp odds and rounds and angles up to about 70 degrees and have double-ended dogs for holding rounds, longs and just about anything at any angle imaginable. It is the all-purpose vise which does not compromise any of the purposes, with the exception of uses involving really heavy pounding. Oliver offers vises both by themselves and with patternmaker's benches. Kindt-Collins (see facing page) distributes both.

**The Oliver Machinery Co.**
**Grand Rapids, Mich. 49504**

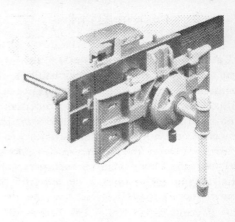

Items from Oliver catalog.

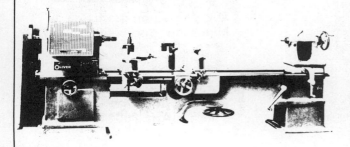

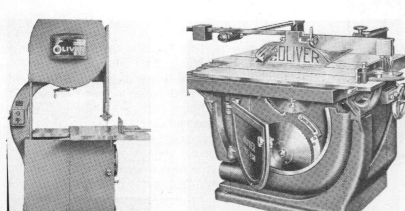

# MOLD MAKING

The use of sand molds is the quickest, easiest and least expensive method of making metal castings, since sand can be used over and over for a large number of castings. Briefly, in order to make the sand mold, the pattern is placed on a flat surface and dusted with flour silica which prevents the pattern from sticking to the sand. The bottom half of the wooden flask is placed around the pattern, the sand which has been previously dampened, is then sprinkled on the pattern and rammed around the pattern until it is firm, the flask is then turned bottom side up and the sand surface and the bottom of the pattern are dusted with silica flour; the top flask is then put in place and rammed with sand. The mold is complete after the pattern is withdrawn.

Pouring a casting with the No. 4 crucible

Above from Pyramid Products Co. brochure.

Below from Kansas City Specialties.

*The Foundryette*

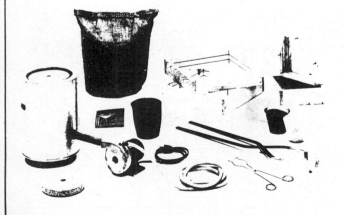

Once you have a proper pattern (oarlocks, cleats and bowchocks are good first projects), you will need a furnace, "flask", molding sand and so forth. Large professional production models are available from K-C and other companies, of course, but these are expensive and probably beyond the practical requirements of small shopmen or home boatbuilders. Two firms offer practical, low-cost kits supplying everything you need for casting up to 50 lbs. of metal up to grey iron in melting temperature. These are:

**Kansas City Specialties Co.**
**2805 Middleton Beach Rd.**
**Middleton, Wisc. 53562**

**Pyramid Products Co.**
**3736 South 7th Ave.**
**Phoenix, Ariz. 85041**

Both firms offer complete kits in varying sizes from about $50 to about $160, 3-50 lbs. metal capacity (red brass). The emphasis of their literature is on "hobbyist" uses; statuettes, etc., but one firm wrote to say that at least one customer had purchased a unit to cast custom yacht fittings in aluminum. Kits include everything you need except the metal and gas and can be used not only for casting, but heat treating and case hardening as well.

Whether you go for casting or not, considerable savings on fittings can be realized if you make your own patterns and have a regular foundry cast them for you.

72

### Casting Kits

We have found two organizations that offer kits with which you can save many dollars by making your own shop tools.

**Casting Specialties**
**Cedarburg, Wisc. 53012**

**HAMMER MOLD HM33**

At last an economical way to mold your own lead hammers in your school shop. With our castings and a little filing and drilling you can make a top quality mold for making your own 2# lead hammers. All rugged cast iron construction.

HM33   Complete parts .................... $5.25
#107H  handle for 2# hammer .............. .52

Casting Specialties, a division of Struck Corp., offers kits for drill presses, table saws, vises and many other tools. Their kits are designed as school projects and involve milling and lathe work. If you have this equipment, the results are sturdy, attractive and really good tools at rock-bottom prices.

American Machine and Tool Co. kits require no mill work and are straight kits, but again at very substantial savings. Their line includes saws, presses, jointers, spindle-molders, lathes and sanders with sundry attachments. They also stock and offer electric motors for their kits.

### MACHINIST'S BENCH VISE MV102

A husky vise for home shop use, using the modern tube guide for sliding surface. Easy to finish on a minimum of machinery.

**SPECIFICATIONS**

3" x 1½" jaw, opening 5 inches, 2½" gap above sliding surface. Cast iron jaw and body ¾" CRS lead screw. Jaws can be faced with tool steel if desired. Anvil tail.

**MACHINE TOOLS REQUIRED**

Lathe with mill attachment and Drill Press.

MV102   Castings only (Shpg. wt. 16#) .............. $ 8.49
MV102X  Complete parts (Shpg. wt. 23#) .............. 11.59

73

---

**American Machine and Tool Co., Inc.**
**Royerford, Pa. 19468**

BRAND NEW

# ELECTRIC MOTOR

**DEVELOPS FULL 1 HP**

Brand new, factory fresh motors for use with any machine in this folder. Limited quantity . . . first come, first served.

**SPECIAL AMCO PRICE**
(when purchased with any unit in this folder) **$19⁹⁰**
f.o.b. factory
Shipping Wt.: 17 lbs.

**\*\*FULL SERVICE 1-YEAR WARRANTY**

". . . found it a genuine bargain." WORKBENCH
**If purchased separately, $24.95**

---

FULL 22" LONG,
4⅛" # JOINTER-PLANER

**Model No. 2433**
complete as shown
f.o.b. factory
Shipping wt.: 18 lbs.

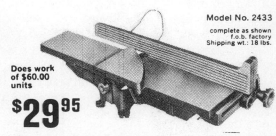

**Does work of $60.00 units**

**$29⁹⁵**

**Precision Ground Tables, All Cast Iron and Steel Construction**

Now, at little more than a hand tool price, a guaranteed professional quality precision machine which does same work as skilled hand planing . . . much faster, more accurately. Makes accurate glue joints: rabetting cuts for doors, window frames, table drawers; square taper cuts for chair legs; extremely accurate beveling. Helps amateurs produce quality work—with the sweat eliminated.

**TOP QUALITY FEATURES SPEAK FOR THEMSELVES**

• Precision ground cast iron tables, adjustable for depth of cut • Rigid cast iron base • New patent-pending design holds clearance between knives and tables at any depth • Rabett depth ⅜" • Hardened, ground high speed steel knives • Patent-pending fence adjustable to any position, any angle 0° to 50° • Patent-pending lift-off guard (nothing to loosen!) • Balanced steel cutter head.

**LISTEN TO THE EXPERTS:**

". . . easily whacked the grooved edge of tongue-and-groove pine in a single pass . . . as fast as you can push the stock through . . . planed (knots) smooth without chipping." . . . POPULAR SCIENCE. "Does a fine job." . . . WORKBENCH

**10-YEAR FULL-SERVICE GUARANTEE°**

**DELUXE 4⅛" BALLBEARING**

# JOINTER-PLANER

**Model No. 2433B**

Precision built for continuous, smooth, high speed, heavy duty production. Sturdy, well ribbed grey iron tables accurately machined, easily controlled by fast-locking convenient controls. Double shielded, lubricated for life bearings.

**$34⁹⁵**
f.o.b. factory
Shipping weight: 19 lbs.

# Forging

And so we continue backwards, in a forwards sort of way. Before you mill, before you cast, why not forge?

Blacksmithing is a great art, a great activity and there are many signs that there is about to be a revival of it in this country. Blacksmithing has always been an intimate part of shipbuilding and it ought to be again for, while years are required to become a journeyman smith, there is no reason why the average shopman and boat-builder cannot learn to make his own gear: hooks, bolts, boat fittings of all kinds and, what the heck, fastenings and those special individual touches on shipboard that make a craft really one's own. Forging is a matter of heating iron or soft steel and pounding it into a desired shape. The pounding not only shapes, it compacts the molecules of the metal, making it strong and surprisingly resistant to deep rust and corrosion, vastly more so than does casting or stamping.

Waldo Howland's fine schooner Integrity was fastened and largely fitted-out in iron and its strength, practicality and serious attractiveness gave the lie to the brass and chrome freaks who view iron with a materialistic racism, entirely unreasonable and unjustified. My Friendship sloop was fastened and fitted with iron and it gave no trouble even after 25 years of more or less creative abuse at sea. Strong, cheap and you can do it yourself.

We looked for a "kit" and information with trepidation. There was no need for it, though, because some of the old blacksmithing tool outfits are still at it—thank heavens! First, a little seduction with three good books:

"The Art of Blacksmithing," by Alex Bealer, Funk and Wagnalls, N.Y.: An illustrated narrative account of the fundamentals of smithing. The novice or would-be smith will be absolutely seduced into further interest. A good first book.

"The Village Blacksmith," by Aldren A. Watson, Thomas Y. Crowell Co., N. Y. Beautifully illustrated and easy to read, this book does for blacksmithing what Eric Sloane does for

Illustration from "Modern Machine Shop Practice," 1892, in "Blacksmithing and Farrier's Tools" at the Shelburne Museum.

woodworking. It is history, art, science and yarning all at once.

"Blacksmithing and Farrier's Tools," by Bradley Smith, the Shelburne Museum, Shelburne, Vermont. This one fills some of the holes left by the other two, giving a dimension of reality that the others trade for nostalgia and romance. Basically it is a compendium of data on hundreds of smithing tools, their form, history and use; a technical treatise on the things themselves.

Out-of-print blacksmithing books have become a very hot item in second-hand bookshops. But they are out there somewhere and demand for them is bound to get some necessary reprinting going. The English, who are much better stewards of the artisan than we, have a government organization called the "Council for Small Industries in Rural Areas " which offers several books and pamphlets with technical data on the tools and techniques of the working blacksmith. A brochure describing these and others can be sent for by writing:

CoSIRA　　　　　　　　　　　　—GP
P.O. Box No. 717
35 Camp Rd.
Wimbleton Common
London SW 19 4UP

74

Blacksmithing tools are offered by the following firms in the U.S.:

The Bicknell Mfg. Co.
Rockland, Me. 04841
or
Elberton, Ga.

An excellent line of cutters, punches, drift pins, hammers, drills, chisels, fullers, swages, tongs and dressers.

Items below from Buffalo catalog.

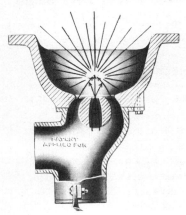

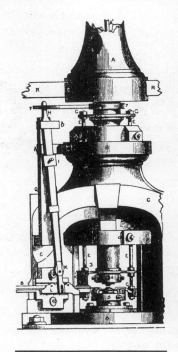

The Buffalo Forge Company
P.O. Box 985
Buffalo, N.Y. 14240

An old and venerable firm, friendly and with fine quality virtually unchanged from the old days when most American villages had a Buffalo working all day somewhere at the edge of town. They offer forges, blowers, fire pots, shears and arbor presses.

75

# SEMI-PORTABLE FORGES
## THE -49 SERIES
### 249 with 200 Hand Blower
### 849 with 2LEH Electric Blower

The -49 Series Buffalo forge is a semi portable unit used for the heaviest type of blacksmith work in railroad shops, garages, and structural iron shops. Featured is a 38″ x 42″ x 7″ deep one-piece cast iron hearth and type RR fire pot. Plain units are available with 3″ blast connection and lever controlled blast gate for operation from a central blower source. Hand or electric blower models are also available. Halfhood and water tank are optional at extra cost. Specify operating voltage when ordering 849 model.

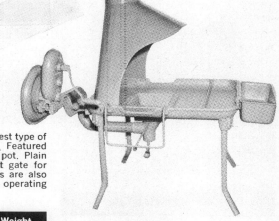

**249H FORGE
WITH WATER TANK**

| Model | Hearth Size | Hood | Blower | Motor | Weight |
|-------|-------------|------|--------|-------|--------|
| 49    | 38″ x 42″ x 7″ | No  | No   | No    | 377#  |
| 49H   | 38″ x 42″ x 7″ | Yes | No   | No    | 397#  |
| 249   | 38″ x 42″ x 7″ | No  | 200  | No    | 437#  |
| 249H  | 38″ x 42″ x 7″ | Yes | 200  | No    | 457#  |
| 849   | 38″ x 42″ x 7″ | No  | 2LEH | 1/5 HP | 445# |
| 849H  | 38″ x 42″ x 7″ | Yes | 2LEH | 1/5 HP | 465# |

**Fisher and Norris, Inc.**
301 Monmouth St.
Trenton, N.J. 08607

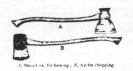

*A*, Broad-ax, for hewing ; *B*, Ax for chopping.

Items below from Fisher & Norris catalog.

## EAGLE ANVILS

### The Guaranteed Kind
### Fully Warranted

First-Class Blacksmiths, Machinists, Toolmakers and craftsmen have used EAGLE Anvils in this country and abroad for more than a century; EAGLE Anvils have no peer! The superior production techniques and high-grade materials used in their manufacture have kept pace with the demands of modern industry for quality tools which give continued superior performance.

Many government purchasing specifications are based on the standards set up by Fisher & Norris for the products they manufacture. The blacksmiths' anvil (pictured above) is typical of these requirements.

HORN - solid piece, tough, untempered, forged steel, guaranteed not to bend nor break.

FACE - one piece, crucible tool steel, ground and tempered edges, perfectly welded to the body. Will not settle.

BODY - solid piece gun iron alloy, warranted not to settle nor break. Will produce satisfactory hammer rebound without unnecessary ringing.

They make the patent "Eagle" anvils and double screw blacksmith vises. These are the best anvils in the world and the firm is the only manufacturer of leg vises left in the U.S. Anvils range from 50 to 500 pounds; prices from $75 to $125. Leg vises are unbelievably powerful, the strongest vise in existence. They are expensive ($300 to $350) but still will be working when our existence is of concern only to archaeologists. F. & N. also offers saw maker's, export doublehorned and chainmaker's anvils.

## SPECIAL ANVILS
## GREY IRON and SEMI-STEEL CASTINGS

In addition to the full line of stock anvils illustrated here, Fisher & Norris can supply special anvils or other grey iron or semi-steel castings of any weight or shape at a slight additional cost above regular patterns.

Send us your specifications. There is no charge for a quotation. We specialize in welding tool steel to cast iron. All work is fully warranted.

**76**

## DIMENSIONS - STOCK ANVILS

| Wt. Lbs. | FACE | | | | HORN |
|---|---|---|---|---|---|
| | Length Inches | Width Inches | Hardie Hole Sq. in. | Pritchel Hole | Length Inches |
| 50 | 10 | 3 | 5/8 | 7/16 | 6½ |
| 80 | 11½ | 3¼ | 3/4 | ½ | 7½ |
| 100 | 12¾ | 3½ | 3/4 | 9/16 | 9 |
| 120 | 13½ | 3½ | 3/4 | 9/16 | 9 |
| 150 | 15¾ | 4 | 7/8 | 9/16 | 10¼ |
| 160 | 16 | 4¼ | 1 | 9/16 | 10¼ |
| 180 | 16½ | 4¼ | 1 | 9/16 | 10¼ |
| 200 | 17¼ | 4¾ | 1⅛ | 5/8 | 11½ |
| 225 | 18 | 4¾ | 1⅛ | 5/8 | 11½ |
| 250 | 18½ | 5¼ | 1¼ | 5/8 | 12½ |
| 300 | 19¾ | 5¼ | 1¼ | 5/8 | 12½ |
| 350 | 21 | 6 | 1¾ | 3/4 | 13¼ |
| 400 | 22 | 6 | 1¾ | 3/4 | 13¼ |
| 450 | 22 | 6 | 1¾ | 3/4 | 13¼ |
| 500 | 23 | 6½ | 1½ | 13/16 | 14½ |
| 600 | 24¼ | 6¾ | 1½ | 13/16 | 14½ |
| 700 | 25½ | 7¼ | 1⅝ | 13/16 | 14½ |

E-269-57

BUILT TO STAND THE HEAVIEST WORK

## THE "FISHER" DOUBLE SCREW
## PARALLEL LEG VISE
## WORLD'S STRONGEST VISE

Main lever operates double screw mechanism which insures absolutely parallel closing of Tool Cast Steel Jaws, file cut, properly hardened and welded in place by a special process. Solid slide prevents front jaw from dropping or twisting.

| NO. | WEIGHT | JAWS | OPENS |
|---|---|---|---|
| 4 | 110 lbs. | 6¼ " x 1¼ " | 7½ " |
| 5 | 150 lbs. | 7 " x 1½ " | 9 " |
| 6 | 200 lbs. | 8 " x 1½ " | 12 " |

**The Kennedy, Foster Co., Inc.**
855 Bloomfield Avenue
Clifton, New Jersey 07012

Primarily a supplier to farriers and jobbers, Kennedy, Foster carries a very complete line of cutters, punches, hammers, fullers, flatters, anvils, tongs, etc. They are also distributers for Buffalo forges.

**The Manhattan Tool Works**
261 First Ave.
Newark, N.J.

Manhattan offers several forged smithing tools along with the boat and shipbuilding tools discussed elsewhere.

**TOOL NO. 18300 BLACKSMITH TOP SWEDGE**

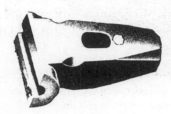

| SIZE | WEIGHT EACH | HANDLE LENGTH | PACKED EACH |
|---|---|---|---|
| 1/2'' | 2½'' | 16'' | 6 |

(ALL SIZES AND PRICES PAGE NO. 19)

**TOOL NO. 18400 BLACKSMITH TOP FULLERS**

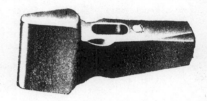

| 1/2'' | 2½'' | 16'' | 6 |
|---|---|---|---|

(ALL SIZES AND PRICES PAGE NO. 19)

**TOOL NO. 18500 BLACKSMITH FLATTERS**

| 3'' | 5 lb. | 16'' | 6 |
|---|---|---|---|

(ALL SIZES AND PRICES PAGE NO. 19)

**TOOL NO. 18200 HALF ROUND HARDIES**

Kennedy. Foster Co., Inc.

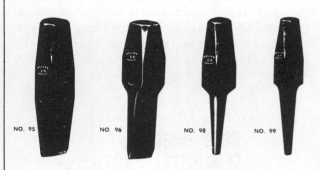

NO. 95    NO. 96    NO. 98    NO. 99

HELLER BLACKSMITHS' ANVIL TOOLS

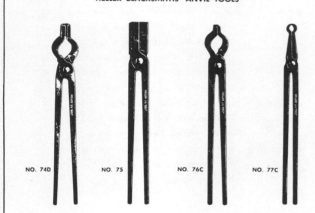

NO. 74D    NO. 75    NO. 76C    NO. 77C

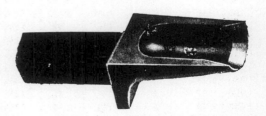

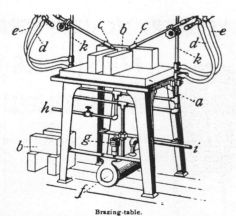

**Brazing-table.**

*a*, fire-brick slab on iron table; *b*, loose fire-brick to concentrate heat; *c*, blowpipes; *d*, gas-pipes; *e*, air-pipes; *f*, compressed-air reservoir; *g*, pressure control; *h*, gas supply; *i*, air supply; *k* standard, with set-screw, supporting pipes.

**From an old print.**

| 1-1/4'' | | 15/16'' | 12 |
|---|---|---|---|

### Quality Plus

Peddinghaus, Inc.
261 First St.
Palisades Park, N.J. 07650

If you too have a secret ecstasy button that is pushed when you get next to sheer quality, it will be pushed by Peddinghaus tools. Drooping dollar exchange values stacked against the mark don't help at all, but, nevertheless, if you have ever made photographs with a Leica or driven a Porsche, you will know that this kind of quality brings no regrets afterwards. Peddinghaus makes anvils, really fine anvils, but its price and configuration make a domestic brand a better buy. But once you see a Peddinghaus shears, bender or vise in action, you'll want one.

**Universal-Bender Model 64/8**
with interchangeable tools for rolling bending pressing

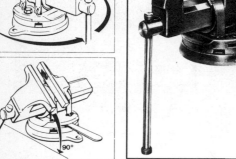

360°

90°

Machinists Vises

Model 5 RP 10
Plate and Section Shears

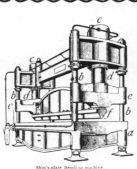

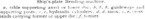

Ship's-plate Bending-machine.
*a*, table supporting anvil or lower die; *A*, *b*, *b*, guideways and supporting posts; *c*, *c*, hydraulic cylinders; *d*, *d*, rams; *e*, *e*, cross heads carrying former or upper die; *f*, former.

### Breeches Buoy Notes: 2

The sense of unreality about the water can be overwhelming. There is so unbelievably much of it! Many fishermen hate fishing, but they love to be out there and that's it. Many boatmen are frightened of the sea, but it dominates their fantasies, like war does for some. How many thousands earn their living writing about boats, watermen and the sea they experience only occasionally and superficially?

The edges, too, are incredible. The beach is a visual canvas; sunbathing and walking along on it are forms of painting and where there are cliffs and rocky seafronts backed by forest, there is no reality at all, not even an artistic one. Stand on or walk along the shore and listen to your mind or, better, watch others do it. They are not even there! They are swept by thought, memory, hope, wonder; almost anything but an honest grasp of it. It is the lone-stallion syndrome, the archtype from childhood.

No, an honest appraisal admits to the total irrelevance of the human presence. It is our indulgence, not the sea's. There is so much to the experience of the sea that to the fully conscious man it is in fact no thing at all.

—GP

Gene Tatten, shipsmith at Mystic Seaport, at the forge preparing the chainplate belts from the whaling vessel Charles Morgan for another century of service.

## Breeches Buoy Notes: 3

Now and again on the shores of the island I'll find a dolphin, a porpoise with a bullet hole in it's back. It is great sport, I am told, to become good enough with a rifle to anticipate the next breech of these creatures and squeeze-off a shot as the hump breaks through the sea's surface.

Now and again we hear that porpoises perhaps speak to one another . . . that porpoises are not easily frustrated. A zoologist friend of mine, doing eighteen month's research on manatees in Florida, became very attached to a herd and developed a love, fellowship and respect for them and they for him, not as animals but as true fellows.

Now and again arrogant nations have "Discovered" new territories, declared them theirs and proceeded to dominate them, beginning with the fraudulent purchase or theft of land and the systematic murder, enslavement and demoralization of the aboriginal inhabitants. The justification was "ownership."

Now and again, and always much later, the conquerors achieve the luxury of embarrassment over their conquest. The African suddenly has a great tradition. The many Indian cultures are finally seen to possess a wisdom, vision and lifestyle enormously appropriate to the continent, showing much of our own to be squanderous and infantile.

The very first explorers found a people who were animals and spoke gibberish and, because "real" clothes were not available here, soon dressed much as the Indians in buckskins and leggins. "Specimens" were now and again captured and sent back to the Royal Courts where they were displayed and taught to perform civilized tricks for the courtiers.

Now and again we don flippers and shiny, slippery black wetsuits, because real clothes are not available there, and we go to sea to claim it for ourselves. And the inhabitants are animals and speak gibberish and, now and again, we capture specimens and send them back to our circuses and courts to be displayed and learn to perform civilized tricks.

And when I find one of these murdered aboriginals I think of the Sioux chief who, when asked by an early explorer what a vast area of the Dakota and Wyoming Territory was called, smiled and replied "mine". He smiles because he had heard of the white man's ways and knew that that was all he could understand. Now and again I wonder what incredible embarrassment awaits us one day at sea.

—GP

79

# SAWS

Wood is the bain and glory of the boatbuilder; bain because so few understand his needs and cut for them, glory because of the variety and quality of woods he gets to work with to complete an appropriate job. It is pointless to review brand names according to quality and value, excepting,

of course, to reiterate that the cheap tool is less then worthless. I am married to imported English handsaws, but that is a personal thing. There are people equally enamored of Swedish and domestic saws. The important thing is that you have good ones and know how to care for them and keep them up yourself — unless you've a reliable pro in the neighborhood.

Stanley offers a saw file guide, set and vise and some few other companies offer tnis and that traditional saw work handtool. A company which specializes in saw work tools for setting, filing and even sawmaking is:

Foley Mfg. Co.
3300 N.E. 5th St.
Minneapolis, Minn. 55418

Items from Foley catalog.

## Foley Hand Saws for Custom Sharpening

Untoothed saws for custom filing. May be used to make any tooth style, rip or crosscut, in any spacing from 4 to 16 points per inch. (These saws will cost up to $10 and more if purchased with teeth.) All blank custom saws by Foley are sold only in packages of four.

| | |
|---|---|
| No. 389503 Extra fine quality, straight. Pkg. of 4 | **$27.00** |
| No. 389502 Professional quality, skew back. Pkg. of 4 | **$24.00** |
| No. 389501 Commercial quality straight back. Pkg. of 4 | **$16.00** |
| No. 389010 Saw handles (extra fine) Pkg. of 4 | **$9.00** |
| No. 389006 Saw handles (professional) Pkg. of 4 | **$8.00** |
| No. 389005 Saw handles (commercial) Pkg. of 4 | **$4.50** |
| No. 389007 Pkg. of 12 small handle screws | **$ .95** |
| No. 389008 Pkg. of 12 large (Medallion) handle screws | **$1.35** |

## Saw Filing Clamp

Moves forward and backward to any angle. Grips saw blade firmly merely by pressure on maleable iron lever.
No. 370700 (No. 2) ... **$18.75**

The Speed Corporation also offers saw filing and setting equipment for both hand and power circular saws. Their line looks very practical and easy to use and at excellent prices.

The Speed Corp.
P.O. Box 3437
Portland, Ore. 97208

Items from Speed Corp. catalog.

## Hand Saw Sharpener

Now you can do expert saw filing at home. Lifetime tool makes precision filing easy for even the most inexperienced. Two simple adjustments for pitch and angle make it fit any type hand saw. Keep your saws extra sharp and true-cutting with a SPEED Saw Filer. Complete with file ready to use.

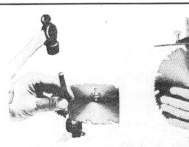

## Circular Saw Blade Jointer and Set

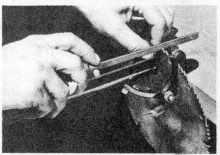

## Circular Saw Blade Sharpener

Most every authority to write about boat-building says that after the electric drill, the most important and useful power tool to own is a bandsaw. No question that this is true, and, if a long look at a few dozen boatshops is any indication, the larger the bandsaw the better. But have you seen the prices? Yowee! By looking around, though, you can find some of the old 30" and 36" veterans for a reasonable price. Sometimes they are a bit roughed-up, but, usually, new wheels or shoes and a new guide will put them in good working order. The Carter Products Company makes all three for large bandsaws. They are reasonably priced and service is fast and personal.

**with TEFLOY Support Blocks**

- 57% less friction
- Wears 10 to 12 times longer than hardened steel blocks.

All items from Carter catalog.

**CARTER 36" SUPER-RIGID WHEELS WITH EXCLUSIVE, INDIVIDUALLY BALANCED 2-INCH LOK-ON TIRES**
- Perfect balance
- Extra heavy-duty construction
- Operates *perfectly* at any speed from 18 RPM to 1800 RPM and from 150 FPM to 15,000 FPM
- Unconditionally guaranteed

Also Carter 30" RIGID WHEELS with QUICK-CHANGE tires

**Carter Micro-Precision Guides** — 3 sizes for any size blade or machine.

CP10    CP20    CP30
(#1)    (#0)    (#00)

Industry's first fully adjustable, fully guarded, precision band saw guide. In complete range of sizes for any standard machine. Now redesigned for extra heavy duty.

Carter Products Co.
50 Market Ave., N.W.
Grand Rapids, Mich. 49502

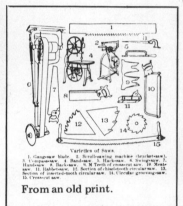

Varieties of Saws.

1. Gang-saw blade. 2. Scroll-sawing machine (bracket-saw). 3. Compass-saw. 4. Band-saw. 5. Hack-saw. 6. Swing-saw. 7. Hand-saw. 8. Back-saw. 9. M Teeth of cross-cut saw. 10. Meat-saw. 11. Rabb-t-saw. 12. Section of chisel-tooth circular saw. 13. Section of inserted-tooth circular saw. 14. Circular grooving-saw. 15. Crosscut saw.

**From an old print.**

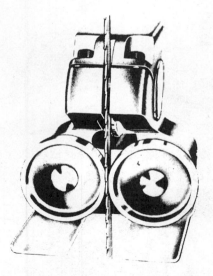

**Carter "Guidall 400"** —for any saw, any speed, any load. Blade speeds up to 15000 fpm — 167% more efficiency. Available with support rollers or support blocks.

**Carter "Guidall 500"** —for 14" - 30" machines. Handles blades ⅛" to ¾".

**Carter "Guidall 600"** —for any 30" - 42" machine. Handles blades ³⁄₁₆" to 2½" wide. Both with sealed ball bearing construction.

81

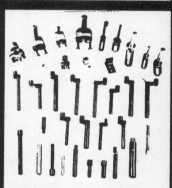

**Carter Mounting Brackets** — adapt Carter guides to any band saw machine for safe, trouble-free operation at any speed or load.

**WRITE FOR FREE CATALOGS**

Two big names in the power sawblade field are Milford, made by the Henry G. Thompson Co., and Simonds, both sold only through distributors.

Simonds is a big one. Their 1¾" commerical catalog (available only to industrial users and distributors) indicates that there is not a cutting operation that they cannot supply. They also make a complete line of files, rotary burrs and rasps.

From the Simonds catalog.

The H.G. Thompson Co. has been responsible for much research in materials cutting problems and not only offers specialized cutting products, but a standing cutting research service to commerical customers. Send them a sample of the material and they will research it and make you an offer based on comprehensive tests. In addition to saws, they also offer taps and dies, drills, flat stock and all manner of cutting stuff.

**The Simonds Saw and Steel Co.**
**Fitchburg, Mass.**

**The Henry G. Thompson Co.**
**P.O. Box 1304**
**New Haven, Conn. 06505**

From H.G. Thompson's Milford catalog.

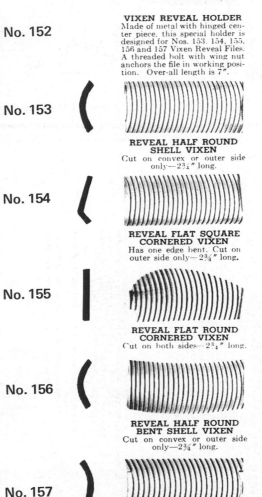

82

No. 152

**VIXEN REVEAL HOLDER**
Made of metal with hinged center piece, this special holder is designed for Nos. 153, 154, 155, 156 and 157 Vixen Reveal Files. A threaded bolt with wing nut anchors the file in working position. Over-all length is 7".

No. 153

**REVEAL HALF ROUND SHELL VIXEN**
Cut on convex or outer side only—2¾" long.

No. 154

**REVEAL FLAT SQUARE CORNERED VIXEN**
Has one edge bent. Cut on outer side only—2¾" long.

No. 155

**REVEAL FLAT ROUND CORNERED VIXEN**
Cut on both sides—2¾" long.

No. 156

**REVEAL HALF ROUND BENT SHELL VIXEN**
Cut on convex or outer side only—2¾" long.

No. 157

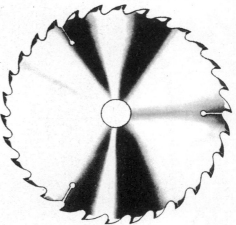

### Sharp and Abrasive

Norton is synonymous with sharpening and grinding. The firm carries thousands of abrasive tools and fixtures (wheels, stones, chuck burrs, diamond wheels and one on one) and those I've used in the shop are "it." Their Multistone, three stones in a covered oil well, completely revolutionized my concept of sharpness and sharpening technique. Their products are sold through distributors.

**Norton Company**
**Worcester, Mass. 01606**

From the Norton catalog.

Grinding and Cut-Off Wheels

Sticks and Bricks

# Now, more than ever, Norton means everything for grinding

Mounted Wheels

Diamond Dressing Tools

The Mystic Seaport Boatshop came up with a wonderful circular saw storage wrinkle. A little dado work in soft pine and some band - or jig-saw work in Masonite will solve the problem (and it _is_ a problem) forever. Right?

83

### Countersinks, Counterbores, Plug Cutters, Drills and Taps:

Just about every tool catalog you read carries a couple of countersinks and plug cutters. This placer-mining made us suspect that there was more to it and we looked for the source. Found it! W. L. Fuller, Inc. of Warwick, Rhode Island, is a major source of these items, a mother lode containing more than you will find anywhere downstream. I've used a set of their high speed taper point drills with countersinks for two years and they are terrific. They also offer a set of plug removal bits which would get much use in a boatshop.

W.L. Fuller, Inc.
1165 Warwick Ave., (for inquiries)
P.O. Box 767 (for sales)
Warwick, R.I. 02888

*Siliquaria anguina.*

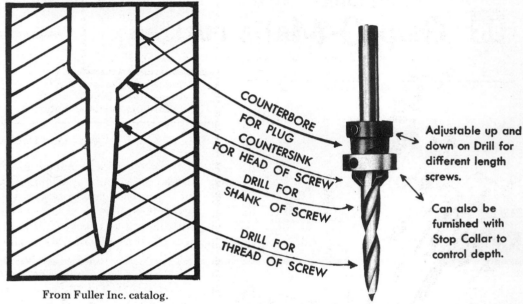

COUNTERBORE FOR PLUG
COUNTERSINK FOR HEAD OF SCREW
DRILL FOR SHANK OF SCREW
DRILL FOR THREAD OF SCREW

Adjustable up and down on Drill for different length screws.

Can also be furnished with Stop Collar to control depth.

From Fuller Inc. catalog.

84

---

⚙ **"Old Ways of Working Wood"**
By Alex W. Bealer.
Barre Publishers, Barre, Mass.
1972, 229 pp. $12.50.

Alex Bealer's books are good stuff. I'm still reading his book on blacksmithing, if ever I can borrow it again from George Putz. It seems George is in the process of building a blacksmith shop, and Bealer's book is a big help. The same can be said for anyone wanting to set up an old-time woodworking shop. Bealer will tell you what you need in "Old Ways of Working Wood."

Most of the old tools and how to use them are covered here, with the excellent text well balanced by lucid drawings by the author. The pride of good workmanship is reflected in the pages of this book, and both woodworker and boatbuilder will find information and inspiration here. Don't let the $12.50 price jar you too hard if old tools, old methods and the artistry of wood are of interest to you.

—DRG

From "Old Ways of Working Wood"

Using the bow drill

Using the auger

At a very early time the auger became the first boring device that was turned continuously in one direction, usually clockwise, to bore a hole. The auger is much more simple in concept than either pump or bow drill but is more effective on thick boards and in boring larger holes. It consists merely of a long bit with one of several different type points and a transverse handle into which the shank of the bit, of square or rectangular section, is inserted and sometimes clinched.

### Mechanic's Tools:

Some people like mucking about in the bilge. Personally, I like speaking to a person's other end, but, being a true liberal, I found two automotive supply outfits that offer tools, parts and gear that have marine applications in the engine room:

Whitney and Co. offers an astounding array of engine parts and tools; really interesting and complete. Owantonna will be of interest to yards that do a lot of marine engine work. Their products are available through distributors only.

J.C. Whitney and Co.
1917-19 Archer Ave.
P.O. Box 8410
Chicago, Ill. 60680
Catalog is $1.

From J.C. Whitney catalog.

**BODY and FENDER REPAIR KITS & TOOLS**
20 Piece SUPER DELUXE BODY & FENDER TOOL KIT

Our most complete body and fender kit. Contains all of the following high grade, drop forged tools with highly polished surfaces: Bumping anvil, finishing and dinging hammers, combination rubberset hammer—short and long picks— fender flange—mushroom, cartrack, heel, toe, double-end, wedge, rolling, oval, utility, comma, shrinking and general purpose dollies.
75-3061—Shpg. wt. 33 lbs. . . . . . . Set **$54.50**

### Long Line
### Grip-O-Matic® PULLERS

**OTC** RESEARCH ENGINEERING DEVELOPMENT

Fed. Spec.: GGG-P-00781D

GEARS, BEARINGS, PULLEYS, WHEELS, ETC.,

Owatonna Tool Co.
Owatonna, Minn. 55060
They distribute to jobbers only.

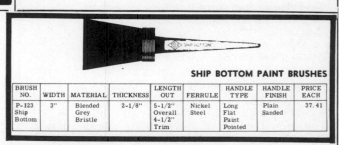

**2-JAW**

**3-JAW**

Even the most stubborn pulling job becomes easy with OTC hydraulic power! Available in both 2-jaw and 3-jaw models, these "Grip-O-Matic" pullers are equipped with OTC's famous "Power-Twin" center-hole ram. Four capacities: 17½, 30, 50 and 100 tons. Ram is easily removed from puller for use in other applications, also!

### A Very Good Book:

You can go bananas getting through the books. This catalog has mostly marine books, and shop and wood books are perhaps best discussed elsewhere or in later "Mariner's Catalogs." But one book is so good it requires special mention. That is "Planecraft." The English edition, published by C. & J. Hampton, Ltd., is now out of print we understand, but a reprint of it is offered by Woodcraft Supply Corp.,of Woburn, Mass. Reading it will change your shop technique beyond measure. Even though the emphasis is on planes, the lessons in the book will carry over into every aspect of your woodwork. Your tools and your boat will love you for it.

85

### Brushes:

The Solo-Horton Brush Company makes over 9,500 types of brushes. They sent us catalogs of hand wire brushes, power wheel brushes, painting brushes and maintenance brushes. Friends, these guys have brushes!

Solo-Horton Brush Co.
940 Eighth Ave.
New York, N.Y. 10019

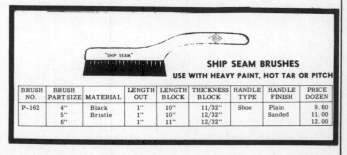

**SHIP BOTTOM PAINT BRUSHES**

| BRUSH NO. | WIDTH | MATERIAL | THICKNESS | LENGTH OUT | FERRULE | HANDLE TYPE | HANDLE FINISH | PRICE EACH |
|---|---|---|---|---|---|---|---|---|
| P-123 Ship Bottom | 3" | Blended Grey Bristle | 2-1/8" | 5-1/2" Overall 4-1/2" Trim | Nickel Steel | Long Flat Paint Pointed | Plain Sanded | 37.41 |

**SHIP SEAM BRUSHES**
USE WITH HEAVY PAINT, HOT TAR OR PITCH

| BRUSH NO. | BRUSH PART SIZE | MATERIAL | LENGTH OUT | LENGTH BLOCK | THICKNESS BLOCK | HANDLE TYPE | HANDLE FINISH | PRICE DOZEN |
|---|---|---|---|---|---|---|---|---|
| P-162 | 4" | Black Bristle | 1" | 10" | 11/32" | Shoe | Plain Sanded | 9.60 |
| | 5" | | 1" | 10" | 12/32" | | | 11.00 |
| | 6" | | 1" | 11" | 12/32" | | | 12.00 |

## Breeches Buoy Notes: 4

Throughout the catalog there rings a note of discontent about the quality of nautical experience that too many people somehow get stuck with. Certainly the old adage about how people create their own hell applies and, too, the genuine fun on the water that is being had by all makes the discontent a kind of disreputable sour grapes. Sure, things are temporarily tough in the inflation squeeze but we'll get it worked out, right? So the old tarred-rope, do-it-yourself, well-now-shipmates routine is really just a peculiar indulgence of the marine fringe, inter-tidal gurglings of the too-moderately healed. There is truth in this.

There is reason too. The pleasure and professional boatmen are both becoming too out-of-touch with the resources necessary to their pleasure and work. The hundreds and thousands of decisions that go into what a boat is to become and where and how its use shall be exercised are more and more being made by people other than the user. So these sour grapes are neither nostalgia, impractical harping nor politics. It is really about our experience. That some pay $3,000 for a 15' sailboat and this for a boat with cheapo, chromed, undersized deck fittings is really an exploitation of ignorance, and the fact that the buyer may be able to afford and get much pleasure from the boat does not make it less so.

Experience on the sea must be seamanly, competent. The traditional standard designation for this competence was "able bodied", A.B. To be able one had to understand and respond appropriately to all manner of phenomena of earth, air, fire and water. To be sure, this ability was never all there, never complete. Before in-

industry and government made mariners' decisions for them, there were greedy, ruthless, and stupid owners, masters and officers. But the standard was there and some few saw their way to meeting it. The some few continue on, but now there are millions of people on the water and, to the extent that they do not understand the materials and the techniques in the fabrication and use of their materials, they are incompetent, disabled, D. A.

Our boats and wharves are our tools, our crutch and shield between us and the experience we look for on the water, at sea. They are our media for seeing and being watermen and either we or others shall decide whether it is we who are in control, are A. B. Only we will decide that we are.

The professional is either A. B. or he's broke. But a lobsterman needs 300 horsepower? His boat has to cost $15,000? The underworld has to control the price he gets for his catch? What percentage, we ask of a man's thousand-pot string goes to pay for the fact of a thousand-pot string? How much waste of fish and capital is created by corroded, obsolete, faulty equipment and/or ill-articled crews? We figured out once that it takes roughly one chock-full hold of a vessel to pay for one foot of the vessel, viz., 300 lobsters for one foot of a lobster boat, 60 hogsheads of herring for one foot of a sardine carrier, etc. etc. We couldn't figure what the hold would be full of to pay for one foot of cruising yacht; Mount Gay Rum, perhaps?

—GP

---

**"Catalog No. 34"**
**C. Drew & Co., Kingston, Mass.**
**Re-issued by The Marine Historical Association,**
**Mystic, Conn. and Antique Trades and Tools of**
**Connecticut, 1972.**
**Available from Mystic Seaport Store,**
**Mystic, Conn., $1.50.**

This catalog, originally published in the 1920s, was republished to show some of the common tools used for building wooden boats. In it, you will find expert renderings of augers, caulking irons, caulking mallets, hawsing irons, reaming irons, marline spikes, coppering hammers, ship scrapers, rivet punches and many more; in short, many of the **tools** that can still be used today but are not easily found. The Drew Company was noted for the excellence of its tools (the company still exists but no longer makes ship's tools). The catalog still has use, since it is a handy guide for identifying used tools you might pick up here and there.

—PHS

### Stabilizing the Unstable

If you have chosen to use exotic or particularly hard woods in your model, it is best to keep in mind that many of these woods are subject to the vicissitudes of climate, especially moisture. Some part of the wooden object, usually the outside, will shrink faster than the cellulose can stretch or compress. Cracks open up, and warp and wind destroy the object so carefully crafted.

Polyethelene glycol (PEG) is a white, wax-like, water-soluble chemical that stabilizes wood against the effects of moisture, sunlight and heat. Sailing models, models displayed near windows, over fireplaces or which have parts made of exotic or hard wood can benefit from PEG treatment. The U.S.D.A. has a pamphlet on the use of this handy substance.

—GP

**"How PEG Helps the Hobbyist**
**Who Works With Wood." by H.L. Mitchell.**
**U.S. Dept. of Agriculture**
**U.S. Government Printing Office**
**Washington 25, D.C. $.45.**

# Winches

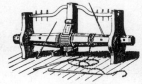

.Fig. 1.—Ship's Windlass.

# Hoists

Fig. 2.

Our discussion of winches and hoists is confined here to a brief review of some devices we think will be of use to small boatmen, salvagers and beach vehicle owners. We're sidestepping commentary on dock hoists, fishing boat winches and larger lifting devices with the hope that readers will let us know of their own experiences with the Hancocks, Stroudsburgs, Marcos, Gearmatics, etc. Meanwhile, here are some good rigs for the little guy.

—DRG

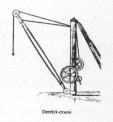

Derrick-crane

## A Powerful Hand-Winder

Anyone working around the waterfront or on the beach with a vehicle, sooner or later (and often sooner) has need of a winch. A conventional vehicle-mounted hauler, either electric, hydraulic or PTO driven, depends on engine power to operate it. These fixed winches are also expensive, heavy and, much of the time, added deadweight in the front-end of your vehicle.

Hand winches have the nice features of light weight and simple, independent operation, but most are limited by a pulling strength of a ton or less. Now comes the Model C 5000-1 Carwinch with a rated pull of 5000 lbs. That's better than

The CarWinch C 5000-1

87

most electrics and right up there with many of the other fixed haulers. Yet, it weighs only 35 lbs., comes with 60' of aircraft cable, can be worked off the trailer hitch or from a portable hitch ball at the other end of the cable. The whole rig costs less than $100. We haven't seen this winch in operation, but if it lives up to the claims of its manufacturer, The Hilmer Co., it has to rate as a worthy piece of gear for anyone working around the water.

The Hilmer Co.
Box 3537
Boulder, Col. 80303

## MITTYS AND BLIGHS

"Most yachtsmen are Walter Mittys, the celebrated character whose day dreams were realities to him. When the quiet living man steps into his dinghy, he becomes a Columbus, Magellan, Drake or Slocum, while quite a few when racing, obviously become Captain Blighs to judge from their language and treatment of their crews."

—J. Hogg in "Self Steering"

### A Tested Gas-Winder

The small boat man with traps and lines to haul, or with other needs for a small powered winch, will find the Nu-Way and E-Z Way haulers a godsend. The E-Z Way has been in service along the New England coast for several years. It's a simple rig, with a wood base, 3 h.p. Briggs & Stratton four cycle engine, belt and pulley and a winch head. It has a lift of 250 lbs. The Nu-Way is a more sophisticated E-Z with metal base and single or double winch heads driven by gears rather than a belt. It exerts a 400-lb. lift. The E-Z lists for $135, the Nu-Way for $259.50 with single winch head and $328 with double head, from:

Gowen Inc.
72 Commercial St.
P.O. Box 3542
Portland, Me. 04104

—DRG

From Gowen Inc. catalog.

## E-Z WAY LOBSTER HAULER

**Adjustable Mounting on Hard Wood Blocks for Quiet Operation**

## RUGGEDIZED NU-WAY LOBSTER HAULERS

88

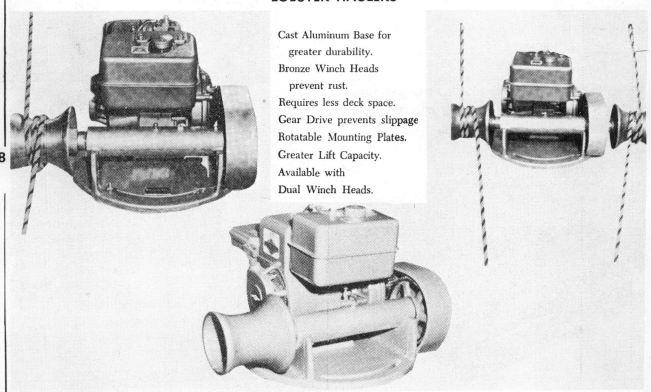

Cast Aluminum Base for
greater durability.
Bronze Winch Heads
prevent rust.
Requires less deck space.
Gear Drive prevents slippage
Rotatable Mounting Plates.
Greater Lift Capacity.
Available with
Dual Winch Heads.

---

## WITH FEELING

Words written by the Italian mariner, T. Serafini, not in his native tongue, on the disillusionments that often accompany a sailor's return to civilization after a long voyage:

"To bend me miserably upon hills of written papers. To handle a pencil or a pen with difficulty because smaller than an oar, to return to tell by phone absurd things, to smile forced to customers, to cross the street running being afraid to be hurted by cars, to be obliged to pay taxes, the rent of the home, the bus, the tailor, invoices of electricity, telephone and many things else."

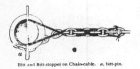

Bitt and Bitt-stopper on Chain-cable. *a*, bitt-pin.

Burtons.
1. Single Spanish.
2. Double Spanish.
3. Top burton.

## A Popular Hoist

Only 90° from lateral movement lies the wonderful world of vertical movement. Funny how so few degrees can make such a difference. A company dealing in this movement is:

**C.M. Hoist
Tonawanda, N.Y. 14150**

Their lines of electrical and hand-operated hoists cover virtually any hoisting requirements a boatshop might encounter and a letter from the president indicates many marine yard customers.

From C.M. Hoist catalog.

Gear Cover Removed

"Spider" Removed

Cluster Gear Removed

Reverse Side
"Spider" and Gear

# MINI-DOZER

89

Small yards must constantly worry about their outdoor moving requirements and there are perhaps more Rube Goldberg setups in them than ways to mix martinis. A possible solution is the Mini-Dozer, sold in kit form by the Struck Corporation of Cedarburg, Wisc.

**Struck Corp.
Cedarburg, Wisc. 53012**

- Rugged, cast iron 12 hp electric start Tecumseh engine.
- Removable hood and clutch compartment covers for easy servicing.
- Heavy-duty clutch belts using new steel cable core design.
- 10 gauge stamped steel interlocking track shoes.
- 6 quart rear mounted gas tank with fuel pump for all angle operation and elimination of vapor lock.
- New design mud fenders to dress up your Dozer and keep it neat and clean.
- New baffling inside Dozer to eliminate engine heat build-up.
- Reinforced track drive and idler sprockets with sleeve bearings and pressure zerk fittings.
- Vibration resistant and reinforced engine mount.
- Improved drive train can transmit full 12 hp load to tracks.
- Remote battery box and controls for "outside" use and easy maintenance.

# Moving Equipment

Steam-crane.

**Standard Handling Devices**
**P.O. Box 13K**
**Medford, Mass. 02155**

Few shop projects offer so many opportunities for sprained backs and hernias as boatbuilding. You don't have to move it all very much or often, but that's the problem; one gets lazy about setting up properly with moving equipment or aids.

Standard Handling Devices of Medford, Mass., carries a large variety of moving gear and aids, from simple casters to complete elevators for warehouse use, 136 pages of it all collected from industries throughout the country. The battle you have going with your table saw can be won by you.

90

All items (except steam crane)
from Standard Handling catalog.

# DRAWER TRUCK

Standard models have 36 shelf drawers, each 5½" W. Prices on request for models with drawer widths of 8¼" or 11". All drawers are 4⅝" high.

## VG SERIES

### CAPACITIES 500 to 7000 LBS. EACH

**Recommended for movement of production jigs or fixtures in straight line assembly, travel in and out of "blind alley" retorts or ovens, for assembly or processing operations where rivets, bolts, or other wheel-stopping hazards might impede normal caster movement.**

V-Grooved wheel casters are the combination of Series 16, 72 and 81 casters and V-grooved wheels.

Wheel face and V-groove fully machined - V-groove permits easy operation on inverted angle track - flat surface of wheel permits equally easy operation over floors.

By grinding down the ends of angle track, casters are easily rolled on and off track. Curves can be installed by using curved channel guides or curved track. Position locks are useful to hold equipment in place.

| *Capacity | Diam-eter | WHEEL Width | Type | Overall Height "B" | Bolt Hole Centers F&G | Top Plate Size D&E | ††Approx. Weight |
|---|---|---|---|---|---|---|---|
| 500 | 4 | 1-3/4 | | 5-5/8 | 2-5/8 x 3-5/8 | | 8 |
| 800 | 5 | 2 | Semi-Steel | 6-1/2 | or | 4 x 4½ | 9 |
| 900 | 6 | 2 | | 7-1/4 | 3 x 3 | | 11 |
| 500 | 4 | 1-3/4 | | 5-5/8 | 2-7/16 x 4-15/16 | | 10 |
| 800 | 5 | 2 | Semi-Steel | 6-1/2 | or | 4½ x 6¾ | 11 |
| 1000 | 6 | 2 | | 7-1/2 | 2-5/8 x 4-7/8 | | 13 |
| 1500 | 6 | 2-1/2 | | 7-1/2 | | | 19 |
| 1650 | 8 | 2-1/2 | Semi-Steel | 10-1/8 | 3-3/8 x 5-1/4 | 5 x 6½ | 26 |
| 6000 | 6 | 3 | Drop Forged | 8-1/2 | | | 44 |
| 4000 | 8 | 3 | Semi-Steel | 10-1/2 | | | 58 |
| 7000 | 8 | 4 | Drop Forged | 10-1/2 | 4-1/2 x 6 | 6 x 7½ | 70 |
| 4000 | 10 | 3 | Semi-Steel | 12-1/2 | | | 54 |
| 6000 | 10 | 3 | Drop Forged | 12-1/2 | | | 46 |
| 7000 | 10 | 4 | Drop Forged | 12-1/2 | | | 79 |

# Heading Off

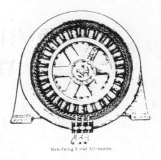

Revolving Field Alternator.

# Electrical Problems

### By Mark White

Almost 90% of electrical troubles and the resulting damage can be laid directly to corrosion. A few extra minutes in the installation of an electrical connection can pay off in years of trouble-free service.

All electrical joints should be soldered with a rosin core solder. Acid core solder leaves corrosive acid in the joint so should never be used. Any terminal clips should be soldered in addition to being crimped. Never mind how new and modern the directions are on the package for terminal clips. They all leave space for salt water or salt mist in the air to get in and start eating away at the metal. Once a little corrosion has formed, a high area of resistance results and this in turn leads to higher heat and increased corrosion. A vicious circle is formed that can only be relieved by hacking the connection out and doing the job right.

Once a soldered joint is formed it should be further protected by a small amount of electrical putty mashed over the bare wire and then taped. Electrical tape (the plastic kind) works fairly well for this and has a very high resistance factor but also tends to unravel, melt in warm areas and crack in very cold areas. Many people use old-fashioned friction tape for low voltage connections (12v to 32v) and cover the plastic tape with friction tape in high voltage connections. In a really exposed area it may be wise to hold the tape shut with a turn or two of a piece of fine seine twine tied tightly.

Areas that are not designed to be taped can be protected with a special electrical grease that will keep salt water and air away from the metal. Vasoline or water pump grease seems to work almost as well. Many think that the grease, being an insulator (which it is) will prevent the flow of electricity. It doesn't because the metal parts of the connection mash the grease out of the way and permit intimate contact through which power flows easily. The grease is especially valuable in areas such as battery terminals, and on knife switches. It also works well where terminal clips are tied into an electrical device such as a starter solenoid or a power panel. It should be applied so as to form a thin shield over every exposed metal surface that carries power.

The old-fashioned exposed knife switch is a bad actor in the nautical field. It has too many exposed pieces to work loose and get corrosion build-up. Enclosed switches are much better. If in doubt as to whether a switch or other connection is giving trouble, simply hold a hand near while power is being used. If it gets warm (or worse, hot) then the corroded area is acting like a heating element and robbing power. Yank the offending area out and clean it or replace it.

Out at sea a large stranded wire may suddenly give trouble where it's tied to a connection. Sometimes a permanent repair can be made by chopping the wire back to clean metal and soldering a terminal clip in place made from a piece of clean copper tubing of about the right diameter. The terminal end is made by mashing the copper tube flat with a hammer and drilling it for a screw hole. The tube can be left a little long to bridge the gap left by chopping the bad section out. The tube is carefully cleaned inside with a tight roll of sandpaper or a small file and the entire inside is filled with solder. The wire is heated and tinned and pushed into the solder in the tube and left to cool. The whole unit is taped, to keep the newly formed terminal from grounding to a nearby wire, and installed. If the area still gets hot it may be necessary to replace the whole thing when the boat gets back to port or to find another hot spot. Properly done, this type of repair is permanent and trouble-free.

One last thing; be sure to grease the base of all light bulbs. If the socket is already corroded it can be cleaned with a specially shaped wire brush. The grease will not only keep the connections from heating but will allow easy removal of a bad bulb. Special hi-temp grease can be used for really powerful bulbs. The newer quartz-iodine lamps get too hot for any grease so it is best to simply seal them carefully and keep salt out.

---

### GREASE TIP

Cup grease (the stiffer or harder the better) rubbed onto a propeller will keep it remarkably free of barnacles. With the boat hauled for bottom painting, scrape the prop and scour clean with old sandpaper. Then smear the blade and hub with a thick coat of the stiff grease, smoothing it out and rubbing well in with the fingers. Don't ask me why it doesn't wash off: even in steadier than usual use of a boat, enough seems to cling to the bronze to discourage fouling.

—Jim Emmett

91

---

"Marine Fouling and its Prevention" by Woods Hole Oceanographic Institution.
U.S. Naval Institute, Annapolis, Md.
1952, 388 pp., illustrated, bibliography, index, $12.

Though a lot more is now known about the subject (the research for this book was done during 1940-1946), you'll have to ferret it out yourself from scientific journals and learned papers. This is the only book I know of that addresses itself solely to the subject — it's hard to believe when you consider that marine fouling is on the minds of everyone who operates a boat in salt water.

At any rate, this is a very good book on the subject. Divided into three parts — problems of fouling, biology of fouling and prevention of fouling — it's worth reading by anyone who really gets interested in he subject. It's not a book for curling up with in front of the fireplace, though, since most of it is fairly technical.

—PHS

A CHEAP YARD.                    AN EXPENSIVE YARD.

From "Boatowner's Sheet Anchor"

✪ "Boatowner's Sheet Anchor" by Carl D. Lane.
Thomas Y. Crowell Co., N.Y.
1969, 304 pp., illustrated with sketches, $7.95.

The sub-title is "A Practical Guide to Fitting Out, Upkeep and Alteration of the Small Wooden Yacht," and the book is just that. Lane is a traditionalist who is not necessarily wedded to the old ways. If a new idea or method comes along, he'll try it; and if it works, he is more than happy to pass it along.

The book is loaded with useful information, much of it you won't find anywhere else. You can "read" this book in the conventional sense; in other words, it is not dry and technical. As a matter of fact, I recommend that you start at the beginning and go right through to the end. There is so much good information, humor, truth and priceless gems buried in Lane's writing that it would be a shame not to read it all.

—PHS

92

To keep it out of the boat altogether is the ideal, if you can do it. No man has yet found out the sure-fire trick of doing this. Dry rot is a fungus, attacking the fibrous walls of the wood cells. The fungus can feed only under certain moisture conditions, and the trick seems to be to keep wood reasonably dry. On shipboard, this is well-nigh impossible. Recommended, then, as the next best thing, is ample and positive ventilation, on the theory that while we must have a certain amount of moisture, we can take steps to immediately disperse it and thus destroy a condition favorable to dry rot.

Very seldom does salt water encourage dry rot. The old ship-masters understood this well, going so far as to place salt boxes between timberheads and, by means of a deck filler-plug, keeping them filled with rock salt which went into solution with any water approaching its neighborhood. On salt water, a vessel almost invariably will develop her rotten spots high above the water line, very likely in the vicinity of the quarters, bow, or her clamps and covering board—places which are likely to suffer from lack of free air passage, fresh water deck leaks, and the heat of the sun.

> "Animal or mineral?" asked the Bosun.
> "Neither," replied Alice. "Guess some more."
> "Bird, beast, fish, or devil?"
> "D-devil," Alice admitted.
> "I know," cried the Bosun, "it's a dinghy!"
>
> —FROM Alice in Boatland

✪ "Fitting Out: Maintenance and Repair of Small Craft"
   by J.D. Sleightholme.
Adlard Coles, London, England.
1972 (2nd edition), 130 pp., illustrated.

The author makes no secret about it, this book is for making minor repairs and doing basic chores. But for anyone who will be leaving the major overhauls to the yard, it's a handy volume to have around.

Most boatbuilders will disagree with Sleighthome's recommendation to butt planks on a frame, but the rest of his advice is reliable. The chapters are maintenance, repair of wooden hulls, painting, bosunry work, sail repair and the auxiliary engine.

—PHS

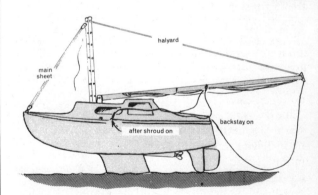

Tabernacle masts in small craft can be raised by hand quite easily. The after shrouds can be attached also the backstay while the mast is lying on deck with its heel ready positioned in the tabernacle. There will be a struggle to raise the mast high enough for the men on the forestay to begin hauling, but thereafter it will go up easily. A simpler canti-lever can be rigged by standing a short ladder on deck forward of the mast heel and passing the forestay (or a rope) over it, attaching it at that point, and thence down to the deck. This arrangement allows the forestay party to take charge of the load early in the lift (41). The same method can be used for lowering.

# BOATBUILDING

*31' ketch design by E.R. Frost, 2 O'Byrne Dr., Anchorage Point, Somers Point, N.J. 08244.*

Here is a subject of endless length and bottomless depth, the culmination of one's thinking about boat types, the materials to build them with and the tools with which to do the job. One can fill shelves with books on how to build boats, can blow his mind with information both helpful and confusing from friends and experts, can look and feel and dream and ponder. But somewhere along the way he must make his decision, draw his first serious line, bend his first board. Experience is ever the best teacher.

What follows on these pages is aimed at helping both the beginning boatbuilder and the expert — a selection of some of the best books on the subject, hard-won tips from both amateurs and veterans and even some sources of good custom boats if hull-building isn't your bag. But as we point out so often in this first round of "The Mariner's Catalog," this is just a start. Thousands upon thousands of boats have been built over the years and many of you who are reading this now have gained insights into the boatbuilding art that should be shared with others. In later "Catalogs" we would welcome your participation through letters, drawings and photos. Meanwhile, let's start with the basics:
—DRG

○ "Boatbuilding" by Howard I. Chapelle.
W.W. Norton, New York.
1941, 624 pp., illustrated, $15.

○ "Boatbuilding Manual" by Robert M. Steward.
International Marine Publishing Co.,
Camden, Maine.
1970, 220 pages, illustrated, bibliography, index, $9.50.

These are the "heavies" on wooden boatbuilding. Both of them are extremely valuable for anyone seriously interested in building his own boat. Of the two, Steward is the more modern, not in the sense that wooden construction has changed in any appreciable way since 1941 — only that he details the new waterproof glues, plywood, caulking compounds, etc., that have come on the market since then.

Two of the best features of Chapelle's book are the first two chapters on what to look for in your plans and how to loft your plans full size. For most amateurs, lofting looks very mysterious, but Chapelle's in-depth discussion (69 pages in all) should answer practically any questions that might arise. The rest of the book is divided up into chapters on setting up the backbone,

93

*Contd. on next page*

*Contd. from preceding page*

flat-bottom construction, V-bottom construction, round-bottom construction, lapstrake and other methods, finish work (including spar-making, mechanical installations, joinerwork) and tools. There are plans for 19 boats in the book, all of which are traditional in design. The diagrams and sketches are as detailed as the text.

Steward's book is as comprehensive as Chapelle's, but doesn't go into as great detail. For this reason, it might have greater appeal to the amateur, since it is easier to follow. I guess a better way to make the point is to say that Chapelle has written a treatise on boatbuilding, while Steward has written a practical guide. Steward has lots of excellent illustrations, but no building plans. There are chapters on plans, tools, wood, fiberglass and other materials (in the general sense only — not how to build with them), fastenings, lofting, molds and templates, setting up, framing, planking, joinerwork and miscellaneous fitting-out details.

I guess I don't have to tell you that you should get, or read, both.

—PHS

**From "Boatbuilding Manual"**

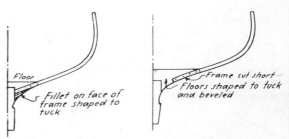

FIGURE 11-4.

### PLANKING SCALE

Example: Assume 8 strakes remaining.
Greatest girth divided by 8 = 4½"
Least " " " 8 = 3"
4½" - 3" = 1½" = 12 eighths
Divide space between girth marks on scale batten into 12 equal parts
Scale applied to any frame will give plank width at that frame.

**Width Scale for Remaining Planks**

The planks between the last of the bottom planks and the sheer strake may be lined out by dividing into equal spaces the girth to be planked at each spiling frame, but the work is easier with what is called a planking scale made with a batten about ⅛ by 1 inch. Mark on the batten the greatest space still to be planked, which will be near the middle of the boat, and also the shortest space wherever it may be. Measure the greatest girth with a rule, and on something besides the batten arithmetically divide the distance by the number of strakes still to go on. Let us say the answer is 4½ inches, therefore call the corresponding mark on the scale 4½ inches. Do the same with the shortest girth and, assuming the answer is 3 inches, call the corresponding mark on the scale 3 inches. Now find the number of eighths of an inch there are between the two girth marks on the scale, twelve in this case. Divide the space on the scale between 3 inches and 4½ inches into twelve equal spaces and label them so each one represents ⅛ inch. See Figure 11-4. You will see that the scale when bent on any frame will give the width of the strake at that frame. It only takes a few minutes' time to make a planking scale, and with it you can go along and note the plank widths on as many of the frames as you like for reference when making the remainder of the strakes.

**From "Boatbuilding"**

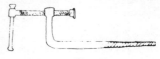

*111. Ceiling Clamp*

The ceiling is clamped in position with a special ceiling clamp; this is like an ordinary steel C-clamp except that the lower portion of the C is not formed—in fact, the shape is like half a T (⊤), or an L upside down. The lower stem is coarsely threaded and is tapered. A hole is drilled into the frame on which the clamp will be used, then the stem is screwed into the hole. When deep enough to hold, the clamp is set up like the ordinary C-clamp, with a screw in the top arm of the clamp. As pressure grows on the clamp the stem binds in its hole in the frame. When the clamp is removed, the hole in the frame is plugged. The ceiling is spiked to the frames with occasional through-fastenings in the thick strakes, as before mentioned. After the ceiling is in place, in a large vessel, it is calked; large seams are wedged with white cedar strips, or wedges. This serves to prevent the ceiling from working and so stiffens the vessel longitudinally. As the ceiling is put on, the inside of the planking, the frames, and the outboard faces of the ceiling planks are treated with some wood preservative, but should never be painted. When the ceiling is in place, in a large vessel, "strong-backs" are run athwartships over the after frames, say, on every other after cant on top of the ceiling, and through-drifted to the frames. These serve as floor timbers in, or near, the counter.

*105. Forming Sharp Reverse in Frames*

### On The Beach

"Timber and materials were collected or bought well before I needed them. Before the boat was started, I used to stroll along the beach near our home. Sometimes, though not often, there would be good, usable pieces of timber washed up by the sea. These I would carry home.

"Every piece of timber was carefully examined, measured, and earmarked for a particular purpose. Under these circumstances, one tends to become an unforgivable hoarder with an eagle eye for any junk, rubbish or lumber which might conceivably be of some use to someone somewhere. If the boat could have been built out of twigs, the birds in the village would have had no nests."

—Donald Ridler in "Eric the Red"

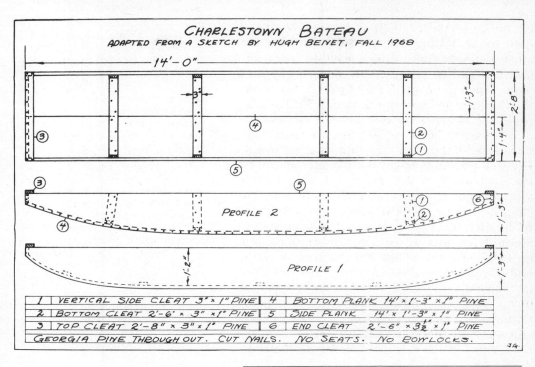

**CHARLESTOWN BATEAU**
ADAPTED FROM A SKETCH BY HUGH BENET, FALL 1968

PROFILE 2

PROFILE 1

| 1 | VERTICAL SIDE CLEAT 3" x 1" PINE | 4 | BOTTOM PLANK 14' x 1'-3" x 1" PINE |
|---|---|---|---|
| 2 | BOTTOM CLEAT 2'-6" x 3" x 1" PINE | 5 | SIDE PLANK 14' x 1'-3" x 1" PINE |
| 3 | TOP CLEAT 2'-8" x 3" x 1" PINE | 6 | END CLEAT 2'-6" x 3½" x 1" PINE |

GEORGIA PINE THROUGH OUT. CUT NAILS. NO SEATS. NO ROWLOCKS.

# THE
## Simplest
# BOAT

## The Common Punt

The lengthwise planking of the bottom is not what I am familiar with for small scows or punts like this. I believe that cross-planked construction is the more usual. Yet fore-and-aft bottom is probably better, and certainly it should offer less resistance in sliding over mud, if there was much of this. Also there would be fewer seams to open and leak.

As we have already seen, W.P. Stephens designed his rather nicely modeled punt with the bottom plank running lengthwise.

There might be some difficulty in bending these bottom planks if the curve or "rocker" was too abruptly rounded. The bottom curve I have shown in Profile 1 on the drawing closely reproduces the curve on Benet's sketch, and in my judgment might require steaming of the planks.

In Profile 2, I have eased this curve enough so I think that softwood boards (pine, cedar, cypress), if not too dry, could be sprung in place without steaming, and in a second sketch I show the proper way of going about this. Nail one end securely, and then use the length of the board as a lever to spring the board down in place gradually, nailing securely as this proceeds, both through the cross cleats of the bottom and through the side edges. Boards several feet longer than the bottom should be used in order to gain leverage and to get the last end down into place. When this is securely nailed the excess is sawed off.

Boards as wide as were used originally, as shown in the drawings, are not necessary. The bottom could well be made of four boards instead of two, and the sides of two boards each instead of the one wide one. And the narrower boards would bend into place a lot easier.

Benet in his sketch does not show any cleats on the sides. Possibly these are not absolutely necessary, and were not used for the cheapest construction, but I have put them in. They support the bottom cross cleats during construction when a lot of pressure is put on the cross cleats in springing the bottom boards into place. Also the side cleats brace the sides and help to keep the wide side planks from warping or splitting. If two planks were used

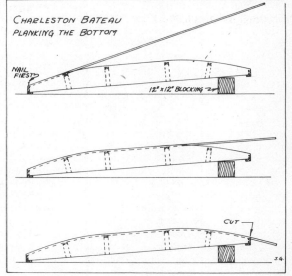

**CHARLESTON BATEAU PLANKING THE BOTTOM**

NAIL FIRST

12" x 12" BLOCKING

CUT

for the side instead of one wide one, side cleats would of course be required.

This would be a very easy and inexpensive boat to build, and either as it is, or with minor modifications, could prove a most useful craft under many different conditions and circumstances.

It is capable of carrying heavy loads, it is extremely stable in calm water, and will row or paddle easier than might appear. It will take a lot of abuse and should not require much care or upkeep.

As a utility craft or small workboat on the waterfront, whether it be on a river, a lake or the ocean, this bateau, small scow, punt or whatever else you choose to call it, has real possibilities. Besides, it could be used with an outboard motor, if one wished, and would even sail with a few slight modifications. With its fore-and-aft bottom plank it would be very easy to install a centerboard.

In a word, this is a basic hull with which a great deal can be done for very little.

—John Gardner

Band-saw.

# Old
# Ways
# Work

## By Pete Culler

In these modern days of wonder materials, new methods and what seems at times total reliance on the chemical industry, it may seem strange, not to say foolish, to urge going back to some of the more simple things of the past. Many of these apply to boats and vessels, as well as finding uses in other applications.

Just why should we go back? The main reason is, old ways and materials work, are for the most part readily available, not expensive as things go now, usually are non toxic (some may be even somewhat digestible!), are easy to use and are a satisfaction to work with — something which is not always so when using some packaged thing out of a spray can. There is no problem of disposal for instance, which can be a danger with a spray can. I always wonder what trouble one of these things might cause when I send an empty on its way to the dump. Personal notion only. I feel anything in a spray can is just a way of doing an inferior job quickly and paying the price of the contraption to boot.

Linseed oil, and I refer mostly to boiled oil, is a most useful thing to have around a boat, shop, shipyard or any place things are built or repaired. Cut, added to or mixed with some other simple things, it can do a lot. Cut with kerosene "to make it drive in," it's a fine primer for new, exposed woodwork. Turpentine can be used just as well, but kero is cheaper if it's to be used in large amounts. Some say a paint primer is better, and in some cases it is; but where marks and figures can be lost by covering with paint, as is common in boat work, oil and kero do just fine. Nothing is more irritating, to me at least, than when work has been carefully laid out, marks made so no mistake is apt to happen, then some dope paints them out!

A gallon of boiled linseed oil, a pint of turps and a pint of pine tar, mixed, preferably when the oil is warm, is what I call "deck oil." This is fine for unpainted decks of working craft, inside of skiff and bateau bottoms which are unpainted, and, in the past, bottoms of log canoes. The same mix is also fine for a starter coat for wooden spars and other woodwork which will not be painted very soon. Wooden cleats, pins, ship's blocks, and any other small wooden items soaked for a month in this stuff become extremely hard in time and nearly weather proof. It's good for the bed of an elderly pickup truck — puts new life in the box, which then outlasts the rest of the rig. Apply to a dry box, under a blazing sun, and don't spare it, and it does real business. Another, and lesser coat, later on finishes the job.

A much used and aging boat trailer can be a discouraging sight — you are going to paint it but don't get around to it. Long drawnout business to do it right anyhow. Probably needs sandblasting. So if she's real bad, bang on her with a hammer enough to get the big rust flakes off and follow with a good blasting with a hose to get any salt out of all the corners, then let dry. Pick a dry nor'west day, if possible, and tuck the deck oil to the rig. It seems to like some rust and runs and penetrates where no paint ever can. A second coat sometime later is a good idea. Not pretty, but it sure takes to rust.

This, of course, applies to any metal work. If you do metal work requiring heat, when the job is done and still hot, say a black heat, quench it in the oil and you have even better protection. This was an old-time smith's trick and as explained to me by an old master at it, "heat opens the pores in the iron and it drinks in the oil, which immediately oxidizes under the heat." If it's so or not, I don't know, but it works!

I feel timber for bent boat frames takes steam and bends better if soused, say the night before steaming, with kerosene, cut with just enough oil so the kero stays around for a spell. Certainly kerosene has the ability to penetrate dry, or reasonably dry wood, as a simple test will show, kero, or something very smiliar (mineral spirits) is the base for many wood perservatives.

Some old-timers claim kerosene alone will drive the moisture out of green wood — my experience has been that it does to a great extent. No steam box being handy, a plank well soaked in kero, say overnight, will usually bend into place when, if left dry or even soaked in water, it might not go without breaking. Personally, I rely on this method very much, with or without steam.

To get back to using this deck oil mix on metal. A mooring which is pulled up and hauled ashore for the winter rusts and scales rather badly, much salt being in the iron. Here again, what's needed is a good pounding and much washing with fresh water under pressure, then a spell of drying and a coat of oil, which bites right in and carries things till spring, when the mooring is far less messy to handle.

Pine tar now seems unknown to most people, yet it's quite commonly available. Put a dab of it on a mooring or anchor shackle and the fitting will unscrew with ease years later. Same applies to turnbuckles, galvanized iron or bronze, or any outdoor screw thread. Total submerging over long periods seems to have no effect on pine tar. (Naturally, shackles for serious work should be wired.)

Tallow seems now to be totally forgotten as a shop lubricant, or for the same use on boats and vessels. Many people don't seem to know just what it is anymore, let alone where to get it.

Some butchers still try-out tallow, but it's very simple to make your own, as all it is is the fat scrap from meat melted down and cleaned up. Trying-out fat scraps slowly is no chore in an iron skillet — most kitchens tend to produce waste fat anyhow. To clean it up, simply simmer it very slowly in a large amount of water. This lets the dark burnt stuff, salt and other impurities settle out. A long simmer is good, then let it cool and simply lift the congealed tallow from the water in chunks. For places of chafe, say oarlocks, gaff jaws, mast hoops, etc., nothing seems to work so well. This was the stuff of the days of sail. The cook set aside what the ship did not use. He often sold it on making port, unless the skipper was a tight-fisted sort, in which case HE got the graft.

For shop use, I mostly dilute tallow with kerosene so

*Contd. on next page*

From "Complete Amateur Boatbuilding"

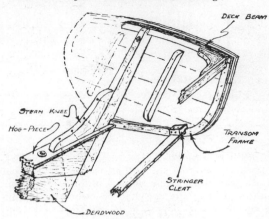

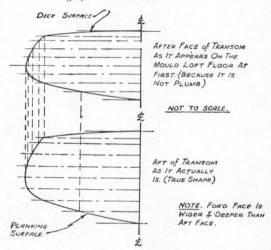

Fig. 42. Stern knee and transom.

Fig. 43. Raked transom pattern.

⚫"Complete Amateur Boat Building" by Michael
  Verney.
The Macmillan Co., New York.
1967 (second edition), 309 pp., illustrated
  bibliography, index, $6.95.

Covers wood, fiberglass and metal
construction, but the primary emphasis is on
wood. If you are interested in building a boat
and uncertain about which method to use as
well as what material to build with, this book is
worth looking at. Verney's discussions of
fiberglass and metal are short and not too
detailed, but they do give an indication of what
might be expected if you choose those materials
(you will have to look elsewhere for more
specific information on these subjects).

This is a British book so the terminology
might throw you here and there and the sources
of supply are generally meaningless to an
American. The things you expect to see covered
on wooden boat construction are here all right,
but there are a few extra wrinkles you might not
see elsewhere. For instance, there is a detailed
explanation, with illustrations, on how to build
a slipway if you are fortunate enough to be able
to build your boat where she will be launched.
—PHS

97

## Old Ways Work

### Contd. from preceding page

it can be used in an oil can; say, a good big tablespoon,
melted, poured into a pint or less of oil. Nothing does
quite as well keeping power tool tables in good shape
while insuring an easy and steady feed. For sawing heavy
timber, it's the next best thing to proper rollers.

I use tallow a lot for the dumb center of a
wood-cutting lathe, and it's useful in metal turning and
thread cutting with these additions: some white lead and
enough tallow added to oil to make a thin paste. (Note
that now white lead seems to go on the "No" list, like
bootleg whiskey.) Powdered sulfur will do the same job.
This is not the best cutting oil, but it's pretty good, and
you can get by if the manufactured stuff is not on hand.
In fact, some old-time machinist books go into detail on
making cutting oil. Though a small matter, I find

modern auto lube oil not too good for some shop work
— it's intended for high-speed bearings under high heat
and somehow does not have the slip that the above
mixes have for crude work.

Modern quick-dry paints have some very good points.
"Skinning over" once a can is opened is not one of the
good ones. When about to close up the can after use,
clap the lid partly on, and carefully blow a long breath
into the can and button it up quick; this is supposed to
displace some oxygen. It's by no means perfect, but does
help some when working out of the same can every day
or so. I imagine a breath smelling strong of onions and
tobacco might be just the thing.

Most people have some interest in wood, varying
from passive to very active. A large number are sort of in
between because they think wood is hard to come by,
especially if exotic. So much good stuff goes to waste,
just because it's misunderstood or can't be seen for the
trees! If you tend to look up instead of always at your
feet, you may often spot a few boards, long forgotten,
stored overhead in a barn or shed where it's had a good
cooking for years, being close to the roof. Often it's
some very interesting type of wood, or just pine boards.
Sometimes it can be had for the asking, or a very small

_Contd. on next page_

# Old Ways Work

*Contd. from preceding page*

sum, since it may be cracked, warped and way too dry.

If it's likely looking stuff otherwise, get it, then put down sleepers, level both ways, outdoors. Stick and stack the stuff carefully, weighed down heavily and put on a good cover — tar paper will do, but fix it so it won't blow off. Cover so ends and sides get plenty of air.

Put down this way in the fall, and going through till April, the pile will pick up its moisture content again and much of the warp will be pressed out. The result will be a lot of quite useful wood. The rents will still be there, and other lumber defects, but it's now pretty nice stock.

Not including lumbering operations, trees are being felled all the time — for firewood, clearing land, house lots and "developments." Much of this goes to waste. These tree destructors nearly always spoil any possible knees, for they saw at the elbows, never clear of them, for a crooked knee is most unhandy to throw into a truck. A good lookout, your own tools, the right approach and you may be allowed to help destroy a likely apple tree, cutting it properly so as to save the knees and often getting a passable piece of trunk for real timber. I've found if you explain just what you are after, most tree-cutters will cooperate to a great extent — they don't quite understand it, but if you don't slow things up much they go along with it.

Nice apple, cherry, locust, walnut, elm and many other woods are excellent for so many projects, and all of these take kindly to use in boats as well as cabinet work. Often someone's woodpile can turn up likely stock for all sorts of parts and fittings, at no cost for superior material. All it takes is a sharp eye, a rag-picker's makeup and some knowhow to work the stuff up, and this last is not at all difficult to learn.

Let's assume you've acquired a chunk about 3' or 4' long, and 12" or more in diameter. It can be split lengthways with a chain saw. Then it's quite possible to saw it through quartering with the aid of a table saw or a

*Square Rabbet-plane.*

hand electric saw, partly finishing it with a hand or band saw. If the bandsaw will take something more than 6" it will do the whole job, and of course quarter sawing can be continued for all of it.

Smaller diameter stuff can have a flat hewed on one side with an axe, no chainsaw being handy, and finished up as before. It's not the hardest work to do it all with

98

---

● "Simple Boat-Building" by Geoffrey Prout.
Brown, Son & Ferguson, 52 Darnley St.
Glasgow, Scotland.
1960 (2nd edition), 149 pp., index, $2.

A delightful little book with the ten-thumbed amateur in mind. Prout is aware of the obstacles the backyard builder must face (lack of space, limited ability, few tools, fewer funds) and consequently doesn't scare the reader off with demands for the perfection usually attained only by master boatbuilders.

The chapters tell the story: Hints on Designing, Sequence and Method in Building, How to Build a Dinghy Flattie (skiff), Finishing Details, A V-Quartered Sailing Dinghy, A Moulded Pram Dinghy, An Outboard Runabout, How to Build a Daggerboard Trunk, A Standing Lugsail You Can Make.

The method Prout is advocating here is the one where the bottom is built first and then jammed down on stocks to gain the proper rocker. The stem and transom are fixed, and then the planks (lapstraked) are bent around. The molded pram dinghy, however, is not built this way but over molds. One of the best parts of the book is the chapter on designing, in which the critical dimensions necessary for a well-found skiff are given. Where else can you find help on designing your own skiff?

—PHS

hand tools, provided they are sharp. Locust is especially good — handsome to look at, shrinks practically not at all, turns well, takes a nice finish and is excellent for pins, cleats and anywhere that strength, durability, along with good looks are required. Apple is excellent for knees — nothing quite like it — as apple as well as pear grow crooked by nature. Both have handsome grain, hard and durable, but require some drying. The common elm of New England is very hard and tough, is not a handsome wood. Still it makes fine wood bullseyes, deadeyes and things requiring great strength. A usable knee can often be got out of a crotch.

All sorts of wood turns up on woodpiles — it's a matter of locality. Occasionally one finds ash, walnut, tupelo, and others which are considered very hard to come by. I have made mallets and got knees of mulberry from a woodpile, and nice stuff it is. Some old railroad ties from certain parts of the country are walnut — which is quite durable. Really old Cape Cod light poles are often chestnut. Cedar short stuff, to be worked over, is now available from most fence companies in the New England states. Cherry of various kinds is usually available for the taking where trees are being removed.

Old buildings coming down may have excellent timber, and some big craft have taken benefit of the big hard pine timbers, professionally resawed. There is also

*Contd. on next page*

### Glass Windows

To the Editor:

I would like to draw the attention of your readers to a serious danger. This involves the integrity of the rectangular "yacht windows" that are installed in the hulls of so many yachts.

Our yacht Passagemaker, while crossing the Trades north of Hawaii en route to Seattle under conditions by no means more rugged than a yacht should be able to handle, was struck forward by a combination of two or three small waves with sufficient force to break in the forward port in the hull. The glass fragments were hurled across the boat and severely cut one of the passengers on the face. Subsequent examination of the fragment pattern showed she was lucky not to have lost one or both eyes.

It was disturbing to find out in this abrupt manner two things. That a port of this size, 8" x 10", was equipped with ¼" thick glass. And that this was ordinary glass that quite literally shattered into a thousand fragments.

This is not an isolated case. The yachting press ("Yachting" January 1966) recently carried the story of a similar incident. Their subsequent troubles were much more serious. It is apparent that the type of yacht window sold in this country is not seaworthy in the accepted sense of the word.

The manufacturer of this port, a well known Connecticut firm, was informed with suggestions that a stronger port was needed for the growing number of seagoing motorboats. They replied that competitive conditions within the industry were such they found it impracticable to offer a port that would have a stronger glass — or even to switch to shatterproof plate in the ¼" thickness.

This is an astonishing statement. But observation of current yachts, many of which have extensive areas of glass of the smallest possible thickness and plain glass at that, shows it is undoubtedly quite true. The only way to change this situation is for the public to be aware of the danger and to demand glass more in keeping with the seaworthiness of the rest of the vessel — and be willing to pay the price.

Remember, what happened to us can happen to you.

Robert P. Beebe, N.A.

"A bow-legged boat!!! That does it!"

---

_Contd. from preceding page_

much good smaller stuff: hard pine, cypress and excellent trim pine. Occasionally walnut and cherry come from what was once a first-class dwelling. Nail and bolt holes there are, to be sure, but boring out and bunging take care of this. I've seen very nice wide pine tables made from an attic floor probably 175 years old. The rusty nail holes were covered by graving pieces of various shapes and colors of wood. No one was the wiser; they thought this gave considerable charm!

Usable iron and steel go to waste like wood these days. Much excellent tool steel hits the scrap pile. Working tool steel brings to mind the picture of a craftsman of much skill and training — few think they dare attempt it. Yet, to make simple things takes little skill; more skill develops as you go. Besides, the stock is junk, and free, so you can afford mistakes in learning. For one thing, I refer to wornout files; they come in all sizes and shapes, from tiny to big old soakers. These are prime stuff for some tools, and in small and modest sizes, at least, are easly worked (you will spoil a couple at first) with readily available heat.

Anything, including a gas stove, which will give a red heat on modest-size files is adequate. More heat than this, and you can easily burn and ruin this type of steel. If you lack regular blacksmith tongs, a big stout pair of pliers will do. Also needed is a hammer, any hammer, though there is often more than one, so one may be more suitable than another. A chunk of iron, more or less flat on one side — a short piece of rail is OK — will serve as an anvil. A grinder, and a cold chisel to cut off a hot end, will get you started. Later on, if your interest holds and increases, a small forge may be wanted.

Two very useful tools require no heat at all. The first is what used to be known as a bearing scraper; few scrape bearings anymore, but I find this item much used in my shop as a deburring tool. Simply choose a three-corner file, worn out naturally, or more than one so as to have different sizes, and grind all three sides, fore and aft, not sideways, until the teeth are entirely gone and the edges are sharp (they will be very sharp). The tool can be whetted on a stone for fine edge. Put on a wooden handle — you may want to tape the point for two-hand use. This whole operation has taken only a few minutes. It can even be done on a water stone, though it takes longer. This is a fine tool for deburring any sharp metal edges, and in some cases scraping of soft metals, and has cost nothing but time.

With the second tool, you start as above, and here you may want three or four sizes. Grind the file, then grind around the tang near where it thickens, and break off — the file is usually soft here. What you now have

_Contd. on next page_

"Small Boats" by Philip C. Bolger
International Marine Publishing Co.,
Camden, Maine
1973, illustrated, $12.50.

First off, let me confess — I handled the editorial production of this book, so my point of view could hardly be considered objective. But you can offset this built-in bias by understanding that I seldom give books that I edit high praise because my almost fanatical familiarity with them makes their flaws (and all books have them) seem like the San Andreas Fault.

Phil Bolger's book is a cut above most others for two very good reasons: he is an excellent writer and, as a boat designer, he is not intimidated by his profession. He's not afraid to throw out obsolete ideas, try new concepts, borrow from time-tested designs, claim victory, and admit defeat. Is there another serious naval architect who would dare design a 32' folding schooner, have it built and launch it for the first time in front of the press without a trial run to see if it would work? (It did, and readers of the "National Fisherman" will probably remember Burt Coffey's reporting on the event in the May 1973 issue). Is it possible that a designer could be as conservative as to offer Monhegan, a Friendship Sloop, and then turn right around and be radical enough to design Nina, a sailboard specifically intended for sport swordfishing off the coast of Florida? Would Olin Stephens? Or Pete Culler? Or Bruce King?

Phil Bolger's book is really three: an essay

on his feelings about boats, a description of his designs (31 of them here) and a collection of plans and specifications to build those designs. Among the boats in this book are Defender, a classic 11' yacht tender; Thomaston Galley, a 15'6" motor/sail/oar boat; Kotick, a 15' kayak; Vanitie, a lovely 19'8" daysailer; Quickstep, a 19'10" canoe yawl; Yarrow, a 16'1" Tancook Whaler; Sea Hawk, a 15'6" dory skiff; and Seguin, a 15'6" utility outboard. Which says it all about Phil Bolger -- he's diverse.

—PHS

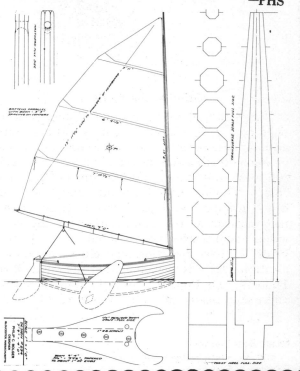

**100**

# Old
# Ways
# Work

*Contd. from preceding page*

will fit nicely into a standard three-jaw electric drill chuck; if the file butt is too big, reduce it by grinding, and try and remove the same amount on each side. This makes a red hot and rapid tool for drilling out loose knots in say, cedar planking. The sharp point searches out the run of the knot, and the tool leaves a clean, tapered hole, just what you want for plugging. It's also not a bad drill for boring thin stock if you don't happen to have the real thing in the proper size; a stopgap to be sure. but it gets the job along.

While on the subject of drills, if small holes are needed and a drill the right size is not on hand, various sizes of common nails, with the heads cut off, points beaten cold to a spear shape, and then ground to

approximately an included angle of 90 degrees, with some back relief, will do the job. The diameter can be controlled by grinding. Being soft, they don't last, but often get the job done.

I hang on to sail needles with broken eyes. Being quite hard, they make fine small drills, especially for clinch fastening light lapstrake boats where plank is so thin the common copper tack is used. A small wood stop on the needle controls the depth of bore. The hole is tapered, which is just what you want for a tack, so it completely fills the hole, leaving no slack on the inside. Of course, you can grind standard drills to a taper, but then they don't suit another job — the altered sail needle is all you need.

Flat files come in various sizes; occasionally you get a real big one, often much rusted. These are big enough and long enough to supply stock for a couple of plane irons — narrow, smoothing or rabbet. Many craftsmen end up making planes, and John Gardner has written much about it in "National Fisherman." Plane irons are hard to come by; good wood for them is not, as mentioned earlier in discussing the availability of wood. One of my best working planes is elm — not pretty, but very hard.

For a smoothing plane iron, take the biggest flat file

*Contd. on next page*

## Good Maine Yards

Are you looking for a small, skilled yard to build you a fine wood yacht, a fishing craft, an aluminum racer, a fiberglass cruiser or sailboat or some other custom-designed boat? Such yards still exist, and in considerable number, along the coast of Maine, and the steady parade of new boats heading south each year testifies to the fact that not all the boats come from the same mold. Instant information about some of these yards -- their facilities, capacities, personnel, location, etc. -- is available from the Maine Boat Builders And Repairers Association. Their brochure lists nearly 50 yards and related facilities.

—DRG

**Maine Boat Builders
   and Repairers Association
Frederic L. Felton
Executive Secretary
Cumberland Foreside,
Portland, Me. 04110**

for plane irons and will chip and be difficult to whet. Not so. A little judicious "burning" in grinding will sufficiently soften the edge.

It's said a plane won't work without a cap iron. With a thin iron, this is so, but these extra-thick irons don't need any. Being very stiff and rigid, they hold an edge.

I have several planes of various models made this way. I have found out this: Besides cutting the throat and wedge ways, as explained before in "National Fisherman," and to suit the thickness of the new iron, I like my smoothing planes at a 50 degree angle. Lengths simply suit the fancy, and sometimes the particular block of wood — this goes for the general shape, too. Some manufactured wooden planes are very uncomfortable to hold and work with. I frequently put a wood handle and knob on even a smoothing plane. The German horn instead of a knob is good, too. The bed in the block for the iron to rest on should be dead flat or very slightly hollow — never rockered even a little or the plane will chatter. I like to grind the bevel on the iron only slightly less than the angle it makes with the bottom of the plane — just so the heel never drags. And grind it HOLLOW, using the natural round of the grinding wheel. With the above bevel, a 50 degree angle, and the plane otherwise right, there is a great deal of metal backing the cutting edge, which lasts and lasts with no chipping unless you strike an open knot with sand in it. This ruins any edge.

Rabbet and beading planes can be made the same way, using smaller flat files. I find the narrower-than-standard, lower-angle smoothing plane superior to the standard angle and width for most work, especially spar work. Imagination can run wild with designs and models of planes and other special use tools.

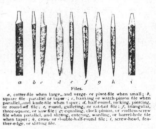

Files.

*a,* cotter-file when large, and verge- or pivot-file when small; *b,* square file parallel or taper; *c,* banking or watch-pinion file when parallel, and knife-file when taper; *d,* half-round, nicking, piercing, or round-off file; *e,* round, gulleting, or rat-tail file; *f,* triangular, three-square, or saw-file; *g,* equaling, clock-pinion, or endless-screw file when parallel, and slitting, entering, warding, or barrel-hole file when taper; *h,* cross- or double-half-round file; *i,* screw-head, feather-edge, or slitting file.

To get back to files as source of material for other tools. Now we need some heat; red is enough. I have, through the years, collected some good carving and light-work cutting tools, mostly English and very good. Many needed much restoring. Still, there were shapes not on hand I felt need of (or maybe it was the need of just making). Small files do fine here, and again I say only a red heat — too much and some of this metal turns to mush. While a forge can be used, it requires some practice with its use, as you have at hand far more heat than needed. Gas stove, wood or coal fire, propane torch, any will do fine. After all, in far-off places forging is still done squatting in the open before a small charcoal fire, bamboo bellows, all very primitive. But nice work is turned out.

Heat and hammer, heat and hammer, as this light metal does not hold heat long, and beating it when it's too cool can break it. Small paring tools — straight, skew, angle, vee — can be made as well as gouges of all shapes and bevels. Lengths are made to suit, and in all shapes, bent, half bent, spoon, etc. No limit. Finish by grinding.

Now the matter of cutting edge. Grind to shape and

_Contd. from preceding page_

and grind off the tang. Half way along its length, grind with the edge of the wheel all around it, at least halfway through. Put it in the vise at this point and a sharp blow on the upper half will break it off. You now have stock for two irons.

Now grind off the teeth. The pattern does not have to totally disappear except near what will be the top of the cutting edge — if this is not smooth, naturally you will end up with a serrated cutting edge. If the rest of it feels smooth to the hand even though the pattern has not been totally removed, it is sufficient. One end will have a taper. Keep this up in the plane and square off the lower end with the other piece, round up the soft tang end and square the other. Then grind the square ends to a plane iron bevel.

This is a lot of grinding but worth it. A big, powerful grinding wheel is an advantage, especially with a rather course stone, as it makes less heat. Have plenty of water for quenching. Some will say this file stuff is too hard

_Contd. on next page_

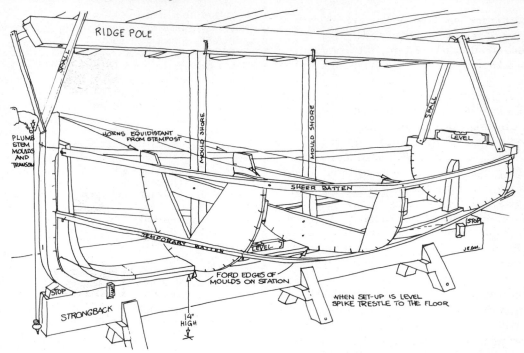

⊛"Clenched Lap or Clinker" by Eric McKee.
National Maritime Museum, Greenwich, England.
1972, 30 pp., illustrated, softbound, $2.

A museum publication you can actually do something with. For starters, you can take out the special cardboard insert, cut on the dotted lines, and put together your very own scale half-model of a 10' workboat. While you're doing it you can follow McKee's step-by-step description of the building of a lapstrake boat. By the time you're finished, you'll probably be a lapstrake (Clinker is a British term for the same thing) freak, and the only thing left to do is build that 10' workboat in real life. To pick up on the finer details of this type of construction, your next book should be "Clinker Boatbuilding" by John Leather (International Marine Publishing Co., Camden, Me. $8.95).

—PHS

# Old Ways Work

*Contd. from preceding page*

whet, then try for hardness. Some of this material is air hardened and you may find things just right. If not, brighten up the working end and experiment with heat and water. Watch for the color near the working end. This is not a how-to on tempering — if you have gotten this far, you will no doubt pick up the rest. Most old machinist books go considerably into tempering. For such woodworking tools, I use a color somewhere between light and a dark straw. Simply experiment until you get an edge that will hold.

Now, if you get taken up by this sort of thing, and a forge is available, possibilities are unlimited, as is the stock to work with. A garage which works on big vehicles often has broken truck springs out back. This is prime stuff for big tools. Need I say more?

Often some sort of wood-turning lathe is around, or a beat-up metal one is converted for wood. Actually, a homemade wood lathe of considerable ability is not difficult to build. Many have no doubt seen small lathes in museums which were built aboard sailing vessels on long voyages, notably whalers. Cutting tools for such machines I make totally from files, usually just by grinding and fitting a stout wood handle, with a pipe or tubing ferrule. The handiest ferrule stock for any tool handle is common galvanized steel electric conduit — it comes in several diameters and scraps are readily available.

I am no great ecology nut, or maybe I always was without being aware of it, as the word was not known in every household when I started in. The various approaches above mentioned have been a great source of satisfaction, and give a feeling of independence. A knowledge of being able to work over what appear to be useless things can, at some time in one's life, be a real life-saver. My preachings along this line are often not taken seriously, for now many consider it "work," something to be avoided at all costs. Idling away at the boob tube may be some people's idea of living — after all, their set is the most expensive in the neighborhood. Different ships, different long splices, but somehow I feel they miss a lot.

⊕ "Boat Carpentry" by Hervey Garrett Smith.
Van Nostrand Reinhold, New York.
1965 (second edition), 178 pp., illustrated,
    index, $7.50.

Hervey Garrett Smith is one of my favorite writers on practical marine subjects. I especially like his drawings, which are clear and show as much detail as necessary to understand the principle being illustrated and nothing more.

This is not a book on how to build a boat, but rather a book on the techniques and tools to use if you will be building a boat. In other words, it is a collection of information on methods, tools, fastenings, joinery, etc., that will serve you in good stead if you should build or repair a boat.

The best material here is on fastenings, glues and adhesives and wood preservatives. A lot of misinformation and/or vague information is passed around on these subjects, and Smith cuts right through the double-talk. His strength is that he gives the traditional boatman modern techniques — too many lovers of the old ways tell you that there's nothing like oakum for a seam, which is OK with me, but how many boatyards carry the stuff? So, if you want to read about modern adhesives, Smith will tell you about them (he believes that those sold now are better than anything produced in the past).

With all these words of praise for this book, I can't help tempering them a bit. Smith goes into detail about caulking but then gives us only three short sentences on seam compounds.

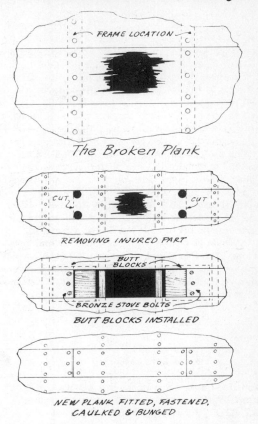

The Broken Plank

REMOVING INJURED PART

BUTT BLOCKS INSTALLED

NEW PLANK FITTED, FASTENED, CAULKED & BUNGED

There's more to the subject than that, especially with the arrival of the new synthetics.

Other subjects covered in this book are woods, fiberglass, steam bending, wood finishing and the application of gold leaf. The latter is truly fascinating.

**103**

—PHS

**Quote and sketch from "Boat Carpentry"**

When a damaged member must be replaced, the first thing to do is to analyze every step of the operation, find out what is involved, and how you are going to do it. Use your imagination, and anticipate every possible trouble. Determine how and where the piece is fastened, and if the fastenings are accessible. Suppose they break or are frozen in the wood. How are you going to treat them? Are you going to have to remove *other* members, because they may be fastened to the first piece, or to get room to work? Decide how you are going to cut the damaged piece out, where you are going to cut it, and finally, how you are going to fit and fasten the new piece.

These things may seem very elementary—indeed, they are meant to be. But I had to make a good many mistakes and spoil an awful lot of nice wood before I learned that the time to make mistakes and to do your best thinking is before you start to work. Meticulous planning beforehand can make any job simpler.

**Decide Yourself**

". . . the sensible way to go about seeking a proper cruiser is to begin by formulating one's own requirements and not by wandering through a boat show with checkbook in hand."

—Arthur Beiser in "The Proper Yacht"

## Keel Casting

A few years ago, John Baker of Cranston R.I., built the H28 ketch Cockerwitter from an L. Francis Herreshoff design obtained through "Rudder" magazine.

"The plans are in excellent detail," says Baker, "and very easy to follow. We are very pleased with the boat."

Of interest to backyard builders is the fact that nearly all of the boat from keel to masts was built by Baker. Of special note is the 3000-lb. keel which he cast himself.

Baker describes the keel project as follows:

"The mold was made of one-inch boards, as green as possible, and painted with water glass to help reduce burning. The upright sides of the mold are straight lines but set at an angle, with a length of about 12', a width at center of some 12" and tapering to about 4" at each end. It was a really easy form to make with measurements taken off the table of offsets.

"A shallow trench was dug close to and below the bottom of the lead pot to receive the mold, which was then bedded and tamped in the trench evenly to minimize lead leaks. It was important that the mold be level as it was left open the full length.

"After the lead was poured and had set (at least 48 hours), an A-frame was rigged with a chain hoist over the center of the lead and the casting was pulled from the ground, the mold knocked off, lead cleaned and then set up on blocks for the oak keel.

"Scrap lead was used for the casting as this drills and cuts much better than pure lead. I had no trouble drilling the fourteen 7/16" holes through the oak keel and lead for the silicon bronze bolts. If pure lead was used, I had been advised to add about 1% antimony for the same reason.

"During the heating process none of the enamel came off the tub although I would advise getting a tub from a scrap yard rather than using the house tub."

Baker's H28 is of strip-plank construction.

Auxiliary power is a 16 h.p., four-cylinder Graymarine Lugger engine which turns a two-blade 14" x 8" propeller set at a 15-degree angle to the centerline in order to avoid having to bore through the deadwood. Speed under power is five knots.

—"National Fisherman"

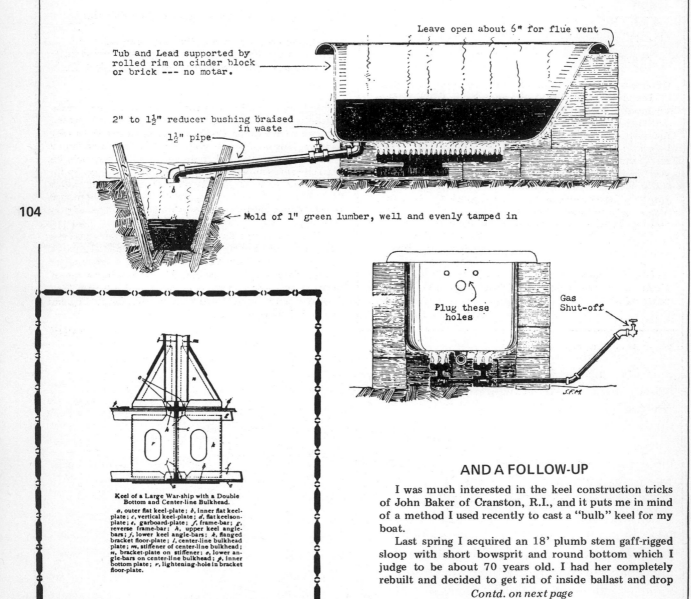

Tub and Lead supported by rolled rim on cinder block or brick --- no motar.

Leave open about 6" for flue vent

2" to 1½" reducer bushing braised in waste

1½" pipe

← Mold of 1" green lumber, well and evenly tamped in

104

Plug these holes

Gas Shut-off

Keel of a Large War-ship with a Double Bottom and Center-line Bulkhead.

*a*, outer flat keel-plate; *b*, inner flat keel-plate; *c*, vertical keel-plate; *d*, flat keelson-plate; *e*, garboard-plate; *f*, frame-bar; *g*, reverse frame-bar; *h*, upper keel angle-bars; *j*, lower keel angle-bars; *k*, flanged bracket floor-plate; *l*, center-line bulkhead plate; *m*, stiffener of center-line bulkhead; *n*, bracket-plate on stiffener; *o*, lower angle-bars on center-line bulkhead; *p*, inner bottom plate; *r*, lightening-hole in bracket floor-plate.

## AND A FOLLOW-UP

I was much interested in the keel construction tricks of John Baker of Cranston, R.I., and it puts me in mind of a method I used recently to cast a "bulb" keel for my boat.

Last spring I acquired an 18' plumb stem gaff-rigged sloop with short bowsprit and round bottom which I judge to be about 70 years old. I had her completely rebuilt and decided to get rid of inside ballast and drop

*Contd. on next page*

*Contd. from preceding page*

it to the false keel which has a long straight run as shown in the sketch.

I took a gallon anti-freeze can (any kind will do) and cut it in half the long way and propped it up. (See sketch). I melted scrap lead on a regular plumber's rig and poured into this mold to a depth of 2" or so, taking care to line the can each time with aluminum foil to prevent sticking to the tin. Each cast came out in a half-cylinder form and weighed roughly 20 lbs. I bored a single hole through the middle of each, oiling the bit to keep it from fouling, and counter-sunk. Then I bolted these along the bottom of the keel with 3/8" brass bolts

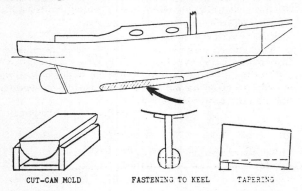

CUT-CAN MOLD       FASTENING TO KEEL       TAPERING

(bronze would be even better, but don't use galvanized).

The ends are feathered fore and aft simply by tipping the mold.

Fill the spaces between the casts with plastic steel and file with rough file and wire brush and you have a nice bulb keel which doesn't increase your draft. One of the nicest things about it is that you can balance her just as you like by distributing the casts fore or aft.

Be sure to locate your keel bolts in advance so that you won't strike one as you bore through for the casts! The weight, of course, can be substantially increased by pouring the lead to a greater depth in the can.

> Joseph E. Garland
> Eastern Point Blvd.
> Gloucester, Mass.

P.S. The idea, incidentally, came from Capt. Tom Morse, Rocky Neck gill-netter, from whom I bought the boat. —JEG.

—"National Fisherman"

**"The Bark Canoes and Skin Boats of North America"** by Edwin Tappan Adney and Howard I. Chapelle.
Supt. of Documents, GPO, Washington D.C.
1964, 242 pp., illustrated, bibliography, index, $3.25.

Part history, part building instructions, this book will have you dreaming about your own birch-bark canoe. There are photographs, construction details, lines drawings and fine text on bark canoes, skin boats, kayaks and umiaks. At $3.25 for a hardbound book of immense value to canoe historians and builders, this has to be a bargain.

—PHS

Kaiak or Baidarka of an Alaskan Eskimo.

**"How to Build and Manage a Canoe"** by Ellis and Beams.
Brown, Son and Ferguson, Glasgow, Scotland.
1963 (3rd edition), 2 volumes, 142 pages, illustrated, 7 sheets of plans, glossary. Vol. 1, $2.25; Vol. 2, $2.75.

Volume I is a book in the conventional sense, with instructions on building and handling a two-seater canvas-covered canoe (looks more like a kayak to me). Volume II is a surprise - you turn the cover and find a pocket with seven folded sheets of plans for building the self-same canoe. The renderings are true joys to behold. In other words, the book isn't on building canoes in general, but on building one in particular (though the principles naturally can be applied to another of your choosing).

Ellis has written another book by the same publisher, "The Book of Canoeing" (1957, 4th edition, 212 pages, index). In it are instructions for building a single-seater kayak. This book is very English, with quite a bit of material on where to take your canoe in the British Isles. If you're a canoe buff and plan to vacation in England, maybe this book would be of interest.

—PHS

105

From "How to Build and Manage a Canoe"

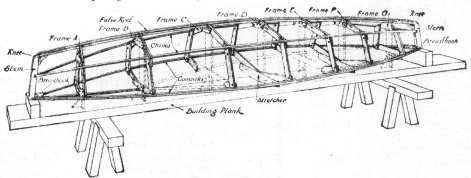

TWO SEATER KAYAK
*Framework of kayak before being covered*

FIG 1

**"Boatbuilding in Your Own Backyard"** by S.S. Rabl.
Cornell Maritime Press, Cambridge, Md.
1958, 224 pp., illustrated, plans. $10.

As the title suggests, this book is for the genuine backyard boatbuilder. Rabl makes no bones about it. He assumes that the reader (and thus the builder) is a plain, ordinary, everyday Joe, without an array of power tools, a heated building shed and an intimate knowledge of cabinetmaker's joints. As a consequence, he tells you how to do everything yourself, including how to make your own tools. For instance, on page 14 he shows you how to make a "Swedish band saw," one of the weirdest contraptions I ever saw, but from the looks of it, it's definitely something you could build in your kitchen, and my high school physics course says it should work. See also some of the other homemade tools he describes, such as planes, clamps (you can save some money with these) and bevels.

Rabl includes quite a few plans, which the publisher will provide blueprints for after the payment of a modest fee. Among them is Rabl's well-known tabloid cruiser Picaroon, one of the saltiest 18-footers you'll ever want to see.

Kittiwake is an inexpensive 24' inboard boat designed by Sam Rabl. Plans are included in "Boatbuilding in Your Own Backyard."

He also shows a 7' plywood dink "that everybody needs." I decided I needed one and can attest that building it is as Rabl promises: "The acme of simplicity."

The author features wooden construction, but does have a good section on fiberglass building. You can tell his heart isn't in it, though. Another nice touch in this book is a design for a trailer, with a fair description on how to build it. Considering the price of a new trailer, it is a design well worth considering.

—PHS

From "Boatbuilding in Your Own Backyard."

106

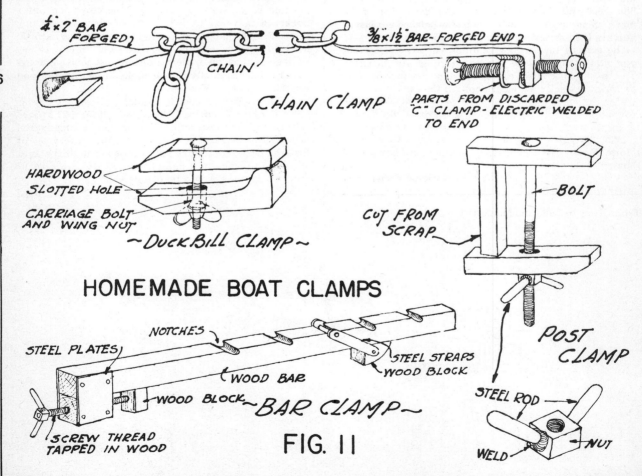

HOMEMADE BOAT CLAMPS

FIG. II

### Texas Dory Boat Plans

A man named Capt. Jim Orrell is apparently much enamored of a simple boat called a dory. He has undertaken to revive a raft of old plans and has added to them by having had new variations drawn up. He puts out sets of plans at a very modest cost for everything from the 15½' rowing dory to large sailing dories and speed skiffs, to very large cabin cruising-type dories. Most seem to be very able and practical hulls.

Perhaps the most popular has been the Gloucester Gull Rowing Dory considered by its designer, Phil Bolger, as one of his best boats. This is an extremely pretty boat designed especially for easy rowing. It is an honest hull that moves smoothly under oar and would be a good first boat for a youngster. I've had mine for a few years in Alaskan waters and find it to be seaworthy and a real workhorse for moving gear and supplies from one place to another.

My only criticism of the plans is that they call for oak whenever possible and that they seem to lack well-gusseted frames amply supplied. It has been my experience that oak works well for guards and areas subject to chafe and that it is a very strong wood, but that it also tends to check heavily when used for such things as seats, frames, etc. A softer wood such as Douglas fir seems to hold up better for parts that get baked by the sun and are thus subject to checking. On the subject of frames; one would do well to build permanent frames instead of the temporary station frames mentioned often in the plans. This would make the boats easier to build and would also prevent the sides from working at the chines and leaking.

Jim Orrell seems to be the dory man in the U.S. and he has a wide variety of dory plans and study sheets. I was amazed at the amount of dory lore and history and descriptions he's collected and reprinted.

—Mark White

**Mark White's Rowing Dory**

As a footnote, we should mention that most of the Texas Dories are made from the boards of designer Phil Bolger, 250 Washington St., Gloucester, Mass., one of the country's most innovative naval architects. Typically, Bolger has taken the basic banks dory and Swampscott dory hulls and modified them for use with power — usually outboard motors. The boats are designed with the backyard builder in mind, using plywood and local lumber in the construction. The Texas Dories have proved to be fast and seaworthy and are very much worth the consideration of anyone looking for good, sound designs.

—DRG

Offshore 26, below, is one of the most popular Texas Dories. The one shown is powered by a 100 h.p. outboard and was clocked at 28½ m.p.h.

**Texas Dory Boat Plans**
P. O. BOX 720
GALVESTON, TEXAS 77550

Bending in a fresh piece of ceiling.

Photo from "Building of a Wooden Ship"

● "The Building of a Wooden Ship" by Dana A. Story.
Barre Publishers, Barre, Mass.
1971, photographs by John M. Clayton, $12.50.

This is a collection of 85 photographs taken between 1938 and 1947 of wooden shipbuilding at the famous Story shipyard in Essex, Mass. The photos are arranged in sequence to show the building of a ship from half-model, to mold-loft floor, to the laying down, framing-up, planking, decking, caulking, joining and launching. The text by Story is really expanded captions with lots of fascinating detail and plenty of color.

The two boats featured here are poles apart — a 55' schooner yacht and a large dragger — but the building methods are essentially the same. If you're interested in wooden shipbuilding from an academic viewpoint, you'll like the book; if you're in the throes of building your own wooden boat and need inspiration, you'll love it.

—PHS

● "Boatbuilding with Plywood" by Glen L. Witt.
Glen L Marine Design, Bellflower, Calif.
1962, 214 pp., illustrated, $7.50.

Good, solid information on plywood boatbuilding, from selecting the wood to finishing off the boat. Witt knows what he is talking about, and though his writing doesn't have much style, he gets the details across without confusion. He covers just about everything required to build a plywood boat and his illustrations and step-by-step photographs are excellent.

For instance, his illustration on how to make a scarf joint to join two plywood panels is the best I've ever seen. His chapter on fiberglassing a plywood boat is good, too; he covers both the dry and wet processes. I think it is safe to say that the average amateur builder could easily build a quality plywood boat if he has a clear head and this book in hand. There's no index; a book like this needs one.

—PHS

*New support for the mast step. The timber is through-bolted to the keel.*

"Restoration of the Smack Emma C. Berry" by Willits
   D. Ansel.
Mystic Seaport, Mystic, Conn.
1973, 94 pp., illustrated, glossary, bibliography, fold-
   out plans, paperbound, $5.95.

A better title for this book would be "The Restoration of a Wooden Ship, with Special Attention Paid to the Smack Emma C. Berry," because the subject is ship repair when you get right down to it. That the victim happens to be the Emma C. Berry is incidental. A better discussion of the subject would be hard to find, and should be especially helpful to the person who is long on desire and short on cash, and who tackles a restoration job without guidance from the pros. This is a heartening book for the boat rebuilder who might be sick at heart — if they could do it to the Emma C. Berry, it can be done to the good ol' Lollipop.

—PHS

109

## THE AMATEUR YACHT RESEARCH SOCIETY

Life's affairs seem progressively to emphasize and even to aggravate the differences we see between people. All those little differences and games of coalition and strategy school children build about themselves in micro-emulation of their folks and faculty seem to become blown way out of proportion in later life. Once in awhile it is nice to reflect that all this foolishness surrounding us began in childhood; that in fact, everyone was a kid once and largely remains one still.

It is disturbing, though, that only some of the old chums seem to be still about. There is a group missing it seems. The opportunely serious hall-monitor-safety-patrol-jocks are still around and still running things, I notice. The class geniuses are no doubt being housed and fed by Military contracts somewhere. All the C-plussers have run off to become teachers and social scientists. The music types have either died or are now up to second chair. And so on.

Missing are the incorrigible goofs; the bright, over-mothered, creative kids who did some of everything and got a kick out of it when they weren't being emotionally blackmailed too much. You know, the guy who really felt life was pretty keen, discovered girls late and then only because one was really nice and liked what he liked, who took walks, collected and sent for stuff and kept a notebook of robot diagrams and lists of what he needed to build a sailboat.

Except for a junior high science teacher here and there, my impression has been that this exemplary sub-species has become rare, endangered even. That is, this was my impression until I found the Amateur Yacht Research Society.

*Contd. on next page*

*Contd. from preceding page*

What relief that they made it, for they are better men than most!

The A.Y.R.S. has a zest, the spirit of the doodler-designer-dreamer-nut-rigorous scientist, that is all at the same time silly-infectious, creative-good, fun-utterly, human-terribly valuable. They are full of diagrams, formulas, theorums, inspirations, brainstorms and chimeras. They are also full of hard work, experiment, hundreds of thousands of hours of real experience, delight and learning from success and failure alike. They take ideas wherever they find them and put them together and then try them.

Anything is allowed and, if you can believe it, you may in print be warm, personal and sentimental, make mistakes, be stuffy and the whole thing makes me wish you could get a good pint of fresh stout in the U. S. Alas, you cannot. You can join the A.Y.R.S., though, and if you are into cats, tris, hydrofoils, proas, new sail and hull configurations and scaring hell out of yourself, you ought to.

—GP

Information and books and membership ($10/yr.):
**A.Y.R.S.**
**Hermitage, Newbury**
**Berkshire, England**
American National Organizer:
**W. Dorwin Teague**
**375 Sylvan Ave.**
**Englewood Cliffs, N.J. 07632**

110

## Wood Boat Builders List

While the majority of boats today are being built by a relatively few large manufacturers, there still exists an "underground" of small shops and medium-sized yards which devote at least part of their efforts to the building of commercial and pleasure boats in wood and, ever more commonly, other materials. Many of these builders turn out excellent hulls at surprisingly low cost, especially if you are willing to settle for "workboat finish" rather than yachting gloss.

Some fishing boat hulls are quite easily converted for pleasure use and with reasonable care will give their owners long service. The boats are designed for the waters of their areas, too, thus assuring the buyer of a seakeeping reliability he might not get with a big-name stock boat of the same size.

The big problem is finding these workboat builders. A few may advertise in such publications as "National Fisherman," "Workboat," "Soundings" or some of the other smaller marine publications, but most rely on word-of-mouth for their orders. The only national listing of any kind which we have seen is the "Partial List of Fishing Boat Builders," Fishery Leaflet 618, published in 1968 by the U.S. Bureau of Commercial Fisheries. The leaflet should now be available from the Publications Division, National Marine Fisheries Service, NOAA, U.S. Dept. of Commerce, Washington, D.C. 20235. It lists 238 shipyards in 26 coastal and inland states, and includes the name of the firm, its address and the material(s) in which it builds.

Unfortunately, the hazards of trying to run a small yard in today's swiftly changing world are evidenced by the attrition to this list since it was published some five years ago. Several of the yards with which we are familiar are no longer operating or, at best, are no longer building boats. We would guess that from 20% to 25% of the firms on the list are defunct, but this still leaves a sizable seed list to work with.

A closing note: A fair number of these builders remain in boatbuilding simply because they like

Partial List of
**Fishing Boat Builders**

UNITED STATES DEPARTMENT OF THE INTERIOR
FISH AND WILDLIFE SERVICE
BUREAU OF COMMERCIAL FISHERIES          Fishery Leaflet 618

it; in short, they're rugged individualists and will not be pushed. If they like you, they may build you a boat. If they don't, they may have orders ahead for one helluva long period. If you want to save money, don't ask the builder to deviate from his usual work.

He probably has several choices of hull and layout, but if you begin making a lot of changes before or after construction begins, be prepared for an irritated builder and a jump in the cost of the boat.

Of course, if you have the time, you'll be ahead by going to the general area where you want your boat built, ask around for builders, check with them about hull types and generally become acquainted with the marine outlook of the people. This background work will tell you something about the boat you can expect that no slick sales brochure could ever do.

DRG

## Chapelle on Lofting

I have been following the discussion of the design of home-built boats with much interest. As one who has had some experience with home-builders, I should like to pitch in my five-cents' worth.

I think the home-builders of boats are very hard guys to classify. Not only do they vary widely in intelligence, common sense, skill and financial worth, but also, Allah protect us, in what they desire. This is why "plans for home builders" vary so much, I suppose.

It has long been my opinion that the past 30 years have produced lowered skill and common sense in boatbuilding and in this I see damned little difference between many small "professional builders" and home-builders. In the first place, both want to cross-out mold-loft work. The boat set up is the only gauge of progress in building that they will accept. I am in full agreement with the naval architects who have complained about a lack of concern in complete lofting by home-builders. This complaint will apply to many one-man professional boat shops.

The one-man shop, whether amateur or professional, produces a common problem. The builder must get material, puzzle over the plans, and build the boat — and

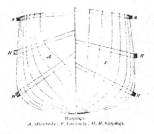

Harpings.
*A,* afterbody; *F,* fore-body; *H, H,* harpings.

almost invariably there is a deadline, real or imaginary, to be met. The one-man shop, therefore, is the place where lofting, particularly extensive lofting, is a "delay factor" and the recent trend is to get along without it if possible, with often very sad results.

Yet, if the plans are drawn with very great precision, a passable job might possibly result. But it is somewhat rare, I judge, to make plans scale-accurate enough to allow this — hence the often sad results.

It is true that chine-model hulls are easiest to loft and the plans can be drawn with great precision if the scale is 3/4" — 1" or upward. Unfortunately, however, after lofting you have to build the contraption. It is not true that all V-bottom hulls are easier to build than round-bottom hulls. This popular assumption has raised the devil with many a promising amateur builder.

Fore-and-aft planking of V-bottom hulls requires complete framing with bevelling, and there is often a hellish twist in the garboard that steaming does not solve. Or, in Chesapeake skipjacks, the traditional easy planking, herringbone fashion, is cancelled out by the need for a large, heavy keelson which few amateurs can handle, lacking heavy tools or skill with broadaxe and adz as most do. A special framing plan for the amateur is therefore necessary.

I have had many an "expectant" home-builder write that he wished to build, with sheet plywood, a boat designed to be planked. Sheet plywood requires complete framing, of course, and for this plans should be drawn. Again, all chine-model hulls are not easy to build of sheet plywood — I wonder why the plywood industry

## Pinching the Forefoot

Of all the joints of seams of a boat's backbone structure, the forefoot one is possibly the most difficult to make up in a way that it will remain closed. The proof of this is in so many boats on the railway showing a wide filling or even a graving piece let in to at least make the open joint less apparent.

Providing the wood is decently seasoned this method

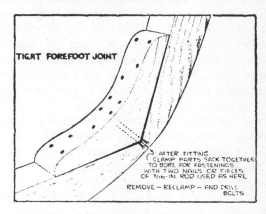

of making up the joint gives a seam that should stay permanently tight. The size of the nails or diameter of rod used should be in keeping with the heft of the members, from 1/8" to 1/3" diameter ordinarily sufficing. Naturally, the nails, we'll say, should be long enough to project both sides.

—Jim Emmett

has been of so little help to the boatbuilder in solving the problems of this type of construction?

Home building of plastic boats has been the latest activity and some horrifying craft have resulted. In this area, the hull must be lofted accurately if a satisfactory boat is to result; there is no alternate.

I don't think "stock plans" are the answer to the problems of home-building or amateur construction. The builder needs to have a special design that meets his real or imaginary use-requirements and is fitted to his skills and available tools. Otherwise, there will be grief.

But such plans are expensive — this subject has been well covered so there is no need to discuss it again. The point of the reference is that the relationship of naval architect and home-builder or one-man shop ought probably be that of psychiatrist and patient!

This is a matter of real concern — one of my clients shot and killed his boatbuilder; which I had not advised, I should add.

——Howard I. Chapelle, Curator, Division of Transportation, Smithsonian Institution, Washington, D.C. 20560, in a letter to "National Fisherman," June 1966.

Sagitta.

## Ouch!

"Right off, somebody recalled kind of quietly that L. Francis Herreshoff had said glass boats inside looked like frozen snot."
—Capt. R.D. (Pete) Culler in
"The Telltale Compass"

# METAL BOATBUILDING

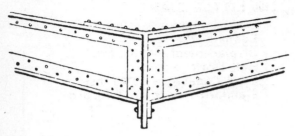

—Keel of an Iron Ship.

"Hull Welding Manual" (AWS D3.5-62).
American Welding Society, 345 East 47th St.
New York, N.Y.
1962, 62 pp., illustrated, paperbound, $2.50.

This booklet is directed toward large-ship construction, but there is plenty of information here for the steel or aluminum boatbuilder. The chapters are Materials, Design of Structural Details, Hull Construction and Inspection and Qualification. The diagrams are very good, especially those showing cross sections of welds.

If you plan on building in metal, it might be a good idea to check out the various publications of the American Welding Society. They distribute an annual catalog listing what's available, much of which you won't find elsewhere. For instance: "Standard Methods for Mechanical Testing of Welds," "Safe Practices for Welding and Cutting Containers that Have Held Combustibles," "Application of Aluminum and Zinc for Protection of Iron and Steel," and "Brazing Manual."

—PHS

From "Hull Welding Manual"

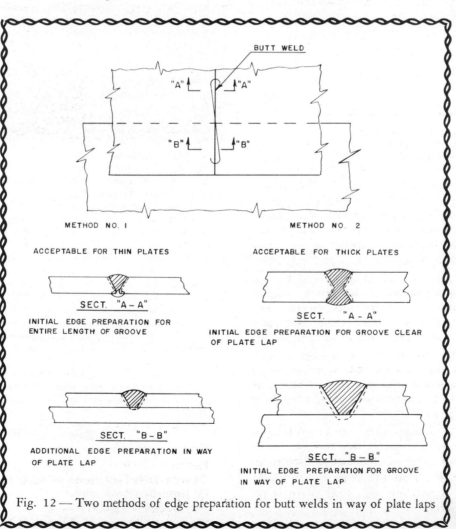

Fig. 12 — Two methods of edge preparation for butt welds in way of plate laps

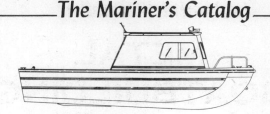

**MonArk Boat Co.**
**P.O. Box 210**
**Monticello, Ark. 71655**

Small workboats, large ones, pleasure boats, hulls and pontooons, runabouts and sportfishermen — all built of aluminum — make up one of the broadest lines of boats we've seen anywhere. MonArk is a modern, big-time boat manufacturer, but if you're thinking in terms of an aluminum craft, chances are they can supply you with it, including custom alterations. It's not easy to just go out and order a bare aluminum hull for completion in your own backyard, but the huge variety of models offered by MonArk are available for the choosing, from bare hull to finished vessel. They have several catalogs, so state your interests when writing.

—DRG

**2100 LITTLE GIANT**
**LOA** — 21'3''
**Beam** — 7'8''
**Displacement** — 2100 lbs.
**Hull Draft** — 9''
**Load Capacity** — 3200 lbs.
**Standard Power** — Outboard

2408-V-

113

● **"Small Steel Craft" by Ian Nicolson.**
**Adlard Coles, London, England.**
**1971, 206 pp., illustrated, $12.**

There's so little available on the construction of small boats in steel that it's great to see a book like this. For some reason, steel boats don't get the attention they deserve. Maybe it's peoples' fear of corrosion, which is generally unfounded if steel boats are finished properly.

At any rate, if you are going to build, have someone else build, or buy a steel boat, I highly recommend that you read this book. The sub-title is "Design, Construction and Maintenance" and the scope is just that. Nicolson answers most of the questions you might have on the subject, and when you are finished, you wonder why you didn't think of steel in the first place when you started thinking about getting a boat.

This is a British book, and while the terminology is easy enough to follow, when Nicolson suggests sources of supply, they're in England or Europe. That the book doesn't have a bibliography is bad enough; that there is no index is inexcusable.

—PHS

**2810-V-S-F-11-S**

**LOA** — 28'0''
**Beam** — 10'0''
**Design Displacement** — 8500 lbs.
**Design Draft** — 2'9''
**Passenger Capacity** — 6
**Standard Power** — Twin GM-453

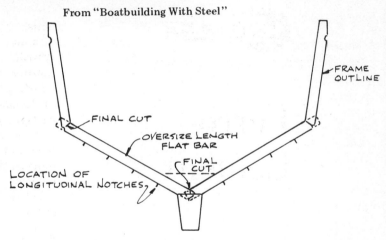

From "Boatbuilding With Steel"

6-5. A frame made from flat bar stock, with final cuts made after the parts are matched to the scribed frame lines.

"It is strange that an age which accepts without question the undeniable success of large ships of steel (how many wood or plastic ocean-going cargo vessels exist?) should have any doubt about steel for small vessels or for pleasure craft."

⊛ "Boatbuilding with Steel" by Gilbert C. Klingel. (incl. "Boatbuilding with Aluminum" by Thomas Colvin)
International Marine Publishing Co. Camden, Me.
1973, 248 pp., illustrated, index, $12.50.

When I finished reading this book, my immediate reaction was: If the day ever came that I would have a custom-built boat it would (1) be steel, and (2) be fabricated by Gilbert Klingel. The author's dedication to his material, and his craft (Klingel is by profession a steel boatbuilder), comes through so strongly in this book that you wonder why you ever considered anything else.

The problems with using steel for boats are obvious and have been belabored for years. There's hardly a boatman alive who doesn't have a favorite horror story. Klingel makes no effort to hide these problems; in fact, he takes the offensive. His argument is detailed and convincing — the secret to a successful steel boat is quality. Quality in design, construction and maintenance. I have never seen a boat built by Gilbert Klingel, but if he builds them the way he recommends they be built in this book (and there is no reason to disbelieve him), then he must have one heck of a long list of delighted owners.

The introduction says it all — anyone who builds boats, whether he is an amateur or a professional, whether he builds in steel, or wood, or aluminum, or fiberglass, or walrus hide, should commit those four pages to memory. For instance: "We should believe that when we build, we build forever, and that what we build should be as lovely or as graceful in ten years as it was when it was produced."

But don't get the idea that this is a book of flowery prose on the heaven-sent qualities of steel for boats. Far from it. "Boatbuilding with Steel" is a practical manual on all facets of the craft: selecting a design, lofting, picking a building site, cutting, welding, handling heavy steel plates, metalizing, painting, installing fittings, etc. To cap it all off, Thomas Colvin, no lightweight in the field (no pun intended), adds a chapter on aluminum for those who would like to compare one metal to another.

Read it.

—PHS

**114** From "Boatbuilding With Steel"

**Flame-spraying**

As the hull, a section at a time, is sandblasted, and before it can become contaminated with moisture, it should be anodically protected by flame-spraying of either aluminum or zinc. I regard this "anodic treatment" as of the essence. It is essential for both long life of the boat and for freedom from annoying minor incidental corrosive attack from abrasion, scratches, or other mechanical mishaps that will inevitably occur unless the boat never leaves the launching dock. Both zinc and aluminum act as anodic materials; they are lower in the "Electromotive Series" than steel and serve to protect it in the presence of sea water, the ever-present electrolyte in which every boat rests.

It may be argued that flame-spraying, in view of some of the modern paint systems, is unnecessary, needlessly expensive, and, at the extreme, a matter of gilding the lily. It is true that there are a number of steel-hulled vessels which seem quite adequately protected without it, but critical examination of each case will reveal that the owners either lavish constant care on their boats, immediately touching up each rust spot as it appears, maintain their craft in fresh waters, such as the Great Lakes, or keep them under constant cover; many rue the day they did not go an extra step further to avoid the constant touch-up work. Each year, craft are brought to my yard by owners seeking correction for annoying problems which should never have occurred in the first place. No matter how good a paint system may be, or how carefully it may be applied, sooner or later it is going to be scratched or chipped, or it will locally blister, peel, or crack. Unless it is immediately taken care of, the inevitable streak of rust appears and becomes unsightly; neglected, it becomes a potential source of trouble. Few boats are hauled for painting more than twice a year, most only once; unless there is an auxiliary method of protection to carry over between hauls, the defect becomes aggravated, the unsightly spot more so. Beyond the general anodic protection it affords to the entire hull, flame-spraying provides anodic local protection from painting defects for at least a year and slows down the possible damage to such a degree that correction is easy, the expense minimal.

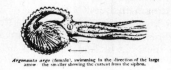

*Argonauta argo (female), swimming in the direction of the large arrow the smaller showing the current from the siphon.*

# Ferro-Cement

○ **"Ferrocement Boat Construction" by Chris Cairncross.**
International Marine Publishing Co., Camden, Me.
1972, 192 pp., illustrated, bibliography, $9.95.

A good book to start with. Cairncross puts ferro-cement in perspective by taking the first 61 pages for a brief history of the material and a discussion of boat designs suitable for construction in it. In that section are interesting comments by Maurice Griffiths, the noted British designer, yachtsman, editor and writer. Cairncross then goes on to give you a choice of construction methods — pipe frame, male mold or female mold — and discusses the merits of each (he favors pipe-frame construction).

The rest of the book is devoted to site selection, construction, lofting, reinforcement, mortar, plastering the hull, curing, finishing and painting and construction details. There is an excellent bibliography but unfortunately no index.

The thing I like about this book is that Cairncross gives reasoned arguments. Too many writers in the field tend to be dogmatic: "Take my word for it, this method is best." His practical information is just that, based on practice rather than theory. He gives numerous examples to back up his suggestions; when he tells you not to do something, he'll give you a concrete (no pun intended) example of what happened when somebody did.

—PHS

○ **"Practical Ferro-Cement Boatbuilding" by Jay R. Benford and Herman Husen.**
International Marine Publishing Co., Camden, Me.
1971 (3rd edition), 216 pp., illustrated, index, $10.

This straight-forward, practical, eminently useful book is not offered as the last and final word on ferro-cement boatbuilding, say the authors.

Nevertheless it is outstandingly one of the best of a spate of publications recently to appear on the ferro-cement frontier. It takes ferro-cement beyond the chicken wire stage — a real advance.

The use of square, welded, half-inch steel mesh, specially designed and produced for boatbuilding indicates the application of new and improved engineering practice to ferro-cement construction.

Mainly the book is a detailed, stage-to-stage record of the building of the Harambee, a 60' ferro-cement ketch designed by Jay R. Benford for Herman and Gail Husen both to live aboard and for paying guest and charter parties for summer cruises in the San Juan Islands. The Husens were on the beach for over a year building their new home.

Herman Husen's background of teaching and charter skippering, according to Benford, made him invaluable as a collaborator. In any case, Husen's exacting and methodical application to the job in hand is evident on every page of this book. Benford, himself, besides furnishing the design, supervised the construction throughout.

It is clear the authors practice what they preach. One of their recommendations is that builders keep accurate and organized notes both for their own benefit and for others, and it is apparent that these builders did just that. The numerous photographs by Steve Kennedy of Port Angeles add immeasurably to the clarity and impact of the book.

Printed by photo-offset with a simple binding which allows the pages to lie flat for easy reading and reference, this unpretentious volume is both functional and pleasing.

Having gone through its pages rather carefully, I can discover little to find fault with. While it is not an exhaustive treatise and does not pretend to be, it is still surprisingly complete, and I venture there are few practical building situations or problems on which it does not shed some useful illumination.

—John Gardner

115

# Modern ADHESIVES

### By John Gardner

Within the short space of the past three decades, chemistry has brought more radical and far-reaching changes to boatbuilding than took place in the previous 3,000 years. Since World War II, a large number of synthetic, man-made materials have gained acceptance, and in some cases have replaced to a considerable extent older boatbuilding materials of natural origin, that is to say, wood, hemp, manila, cotton, turpentine, pitch, tar, linseed oil,and others.

Sails and cordage for yachts are now largely made from synthetic fibers — nylon, dacron, polypropylene. Modern marine paints and finishes are synthetic for the greater part. The most extensive and important application of plastics in boatbuilding to date is fiberglass, a combination of polyester resin and glass fiber reinforcement (GRP). Plastic foams are rapidly coming to the fore in boatbuilding for a variety of applications. Flexible compounds of polysulfides, urethane resin, or silicone rubber are replacing older caulking and bedding materials.

Traditionalists who are partisans of wood and who would insure the continuation of our heritage of wooden boats, usually deplore plastics of every sort and want no part of them. This is a mistake. Some of the new plastics are not only compatible with wood, but when used properly, serve to strengthen and to reinforce it, and to extend its usefulness. In fact, when applied to wood, the resulting combination is ideal for many boatbuilding uses and needs. What is being considered, of course, are the new thermoplastic glues, and the epoxy adhesives in particular. When correctly used, epoxy glue and adhesives can do things for wood which wood cannot possibly do for itself.

Over fifteen years ago, the late Sam Rabl in his now classic how-to manual, "Boatbuilding In Your Own Backyard," sang the praises of a "miracle adhesive" used for the construction of Fish Hawk, 18'x7'x1' 8" sportfisherman which Rabl designed and built for his own use.

That "miracle adhesive", so called, whose qualities did seem miraculous then, was an epoxy formulation. Epoxy glues were quite new at the time and all but unknown to the boatbuilding trade.

Epoxy glue is so good and so far superior to any and all boatbuilding adhesives which preceded it, that it should have been immediately and universally adopted throughout the trade, but it wasn't. On the contrary, its acceptance has been slow and spotty, and today after nearly two decades, there are still boat builders who are not using epoxy glue. Believe it or not, even to this day you will occasionally run across boatbuilders who have never heard of it. But more often, builders shy away from epoxy because they have been told that it is a health hazard, or they have picked up the mistaken notion that epoxy is very expensive. More often than not, detailed and reliable information about epoxy adhesives is unavailable, and sources of supply are not always easy to locate. It is almost as if there were a conspiracy to withhold epoxy from home builders and the small boat shop. Of course this is not so, but the effect of existing conditions of distribution is much the same.

Wood, the original boatbuilding material, is in trouble. Lumber is getting more expensive all the time, while quality declines. Dimensions, grades and species, long standard in the boat building trade are no longer to be found. The builder today must make do with what he can get, and often the pickings are slim.

This is where glue comes in. Short pieces can be spliced to get the longer lengths desired, and narrow strips, that often would otherwise be wasted, can be laminated to give curved shapes of exceptional strength and stiffness. For instance, where extra long, wide boards were once required for planking small boats with continuous, full-length strakes, the same or superior results can now be achieved by glue-splicing continuous strakes from two or even three short lengths. For strakes with large amounts of curve and twist, those spliced from several short pieces will be stronger, because in splicing, cross grain which splits easily can be avoided, as is not possible when a curved strake is cut from a single length of wide, straight board. No steambox at hand, laminated ribs glued up from thin strips bent to shape and clamped on forms until the glue hardens will serve just as well, and may even prove stiffer and stronger when properly done. Superior deck beams can be laminated to shape from relatively inexpensive spruce or Douglas fir construction lumber stripped on the circular saw while avoiding knots and other defects. Excellent substitutes for natural crook knees, breast hooks and other curved members can often be laminated from odds and ends of scrap lumber.

Although solid timber as grown is best for stems and keels and other large members exposed to wear and weather, these may be laminated, as a second choice. Oak can be glued reliably with epoxy glue, while joints in oak made with resorcinol glues are not to be trusted, especially if subjected to alternate soaking and drying out. The alternate expansion and contraction resulting from frequent and extensive changes in moisture content of wood subject glued joints to powerful strains which in time can cause failure if the joints are not perfectly made, and oak moves a lot in swelling and shrinking. This should be taken into account when considering large glued-up laminations of oak. Further, laminating large pieces is a relatively lengthy and expensive process. New converts to glue frequently want to glue everything, and have been known to go to extra trouble and expense to make up laminations when perfectly good sticks of solid timber could have been had for less money.

One other special application of the new glue, specifically epoxy glue, should be mentioned here. That is its use for mending splits and breaks in small craft planking. Formerly when splits or rents developed in the thin, softwood planking of small boats, it was necessary to replace the damaged planks, usually a difficult and lengthy operation. With epoxy, split planks are easily repaired on the boat, in most cases. The crack is filled with epoxy mix generally thickened to prevent it from leaking out before it sets, or it may be overlaid, or dammed, with masking tape to hold the glue in place until it sets. After the glue has hardened, the plank is as strong, or stronger than it was originally. A repair of this sort is possible with epoxy, as it is not with other glues which do not have epoxy's property of retaining full strength in wide applications.

Glue as an important boatbuilding material dates from the early decade of this century when casein glue came into general use for making hollow spruce spars. Previous to that casein glue had gained some acceptance

*Contd. from preceding page*

in Europe from laminated roof trusses. For best results, joints for casein glue must fit perfectly, and require forceful clamping pressure until the glue sets. Casein glue is not waterproof and must be protected from moisture. When these conditions are met, joints so glued are strong, reliable and lasting, and casein glue came into general use for hollow spars.

In the early 1940s shortly after the start of World War II, a new plastic glue was introduced into American boat yards engaged in war work. This was a urea resin glue in the form of a dry powder which was mixed with water before using. The first to make its appearance was colored with a green dye, and so became known in the boatyards as "green" glue. Later it took the form of a brown powder still sold today. Urea resin, while not waterproof, is considerably more water resistant than casein glue, as well as easier to mix and to use in small, quantities, and so it rather quickly replaced casein glue for boatyard use. Like casein, however, urea resin required close fitting joints and ample clamping pressure.

A few years after the appearance of urea resin, phenolic-resorcinol glues were introduced in American boatyards. To begin with there were a number of different formulations on the market, but all of them came to the boatbuilder as two separate components for mixing when used, consisting of a liquid resin reddish purple in color, and a catalyst in the form of a brownish powder. In one

To stiffen the mix to prevent it from sagging or running out of vertical joints before hardening, a thickening agent may be added, one of the best of which is Cab-O-Sil by the Cabot Co. of Boston. An excellent all-purpose surfacer and putty is made by working Union Carbide's phenolic microballoons into a Versamid-epoxy mix until the desired consistency is achieved. For bonding fabric of glass or synthetic fibers to wood, a thinner mix is desirable. Resins which have been thinned by dilutents should be avoided.

Fiberglass is quite a different ball game, that is to say molded fiberglass with polyester resin. It is not advisable to use polyester resin to bond to wood, as it does not have the adhesive of epoxy. For reinforcing plastic overlays on wood, polypropylene fabric is better than glass, as the former is more elastic, and can adjust better to dimensional changes in wood as the latter swells and shrinks. Dynel fabric may be laminated over polypropylene to take wear, as Dynel has superior abrasion resistance; yet, Dynel used alone over seamed construction like wood decking, splits easily along the seams. Polypropylene exposed to sunlight should be well painted to protect it from ultra-violet rays.

There are four main uses for plastics in wood, and composite wood-and-plastic, boatbuilding; (1) for gluing, as adhesives; (2) for sheathing, or overlaying, with fabric reinforcements; (3) for foams mainly for flotation (plastic foams are structural material competitive with

---

## "Plywood Boat Plan Directory"
**American Plywood Association,**
**Tacoma, Washington**
**1970, 47 pages, illustrated, paperbound $.25.**

This little booklet lists sources for plans of plywood boats. Listed, with brief descriptions

and outboard profiles, are six rowing boats, 27 outboard boats, 18 daysailers, 42 cruising sailboats, 45 power cruisers, 18 multihulls and 18 houseboats. In addition, there are general lists of boat plan suppliers, kit sources and one-design class associations.

---

particular respect these glues marked a great advance over all previous boatbuilding glues, except the cement developed for repairing canvas canoes. They were waterproof, or practically so. In other respects, clamping pressure and closely fitting joints, they were no improvement over urea resin. Both urea resin and resorcinol are thermosetting glues, that is, curing depends upon the temperature. Formulations of these glues distributed for boatyard use in general require working temperatures of 70 degrees F. and higher, a decided drawback for wintertime use in unheated buildings. Besides, resorcinol stains wood badly.

Fortunately, one of the best hardeners of all for general purpose adhesive formulations of epoxy is quite free of sensitizing effects and has been proven safe by wide and continued use. This is the polyamid co-reactant, Versamid 140, developed by General Mills and widely distributed under the name of Versamid, but also the same as Shell's Epon Hardener V-40, and CIBA's Pentamid 840.

Versamid 140, in combination with a standard medium-high viscosity epoxy resin such as Union Carbide's Bakelite ERL-2774 or Shell's Epon 828, will satisfy most boatbuilding needs.

As time goes on, the builder can try out more specialized mixes and formulations. Versamid mixes are especially suitable for boat work, giving a glue line which is tough and shock resistant. Mixing proportions are not critical. While 40 parts Versamid to 60 parts resin is normal for most boat yard uses, a half-and-half mix is frequently used.

wood and are a separate category like molded fiberglass); (4) for caulking, sealing and bedding compounds.

The market is flooded with an almost endless variety of flexible caulking and sealing compounds derived from polysulfides, silicon rubber and urethane. They are designed to stop leaks, which they sometimes accomplish and sometimes do not. In the latter instance they can do more harm than good, frequently contributing to rot. Not infrequently these flexible caulking compounds come loose in spots, admitting moisture into the seam, although it appears to be tight. Without solid caulking, beneath, this hidden break becomes a likely focus for rot. Frequently, a similar situation occurs when old decks are covered with polyester fiberglass to stop leaks. Water entering through small unobserved breaks, as almost inevitably develop, is trapped beneath the glass. Rot ensues and spreads rapidly, often hidden until well advanced.

Although wood-plastic composite construction has not been considered in detail, the essentials have been covered above. Composite construction is a matter of degree. When the use of plastic adhesives and fabric reinforcements and coverings enter into the structure to an important and indispensable extent, a new dimension in the utilization of wood as a boatbuilding material is attained. Composite wood-plastic construction is flexible and versatile. The superior qualities of the two materials supplement and reinforce each other. The inherent possibilities have not yet been grasped by designers to anything near the full extent of their potential.

*Contd. on next page*

*Contd. from preceding page*

Various formulations of epoxy resins were developed and used by industry during World War II, but for various reasons, epoxy glue, in spite of its superiority over previous boatbuilding glues, did not find its way into American boatyards until well into the 1950s, and then only in a few scattered instances at the start. The chemistry of epoxy is complex, and a great many different adhesive formulations, each with its own distinctive characteristics, are possible. By and large, private industry was not interested in publicizing the composition of formulations worked out for its various special requirements. And concerns offering epoxy formulations for sale to the boatbuilding trade rarely, if ever, tell what is in them.

It is quite true that epoxy glue purchased in this way is expensive and unnecessarily so. However, this is not the case when epoxy resins and hardeners are purchased in gallons or even quarts from plastic distributing firms which supply industry. Such concerns distribute the standard plastic products manufactured by the chemical giants, including Union Carbide, Shell, Ciba, Dow, General Mills, Koppers and some       ers. While they are prepared to furnish resins in tank car lots, most will sell by the gallon and even by the quart. Such secondary distributors are situated throughout the country, and may be located by consulting the standard business directories. Some of these distributors in addition to supplying plastics products, are also helpful sources of information about plastics. One such in the Northeast deserving mention is Allied Resin Corporation, East Weymouth, Massachusetts. Another is the Miller-Stephenson Chemical Co. Inc. of Danbury, Conn., also located in Los Angeles, Chicago and Toronto.

Most of the large chemical corporations manufacturing thermosetting resins and other plastic materials can provide descriptive specifications for their products. These data sheets are worth getting and studying. They are supplied on request. Boatbuilders with an interest in plastics will do well to avail themselves of such information.

There is some published material on fiberglassing, part of which is not wholly reliable, I must add. So far very little on epoxy adhesives is to be found in books, and the same goes for composite construction in which epoxy adhesives and synthetic fiber reinforcements are used with wood. Worth noting in this connection is "The Use Of Plastics in Boatbuilding," an International Marine Publishing Co. reprint of articles appearing some years previous in the "National Fisherman." While some of the addresses given are no longer operative, most of the information is still valid and useful, with some of them not to be found in print elsewhere.

To sum up on the matter of cost, if epoxy resins and hardeners are purchased from plastics distributors in the amount of quarts and gallons, as will be needed for almost any building or repair project of any size, the materials required need not be expensive, at least no more so then most other materials, and relatively less than some, for instance bronze screws. Considering possible savings in the cost of boat lumber when epoxy adhesives are used, their use may even be economy.

As for epoxy being a health hazard, this need not be so, and I for one, and numerous others that I know, have been using epoxy adhesives for years with no observable ill effects. The epoxy resins in themselves are quite harmless, I am convinced, although it is conceivable that an occasional individual could be allergic to epoxy resin, as a few individuals are allergic to milk, lobsters, cat fur and other usually harmless things.

118

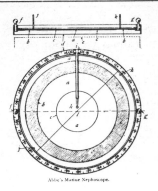

Abbe's Marine Nephoscope.

## Nautical Charts

Basically, there are three sources of nautical charts in this country -- the National Ocean Survey (formerly known as the Coast and Geodetic Survey), the U. S. Naval Oceanographic Office and the Lake Survey Center. The National Ocean Survey publishes charts covering the coast of the U. S. and its territories and possessions. The Naval Oceanographic Office publishes and distributes charts covering the oceans and foreign coasts. The Lake Survey Center publishes and distributes charts covering the Great Lakes and other major lakes.

For a free list of U. S. Naval Oceanography Office charts and publications, send for "Catalog of Nautical Charts." This comes in two parts -- Special Purpose Navigational Charts and Publications ( N. O. Pub. No. 1-N-A) and Miscellaneous Charts and Sheets (N. O. Pub. No. 1-N-B). The catalog will tell you what is available, how much it costs and whom it can be ordered from. U. S. Naval Oceanographic Office, Washington, D. C. 20390.

For a free list of National Ocean Survey charts and selected publications relating to charts, send for the "Nautical Chart Catalog." This comes in three parts -- # 1 covers the Atlantic and Gulf Coasts, # 2 covers the Pacific Coast (including Hawaii, Guam and Samoa Islands), and # 3 covers Alaska and the Aleutian Islands. National Ocean Survey, Rockville, Maryland 20852.

For a free list of charts and selected publications put out by the Lake Survey Center, send for the "Chart Catalog," which comes in one part only. Lake Survey Center, 630 Federal Bldg., Detroit, Michigan 48226.

In addition, for charts of Canadian waters published by the Canadian government, send for "Coastal and Inland Waters Catalog." Canadian Hydrographic Service,   Department of Mines and Technical Surveys, 615 Booth Street, Ottawa, Canada.

## FIBERGLASS KIT BOATS AND BARE HULLS

### By Jack Wiley

The following is a list of manufacturers of fiberglass kit boats and bare hulls. These companies regularly supply fiberglass moldings for home completion: many offer complete kits. Sample prices are included for some boats. These are intended only as approximations at the time of writing and prices, as well as specifications, are subject to change without notice. In most cases the prices are FOB.

**Blue Buoy Yacht Corp.**
**1922 Oak St.**
**Torrance, Calif. 90501**
—24' to 50' cruising auxiliary sailboats

**Blue Water Boats**
**21920 75th Ave., S.E.**
**Woodinville, Wash. 98072**
—38' Colin Archer-type double-ender designed by William W. Atkin, Ingrid (boat name). Ideal for world cruising. Basic hull with sheer clamp, $6,000; shipping cradle, $200; plans $30.

**Cox Marine Ltd.**
**The Shipyard**
**Brightlingsea, Essex, England**
—32' cruising/racing trimaran. One of the first fiberglass ocean-going trimarans to be available for home completion. Name of boat, Cox 32.

**Dreadnought Boatworks**
**P.O. Box 221**
**Carpinteria, Calif. 93013**
—16'6" Norwegian rowing dory. Bare hull, $185.
—32' version of John G. Hanna's Tahiti. Name of boat, Dreadnought 32. Ideal design for world cruising. Basic hull (balsa core sandwich construction), $3,880; major bulkhead, $75; bilge stringers, $65; engine base/sump, $165 (installation, $25); shaft log, $25 (installation, $25); ballast (6000 lbs. bonded into keel ), $1,000; deck installed (with molded-in non-skid, balsa core sandwich construction, and hatch cover), $3,300; cockpit, $95; rudder and fittings installed, $400; chainplates installed, $250; fitted tanks installed (fiberglass, fuel and water, 40 gals.) each, $125; engine installation of your choice, $250. First Dreadnought 32 to be launched sailed from San Francisco to Hawaii in 21 days.

**Easterly Yachts**
**P.O. Box 9104**
**(1729 Lake Ave.)**
**Metairie, La. 70005**
—30' auxiliary sailboat. Name of boat, Easterly 30. Basic kit, $4,250. Price includes hull and deck bonded together with 4 basic bulkheads in place; furnished loose are 3 hatches, 8 windows and rudder. All construction is the same as is used in factory-completed Easterly 30.

**Glander Boats, Inc.**
**R.R. No. 1, Box 140**
**Tavernier, Fla. 33070**
—23' and 33' cruising auxiliary sailboats.

**Hughes Boat Works Ltd.**
**Centralia Industrial Park**
**Huron Park, Ont., Canada**
—25' to 48' cruising/racing auxiliary sailboats. Name of boats, North Star. North Star 38, bare hull, $5,000; deck and cabin, $3,000; other components available.

**Lakeview Boat Co.**
**Box 5595**
**Riverside, Calif. 92507**
—15' canoe kit, $130; also 17' canoe and 13' kayak.

**Luger Industries, Inc.**
**3800 West Highway 13**
**Burnsville, Minn. 55378**
—14' to 20' sailboats. Complete kit for 14', $299.
—14' to 32' powerboats. Complete kit for 14' outboard, less motor, $399.

**McCutcheon Boat Works**
**Ferry Avenue**
**Charlevoix, Mich. 49720**
—30' racing/cruising ketch. Bare hull, $3,000; available in any stage of completion.

**Mount Desert Yacht Yard, Inc.**
**Mount Desert, Me.**
—24' to 36' cruising auxiliary sailboats.

**Plastrend (Division of Dan Ray, Inc.)**
**1005 Blue Mound Rd.**
**(Hwy. 156)**
**Ft. Worth, Tex. 76131**
—40' auxiliary sailboat. Kit is ready to sail with bare interior.

**Reliance Sailing Craft Co.**
**P.O. Box 693**
**St. Laurent (Montreal), P.Q., Canada**
—44' auxiliary sailboat. Name of boat, Reliance 44. Bare hull (deep keel model), $6,500; bare hull (keel centerboard), $7,000; deck and superstructure, $4,500. Designed mainly with offshore cruising in mind.

**Ron Rawson, Inc.**
**15014 N.E. 90 St.**
**Redmond, Wash. 98052**
—30'6" cruising auxiliary sailboat. Boat name, Rawson 30. All fiberglass components, $5,200.
—32' powerboat.

**Sailcrafter Yachts (Columbia and Coronado Yacht Corp.)**
**275 McCormick Ave.**
**Costa Mesa, Calif. 92626**
—22' to 57' cruising/racing auxiliary sailboats. All materials are furnished for completion; also available at any stage of completion from hull only to nearly finished boat. Many special features simplify assembly.

**Sailing Kit Kraft (Morgan Yacht Corp.)**
**P.O. Box 13247**
**St. Petersburg, Fla. 33733**
—22' to 41' cruising/racing auxiliary sailboats. Bare hull for 22' $1,254; other components available.

119

Snap-link.

_Contd. on next page_

*Contd. from preceding page*

**Sea and Air Products, Inc.**
**P.O. Box 821**
**Rockland R.**
**So. Norwalk, Conn. 06856**
—18' to 26' catamaran deck and cabin boats. Hulls for 18', $438. Ideal for houseboats.

**Seafarer Fiberglass Yachts, Inc.**
**Huntington, N.Y. 11743**
—7'1" dinghy, rowing and sailing models.
—23' to 48' auxiliary sailboats. Hull for 23', $950; other components available.

**South Coast Seacraft, Inc.**
**P.O. Box 1674**
**Shreveport, La. 71102**
—21' to 28' sailboats. Hull and deck assembled for 22', $1595.

**Spencer Boats, Ltd.**
**1240 Twigg Road**
**Richmond, B.C.**
—31' to 51' sailboats. Name of boats, Spencer. Hull for 31', $3,268; hull, rudder, lead ballast in place, fuel and water tanks molded in, $4,985. A Spencer 35 was sailed around the Pacific Rim by Hal Roth and his wife. The cruise was chronicled in "Two on a Big Ocean." $8.95.

**Trailcraft, Inc.**
**P.O. Box 606**
**Concordia, Kan. 66901**
—13'6" kayak. Complete kit, $89.
—12' crossbreed canoe. Complete kit, $119.
—14' to 18' canoes. Complete kits, $129 to $144.

**Tyler Boat Co. Ltd.**
**Sovereign Close**
**Tonbridge, Kent, England**
—21' to 49' auxiliary sailboats. Both cruising and racing designs. Designs under 30' that are suitable for world cruising.
—18' to 75' powerboats.

**Tylercraft, Inc.**
**1439 Montauk Hwy.**
**Oakdale, Long Island, N.Y. 11769**
—24' to 29' cruising/racing auxiliary sailboats.

**Vineyard Yachts, Inc.**
**Beach Road**
**Vineyard Haven, Mass. 02568**
—21'7" and 32' powerboats with displacement-type hulls. Basic hull for 21'7", $2,000; deck and cabin, $1,100. Basic hull for 32', $4,200; deck and cabin, $1,900.

**Westsail Corp.**
**177 Monrovia Ave.**
**Costa Mesa, Calif. 92626**
—32' cruising auxiliary sailboat. Name of boat, Westsail 32. Hull with main and engine room bulkheads, $4,200; trunk cabin including cockpit but without trim or windows, $2,063. Ideal for living aboard or world cruising. Double-ender with long keel and 19,000 lbs. of displacement.

120

**Yacht Constructors, Inc.**
**7031 N.E. 42nd Ave.**
**Portland, Ore. 97218**
29', 36' and 42' auxiliary sailboats. Name of boat, Cascade. Bare hull for 29', $1,775. Bare hull for 36', $3,650. Bare hull for 42', $4,950. Known for high quality moldings. Have modules to simplify interior construction.

**Yachtcraft (Islander Yachts, Inc.)**
**1682 Placentia Ave.**
**Costa Mesa, Calif. 92627**
—23' to 55' auxiliary sailboats, many designs. Hull, cradle, and deck for 23' swing keel, $1,145.

**Yorktown Yachts**
**700 Henry Ford Ave.**
**Long Beach, Calif. 90813**
—33' and 35' cruising auxiliary sailboats. Builders who have completed these boats seemed very satisfied. Space is available for building at the plant.

**Recommended book:**

Hundreds of these boats have already been launched. Thousands of others are now being constructed. It is difficult to estimate how many people there are who are dreaming of starting. "Fiberglass Kit Boats" by Jack Wiley (published by International Marine Publishing Co., Camden, Me. 04843) is the first comprehensive source of information of this exciting new approach to owning the fiberglass boat of your dreams.

Raceabout.

## Shore Leave

The average crew of a deepwater racing sailboat will generate $650 in incidental sales ashore per week, according to a study completed by the Marine Advisory Service, University of Rhode Island, Narragansett Bay Campus, Narragansett, R. I. 02882.

The data is but one item in the analysis titled - "Economic Impact of Block Island Race Week." The author, Joseph F. Farrell, sought to identify the amount of shore-side business that the bi-annual regatta brought to the small island off the Rhode Island coast. The $650 includes expenditures for marina fees, registration, groceries, souvenirs, clothing, meals ashore, beverages, fuel, phone calls, tips etc.

The fleet of 196 boats spent $127,400 on the above plus an additional $19,750 on lodgings. The estimate Race Week income for the island is put at $219,238. The impact on the June business was 35% higher than during the same month in non-race years.

—NAEBM Intercom

"Shipshape and Bristol Fashion" by Loren R. Borland.
Van Nostrand Reinhold, New York.
1969, 214 pp., illustrated, $5.95.

When you get right down to it, most practical books on small-boat seamanship repeat the same basic information — the difference among them being how well they do the job. This book is a departure from that state of affairs. Most of the information presented by Borland can't be found elsewhere; it is a distillation of the knowledge he has acquired over the years as a cruising man.

The book consists of 65 articles on diverse subjects, each a contribution of real merit. There are 11 chapters: Sails and Rigging, Spars and Bowsprits, Deck Fittings, Engines and Machinery, Instruments and Electrical Systems, Interiors, Ground Tackle, Canvas Work and Marlinespike Seamanship, The Dinghy, Navigation and Miscellaneous.

To give you an idea of how unique Barland's contributions are, here are a few I like best: A toggle and becket for a headsail sheet fastening rather than a snap shackle; a combination mooring-bitt and ventilator; two designs for sinks that will drain regardless of what tack a sailboat is on; the uses of the clothespin at sea; a steering extension for an outboard motor that will also control the throttle; and a short list of American terms with their English equivalents.

Another book which does the same thing, but with different content, is "Handyman Afloat and Ashore" by Ken Bramham (Adlard Coles, London, 1970, 192 pp., illustrated, $6.95).
Among other things — electric lighting

## Hate to Clean Brushes?

Many times you'll be wanting to apply another coat of the same paint tomorrow. Instead of bothering to clean the brush it is often easier to drop it into a small can of plain water. The water will keep the brush from hardening for a day or so and can be easily shaken out or wiped off before using the brush to paint with again.

The polyester resins used in fiberglass can also be kept from hardening on brushes for a day or two by liberally mashing the bristles into a wet bar of soap (Ivory or Lava will do) and placing them in a small jar of water which has been heavily laced with the same soap. Be sure to wash the soap off thoroughly the next day before use.

Fiberlay, Inc. of 1158 Fairview Ave. N., Seattle, Wash. 98109, sells what they call "Resin Rinse." This stuff is used for cleaning hands and brushes of polyester resin and works well. A few drops on a brush and worked in well by hand enables water to wash everything away. Two or three applications and washings cleans things up much faster and better than acetone. Resin Rinse sells for about $3 a pint and lasts quite a long time.

—Mark White

without an engine, homemade ventilators, cabin tables, homemade water tanks, homemade through-hull fittings, homemade stern tube, two pails for stowing anchor warp, molding your own cleats and other fittings from fiberglass.

—PHS

**121**

From "Shipshape and Bristol Fashion"

An outboard motor for the dinghy is a very convenient thing to have aboard a cruising boat, but it must be small and light in weight to be practical. This usually means that its fuel tank is very small, so one is compelled to carry some spare fuel in the dinghy and to expect to have to fill the tank occasionally while under way.

In even the slightest chop, pouring fuel from a can into the fuel tank becomes an almost hopeless job, with a large part of the fuel going overboard or, worse yet, into the dinghy. We have found an almost ideal solution in quart size plastic "squeeze bottles" with mouths small enough to be easily inserted into the filler opening. Our little motor's tank is not quite filled by one of these bottles, so we never need worry about the tank overflowing while it is being filled. We just run it dry, and then we know it will hold more than the contents of one of the bottles.

The cap is removed, the neck of the bottle is quickly inserted into the filler opening, and the bottle is squeezed until it is empty. A rack for four of these bottles with a length of shock-cord to hold them in place, can usually be fitted to the underside of a thwart or in some other unused space in the dinghy, and will provide a reserve supply of fuel, always at hand and with no need for the always missing funnel.

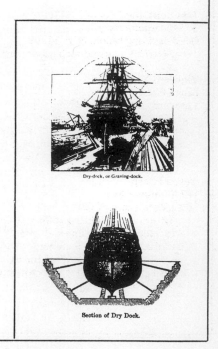

Dry-dock, or Graving-dock.

Section of Dry Dock.

⊕ "Boatbuilding and Repairing with Fiberglass" by
   Melvin D.C. Willis.
**International Marine Publishing Co., Camden, Me.
1972, 178 pp., illustrated, bibliography, index, $9.95.**

⊕ "Foam Sandwich Boatbuilding" by Peter Wynn.
**International Marine Publishing Co., Camden, Me
1972, illustrated, $9.95.**

There are easily more fiberglass boats built these days than wood ones, yet there are many, many more boatbuilding books on wood than on fiberglass. Why this is true is hard to imagine. Maybe book publishers operate under the erroneous assumption that fiberglass construction isn't for the amateur. Either one of

these books will convince you that you, too, can build a fiberglass boat in your own backyard.

Willis deals primarily with molded fiberglass construction — you build a mold and then hand lay-up the hull in the mold. This is the method used by most production boatbuilders.

The author takes you from the beginning to the end and includes facts most authors leave out and most readers want in: costs and sources of supply. He gives you honest analyses of what it will cost you to build various types of fiberglass boats. Willis also devotes a large amount of space to repairing damaged fiberglass boats, a subject seldom discussed elsewhere (Yes, Madison Avenue, it's true. Fiberglass boats

*Contd. on next page*

From "Boatbuilding and Repairing . . . "

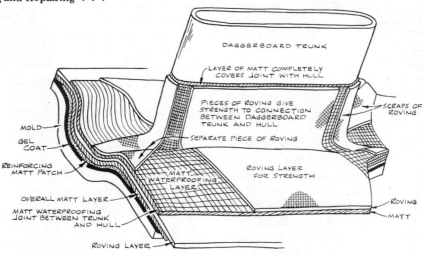

FIGURE 2-38. *The daggerboard trunk attached to the hull.*

### DYNEL

Dynel is a synthetic fabric about one-half the weight of fiberglass cloth. It is compatible with both polyester and epoxy resins. It has good abrasion resistance, high tensile strength, is soft to the touch, and is not irritating to the skin when sanded. The most easily worked of the fabrics presently available, Dynel can be stretched around curves and sharp corners more easily than Vectra or fiberglass. However, despite its good tensile strength, several experts say it should not be used alone because of lack of strength. Except on small plywood boats, Dynel should be used only over a layer of fiberglass. It is recommended primarily as an overlay because it produces a slick finish when sanded, or a canvas-like finish when applied to walkways or decks with a minimum of resin. Also, it has high abrasion resistance, as it is four times as tough as fiberglass. Dynel is a very subdued tan or buff color before it is wetted out, whereas fiberglass is a silver color.

### PRICE OF DYNEL

Dynel comes in one weight from Defender Industries that seems comparable to 10 oz. fiberglass cloth. It is available in widths of 38", 42", 48", and 60". Prices for the 48" width are as follows: $1.57 per yard when bought by the yard, and $1.12 per yard when over 125 yards are purchased. See the Defender Industries catalog for a further price breakdown and an interesting discussion of Dynel's properties and use.

*Contd. from preceding page*

have been known to leak, crack, craze, become holed, and come apart at the seams).

Wynn is a true amateur who decided to learn everything he could about foam sandwich construction and then build his own boat. This book is the result of that experience and is most valuable because of it. The author fell into many pits and is good enough to pass the information on to the reader, who, armed with it, should gain from the knowledge.

Foam sandwich construction is just that; you are sandwiching a layer of foam between two layers of fiberglass. The result is a strong,

buoyant hull that does not require expensive and time-consuming molds. Much of the custom boatbuilding done today in fiberglass utilizes this method, which is tailor-made for the amateur (Sir Thomas Lipton, the boat that won the 1968 singlehanded transatlantic race, was built in foam sandwich).

The one fault in Wynn's excellent book is that the suppliers listed in the back are all in Britain (the author is an Englishman). But then again, you can save money ordering from England, so the fault could very well turn into an asset.

—PHS

From "Foam Sandwich Boatbuilding"

14. The first piece of foam has been screwed into place while the second piece has been screwed on at the keel and is ready for cutting. Because the curves on the dinghy were so tight we had to use narrow pieces of foam; on a larger boat larger pieces of foam can be used, which is much quicker.

It is possible that an amateur built foam sandwich boat will not be quite as symmetrical and as well finished as the professional job. And it will almost certainly be heavier because amateurs tend to increase the sizes of fitting and to add extra pieces of unnecessary resinglass all over the place (I have to plead guilty I am afraid). It is, however, extremely unlikely that an amateur will ever make a leaky or unsafe foam sandwich boat (provided the design is good).

Leaks in a foam sandwich craft are very rare. There are virtually two boats, one inside the other, and both of them are made from resinglass, which, for all practical purposes, can be considered impervious to water.

# Models and Modeling

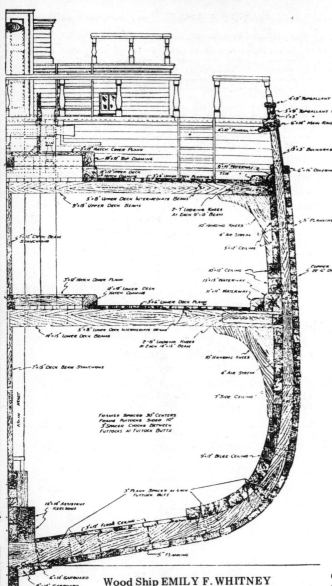

Wood Ship EMILY F. WHITNEY
from Underhill's "Deep Water Sail."

124

## SUPPLIERS

### Just Kits:

When you begin to look about for ship and boat model kits your eyes are opened to how many people must be enjoying this hobby and, for some, profession. There are hundreds available. Most firms which sell the kits also sell materials; fittings, various woods, tools and specialty items. The larger and better-known firms are these:

A.J. Fisher, Inc.
1002 Etowah Ave.
Royal Oak, Michigan 48067

For almost 50 years Fisher has manufactured and sold good ship model kits and fittings. In fact, they are the manufacturers of the fittings many other model firms carry.

**From Fisher catalog.**

FISHER SELF TACKING VANE STEERING GEAR

Brass material used; stampings and machined parts eliminate use of wire construction, except on tiller. Balsa wood Feather furnished. The gear is attached to your deck with three small screws; tiller clamps to rudder post. Complete ready to use, with sailing instructions.

No. 541 Fisher Self Tacking Vane Gear, brass finish.............. $30.00

## On Models

Only a W. C. Fields could hate ship models and get away with it and, even then, only because we somehow knew he was being paid. What can you say? Whether it is an exquisite better-than-perfect museum piece or the crudest of toy block boats, there is something very compelling about models. They are so reasonable! You can buy one completed by a master. You can make one from scratch. You can split the difference and make one from a kit. This is a boat and ship model information kit.

—GP

### Baltimore Clipper Schooner **DAPPER TOM**     An 8 Gun Privateer of 1815

Over All Model Specifications: LENGTH 24"—HEIGHT 18"—SCALE $\frac{3}{32}$"=1 Ft.

This model represents a popular type of privateer during the first decades of the 19th century. Only a fast, well handled ship could be reasonably sure of reaching its destination, since all commerce was subjected to the legalized banditry of privateers. The privateer depended upon its sailing qualities and fire power to prey upon foreign ships, and also to escape men-of-war (mainly British) which patroled the seas.

#MS3162 — Machine carved hull, with accurately carved bulwarks and transom; material for deck furniture, keel, stem, shaped spars, and other woods parts. Pine hull. Complete kit, consisting of hull set, fittings, plans, and instructions .........$30.50

#MS3163 — Complete kit, same as above but with mahogany hull.............................. 34.00

#MS3164 — Plans (set of 2 including 2-color rigging plan by Da Vinci) and instructions $ 1.50

The Bliss people do not make their own, but they sell several lines of both imported and domestic model kits, tools and fittings. Their lines are very complete, but a bit high-priced and their popularity causes them to be out-of-stock now and again. Their lines of miniature working steam-engines, boilers and fittings will capture your imagination, your heart and your wallet.

Above and below items from Bliss catalog.

James Bliss & Co., Inc.
Route 128 (Exit 61)
Dedham, Mass. 02026.
Catalog is 60 cents

## STUART ENGINES

## LAUNCH TWIN ENGINE
### With Cast Iron Cylinders
### Castings and all Materials
Single Expansion— 1-in. Bore, $\frac{7}{8}$-in. Stroke
Height, 5½-in.   Length, 5¼-in.   Weight, 4-lb.

The Single Expansion Engine has the advantage of having no dead centres.

The Launch Engines are designed for boats 4-ft. 6-in. to 6-ft. long and are really beautiful "Exhibition" Models.

**Parts include**—Cylinder Casting, 2 Valve Chests and Covers, 2 Valves, 2 Cylinder Covers, 2 Cylinder Bottoms, 2 Crossheads, 2 Eccentric Sheaves, Straps and Rods, 2 Connecting Rods, Sole Plate, 3 Bearing Caps, 2 Steam and Exhaust Tee Flanges, Slide Bar Bracket, 4 Glands, 2 Steam Flanges, 2 Pistons.

**Sundries.**—Crankshaft, Cast Iron Disc Wheel, 5 Steel Columns, 2 Slide Bars, Steel, for Lagging, 2 each Piston and Valve Rods, Steam and Exhaust Pipes, Hard Brass for Valve Rod Heads, 4 Piston Rings.

**Bolts,** Studs, Nuts and Screws    **Drawings.**—Fully dimensioned.    11-lb.

W. D. writes :—

"I must compliment you on the very thorough way you send these sets of castings out and the excellent quality of the material supplied ; from the clear measurements given on the Blue Print, it should not be difficult to make up this Twin Cylinder Launch Engine."

**Fig. 3837** Reversing Gear Castings ............................................................... $ 9.50

**Fig. 3836** Drawings and materials for Launch Engine Castings ...................... 44.50

125

Model Shipways carries a relatively small but solid line of models and fittings. A nice touch featured in their catalog is .001"-and .002"-thick copper sheathing for the ultimate touch on the ship's bottom!

Model Shipways Co., Inc.
39 W. Fort Lee Road.
Bogota, N.J. 07603.
Catalog is 60 cents

Above and below from Model Shipways catalog.

### COPPER SHEATHING PLATES

In sizes practical for sheathing models ⅛" scale and larger. Saves the scissoring, pressing, wastage, time. Apply with contact cement. .002" thick, in ½ oz. packets.

| No. | Size | Pieces per pkt. | | Per pkt. |
|---|---|---|---|---|
| 976—¼" x ½" | | 375, approx. | ........................... | $1.75 |
| 977—5/16" x ¾" | | 200, approx. | ........................... | $1.25 |

Each packet of plates, allowing for 10% overlap, will cover approximately 42 sq. in.

### SHEATHING COPPER

The .001 and .002 can be cemented to the hull of a smaller model.
Sheets are 6" x 12".

| No. 950 Thickness | Per Sheet |
|---|---|
| .001" | $.55 |
| .002" | .65 |
| .005" | .75 |

The people at Ships Unlimited seem to love their work because they have put out the best catalog in the business and if you are serious about models, or want to be, you should have them on tap. They have several lines of excellent kits, the best and then some, for they are distributors of "The Lumber Addition," the North Shire Deadeyes model club supply of fine seasoned cut-to-scale lumber stock of woods you can get nowhere else.

Ships Unlimited
Ship Model Dept.
P.O. Box 32,
Morton Grove, III. 60053

No. 606
JOLLY ROGER
19" h, 4 lbs.
**$24.95**
Plus $2.00 Shipping Charge

## SHIPS UNLIMITED

Items above and right from Ships Unlimited catalog.

Scientific has a line of relatively inexpensive, slightly simplified wood model kits. As-is, they are a bit rough but good values and, with a bit of extra care, excellent values.

126

Scientific Models, Inc.
340 Snyder Ave.
Berkley Heights, N.J. 07922.
Catalog is 25 cents.

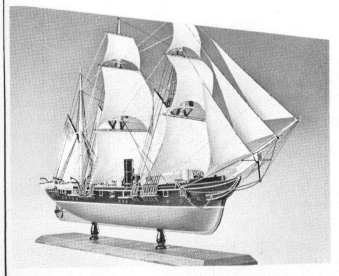

From Scientific Models catalog.

### Kit 166 U.S.S. KEARSARGE, CIVIL WAR GUNBOAT

The U.S.S. Kearsarge was one of the first gunboats built for the American Navy. During the Civil War, she engaged the Confederate vessel, "Alabama" in a famous battle off the coast of France (June 19th, 1864), where the "Alabama" was left a sinking wreck. Our large (27") authentic scale model is an exact replica of the original. The prefabricated kit features a carved wood hull and many precision cast metal fittings — including: combination deadeyes, cannons, carronades, running lights, realistic cloth sails, ladder, steering wheels, kedge anchors, etc. Also included are brass belaying pins, chain, metal nameplate, wood display stand and complete assembly instructions. Display it in your home.

**Length 27"; Height 14¼"**
**price $24.95**

# 1/96 Scale Beautifully Detailed
## Sailing Ships

Items from Revell catalog.

Plastic models. Yes, I know what you mean but, you know, some of them are very good and, technically, some of them are superb if you research your model, add the appropriate rigging and take special care in finishing. Surely there is something not quite the same, but for 10% of the cost of a wood kit and vast savings in construction time, if that's important to you, it gets an acceptable model on the mantle and may make a model-builder of someone you love. You have seen Revell model kits in the local toy department but the offerings are generally incomplete. Best get their catalog. Someone once told me that Eastern-bloc intelligence agents would be first in line for their latest kits. That would seem to be a reasonable standard for accuracy!

**DEFIANCE Jet Propelled Boat**   H-435   Length 15".
The most modern and versatile craft in the U.S. Navy.

Revell Incorporated.
4223 Glencoe Ave.
Venice, Calif. 90292

Ice scooter.
A, boat in motion; B, boat placed so as to show bottom of hull with steel runners.

## Modeling Tools

Most of the firms which sell model kits and supplies also sell tools, but the tools are a sideline for them. Here are the outfits which deal in tools exclusively. Their range of tools for the model-builder is bigger, better and usually cheaper when tools and not other stuff are the order of the day.

Items from Brookstone catalog.

### AT LAST! A MINIATURE WELDING TORCH AT A REASONABLE PRICE!

Brookstone is wonderful, a young-feeling organization daring you to name something it won't carry if given a chance. They comb the tool industry looking for reasonable tools that "don't exist" or which "do exist somewhere" but are scattered all over the marketplace. They have found them and put them in one catalog. The prices are fair and the service is excellent. The model-builder without this catalog is either very fortunate, a good make-doer or uninformed.

127

Brookstone Company
Peterborough, N.H.
Their catalog is free.

**H-2042.0-A**   Miniature welding torch.
SPECIFY STRAIGHT OR CURVED TIPS.
SPECIFY STANDARD ("B" size) OR AIRCRAFT
("A" size) FITTINGS . . . . . . . . . . . . . . . $49.95

**J-1297.1** Miniature anvil . . . . . . . . . . . . . . . $6.95
Three & up . . . . . . . . . . . . . . . . . . Each $5.95

### Specialty Tools and Supplies

Most specialty materials required by the model-maker are available from the outfits listed earlier. Some few are not. Those which sometimes seem impossible to locate are listed here:

Ideas and sources in this department are needed and wanted.

High-quality rigging thread — linen, silk and hemp:

Thomas Hornsby
537 Boyer Road
Cheltenham, Penn. 19012

Storage and working space modules:

National Camera
2000 West Union Avenue
Englewood, Colorado 80110

### Specialty metal construction shapes and pieces

Milled Shapes, Inc.
1701 N. 33rd
Melrose Park, Ill. 60160

OIL REFINERY SCALE MODEL BUILT WITH M.S. STRUCTURAL BRASS SHAPES

### COMPACT PORTABLE WORK STATIONS

Cleverly designed for organizing jobs so that parts and hand tools can be easily transported, displayed and used. When fully extended becomes a 4' station with over 500 cubic inches of storage space. Provides 48 compartments for easy access and visibility. Each tray divides into 4 sections -- by use of 12 snuggly fitted dividers. Holds hundreds of parts and tools -- no wasted space. Load and stack or carry to production line. Made of high impact polystyrene. Folds into 12" cube.

**P-0605**                                                      **$32.**⁷⁰

Smaller version of P-0605 -- extends into 31" station with 30 compartments. Complete with 10 dividers.

**P-0606**                                                      **$7.**⁷⁵

**D-2960**              Extra Dividers - Pkg. 10                  .70

### FINISHED MODELS AND PLANS

Model builders interested in sources of model plans of ships and boats will want to add The Channings to their files. They offer several vessels, most in 3/16 scale, and they are excellent. Small craft modelers will be particularly interested in their Beetle Whaleboat Plans With Complete Equipment which they offer at $5 per set.

The Channings
P.O. Box 552
Marion, Mass. 02738

Gorgonia (Gorgonia flabellum).

## Models and Plans

Some will want the completed model, stock or custom-built. Most everyone would like plans but, for some reason, most think that plans and drawings are either not available, or available only through high-priced proprietary sources and so in the now-high-priced marine print department.

Not true. Plans and drawings are available very reasonably. There are companies that specialize in stock plans and drawings and, if you know the name of the designer of a particular vessel, study plans can often be acquired very reasonably, either from the designer himself or from the curator of his estate. In the case of a living designer, write him that you wish to study the plans or build a model only. If the designer is deceased, the estate is either held by an existing derivative firm or is curated by a marine museum or university department of naval architecture. M. I. T., Department of Naval Architecture, maintains a very comprehensive master file on the location of design estates and collections and an inquiry there will usually get you the name and address of where you can write or call for a copy of the design you are seeking, usually a marine museum, the Smithsonian Institution in Washington, D. C., or some such source.

## An Unusual Outfit

CokerCraft is a most unusual organization. It sells imported models, ship's plans and drawings and, what I mean, a lot of them! Hundreds of completed miniature models are offered, most of them of foreign navy vessels, but many commercial and passenger vessels are offered too. The models, drawings and plans are very reasonably priced and the catalog itself is an education. Their plans and drawings will probably give you a touch of acquisitive lust.

Dear Fellow Ship Enthusiasts:

For the past five years we have been offering you the finest naval and marine items that we can find through our international contacts. We deeply appreciate the confidence that you have shown in us with your comments, referrals and assistance. We will continue to obtain new material for your inspection, vigorously press our own development of new items and give you the best personal service possible.

Henceforth we shall publish a new catalog every second year (even years), and during the interims rely on supplements as necessary. It is our policy to publish a top rate product, in itself a collector's item, which will be around long after others are discarded.

Once again our thanks for your support. Drop us a line and tell us about your projects. Remember we are model builders too, and appreciate knowing what you are doing and seeing photos of your work. If you have any questions, we will be happy to answer them, but to facilitate a reply, please enclose a stamped self-addressed envelope.

**129**

CokerCraft
P.O. Box 124
Charleston, S.C. 29402

Yours truly,

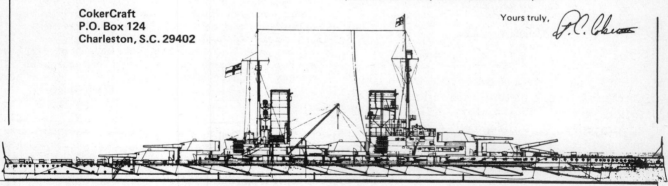

## Selected U.S. Publications

Uncle Sam's Printing Office is one of the greatest sources of useful information in ready-to-read form that we know of. Books, booklets, pamphlets and prints are offered for sale at prices so low that it makes the national debt readily understandable. Information on virtually everything is here, but reaching paydirt in this mountain of words is something else. One easy way to stay abreast of current production (and even this only skims the surface) is to subscribe (free) to "Selected U. S. Government Publications," an 8-page twice-monthly listing. Not only will you find publications of marine interest here on occasion, but you'll also discover information for which the government has paid thousands to make life easier (and perhaps more rewarding) for you.

—DRG

## Inlaid Artistry

F. Kerridge
41 Beverley Road
South Cave
Brough, Yorkshire
England

This fellow's craft is marquetry, which is the process of making pictures with various types of inlaid wood. The color version of the accompanying photograph gives a better indication of the quality of his work, which is remarkable.

—PHS

Dear Mr. Spectre:

I mainly specialize in reproducing photographs of ships in marquetry. I first enlarge the picture to the size commissioned by the customer. The drawing is then transferred to the wood. The veneers are then cut in accordance with the drawing. This means that in the old type sailing ships and clippers I would insert thousands of small pieces of veneer for the rigging alone. The veneers I use come from all over the world so that I can get the different grains and colours to highlight the particular subject. After every piece of veneer is inserted the subject is then sandpapered and polished.

Any type of boat or ship can be reproduced in the form of a picture or as a design on a table or any other piece of furniture. This work can look particularly impressive in wood-panelled walls. I enclose a photograph of a finished picture done for a shipping Co. for their entrance hall. The finished size was 5 ft. by 3 ft. Of course even larger pictures can be done just from a small photograph.

The price is controlled by the amount of work involved. An estimate can be given free of charge on receipt of the customer's photograph.

Yours sincerely,
F. Kerridge

"Handbook of Knots" by Raoul Graumont.
Cornell Maritime Press, Cambridge, Md.
1945, 194, pp., illustrated, glossary, index,
    softbound, $2.50

Not as bulky and expensive as the principle knot books, but certainly covers all the knots, hitches, bends, splices, whippings and braids most people are ever going to want to use. Graumont also provides good material on such other subjects as barrel slings, rope ladders, methods of securing hawsers, net making and meshing, steps in making a sea bag and blocks and tackles.

—PHS

## Organizations

**Nautical Research Guild, Inc.**
**6413 Dahlonga Rd. MD**
**Washington, D.C. 20016**

Anyone seriously interested in marine models and lore should become a member of the Nautical Research Guild. Their "Nautical Research Journal" is an excellent, highly informative and really well-presented quarterly publication dealing with maritime history, model construction techniques, sources of tools and materials, shop notes, news of active individuals and clubs and is the general forum of interchange between professional and amateur modelers in the U. S. Membership is $7.50 and very worth it.

This little piece does not propose to give you any tips on how to make a jig for anchor stock planking or how to carve a riggol or a figurehead. Those things have been well covered over the years, which is good. However, I don't think I ever saw an article by anyone trying to give reasons for spending hours, sometimes years, on a ship model. In my case there are 8736 hours of work in the completed hull of my VICTORY. That is just working time and does not include hundreds of hours just planning, thinking about problems and solving them. On many occasions I have spent all day just finding out ten different ways that the thing could not be done. With those ten out of the way, the next day was clear to find the solution. An English friend classifies model problems in the range of "one soakers" to "four soakers." When building a model he would sit in the tub and contemplate the problem and the difficulty would be determined by how many times he had to soak before solving it. In my case the only "four soaker" was the head rails which has not been the most difficult part of the ship to others.

**From a "Shop Note" entitled "I Never Would Have the Patience" by H.S. Spaulding in the Fall 1972 Nautical Research Journal.**

We wrote to the Nautical Research Guild asking for a list of the active model clubs in this country and received the following note from Merritt A. Edson, Jr., secretary of the Guild. We hope to have an accurate, comprehensive list available in the near future. Meanwhile, if you know of an active club, please write it up, especially if it makes services, facilities, materials or a publication available to its membership.

Vernon Tate forwarded a copy of your letter to him and suggested that I supply you with a list of ship model clubs. Unfortunately I do not have a list that is reliable.

Since most ship model clubs are private organizations whose officers change yearly, addresses assumed for one year would not be current the following year. Most of the larger cities in the United States have, or have had, clubs. Some have been in existence for many years without a break in continuity, while others have flourished for a few years then quietly disappear to resurface again several years later under a new name.

Clubs have been known to exist in Boston, New York, Long Island, Connecticut, Rhode Island, Philadelphia, Baltimore, Washington, D.C., Richmond, Hampton Roads, Chicago (two at present), San Francisco, Los Angeles and San Diego. Over the years the Journal has made mention of each of these, but membership in them and correspondence from them is rather irregular. I hope that by the end of this year the Guild will have more information to supply you on this subject.

One group with a fine small newsletter called "The Fife Rail" is:

**Nautical Research and**
**Ship Model Society of Chicago**
**5658 South Hermitage**
**Chicago, Ill. 60636**
**Dues and subscription are $3.00**

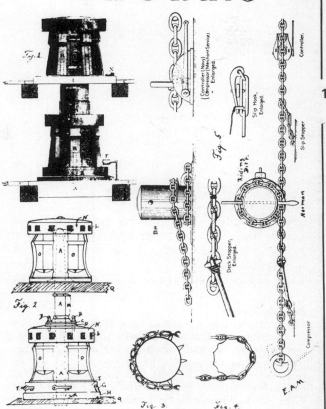

# CAPSTANS

Above from "The Fife Rail," Vol. VII, No. 3.

131

# Journals and Magazines

"Model Shipwright"
2 Nelson Rd.
Greenwich, London SE10
England
$9.50/yr.

A year-old publication with a good reputation among professionals.

Photo by Bil Lingard

**Location** On Mary Street in Clayton near the Municipal Dock on the St. Lawrence River.

**Exhibits** The new Thousand Islands Shipyard Museum is considered the only fresh water museum of its kind with emphasis on antique power craft. Within the main building is an exhibit of 38 small vessels ranging from canoes to larger power boats. There is a unique collection of antique outboard motors as well as many items of nautical hardware. A restoration workshop is engaged in preparing additional small craft for exhibit. Additional nautical displays can be seen at the nearby Thousand Islands Museum located in the Old Town Hall on Riverside Drive.

**Schedule** Daily, June to October, 10:00 A. M. to 9:00 P. M.

**Admission** Adults 50c, Children 25c, under 12 free. Group rate available.

**Special Events** Thousand Islands Antique Boat Show and Antique Outboard Demonstration August 19-20, 1972.

√ Gift Shop
√ Free Parking
√ Picnic Area

Thousand Islands Shipyard Museum
Mary Street
Clayton, N. Y. 13624
Phone (315) 686-4104
Thomas Turgeon, Director

√ Memberships available on request.

"Model Boats"
P.O. Box 35, Bridge Street
Hamel Hempstead
HERTS HP1 1EE
England
$6/yr.

Another English publication with a popular touch. The emphasis tends to be on power, merchant, and navy vessels, especially radio-controlled craft. "Free" sail models are not excluded though, and the model racing class sailor will always find something of interest in it. "Model Boats" is very valuable as an advertiser, for just about every shop and manufacturer in England is listed monthly. This is no small offering because there are more modelers in any one shire of England than there are in this entire country!

Nautical Museum Directory.
Quadrant Press, 19 West 44th St.
New York
Index, illustrated, published annually.

All of the major museums and many of the smaller ones are listed here with information on location, exhibits, schedules, admission fees and special events. Good guide to have in hand as you drive around Seeing America First.

For the most detailed list of nautical museums worldwide (410 to be exact) you'll ever want to see, look in the U.S. Naval Institute "Proceedings," October 1966, beginning on page 4. If you don't subscribe to that publication, most of the larger libraries do.

—PHS

## Museum Collections

Marine museums always feature collections of marine models, and the ship modeler, whether a pro working on his hundredth plank-on-frame piece or a beginner just considering a plastic job, will find the hours spent studying a museum model are worthwhile and very pleasurable. In fact, once you have spent time working on a model, your appreciation for the work of skill is heightened and you develop a sense of concern and stewardship for the legacy of

fine models. Many men and vessels are gone utterly but for their models. Also, museums are more and more becoming less oriented to just preservation. Education is becoming the keynote. Quite probably, it will be the maritime museums of this country that provide the educational spark needed to produce (for the first time) a citizenry that truly cares for the responsible protection and use of our oceans, shorelines and harbors. Become a museum patron.

132

# DICTIONARIES

Chain and Hemp Cables.

♣ "International Maritime Dictionary" by
Rene de Kerchove.
Van Nostrand Reinhold, 450 West 33rd. St.
New York.
1961 (second edition), 1018 pp., illustrations,
$28.50.

—Quote from
"International Mar-
itime Dictonary"

**BOVO.** A Sicilian coasting vessel of comparatively large capacity with an average tonnage ranging from 25 to 40. Length 40 to 60 ft. Breadth 13 to 18 ft. Depth 6 to 7 ft. Draft 5 to 6 ft. Also called *pareggia*.

Bovo

The rig consists of a mainmast without rake stepped slightly forward of amidships, a low bowsprit nearly horizontal, several headsails, and a small jigger mast with gaff or lateen sail. The raking stem is very much like that of the *tartana*. The stern is square or round. The deck has a pronounced round of beam and is nearly at the same height at ends as amidships.

You can sit on a goldmine for years and not even know it. This book is a case in point. I've used this dictionary off and on for quite awhile and never realized how comprehensive it is until I needed to look up the name of a boat type that is the ultimate in obscurity. De Kerchove has it; no other source does.

Actually this dictionary is more of an encyclopedia, since the definitions go into some detail. It is truly international in that the French and German words for each term are given; the terms that are outside the realm of American experience are to be found throughout. The illustrations, where they appear, are nicely detailed. If you can't afford it, but could use the volume from time to time, it may be worth the effort to drop a hint on your local librarian.

Another dictionary is "The Mariner's Dictionary" by Gershom Bradford (1972, Barre Publisher, 307 pp., illus., $12.50). It's not as comprehensive as De Kerchove, but it's not $28.50 either. See review below.

—PHS

♣ "The Mariner's Dictionary" by Gershom Bradford.
Barre Publishers, Barre, Mass. 1972, $12.50.

It is extraordinary how the poor vocabulary is rationalized away. Our eyes do not see the words we don't know. It takes an act of will, a special effort admitting to — the shame of it! — one's own limitations. Opening the mind may be an act of "infinite joy," but the short-term costs are shattering. All of a sudden you are a complete idiot; all the stuff you don't know, and it has been there all along!

But you heal in time, partially through regressing back into blind pride, but some habit of receptivity remains and, with earnest openness, then, one conjures the gall to read a dictionary.

There are a few marine dictionaries and it would not be correct to call any of them good, bad or indifferent. It isn't that it is impossible to edit a poor or excellent dictionary. It's simply that those we have are all O.K., a matter of personality really, each dictionary giving a different slant or tone to the sea-terms which are part of our patrimony. You don't go out to get the best dictionary; you get the most appropriate one.

Bradford's effort is quite complete for its size. Informal and fundamental, only the words and primary definitions are given. Pronunciation, enunciation, derivations, synonyms and rare or obscure usages are deleted. The result is a useful desk and shipboard nautical dictionary of a size you can handle without a constant frustration over marine etymology and orthography. On some slang words, it may be the last word.

I'll take this one aboard and keep Rene de Kerchove's "International Maritime Dictionary" (2nd ed.) for Scrabble and other hard going.

From "The Mariner's Dictionary"
"KELDS, Smooth patches in the midst of ruffled water." (This word just entered your working vocabulary.)

"BOTTOMRY BOND, A lien on a vessel placed by a master who is obliged to raise money for repairs and who is out of communication with his owners. . . . The money revived from such liens can only be used for repairs, takes priority over all mortgages, and is primarily for the purpose of getting a vessel to her home port." (You see a lot of this toward the end of August at Amsterdam's airport.)

"BEATING THE BOOBY," Swinging the arms from side to side to accelerate the blood's circulation." (So that's why it's called a Mae West! Or is it the other way around?)

—GP

133

# Marine  Engines

Marine engines range in size from a tiny hand-operated outboard "motor" (a propeller operated by a hand crank — no longer manufactured) to turbines in excess of 25,000 h.p. that drive today's superships. In between are thousands of makes and scores of types, and we make no effort to cover them here. We do, however, list some interesting types with which our contributors have had personal experience and, finally, some relatively low-cost ways to find the marine power you need in a market that's hypped-up on horsepower and speed — the fast buck, you might say.

Have you found an engine of special interest or particularly good reliability? Let us know about it, and we'll pass the information along in an expanded marine-engine section in later catalogs.
DRG

**From "Inboard Motor Installations . . . "**

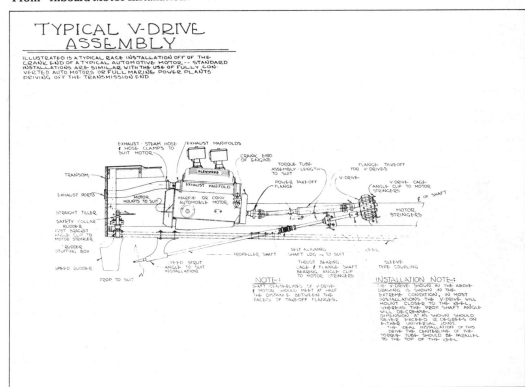

134

---

⊕ "Inboard Motor Installations in Small Boats"
   by Glen L. Witt.
Glen L. Marine Designs, Bellflower, Calif.
1960, 136 pp., illustrated, $6.00.

This has to be the most practical, easily understood book on the subject. You don't have to know anything about marine engines to understand what Witt is talking about. He takes you through the steps of powering a boat, from the engine to the coupling, to the shaft, to the strut, and on to the propeller, including the cooling and exhaust systems. When you're done with this book, you'll be able to install your own or at least be able to talk circles around your local marine engine mechanic.

Best about the book is the illustrations; you can't be mistaken about what the author is describing. For instance, Witt provides a sequence of 28 clear photos on converting an automobile engine to a marine engine. It appears that you actually don't have to be Merlin to do the job.

—PHS

# Old and Modern STEAM

Have you been looking for something in a steam engine lately? Say, a 7 h.p. walking beam or triple expansion, an 18 h.p. single acting twin, a 50 h.p. compound V-4 for your car or a 200 h.p. marine V-4? They're all available, along with the necessary accessories, from Ralph J. Rasmussen, Licensed Engineer, and his Reliable Industries. These lovely looking mills come in kit or complete; the catalog is a day dreamer's quick course in steam engines and steamboating. If we were thinking of steam in small boats, we would turn first to Mr. Rasmussen, and his:

—DRG

**Reliable Industries Inc.**
**34403 Joel St.**
**New Baltimore, Mich. 48047**

From Reliable Industries catalog.

## LARGER AND DIFFERENT
### Single Acting Compound V-4

| | |
|---|---|
| Horsepower Range | 50 to 125 H.P. |
| Working Pressure Range | 600 to 1000 psi. |
| Cylinders | 8 (2 banks of 4 at 90°) |
| Sizes of Cylinders | 1 3/4 & 3 3/8 x 2¼ |
| RPM Range | 0 to 1500 plus |
| Steam Consumption Range | 600 to 1200 lb./hr. |

*RELIABLE* Industries offers this engine to amateur constructors for use as an automotive or marine power plant. The design is of closed crankcase type with spool valves. There are no dead centered positions of the crankshaft, so starting is always positive in response to the throttle. Engine may be arranged in a car with a Pontiac 1961-1963 trans-axle to give reverse and neutral, which may be used for warming engine and running auxiliaries. The design uses many commercial parts which are readily available. The casting kit consists of 19 pieces, including the cast semi-steel crankshaft. Kit weighs about 250 lbs. and finished engine is about 240 lbs. Construction requires use of a 16 inch lathe, milling machine and drill press. Uses steam generator Item 14 on Equipment List.

(SEE LAST PAGES FOR ALL PRICES)

---

**"Questions and Answers on Diesel Engines"**
**by J.N. Seale.**
Drake Publishers, New York.
1972, 128 pp., illustrated, index $2.95.

This book covers non-marine as well as marine engines. Subjects include principles of operation, types, starting methods, fuel-injection pumps, governors, fuel injectors and fuel filters. It is a British book, so the engines discussed are British engines, which is fine, especially since there are quite a few British marine diesels imported by the U.S.

This is a good book for the boatman who is contemplating buying a marine diesel and wants his questions on its operation answered. Not too good for repair and maintenance.

—PHS

From "Questions and Answers . . . "

*What is a "peak" load?*

This is quoted by some engine builders, and is the load which the engine can carry for a few minutes under emergency conditions. The usual practice, however, is to fit a stop on the fuel-injection pumps to prevent them from delivering enough fuel to exceed the one-hour rating.

*In what form is the "rating" of an engine usually given?*

In kilowatts (kW) at revolutions per minute (r.p.m.) of the engine crankshaft.

*What is the brake power of an engine?*

The brake power of an engine is the useful power developed at the engine crankshaft after overcoming the frictional resistance of the engine itself. It is known as "brake" power because the power can be absorbed and measured on a dynamometer—the dynamometer is termed a brake as it absorbs and dissipates the energy developed by the engine.

*What governs the power output of an engine?*

The total power of any engine is dependent upon its design, cylinder bore, piston stroke, number of cylinders and its required application.

*Give a selection of engine power ratings used in large marine propulsion, i.e., general cargo ships, passenger ships and cargo liners*

Without mentioning specific makes, the ratings given in Table 1 apply to a selection of the larger types of two-stroke, turbo-charged, marine-propulsion engines.

*How do marine builders normally provide a range of engine sizes to cater for different requirements?*

By building one or more of their basic designs with a varying number of cylinders.

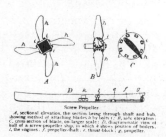

Screw Propeller.
*A*, sectional elevation, the section being through shaft and hub, showing method of attaching blades by bolts *r*; *B*, side elevation; *C*, cross section of blade, on larger scale; *D*, diagrammatic view of hull of a screw-propeller ship, in which *k* shows position of boilers; *l*, the engines; *f*, propeller-shaft; *e*, thrust-block; *g*, propeller.

135

## Small Diesels

The small diesel engine is becoming more and more popular and with that popularity has come a multitude of manufacturers who have cobbled up propulsion systems without the full knowledge and experience of what an engine at sea goes through and what is expected of it. As a result almost all are overpriced and prone to trouble, breakage and hard starting. One notable example was a Japanese engine a friend of mine bought new and which went through three cracked heads, several sets of injectors and two superchargers, all in the course of a year and a half.

Three years ago I was introduced to the Sabb Diesel through another friend who imported one from Norway. The people of Norway have been fishing for thousands of years and Sabb has been making their marine engines for long enough to know what it's doing.

Sabb makes simple reliable engines that last and perform well. Their 10 h.p. seems to be the choice most people make for workboats up to 25' and for sailboats. I ordered mine in 10 h.p. for $956 in U. S. money. Almost everything necessary comes with the engine: throttle control, gearbox, 18" variable pitch prop (as a no-cost option a customer can have a standard 3-bladed fixed pitch prop and the necessary gear box with reverse added) that goes from full forward to full reverse just by moving a lever, 10-gal. stainless steel fuel tank, grease gun, oil can, small tools in box, shaft, stuffing box, nuts & bolts, valves & fittings, etc. A bilge pump was the one extra and it was included in the $965 purchase price.

The engine cost $70 to ship all the way from Norway to Seattle, Wash. It cost another $140 to go the remaining distance to Kodiak, Alaska. It took about a month and a half from Norway to Seattle and another three months to go from Seattle to Kodiak.

The engine was turned over by hand about two months after I got it and it fired and ran immediately. Electric starting is available as an extra but I found it safer to rely on my hands than on a boat battery. The engine would run up to about 1800 r.p.m. and idle down as low as 140 r.p.m. It was very quiet even without the water exhaust fitted and ran smoothly at medium to high r.p.m. It thumped and kicked at very low idle but this was to be expected. One can easily slow a boat down to zero using variable pitch on the prop alone.

The engines I've seen from Sabb are very heavily built and have oversized everything. Just looking at the h.p.-to-weight ratio indicates that they are built to last. Prices seem to be from

From Sabb catalog.

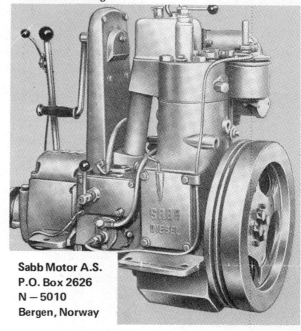

Sabb Motor A.S.
P.O. Box 2626
N — 5010
Bergen, Norway

½ to 1/3 of what most U. S. dealers are getting for their imported stuff.

| | | | |
|---|---|---|---|
| 8 h.p. | - eng. wt. alone | - 364 lbs. | - $700. |
| 10 h.p. | - | - 441 lbs. | - $950. |
| 18 h.p. | (2 cyl.) | - 419 lbs. | - about $1250. |

Note: prices are varying with the rate of exchange.

—Mark White

"Audels Diesel Engine Manual" by Perry O. Black. Theodore Audel and Co., Indianapolis, Ind. 1966, 536 pp., illustrated, glossary, $6.95.

"Diesel Engine Operation and Maintenance" by V.L. Maleev. McGraw-Hill, New York. 1954, 504 pp., illustrated, glossary, index, $8.95. .

Both books deal with diesel engines generally — not specific models and no specific marine applications. Maleev is more technical, textbookish and old (1954); Black is more streamlined and concise. Maleev has questions at the end of each chapter; Black is built around the question-and-answer format. Both cover essentially the same territory, although it is a question of degree: Maleev is more detailed, Black less.

—PHS

## Old Reliable

No discussion of small engines can be held without mention of Lister diesels, the British built engines as familiar as seagulls on the waterfronts of the world. Designed for compatibility with the salt water environment, Listers have compiled an enviable reputation for durability and reliability.

We wrote to Mr. J. E. Barthmaier, office manager of Lister Diesels at Lake Success, asking for a brief rundown on the Lister line. His reply, in part, covers points any potential buyer might want to know:

"You will note that all models are available either as marine propulsion or for marine auxiliary duty. In fact, a large precentage of all commercial fishing vessels produced in the U.S. have Lister-powered auxiliary units installed, covering power generation (electric or hydraulic), refrigeration, pumping, etc. Many of the models are readily hand started.

"All Lister engines are of the heavy duty type and should not be compared with an automotive type engine. They have an excellent reputation for long life and dependability. A point of interest in this respect is the new U.S. Coast Guard Sea Buoys have been powered by Lister engines with the prototype buoy operating in excess of 20,000 hours unattended at sea.

"The only limitation we find in installing Lister engines is in the high speed, light weight type of pleasure craft.

"Our engines are available on a world-wide basis. In the U.S. we have an extensive distributor organization—a list of current distributors is attached. Lister engines are also extensively used by many major U.S. manufacturers to power their products such as generating plants, refrigeration plants, pumping sets and construction equipment."

Like nearly all diesel engines, Listers aren't cheap, and the declining status of the dollar abroad isn't improving the situation. But when you're 500 miles from the nearest dock, in the dark of a stormy night, and much of your navigation and electrical equipment is totally dependent on a little-driven generator barking away in your engineroom, the extra bucks are long forgotten.

SR3MGR engine. 19.5 h.p., 2000 rev/min., with hydraulic servo gearbox.

Lister Diesels
7 Delaware Drive
Lake Success, N.Y. 11040

137

### Un-bung-ling

A foolproof method for removing bungs from wooden boats when refastening: Drill a small pilot hole into the center of the plug; insert a nice, fat screw into the hole and drive it in until it fetches up against the head of the fastening; a few more turns of the screw will draw the bung right out, splitting it in the process (which makes it easy to get the plug off the screw). I've used this system many, many times, and its success has exceeded by wildest dreams. No more damaged planks, nicked chisels, torn fingernails or frustration.

—PHS

### A Diesel Outboard?

Just out of curiosity, I wrote a good diesel engineer I know and asked whether he knew of any possible developments of a diesel outboard. The following excerpt is from his response:

"The diesel outboard looks to be a long way off in the future; nobody wants to talk about it. Engine builders say it's too heavy and runs very hot. Evinrude outboard division never answered my letter or ideas about diesel outboard (power).

"(In) Connecticut, my two friends will not let me in on the development of their (diesel) outboard. I can't really blame them. So the world will just have to wait."

How long can nature?

—GP

### Making Your Own "Marine" Engine

A good number of the marine engines on the market today are conversions of automotive or industrial gasoline or diesel engines. It's perfectly possible to lift that pretty little Slant 6 from the family Valiant, "marine" it with available kits and install it in your 28-footer. Better still, you can order the engine complete from an outfit like Stokes (and keep your Plymouth for other uses) or you can pick up a similar engine — from a wrecking company or an auto dealer, get a conversion kit from Lehman and do it yourself. Either way, you've got yourself reliable inboard power, 145 horses of it, for as little as $5-600 for a bobtail version to about $1200 with a 3:1 reduction gear.

Stokes offers both complete engines and conversion kits, plus used engines and accessories. Lehman does not supply engines, but its Econ-O-Power kits give you everything you need to convert your own. Both of these companies have been in business for a long time — Lehman since 1932; Stokes since 1944 — and each has built up a solid and generally satisfied clientele. Lehman claims to be the oldest firm in the marine engine conversion business. Stokes claims to have the world's largest stock of used and rebuilt inboard marine engines. If you're engine shopping, we'd strongly suggest you start with the highly informative catalogs of both these companies.

—DRG

138

Lehman Mfg. Co. Inc.
800 E. Elizabeth Ave.
Linden, N.J. 07036
Catalog 50 cents.

Stokes Marine Industries
Colwater, Mich. 49036
(Ask for Catalog 360)

From Stokes catalog.

### STOKES 120 H.P. MARINE ENGINE
AS ADAPTED FROM
## FORD FALCON 6

Paragon Gear

Warner Gear

120 H.P. at 4400 RPM
200 Cubic Inch Displacement
3.68 X 3.13 Bore and Stroke
12 Volt Electrical System
8.8 to 1 Compression Ratio

| Dimension | Bob Tail No gear | Paragon 1 to 1 | Paragon 2 to 1 | Warner 1 to 1 | Warner Red. |
|---|---|---|---|---|---|
| Overall length | 34" | 46" | 53" | 44" | 51" |
| Height above centerline | 19" | 19" | 19" | 19" | 19" |
| Depth below centerline | 8" | 8" | 8" | 8" | 8" |
| Mounting width on centers | 22½" | 22½" | 22½" | 22½" | 22½" |
| Weight | 325 | 390 | 420 | 390 | 420 |

Our new Ford Falcon marine engine fills the need for a light weight yet compact six cylinder engine. We start with a new basic Falcon engine and add the widely known Stokes marine equipment consisting of water cooled marine manifold, rubber impeller water pump, motor mounts, back-fire trap and other needed parts. Engine is suitable for runabouts, cruisers, and sailboats. The bob-tail model is also ideal for use with inboard-outboard drives.

44

Below from Lehman catalog.

## "BOBTAIL" ADAPTIONS
## for Inboard-outboard drives and Water-Jet installations.

The popularity of inboard-outboard drives and water-jet units has prompted the offering of a complete line of "bobtail" equipment. As these installations do not require the use of a reverse gear or transmission, the engine is normally connected directly to the propulsion unit. Such engines, not having transmissions, are referred to as "bobtail" models. The bobtail adaption consists of a flywheel housing for enclosing the flywheel and to provide rear engine support and a drive shaft or coupling to connect flywheel to outdrive or jet unit. Bobtail equipment is listed along with other conversion equipment.

FLEX. COUPLING & HOUSING WITH COVER REMOVED

ECON-O-POWER BOBTAIL FLYWHEEL HOUSINGS are gray iron with integral cast wall in the front, lower section and are supplied with cover and gasket for rear opening. Unlike "open-flywheel" models, these housings provide a water-tight lower section to prevent the flywheel from picking up and "throwing" bilge water which often rusts starter mechanisms and other vital parts. An enclosed housing also acts as a safety device by shielding the flywheel from the prying fingers of children and careless adults. Rear engine supports are cast integrally for greatest strength and rigidity.

"Marine Conversions: Car Engine Conversions
for Boats" by Nigel Warren.
**Adlard Coles, London, England.**
**1972, 150 pp., source-of-equipment-list. $7.95.**

A British book with enough general information on engine conversions to be of use to Americans. Of course, if you have a British engine to convert, and there are plenty of them around just waiting, you'll just love this book. Along with subjects like cooling, gearboxes, mountings, electrical systems, tanks, etc., there is a separate chapter on some actual conversions and how they were installed — BMC 948 cc "A" Type; Austin 7; Ford 122E 1500 cc; Volkswagen; 3½ litre Morris Commercial; Ford 100E; BMC 2.2 diesel. I know a guy who put a Ford Cortina engine in a Chesapeake deadrise launch and was delighted with the result.

—PHS

From "Marine Conversions . . . "
Testing

The gearbox adds to the engine's weight quite appreciably, so it may be best to keep them separate and fit them together on the boat. If the engine has been 'reconditioned' at home as described above, it is worth the extra time to rig up a bench test to make sure that everything is in order. The engine can be bolted to some large blocks of wood so that the sump is off the ground. Fill up with oil and fit temporary hoses to feed the Jabsco pump with water and, if applicable, fill up the fresh water side of the cooling. Rig up a temporary starter cable from a battery to the starter motor and wires for the ignition. An old tin can act as a fuel tank with a plastic pipe running to the carburettor. A pipe connection can be soldered to the bottom of the tin. Without a silencer the noise will be incredible, so if the exhaust piping and silencer have been bought they can be temporarily hooked up. Follow the manual's instructions to roughly set the carburettor. Prime the carburettor, switch on the ignition and operate the starter motor. When the engine is running and has warmed up, the carburettor can be finally adjusted and the whole engine checked for oil or water leaks. If the engine has been reconditioned it will be very tight at first and will not idle slowly. It must not be raced during the first few hours of running. Running-in can take place just as well in the boat, but an hour's run in the garage will bring to light any obvious faults.

---

From "Audels Gas Engine Manual"

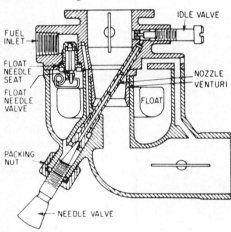

**Fig. 3**—Typical Briggs & Stratton gravity feed carburetor. Float type carburetors are provided with adjustments for both idle and power mixtures. On these, clockwise rotation of the adjusting needle leans the mixture.

"Audels Gas Engine Manual" by Edwin P. Anderson.
**Theodore Audel & Co., Indianapolis, Ind.**
**1961 (repr. 1969), 474 pp., illustrated, glossary, $4.50.**

Covers gasoline engines in general, not necessarily marine engines. The best part of the book is on troubleshooting and servicing a gasoline engine. You'll have to look elsewhere for information, though, on the marine part of gas engines.

Incidentally, Audels has a complete line of books on practical, technical subjects: "Welders Guide," "Wiring Diagrams for Light and Power," "Electric Motor Guide," "Home Workshop and Tool Handy Book," to name but a few. Send for their catalog (4300 West 62nd St., Indianapolis, Ind.) for a complete list. They claim they will send copies of their books for free examination, with no obligation to buy.

—PHS

139

---

"Small Boat Engines, Inboard and Outboard,"
by Conrad Miller.
**Sheridan House, New York.**
**1961 (repr. 1970), 316 pp., illustrated, index, $7.50.**

This book, originally published as a series of articles in "Rudder" magazine, is about the anatomy of the marine engine. It is a general discussion, in that specific engines are neither discussed nor described. Miller covers the principles of operation, cooling, lubrication, ignition systems, starters, tuning up, transmission, troubleshooting, and more. Both gasoline and diesel engines are described.

Even if you're not going to work on your own engine, the book deserves reading since you will have a better understanding of what is going on under your cockpit floor.

—PHS

From "Small Boat Engines . . . "

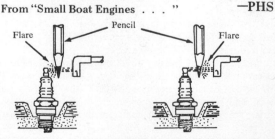

Fig. 63. _How to test a spark polarity with a lead pencil. The left plug, with flare toward terminal, has correct polarity._

# The One-Lunger Lives!

Fifty years or more ago the two-cycle gasoline engine, more commonly known as the one-lunger, was the principal means of propulsion for the small powerboat. Most people today believe that except for a few models scattered around in collector's barns or marine museum displays, one-lungers are long gone — a belief that is the complete opposite of fact. One-lungers are alive and kicking — literally, and are still manufactured in Canada.

Walter C. Hadley is the U.S. distributor of the Acadia engine which is offered in the country in eight models. And don't let the horsepower ratings fool you — two-cycles are not only simple and tough, they are amazingly powerful, to boot, a fact readily ascertained by noting the power ratings of the engines that pushed the pleasure and work boats during the first 25 years of this century.

While the Acadia is most easily obtained in this country, thanks to Mr. Hadley's operation, another manufacturer also turns out one-lungers in Nova Scotia — the Atlantic engine built by Lunenburg Foundry, Lunenburg, N.S.

One-lungers are excellent dory engines and have long been standard equipment in the big fishing dories of the St. Pierre et Miquelon Islands off Newfoundland and other fishing boats in the Maritime Provinces. Because the flat-bottomed boats are frequently drawn up on the beach, a special propeller haul-up device has been developed, a rig still useful and still available. The accompanying letter from Mr. Hadley and other commentary adds to the information available on these old-time engines.

—DRG

Acadia Gas Engines
Mr. Walter G. Hadley
Coanicus Avenue
Jamestown, R.I. 02835

Atlantic Engines
Lunenburg Foundry Ltd.
Lunenburg, N.S.

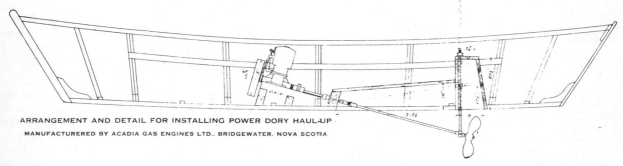

ARRANGEMENT AND DETAIL FOR INSTALLING POWER DORY HAUL-UP
MANUFACTURERED BY ACADIA GAS ENGINES LTD., BRIDGEWATER, NOVA SCOTIA

To the Editor:

Last winter when you started the plans of the St. Pierre dory in NF/MCF, I had some doubt regarding the satisfaction of city folks and juniors in starting the non-gadgeted two-cycle motor recommended. However, this doubt has been somewhat dispelled — quite so, in fact.

One day last August while I was on the wharf of a village waterfront store in the Mahone Bay area, Lunenburg County, N.S., a 25' open powerboat of a local utility type tied up at the wharf. It was manned by three children who had come in from their home on an island three miles along the shore.

The little fellow running the engine was 12 years of age. Asked what kind of a motor he had he replied "A double four! Do you want to see how it works?"

By "double-four" he meant it had two cylinders of the size in single-cylinder 4 h.p. motors. This was a 2-cycle Atlantic (a make mentioned in NF/MCF in June) 8 h.p. with make-and-break ignition.

To the rim of the flywheel the owner had lashed two shaped wood blocks diametrically opposite to each other. When the motor stopped one or the other of these blocks would be about 45 degrees from top center on the port side. The ignition switch was inside the aft wall of the motor box, on port side. Standing on that side abaft the flywheel and putting his right foot on the block, giving it a hard shove downward, the operator could rotate the flywheel enough to start the motor.

The boy certainly knew his motor! By watching the flywheel or outside mechanism of the make-and-break gear and opening and closing the switch at the proper time, he could reverse the rotation back and forth at will. This checks with an article by Harry Sucher some time ago.

The above "cranking system," while most simple, may not be the perfect answer for starting. There is potential danger in the projecting blocks and the operator would have to be very careful to keep positioned so that as his foot slid away from the block no part of him, such as a leg, would be in the orbit of the blocks.

However, the point is that if a small boy can start and run one of these motors, the backyard builder or prospective owner need not worry.

Elmer H. Harris
186 West Brookline St.
Boston 18, Mass.
"National Fisherman" May 1964.

Below, the Atlantic 24 h.p. engine.

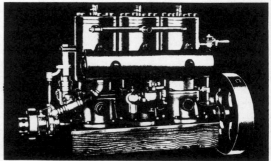

# How to Save Dunked Engines

## and Other Gear

### By Mark White

If, due to any number of circumstances, a boat goes under, here is what to do to save outboard motor, main and/or auxiliary engines, generators, radio, depth sounder, radar, etc.

#### 1. Caution

Remember that most insurance companies, from long and bitter experience with salvaged gear going bad after a few months, consider any electrical/electronic gear that goes under salt water a total loss. Any efforts to save uninsured gear or salvage-purchased gear can be all to the good. An $18,000 radar can often be purchased for $200 — but it will be utterly useless unless promptly and thoroughly treated.

#### 2. Protect The Gear From Air

Wherever the gear and (or) equipment is — as long as it is underwater — leave it there! Don't move it until actually ready to really work on it. Air in combination with salt water is what does things in. If it is possible to get the gear to a fresh water stream or fresh water tank (55-gal. drum, for instance) and completely submerge it, by all means do so. Better to leave the gear in the water an extra two weeks than in open air for a day.

#### 3. Flush

Once the gear has been raised it will be necessary to flush silt, sand, etc. out. In electronic gear this can be done by opening the panels and flooding liberally with a fresh water hose. Keep washing about six times longer than you think necessary. All panels and parts should be open so that everything can be well bathed. A weak solution of vinegar and water splashed on seems to help cut the salt. Follow with more fresh water.

A steam hose will help in cleaning and blasting salt out. Care should be taken not to melt insulation or crack tubes with the stream. Steam can be alternated with fresh water.

#### 4. Quickly Dry And Protect With WD-40

A quick blast with an air hose will remove most of the water. Follow with an application of WD-40, a very light oil type compound with excellent corrosion-inhibiting characteristics. Very few compounds will displace water and protect against metal corrosion as well as WD-40. WD-40 Co., 5390 Napa St., San Diego, Calif., 92110, can give you the name of their nearest distributor.

After the initial application of WD-40, the air hose is directed against every part of the gear and every last drop of moisture must be removed. When the gear is thoroughly dry then every nook and cranny is sprayed liberally with WD-40.

#### 5. Follow Up For Electronic Gear

It isn't much of a trick to get a piece of gear operating soon after it's bath. The trick is to keep it operating later. Gear should be used frequently to keep it warm and dried out. With salvaged gear trouble will usually occur a month to a year or two after salvage. Almost invariably the trouble will arise from salt which has worked its way into stranded wire or small crevices. If the cleaning was not really thorough then trouble will follow. Guaranteed! WD-40 sprayed on the gear from time to time will help but will not entirely eliminate the problem.

#### 6. Main Engines, Outboards etc.

These too, should be protected from air and all tanks and pumps drained, flushed and steam cleaned. It is almost necessary to get the engine running within a day or two of the raising. If the engine will be used daily one can sometimes get away with very frequent oil and coolant changes after everything has been flushed and cleaned. If the engine isn't run frequently then it will be necessary to take everything apart and really clean it. If it's being taken apart then all seals, bearing inserts, etc., should be replaced. Any generators, ignition, etc., are treated as electronics gear.

#### 7. Hydraulic Gear

All tanks and lines should be cleaned and flushed. All pumps and motors should be completely taken apart and thoroughly cleaned. All "O" rings and seals, etc., should be replaced.

Warning — sometimes hydraulic pumps and motors are a lot more complicated than they at first seem to be. Qualified labor may be necessary to put things back together.

A good hydraulic oil with anti-rust additives should be put in the system and everything run for a day or so to heat up the mechanisms and clean out excess and foreign material. This oil should be changed and properly disposed of.

Warning — Don't use WD-40 in hydraulic lines as it may eat seals!

While it is true that many people try salvage and botch the job by not thoroughly removing all the salt, which gives trouble later, it is also true that a careful and conscientious job can save a piece of gear that can go on to give many more years of service. Don Cunning who teaches marine electronics at Ketchikan Community College, Alaska, and who furnished much of the information on saving electrical gear, mentioned a radio-telephone that had been raised and properly treated and is now in its 12th year of service. A boat which had laid on the ocean floor near Kodiak, Alaska for eight years was raised in '72 and in a few days its salvagers had its main engine running.

In warmer waters corrosion takes place much faster but in Alaska it is sometimes possible to get away with raising old wrecks and salvaging the engines. In way of advice to those who want to try to save something off their boat or to fix something from another boat — Don't try it unless you're ready to put forth a lot of time and energy and do the job right.

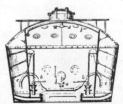

A European form of Diving-bell or Nautilus.

Water admitted through the cock _a_ into the pipes _b b_ flows into the exterior chambers _c c_, causing the apparatus to sink. When the water in _c c_ is displaced by air, the nautilus rises. It may also be hauled up by ropes. Air for ventilation and for displacement of the water-ballast is supplied by air-pumps from above through flexible tubes connected with the interior chamber, and is allowed to pass into the chambers _c c_ by opening valves. Dead-lights in the sides and top admit light to the interior.

141

# Old-Time Outboards

**Seagull Century Plus**

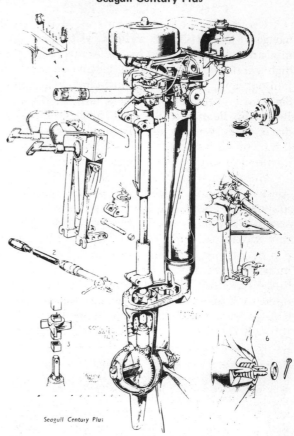

Seagull Century Plus

When you are so far from civilization that the last floating beer bottle was seen weeks ago and the last floating Coca-Cola bottle was seen days ago and you hear the sound of an outboard motor, it's a Seagull. They don't have the zing and zap of the gas-eating-Polluted-gallons-a-minute monsters and the girls in their brochure have intelligence and wear bulky sweaters, but that's part of the reason we take these wonderful motors seriously. Lots of companies import, sell and service them. We got our information from Imtra Corp., 151 Mystic Ave., Medford, Mass. 02155, who specialize in a few high-quality British imports and who carry the clearly-written "British Seagull Handbook".

A motor for the smaller displacement-hull adult. Prices are in the $180 (2 h.p.) to $325 (5½ h.p. long shaft) range at present. Horse power indicators are British standard. A 5½ h.p. Seagull is very nearly 20 h.p. by domestic comparison!

—GP

**Penta U-22**

142

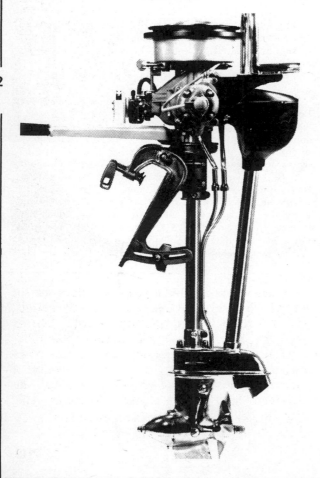

And if you're that far from the nearest MacDonald's and it isn't a Seagull, chances are it's an Archimedes Penta U-22, the Oldtimer, a two-cylinder, 15 h.p., slow-turning (3200 r.p.m.) chunk of bronze and steel that thrives on cheap gas and dirty water. The U-22 is little changed from its original versions in the late 1920s. While it does drink from a remote tank (which is more than you can say for the Seagull), it doesn't have a gear shift because the big prop is also the water pump. It has an exposed flywheel and a hot exhaust box, a couple of hazards one quickly comes to respect. But look at that machinery! There's damn little to go wrong and just about all of it can be handled by a few wrenches and a screwdriver.

Want something more modern? Archimedes turns out a sweet line of up-to-date outboards, 11 in number, ranging from 3½ h.p. to 60 h.p. We got our information from Archimedes East Coast distributor:

Anderson Penta Marine, Inc.
342 W. Ninth St.
Ship Bottom, N.J. 08008

but we understand other dealers are located on the West Coast and in Alaska.

—DRG

### Air Drive Outboard

Every once in a while someone will need to navigate in extremely shallow waters or in a mixture of ice and open water. A good rig where high winds and seas are not a factor is a short 10' jonboat and an air drive outboard. Wards and Sears sell aluminum jonboats and Arrowcraft, Box 700, Pearland, Texas, 77581, sells the air drive. They have many models ranging from 6 h.p. to 45 h.p. and the basic boats can also be included in some of their package deals.

We ordered an 8 h.p. model to try out in Alaska. The unit weighs 55 lbs. and moves our jonboat at about 35 m.p.h. on glare ice and about 4 m.p.h. in water. A more practical solution would have been the 14 h.p. model as the 8 h.p. job just will not move in snow, slush or mud; even with only one man aboard. It does, however, have enough power to go from an open spot of water up on to glare ice and away. This is nice to know if one happens to break through thin ice while moving along. Steering on ice is poor at best and it doesn't take much oversteering to go into a spin or to tip over.

The engine we had was made by Chrysler and started and ran flawlessly. It started easily in cold, wet or rainy weather. Once warm it never faltered and was a joy to run after having had much bad experience with balky outboards. Ours made a great deal of noise, even with two mufflers. Ears rang for hours after only a few minutes use of the motor. Much clothing is needed as the rushing air sets up a very high windchill factor.

In spite of its drawbacks the unit is well worth the money to those who need to go where only the air drive could take them.

8 h.p. — 55 lbs. — $298.
14 h.p. — 69 lbs. — $450.
14 h.p. w/boat — $800.
45 h.p. w/boat — $1600.

Delivery is slow. It took us over 4½ months to get ours.

—Mark White

143

---

"Outboard Motor Service Manual, 1970 (5th Edition)."
Vol. 1, Motors under 30 Horsepower, $5.95.
Vol. 2, Motors 30 Horsepower and above, $5.95.
ABOS Marine Publications, Kansas City, Mo.

For anyone who works on outboards this book is an excellent reference to have on hand. Both volumes begin with general information on outboards and how to repair and maintain them. Then what follows is detailed information and specifications on practically every outboard available today (at least until 1970).

There are exploded diagrams, addresses for procuring parts, overhaul instructions, troubleshooting data and clearly labeled photographs of torn-down motors. Naturally, the most popular models are given more coverage than the rest, but there is plenty of help for those who own or must repair an Apache, Elgin, Guppy, Clinton, Neptune, Gale, Homelite or Mid-Jet to mention but a few.

PHS

In the beginning there is ore rock, and petroleum-derived chemicals. At the other end are our boats, the end of the line. Between beginning and end are thousands of people, tons of gear and that great imponderable — a market economy. That we can buy a marine fitting containing the processed raw ingredients of four or five continents and the work of thousands of men at any price is a wonder. On the other hand, an examination of the marine fittings market is a mixture of fascination, fetishist acquisitiveness, interesting research and moral indignation.

It is almost impossible to examine the industry completely, or fairly, for almost all possible conclusions must be drawn by inference. The catalogs that one must inevitably begin with often do not tell you who manufacturered the product, so you never know for sure whether your comparisons are fair. When the manufacturer is listed, usually because the brand-name stamp is shown in the illustration, the prices are almost always identical because of the fair trade practices.

So our initial intentions to create a price comparison chart, to do some vicarious shopping for the readers, ended in frustration. When it comes to large chandlery shopping, you have to simply go there, look at things yourself, takes your choice and pays your money. No doubt a visible pattern of loyalty to the owner, manager and counter people becomes an aid as time passes.

Meanwhile, beyond the general marketplace, which remains inscrutable, there are discoveries to be made and fun literature to pour over.

# Ship's Fittings

Fore-spencer.

It would be easy to launch into a baroque treatise on the possible connotations of the word "traditional" as it appears in boating literature. They run various gamuts from passe and old-fashioned to functional and plain to rich and beautiful. Here it simply seems a logical place to begin:

Several years ago a young man frustrated at not being able to find traditional fittings created a store that specializes in them. TSYH, Inc. of Portland, is a retail and mail-order outlet for fine wood blocks of all kinds and sizes, rigging and deck fittings of traditional patterns in both bronze and galvanized iron, wood deadeyes, cleats, belaying pins, mast hoops, winches, stoves and both navigation and cabin oil lamps. If they do not carry a particular size or pattern in stock, they also offer a custom fitting service.

From TSYH catalog.

**Policy:**

> To provide a source of hardware and equipment for traditionally minded sailors to outfit their yachts.
> To develop as many items as we can on a standard basis and to maintain these on a stock basis when feasible.
> To provide custom fittings made to your specifications or to suggest custom fitting for your use based on our knowledge of the Traditional Yacht's needs.
>
> All of the items sold by us have been tried by sailors and found to be both as practical and as inexpensive as possible.

**We Need From You:**

> Accurate specifications, sketches, and proposed uses of the items wanted.
> Early orders — we need time to get materials and ship them to you, particularly for the custom-made fittings.

We will be glad to consult with you to recommend fittings and suggest alternatives.

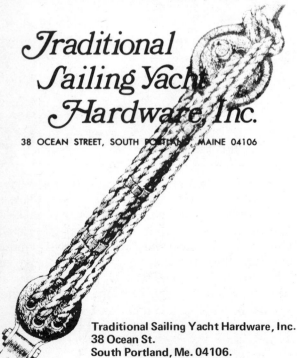

*Traditional Sailing Yacht Hardware, Inc.*

38 OCEAN STREET, SOUTH PORTLAND, MAINE 04106

Traditional Sailing Yacht Hardware, Inc.
38 Ocean St.
South Portland, Me. 04106.

### Lunenburg, N.S.

Lunenburg, Nova Scotia is a town virtually based on the founding of metal, or is it founded on base metal (?). Anyway, there are many firms headquartered there and the patterns and techniques employed are the old ones. Their gear is strong, time-proven and reasonably priced. In most cases, outlets which offer traditional fittings get their supplies from one or another of the Lunenburg foundries.

Two such firms are A. Dauphinee & Sons and Lunenburg Foundry and Engineering Limited. A. Dauphinee and Sons specialize in marine blocks of either ash or lignum vitae with bronze sheaves and galvanized straps, parrels, cleats, belaying pins and deadeyes of ash, greenheart or lignum vitae, whichever you desire or is most appropriate. L. F. & E. Ltd. is a much larger firm offering rugged and functional ship's gear; rudder assemblies, windlasses and capstans, heaving and hoisting gear, chocks, mooring bits, bells, two-cycle engines, struts, hawsepipes, pumps and anon. Just great. Chandler's stock at it's practical best!

**Lunenburg Foundry and**
**Engineering Ltd.**
**Lunenburg, N.S., Canada**

From Lunenburg Foundry catalog.

### YACHT BLOCKS

## A. Dauphinee & Sons
—MANUFACTURERS OF—
### BLOCKS, OARS AND MARINE HARDWARE
LUNENBURG    NOVA SCOTIA    CANADA

# "CENTENNIAL" RACHET GYPSY
# YACHT WINDLASS
## WITH BRAKE

|                        | No. 1 | No. 2 | No. 3 | No. 4 |
| ---------------------- | ----- | ----- | ----- | ----- |
| Length of Winch Head   | 6½″   | 7″    | 8″    | 11″   |
| Diameter outside end   | 6¼″   | 7½″   | 8½″   | 12″   |
| Size of Chain          | 5/16″ | ⅜″    | ½″    | ¾″    |

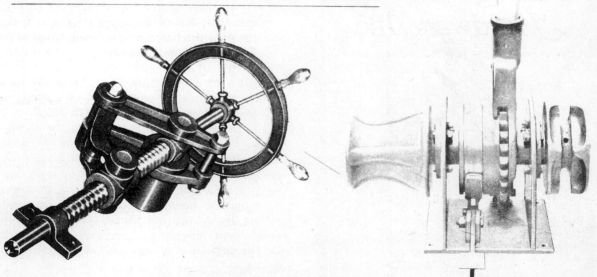

## Worthy of Note

If you share our respect for good old-fashioned foundry work but have a nationalistic streak too, a company here in the U. S. that still manufactures fine cast fittings is The Rostand Mfg. Co. of Milford, Conn. The many fittings shown in their 60-page catalog are most exciting in their form and bronze construction. Unfortunately, much of their line has been discontinued, victims of a changing market and, I suspect, poor marketing and distribution. Their line of beautiful brass bilge pumps, for example, is no longer available, nor is their brass tiller quadrant, nor mast cap, etc. Still, the remainder is fine and should be better known.

**The Rostand Mfg. Co.
Milford, Conn. 06460**

All items from Rostand Mfg. catalog.

### No. 2211
### REFRIGERATOR OR T HINGE

Cast Brass
In Pairs

| Size O.A. | Screws | Polished | Chrome |
|---|---|---|---|
| 3" x 5" | No. 8 | $ 6.00 Pr. | $ 7.50 Pr. |
| 3½" x 6" | No. 10 | 7.00 Pr. | 8.75 Pr. |
| 5" x 8" | No. 10 | 10.00 Pr. | 12.00 Pr. |

Size 3" x 5" has ⅜" or ¾" Offset

### No. 2554
### REFRIGERATOR FASTENER

Cast Brass

Made for a ⅜" offset or flush door and for either a right hand or left hand. Please specify when ordering.
Right hand shown.

| Lever | Screws | Polished | Chrome |
|---|---|---|---|
| 2½" | No. 8 | $2.75 Ea. | $3.50 Ea. |
| 4" | No. 8 | 4.00 Ea. | 5.00 Ea. |

146

### No. 2420 EYE NUT
Cast Brass—Plain or Polished

| Inside dia. of Eye | Tapped for Pipe Size | Plain | Polished |
|---|---|---|---|
| ⅜" | ⅜" | $ .50 Ea. | $ .80 Ea. |
| ½" | ½" | .75 Ea. | 1.10 Ea. |
| ¾" | ¾" | 1.15 Ea. | 1.65 Ea. |
| 1" | 1" | 1.50 Ea. | 2.00 Ea. |
| 1¼" | 1¼" | 1.85 Ea. | 2.85 Ea. |
| 1½" | 1½" | 2.10 Ea. | 3.15 Ea. |

### No. 3292 CAM-ACTION CLEAT
Double Action—Cast Bronze

| Length | Width | Rope Size | Polished | Chrome |
|---|---|---|---|---|
| 3½" | 1⅝" | ¼"-5⁄16" | $7.00 Ea. | $ 9.00 Ea. |
| 4¾" | 2¼" | ⅜"-½" | 9.50 Ea. | 12.00 Ea. |

You can tell when the management of a company really likes what it is doing, whether it is "just a business" to the men who run it or "the apple of their eye." Frankly, the impression you get from many firms is that of a huge junk jewelry outlet preparing to do trade with the indigenous populations of heretofore undiscovered galaxies. Massive improvements would come to the industry if, for one week, the management traded places with the stockroom clerks. Man, would you see a lot of superfluous items get discontinued! It is amazing how many decisions are being made for the sport, indeed for us, by so few individuals, traveling supplier agents and purchasing managers. Anyway, the exceptional firm stands out head and shoulders.

—GP

## Select Supplies

Take Jay Stuart Haft of Milwaukee, for example. This firm sells only selected boat hardware and supplies. But you can tell that they have thought about it, have asked themselves, "Is this worthy of my boat?" Most of their line has to do with windlasses and foredeck gear, but their other items too have that "picked-out" look. Their solid fuel fireplace, folding wash basin, teak wheels, really fine wood gangways, deck lights, door fixtures and cabin lamps all are either the best or unique in the marketplace. The small boat purist will say "rich man's dressings." This isn't so. Prices are competitive and, to the extent that they aren't, it is very often worth sacrificing having two or three second-rate products to having the one really good one. This, of course, is just one point of view, but one that comes from noticing that an awful lot of the best that was once available is no longer, having been replaced in the market by shockingly crumby, undurable, unfunctional and ugly merchandise. Twenty-five cents to Jay Stuart Haft will show you what I mean.

# Skylights and General Woodwork

Teak skylights, hatches and other deck and cabin woodwork of first quality workmanship produced to order in our own workshop, which manufactures S-L steering wheels, side ladders and other standard items.

## Electric Tri-Colour Launch Lamp

Copper.
Size of white lens : 4″ × 3″ (100 mm. × 75 mm.).
**No. 1283**

Jay Stuart Haft
8625 North Tennyson Dr.
Milwaukee, Wisc. 53217

147

All items from Haft catalog

# A handsome light and sturdy Folding wash basin
# *Solid Fuel Fireplace and Stove*

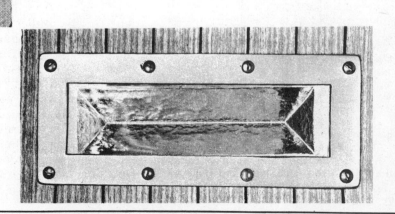

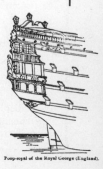

Poop-royal of the Royal George (England).

## Custom Fittings

Before going on to the Big Ones, a word or two about custom builders of fittings. It is extraordinary how many skilled and conscientious men are getting up every morning about this country and spending the day doing their thing, getting by happily doing what they do well and in a small way by word-of-mouth advertising. If you know about one and know that he or she wouldn't mind, let us know. Two that we found are Leslie L. Randall of North Dartmouth, Mass., and John Parker of North Reading, Mass.

Leslie Randall makes ship's wheels. He makes other things too, but wheels are his specialty. After twenty-five years at Concordia's high-quality yard, he "retired" to work on his own. He built the wheel for the replica schooner-yacht America and has built many of the wheels for craft off the ways of Goudy and Stevens.

John Parker is proprietor of Parker Machine and Boat Works. A pattern-maker, founder and machinist by profession, Mr. Parker has focused his skills on the marine field. Read over the enclosed letter he sent to us and share with us the feeling that, "God, it is good to have him!" His price schedule suggests that if a group of people can get together on their building plans, really substantial savings can be realized on custom fittings. We followed-up on his tool-source references and you will find them listed in the tool section.

148

**Parker Machine and Boat Works**
**170 Haverhill St.**
**N. Reading, Mass. 01864.**

Dear Mr. Putz:

Thank you for your interest in my business. I intended to answer much sooner than this but getting out rush orders for customers just seemed to crowd out letter writing time.

I do not have any literature, price lists or schedules, as the nature of my business pretty much precludes this.

I will, however, attempt to describe the nitch in this industrial nation into which I feel I am most qualified to fit. My background is in machine design and machine work, with a life-time hobby of boatbuilding (emphasis on sailboats). I have found with most of the sailboats that anything other than standard pulleys, turnbuckles and metal cleats is hard to find and one usually ends up with some kind of compromise that isn't really right for the boat. Also, since the day has come for the mass-produced, fiberglass, stock boats, the usual items of boat hardware that were usually installed by the builder, seem to have disappeared from the marine catalogs. Therefore, I have found myself designing and building all of this type of hardware for my own boats.

The past mass-produced hardware has probably been displaced by large orders from stock boat builders for specially designed hardware for their own boats. Hence, they are not for sale for anyone else.

I plan to come in here and help out the small boat shops and do-it-yourselfers by supplying the hardware that they need that is right for their boat and that they just can't get anywhere else.

Obviously, I cannot compete, price-wise, with mass-produced items. However, I do think that I can be very competitive with local machine shops which really are not equipped or trained to do the complete job of design, pattern-making and machining necessary. I am completely equipped for drafting, machining and pattern-making, and have over 30 years of experience in each of these fields.

Now for some examples. Since the ad you saw in the "National Fisherman" is my first, I have not had time to fill any of my orders as yet. I will give you my quotes on an inquiry that came in and also treat your example as one. (See enclosed sheet for this.) Just how you can explain all this type of service in your catalog is a mystery to me, but knowing well the knack you Maine people have of boiling a thought down to a few well-understood words, I don't doubt you can do it.

Pattern-making is a trade which usually requires a long apprenticeship and a thorough knowledge of foundry practice and metallurgy; therefore, I don't know of any books on the subject. They teach it at Wentworth Institute in Boston, so they might have a text book they use there. That's one possibility. Another is the U.S. Govt. Printing Office, and last, the English government prints some very well-explained books on the old crafts. I have two of them on hand forging which were recommended to me by a blacksmith in this country. The place to inquire about this is; Rural Industries Bureau, 35 Camp Road, Wimbledon Common, London SW1G.

As for patternmaking tools, I have taken the liberty of calling Woodcraft Supply here in Woburn, Mass., and have given them your name and address to send you their catalog. I highly recommend them. I have quite a few of their tools and especially enjoy using their wooden planes, particularly the general smoothing plane =16D03-0. The Swiss carving tools are excellent. A source for strictly pattern-making supplies is another mail order place and you should write for their catalog. The Kindt-Collins Company, 12651 Elmwood Ave., Cleveland, Ohio. If you need a book on foundry practice, Wentworth Institute would have one or tell you where and what to buy. I wouldn't advise going into the foundry business for profit, but if you intend this as a hobby or side interest, then go ahead.

Illustrations for this letter on next page.

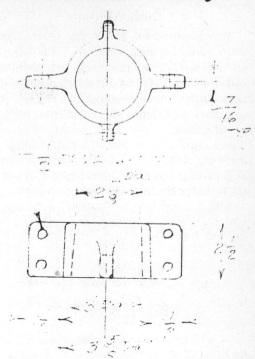

MAST HEAD FITTING

for Heavy Sloop Such

as Friendship

MATERIAL - Manganese Bronze

For strength and to save wt.

> **Quote on custom
> fittings order
> by J.P. Parker.
> See preceding page.**

Design cost for something this simple - No Charge

| | |
|---|---|
| Pattern Cost | $ 50.00 |
| Casting approx. 10 lbs. | 18.00 |
| Finishing and Drilling | 15.00 |
| Total cost for one | 83.00 |
| | |
| Other quotes    Cost each for order of ten | 38.00 |

Parts for a North Haven Dinghy based on an order of four (4) of each:

| | | |
|---|---|---|
| 10 lb. Mast Step | - Plain Commercial Bronze | $ 15.00 ea. |
| Complete Goose neck | - Manganese Bronze | 36.00 ea. |
| Pintles | - Manganese Bronze (4 pr.) | 7.00 ea. |

**149**

### An apology for American booksellers on the pricing of books in dollars that they paid for in pounds

A new book, "In Defence of Sailing Twin-Keeled GRP Craft in the Norfolk Broads" by Sir Cecil Throckmorton has just been published in London by the Lord Nelson Press. The price is 5 pounds.

An American reader of the book page of "Yachting Monthly" notes the fact with glee and calls the bookseller who gets him most of his marine books to place an order. Being a careful soul, our book buyer computes what he will have to pay for the book in dollars. Noting in the "New York Times" that the exchange rate for the day is $2.57 per pound, he multiplies this by the 5 pound price of the book and comes up with $12.85.

Imagine our book buyer's shock when his bookseller tells him he will have to charge him $15 for the title. The bookseller, being a patient soul, explains.

First the seller agrees with the buyer that the list price of the book at the current rate of exchange is indeed $12.85. He then points out that the Lord Nelson Press, like most other English publishers, will give him only a 1/3 discount, instead of the 40% he is accustomed to getting from American publishers — and the 40% he knows he must get on the average if he is to stay in business. This 1/3 discount will make the cost of the book to him, the seller, $8.61. If the seller then takes this cost of $8.61 back up to a list price which will give him his 40% discount, that list price, by arithmetic, will have to be $14.35. And the seller knows that slapping on a 65 cent charge for getting the book in from England will be little enough, so he does so, and comes up with $15.

"So," the bookseller tells the book buyer, "Next time you are converting English book prices from pounds to dollars, why don't you make it easy on yourself, and just multiply by three?"

The book buyer couldn't imagine why anyone would want to defend sailing twin-keel GRP boats on the Norfolk Broads, so he did multiply by three, cheerfully coughed up his money, and, in due course, read all about it.    **—RCT**

### Major Manufacturers and Suppliers

What compels beginning with Perko? It is an old firm which has continued the best of an old line. They have kept up with the field, but kept the best recent developments using the best designs and materials, and have not been tempted into gaudy and cheap lines or into over-proliferating. They have, therefore, kept prices down and the whole sense of their literature gives the feeling that they have maintained pride and pleasure in their merchandise. They continue to offer the old Herreshoff hollow-cast deck cleats, a good line of brass bilge pumps and, of course, their navigation and cabin lamps have lighted four generations of boatmen.

Perkins Marine
16490 Northwest 13th Ave.
P.O. Box D
Miami, Fla. 33164

All items from Perkins catalog.

Fig. 1016

Fig. 1018

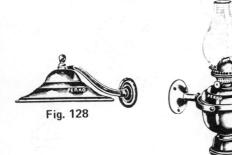

Fig. 128

Fig. 141

150

#### NAVY TYPE BILGE PUMPS
**2-3/4 Inch Brass Cylinder — Cast Bronze Fittings**
**Flax Packed Plunger — Weighted Valve**

**CHAMPION — Figs. 1016 and 1018**
**For Pipe**

| Fig. | Each | Extreme Length Inches | Inlet Pipe Thread Inches | Outlet Pipe Thread Inches | Weight Pounds |
|------|------|------|------|------|------|
| 1016 | $56.00 | 24 | 1-1/4 | 1-1/2 | 8 |
| 1018 | 47.00 | 16-1/4 | 1-1/4 | 1-1/2 | 5-1/2 |

Capacity —
Fig. 1016, 16 Strokes — 5 Gallons
Fig. 1018, 16 Strokes — 3 Gallons

---

Wilcox-Crittenden is another elder firm that maintains something old, something new and, I suppose, something blue. Certainly they have a personality of their own; more "average boatmen"-oriented somehow and broadly aimed at the center of the marine market.

I have always used them for ship's plumbing fixtures and, with the current changes in laws and a vast proliferation of firms and models going for the void, I plan to continue using them, betting on experience and a going thing. A lousy seacock or head fixture can and does sink people all the time. Best save experimentation for the other end of the alimentary canal. Of course, they offer a full line of marine gear and fittings. Their catalog begins with a most interesting piece on metals used in their line.

Wilcox-Crittenden.
Middletown, Conn. 06457

Items here and top of next page from W-C catalog.

**THE "HEAD-MATE"**
**WITH 90° CURVED TAILPIECE**

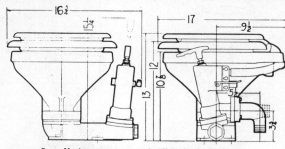

Base: Maximum measurement, 4⅞" wide by 9¼" long.

### "MARINIUM"®

"Marinium" is an alloy of magnesium, titanium, aluminum, beryllium and other metals in various measures. Specifically formulated for use where exposure to deteriorating elements is a problem. "Marinium" is an extraordinary metal, light in weight, and with a dense grain structure that results in an extreme strength to weight ratio. It is in fact, lighter per test strength than anything currently manufactured for marine use. Once formed, its surface is treated to produce additional corrosion and abrasion properties unheard of in other marine metals. "Marinium" fittings will not tarnish like bronze, pit like aluminum, peel like chrome or bleed like stainless.

The streamlined design of this unit — together with its compact size — makes it ideal for use under seats, lockers or bunks.

Rigid P.V.C., Acetal Resin and "Teflon"® are used in the construction of this toilet, together with our famous slow-fired pure-white vitreous china bowl. Comes complete with gleaming white seat and cover. No danger of chipping or peeling. Stainless Steel fasteners are also featured for lasting quality.

The 2-inch diameter pump offers smooth operation — only 6 strokes per quart. The design of the black finish cast aluminum handle assures firm grip. Nickel plated lever is readily accessible for full control. Piston rod packing gland is easily adjustable. Spiral flush action cleans bowl rapidly and efficiently.

"Joker" Backwater Check Valve prevents backflooding, yet opens fully to prevent choking or stoppage. Free-flow, non-clogging waste arm. Full size drain plug permits easy cleaning and thorough draining.

"Buna-N" gaskets and flap valves.

**Connections:** Intake will fit ¾-inch inside diameter rubber hose. Discharge Tailpiece fits 1½-inch inside diameter rubber hose.

**Repair Parts Kit:** Specify Fig. 1520, as described on page 57.

For best installation, use new Basic Seacox, Fig. 1561 and Acetal Resin Thru-Hulls, Fig. 8563.

**Net Weight:** 20 lbs.

### Elegant And Expensive

It is hard to know for sure whether the Merriman-Holbrook trident indicates the best there is or not; likely as not, it does mean the best for winches, blocks and some rigging fittings. Assuming good faith, their prices, and the loyalty of yachtsmen who don't mess around, they should be the best. They are distinctly not "boaty" or in the tradition of ". . .well now, shipmates, lets us set down and spin us a yarn of the days of canvas & hemp and when men were . . ." This is elegant stuff, beautiful, precise, very expensive. Because of the standard and prices, the most likely consideration for the waterman would be their jib furling gear. The strain a headstay must bear to set a jib properly and the circumstances under which a jib must often be controlled indicate no compromise and the Merriman-Holbrook models are powerful, smooth-working and worth the price.

Merriman Holbrook
301 River St.
Grand River, Ohio 44045

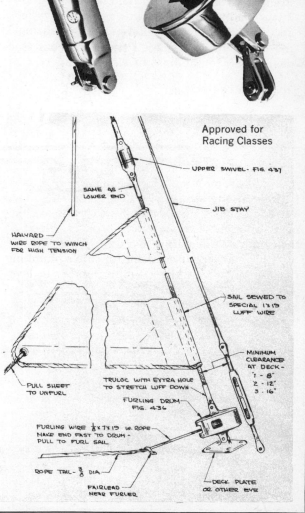

**151**

Approved for Racing Classes

UPPER SWIVEL- FIG. 437

SAME AS LOWER END

JIB STAY

HALYARD WIRE ROPE TO WINCH FOR HIGH TENSION

SAIL SEWED TO SPECIAL 1×19 LUFF WIRE

MINIMUM CLEARANCE AT DECK—
1 - 8"
2 - 12"
3 - 16"

PULL SHEET TO UNFURL

TRULOC WITH EXTRA HOLE TO STRETCH LUFF DOWN

FURLING DRUM FIG. 436

FURLING WIRE ⅛"×7×19 w. ROPE MAKE END FAST TO DRUM- PULL TO FURL SAIL

ROPE TAIL- ⅜ DIA

FAIRLEAD NEAR FURLER

DECK PLATE OR OTHER EYE

### 'Other Type of Fitting'

It would be foolish, probably irresponsible, to neglect "the other type of fitting." These are purely functional, for the most part racing-boat, fittings; alloy manifestations of stress, tension and compression indexes and best-fit curves. Watermen are being silly to denigrate performance. It is not only pointless, it is futile. To go just as fast over the water as is possible is exciting both intellectually and sensually. Our only complaint is that the psychology and much of the sociology that surrounds this interest hurts the environment, aids in the general decay of the aesthetics of maritime traditions and, for economic reasons, inordinately skews the marketplace in favor of a kind of shoddiness that is of use to no one because it is based on exploitation of people's materialistic side and ignorance rather than on integrity and people's best side. This isn't the fault of the things themselves. It is the fault of relatively few merchants and clubs which educate people to this syndrome to everything for everybody allovertheplace, allthetime spending money and having someone else's idea of fun.

In any case, if your interest is to maximize strength to size, windage and weight and absolutely flatback go, you will need fittings for it and there are firms making and specializing in the distribution of these fittings for your stock racing craft, dreamboat or experiment.

**From Nicro-Fice catalog.**

152

Nicro-Fice has a 55-page catalog of fittings for the tuned boat. They are modern, technically sophisticated and very functional. You won't want them on your cutter or Friendship or cruising ketch. You will want them on your racing machine.

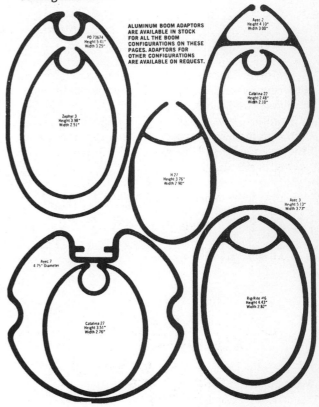

### 3. NM-350 REMOTE OUTHAUL

This powerful outhaul is designed for boats up to 50'. Twenty turns of the handle moves the outhaul slide approximately one inch.

Fabricated of an anodized, high tensile cast aluminum body with mitre gears and a stainless steel screw, the Nicro remote outhaul is fully compatible with aluminum booms and can be built into any boom that has a minimum inside height of $3\frac{1}{4}$" and width of $1\frac{5}{8}$". A maximum clew adjustment of 11" is possible and the retractable crank lies flush with boom surface.

Nicro's remote outhaul is supplied ready for installation with detailed instructions.

The outhaul cable is not included but we recommend $\frac{1}{8}$" flexible stainless steel cable for boats up to 40' and $\frac{3}{16}$" for larger boats. With $\frac{3}{16}$" cable, the NM-313 sheave box with 3" diameter sheave should be used.

**NM-350 Remote Outhaul**      **$64.00**

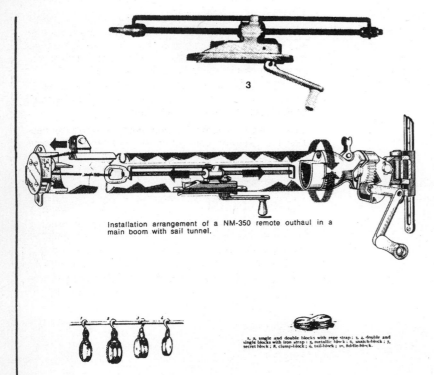

Installation arrangement of a NM-350 remote outhaul in a main boom with sail tunnel.

1, 2, single and double blocks with rope strap; 3, 4, double and single blocks with iron strap; 5, metallic block; 6, snatch-block; 7, secret block; 8, clump-block; 9, tail-block; 10, fiddle-block.

A Siren or Fog-horn.

**SOME OTHER ITEMS
AND FIRMS IN THE GEAR
AND FITTINGS TRADE**

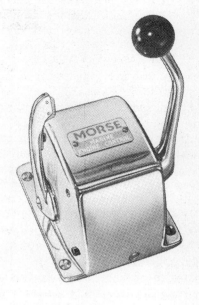

Morse Marine makes engine controls and steering systems. A byword in the field, many builders and boatmen take them for granted, a situation that would be unfortunate if it were not completely justified. Their equipment works, looks good and lasts well, the inboard controls being particularly excellent.

**Morse Controls Division
21 Clinton St.
Hudson, Ohio 44236**

All items from Morse catalog.

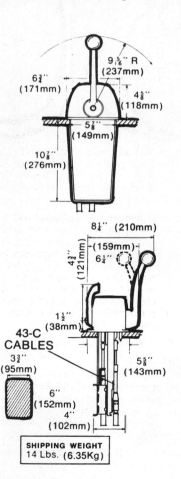

9⅟₁₆″ R
(237mm)
6¾″
(171mm)
4⅝″
(118mm)
5⅞″
(149mm)
10⅞″
(276mm)

8¼″ (210mm)
(159mm)
6¼″
4¾″
(121mm)

**43-C
CABLES**

1½″
(38mm)
3¾″
(95mm)
5⅝″
(143mm)
6″
(152mm)
4″
(102mm)

**SHIPPING WEIGHT
14 Lbs. (6.35Kg)**

The Model MK is a heavy duty control for remote operation of both clutch and throttle of single or twin engines with hydraulic transmissions. The solid bronze housing is chrome plated for corrosion resistance.

Detents are built-in at forward, neutral and reverse for safe one hand operation. Fully adjustable neutral throttle and idle speed control, including a provision for engine shutdown.

This control is ideal for single lever series dual station installations when used with the MD-24 or SS-24 control systems.

10⅞″ (276 mm) depth is required below the mounting surface. The control is available with levers bending inward (for single engines) or outward (for convenient operation of two controls for twin engines).

Throttle cable travel is 2¾″ (70 mm) for push to open operation or 2⅞″ (73 mm) for pull to open operation. Clutch cable travel is 2¾″ (70 mm).

Single engine installation requires a throttle connection kit, a clutch connection kit and two 43-C Morse Red-Jaket® cables which are designed for use with Morse components to insure smooth, instant response to lever movement.

**Model MK** — Chrome finish, lever bending inwards. Uses 2 ea. 43-C cables . . . . . . . . . . . . . . . . . . . . . . **A46008-1**

**Model MK** — Chrome finish, lever bending outward. Uses 2 ea. 43-C cables . . . . . . . . . . . . . . . . . . . . . . **A46011-1**

**Dual Station Kit** — Required to connect SS-24 or MD-24 control to MK for dual station system . . . . . . . . . . **A40167**

**Neutral Safety Switch** — Prevents starting engine while in gear . . . . . . . . . . . . . . . . . . . . . . . . . . . . . . . . . . . . . **A47338**

153

*Screw Propeller.*
*A, sectional elevation, the section being through shaft and hub, showing method of attaching blades h by bolts t ; B, side elevation ; C, cross-section of blade, on larger scale ; D, diagrammatic view of hull of a screw-propeller ship, in which e shows position of boilers, i, the engines ; f, propeller-shaft ; e, thrut-block ; g, propeller.*

Remember the Fuller Brush Man? I have no idea whether he is still pounding the pavement or not, but he is splashing about here and there through Fuller's Marine Division which offers not only a line of boat grooming products, but newly-designed plastic portlights. If anyone has used these ports, we would like to hear from them.

The Fuller Brush Co.
Marine Division
88 Long Hill St.
East Hartford, Conn. 06108

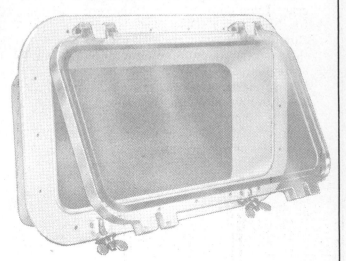

From Fuller catalog.

o  Far lighter in weight than conventional Portlight

o  Frame and spigot made of ABS plastic Injection molded for uniform seamless high quality finish

o  Opening "glass" is one-piece Plexiglass with no leak, no stick, neoprene "O" ring gasket

o  The strength of all components is up to the challenge of blue water cruising

o  15° bevel or slant on spigot

o  Ready to install--no painting

o  No corrosion

o  All fittings are marine-grade brass or bronze with heavy chrome plating

o  Fiberglass screens and plastic finishing rings are included

LIGHTWEIGHT -- STRONG -- READY-TO-GO

and marine designers are choosing this portlight for their own boats!

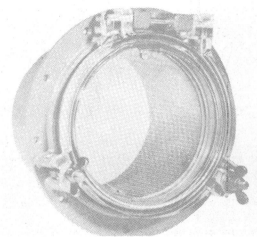

| Item No. | Size of opening in inches | Color | Price each including screen and finishing ring | Shipping Weight |
|---|---|---|---|---|
| 4FM 2005 | 5" x 12" | White | $42.00* | 5 lbs. |
| 4FM 2025 | 5" x 12" | Cream | $42.00* | 5 lbs. |
| 4FM 2007 | 7" x 15" | White | 49.50* | 7-1 2 lbs. |
| 4FM 2017 | 7" x 15" | Cream | 49.50* | 7-1 2 lbs. |
| 4FM 2013 | 7" dia. | White | 38.00* | 4 lbs. |

154

*plus shipping charges from Hartford, Conn., and state taxes if applicable.

## FLOTATION

A most grave potential hazard is built into many boats and is often hidden until a serious capsize occurs. I speak of the air-filled flotation compartment which is built in below the waterline of many small craft.

I know of two instances when loss of stability occurred after water which had leaked into the "sealed" bilges shifted position and caused instability. I have experienced this in an outboard craft. A friend, an experienced sailor, nearly lost his life and that of his wife and crew when a center-boarder lost stability when water which had flooded the hidden bilges shifted causing the boat to capsize and then remain partially submerged with several gallons of water holding her bow down, stern high, in a position from which righting was impossible. Death from exposure was averted only when these people were rescued by a passing boatman who discovered their plight as they were near exhaustion.

Those of us who have discussed these incidents have concluded that any below-waterline sealed compartment of this sort is hazardous for a number of reasons. There is no more difficult task than righting a centerboarder which has her flotation so placed. The experiences described indicated that the undetected leaking may lead to unexpected and irrevocable loss of stability.

I refuse to use any boat which depends upon below-water-line air-filled buoyancy tanks. The British-built Alpha Class sloop made by Mossoms of Oxford is an exemplar for the boating industry. The British Alpha uses above-waterline foam flotation. An Alpha can be righted instantly and sailed while fully flooded. I know of no American sailing dingy which approaches the Alpha safety standards.

I hope you may see fit to publish this warning concerning the hazards inherent in the below-waterline air-filled "flotation" compartments.

Have you ever tried to bail one of these flooded flotation compartments? Right; it can't be done. I got out of it alive by beaching on a sand beach in Southern California. The story might have been different had the loss of stability occurred in the chop of Buzzards Bay.

John Reardon
Southeastern Massachusetts
Technological Institute
North Dartmouth, Mass.

### Imported Gear

We wish "The Mariner's Catalog" had more foreign sources than it does of tools and marine gear. If you know of such, let us know. Several of the firms listed above carry imports, of course, Dutch navigation lamps and the like, but no one in this country has really covered the waterfront to any extent, certainly not adequately.

One firm that carries imported marine fittings exclusively and in a small growing way, is Henry's Marine Buying Service. Henry went abroad, Sweden especially, and found some very choice items for deck and tophamper.

Henry's Marine Buying Service
P.O. Box 301
Coconut Grove, Fla. 33133

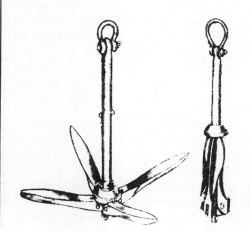

Swedish

## FOLDING

## GRAPNELS

| Cat. No. | Weight | Price |
| --- | --- | --- |
| 501 | 1.5 lbs. | $5.50 |
| 502 | 3.0 lbs. | 7.80 |
| 503 | 5.0 lbs. | 9.30 |
| 504 | 7.7 lbs. | 12.30 |
| 505 | 12.1 lbs. | 21.60 |

155

### Prolonging Life

Lovers, owners and victims of elder wooden boats share a siege of woes and worries. True, the "rather-sail-than-sand" set miss some of the profounder joys, trading them in as they do for logic. But, still, we have a real problem in the veteran craft and we can use all the help we get. Travaco Laboratories is a friend. Their products, sealant paints, caulking and the like work really well. Before going at your craft in a big way, though, experiment in a small place. Very often, the repair or improvement job done this year will require tearing out to get at a larger job later and, in some cases, the better product is the least appropriate where there is a likelihood of having to re-do it in the near future, not only because effort has to be repeated (which is de rigueur in a wooden boat anyway), but because some of the better products really stick like hell and can drive you bananas when you are trying to un-do them. The directions for use of the Travaco products are thorough and, if followed, will give stupendous results on craft old-timers would have burned for their fittings.

# SAILS

⊘✱"Sails" by Jeremy Howard-Williams.
John de Graff, Tuckahoe, N.Y.
1967, 411 pp., illustrated, index, bibliography, $12.50.

If ever there was a complete book on a given subject, this has to be it. Howard-Williams, a former sailmaker with the famed firm of Ratsey and Lapthorn, has written the definitive work on modern sails. He covers sail theory, cloth, design, cutting and sewing, rigging, tuning, maintenance, cleaning, repair, types of sails, alterations and much, much more. The illustrations are simple and clear, and the writing is straightforward.

This is not a beginner's book, however. It should appeal to experienced sailors who are seeking more detailed information on the subject. Since the quest for higher performance sails is largely pursued by racing enthusiasts, this book would be of more interest to them, rather than to cruisers. Howard-Williams describes most of the modern advances in sail technology (to 1967, that is) that nowadays make the difference between the competitive and non-competitive yacht.

If your interests lie more toward cruising, though, don't ignore this book. There is information here on all types of sails of value to all types of craft. Much of it can be put to good, practical use.

—PHS

From "Sails"

156

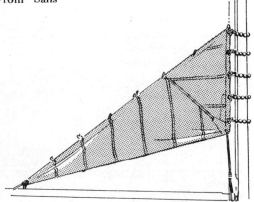

Fig. 64. Headsail acting as a trysail. The foot, reinforced with tape, becomes the luff and is fastened to the mast with parrel beads.

_Battens_

The most common material for battens is wood. Hickory is the best because it combines strength with flexibility; next comes ash. Battens should be well rounded, and they may be tapered towards the inner

end both as to width and thickness, in order to make them bend more at the tip. They should, of course, be well varnished to make them resist water soakage. A good idea, particularly if the end is thin, is to strap the tip with adhesive tape. This both prevents it breaking too easily, and protects the sail if a break does occur. A strip of adhesive tape the full length of the batten serves as a protection from sharp corners in a break, and also enables you to pull the broken end out if the worst should occur.

⊘✱"Make Your Own Sails" by R.M. Bowker and S.A. Budd.
St. Martin's Press, New York.
1960 (second edition), 142 pp., illustrated, index, glossary, $4.95.

There's nothing like being able to beat the system and, because of the high price of quality sails, knowing how to make your own sails should help you do it. Admittedly, there's nothing worse than a poorly made or poorly fitted suit of sails, and some of the worst are made by amateurs. But amateurs are usually at fault from the lack of information more than anything else. After reading this book, I am convinced that most people could make their own and do a creditable job.

"Make Your Own Sails" is a genuine practical book. Subjects covered include theory, sailcloths, sailmaking operations, headsails, Bermudian mainsail, gaff mainsail, gunter lugsail, parachute spinnaker, stormsails, maintenance, renovation, repair, alteration and sailmaking in Dacron. This is a British book, so some of the terminology might be different (such as terylene for Dacron), but the glossary should carry you through.

—PHS

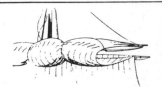

"Everything You Need to 'Do it'."
Kent Sails
Box 7024, Wauwatosa, Wisc.

The "it" referred to above is making your own sails and other items with canvas. Write to Kent Sails and they will send you a free catalog of sailmaking supplies. Send them $2.25 and they will send you a copy of "Guideline Drawings and General Instructions" for the construction of storm sails, jibs, genoas, sunshades, sailcovers and ghosts; this is not a book, but a series of four sheets with sketches and pithy instructions.

—PHS

"Amateur Sailmaker's Catalogue," $1.
"Make Your Own Mainsails," $1.99
"Make Your Own Spinnakers and Staysails," $1.99
"Make Your Own Stormsails," $1.99
"Make Your Own Jibsails," $1.99

**Sailrite Kits, 1650 Verde Vista,
Pomona, Calif. 91767.**

There are kits available for making just about anything these days, and sails are not excepted. Sailrite assembles kits to make custom sails and has ready-made kits on hand for many stock boats, including Blue Jays, Cals, Columbias, El Toros, Ericsons, 5-0-5s, Penguins, Santanas, Ventures, etc.

If you don't want to work from a kit, they're ready to oblige: their catalog lists sailmaking supplies sold individually. Best of all, their four booklets (paperbound) on making sails make amateur work simple and straightforward. These booklets, by James Lowell Grant, have excellent illustrations and are well written.

Each one is divided into three sections: sail design, sail construction procedures and using your sail (including fault detection and correction). The booklet on mainsails, however, doesn't cover gaff sails. A nice feature about Sailrite's service is that they are willing to give you advice by mail if you have difficulties making your sails. Too many companies sell you their products and then ignore all pleas for help.
—PHS

"The Sailmaker," edited and arranged by Robert L. Mickelson, is an attractive and informative booklet of 38 pages, which was assembled in the first place to complement a talk on sailmaking made before a meeting in 1970 of the Early Trades and Crafts Society of New York. The copy I have before me was obtained at the fall meeting of Antique Tools and Trades of Connecticut held at Mystic Seaport at the end of October 1972 at which Bob Mickelson gave a sailmaking demonstration.

Bob Mickelson's ancestors, as far back as is remembered, were sailmakers and shipbuilders. The booklet is dedicated to them and to his father in particular who served his apprenticeship as a sailmaker with the firm of William H. Griffin of City Island, N.Y.

In addition to an historical sketch and a description of various rigs, there is an excellent section on sail cloth, another on sailmaking equipment, as well as descriptions of various techniques for sewing, stitching, roping and so forth. Numerous illustrations supplement the text and add to the attractiveness of this booklet.

No price is given, nor do I know for sure if copies are still to be had. However, for those interested, inquiries should be addressed to Robert L. Mickelson, 174 Rochelle St., City Island, N.Y. 10464.

—John Gardner

**From "Making Your Own Jibsails"**

V.  Fashion the foot portion of the sail next. If you earlier set aside a split panel which covers the exposed foot portion of the sail plan, proceed to "C" below. If you have not yet cut panels for this part of the sail, go to "A" below.

A.  Place the sewn panels over the floor plan. Unroll the cloth bolt from the leech to the tack over the portion of the sail plan left exposed (if any). Allow a two inch overlap at the leech and a three inch overlap along the foot tape. Turn the bolt, if necessary, and unroll it until the foot portion of the sail plan is covered.

B.  Glue and sew these panels together with constant one-half inch seams.

C.  Split the foot section vertically into three pieces as has been illustrated in the case of the Cal 20 jib in Figure 18. Overlap the three panels to form two one-half inch seams. Start broadseaming each seam up from the foot edge of the cloth a distance equal to the depth of your foot roach plus three inches (the allowance of extra cloth outside the tape) plus either two, three, or four inches depending upon whether your cloth is firm, medium, or soft. The broadseams should widen one inch for every twelve inches of their length (counting the tappered part of the seam only).

D.  Now glue the foot roach section of the sail to the main assembly. Use the appropriate broadseam for your particular cloth. Start this broadseam 50% of the length of the seam from the tack.

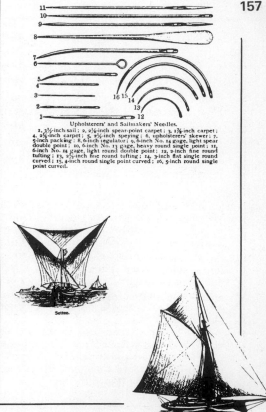

**Upholsterers' and Sailmakers' Needles.**
1, 3½-inch sail; 2, 2⅜-inch spear-point carpet; 3, 1⅞-inch carpet; 4, 2¾-inch carpet; 5, 2½-inch speying; 6, upholsterers' skewer; 7, 5-inch packing; 8, 6-inch regulator; 9, 6-inch No. 14 gage, light spear double point; 10, 6-inch No. 13 gage, heavy round single point; 11, 6-inch No. 14 gage, light round double point; 12, 2-inch fine round tufting; 13, 2½-inch fine round tufting; 14, 3-inch flat single round curved; 15, 4-inch round single point curved; 16, 5-inch round single point curved.

Settee.

Sloop.

157

# Sails  *BOUGHT AND SOLD*

Bacon & Associates Inc.
528 2nd Street
Annapolis, Maryland 21203
Phone: 301-263-4880

Recently I sailed with a happy man. He occasionally races his big, old Alden sloop, and was not entirely satisfied with the good-but-not-perfect big Genoa jib he had. But then he found as perfect-setting a jib as I've ever seen. It should have cost him well over a thousand dollars, but he paid $200 for it instead. He just loves that sail.

He got it from the Bacon people. It's one of those businesses where the people know what they're doing and have kept the thing small enough to be able to keep doing it, rather than merely "administer" somebody else doing it who is less competent than they are.

Bacon typically has an inventory of 3,000 to 4,000 sails in his loft. The high point is in January, the low at the end of the summer. These are mainsails, mizzens, all kinds of headsails, spinnakers, mizzen staysails, and a few gaff sails, varying in luff length from 10' to 80'.

You find out what's in the inventory by writing for a free monthly listing, which is sent by first-class mail. You can ask to get it two months running, but then you must request it again.

The only way to get a sail from Bacon is to choose it from their list. They describe the sail and you choose it, rather than the other way around.

On big sails, like my friend's beautiful Genoa, there are very large savings. On smaller sails in the more popular sizes, the savings are less, but are still well worth thinking about.

Some of the sails are brand new. (Sailmakers sometimes get stuck, having built a sail that the customer, for whatever reason, decides he no longer wants.) There is a saving, too, on these new sails.

You can also get from Bacon fittings that attach to the sail, such as slides or hanks. And they carry the English Marlowe braided dacron rope for sheets. Thus you can get everything you might need to complete the sail.

Normal shipment is by UPS at 2:30 p.m. If an order isn't received in time to make today's UPS pickup, it will certainly get on the truck tomorrow. Bacon can ship C.O.D., or you can pay for the sail in advance. They charge 3% of the price for packing and shipping.

All of the sails at Bacon are taken in on consignment. They must have your sail in their loft before they can describe it accurately in their list and before they can ship it quickly to a customer. You can send your sail to them without any prior communication. They will acknowledge its receipt and tell you exactly how they will list it, including the price. You can quibble with the price they put on your sail, but they know the market and will try to sell your sail for a fair price.

For their efforts, Bacon & Associates take a 30% commission.

The Bacon telephone is always answered by people who know their business; you don't find yourself calling from Maine or California and talking to someone who doesn't know a luff wire from a batten pocket.

Roger C. Taylor

158

## Don't—Forget—Me Knot

The following handy bit of advice came to us "over the counter," so to speak, in a release from Samson Cordage Works, 470 Atlantic Ave., Boston, Mass. 02210. It's easy to assume that rope is rope, and even those who use rope a lot fail to take into full account the weakening factor of knots. In a genuine service to rope users, Samson has come up with the following:

—DRG

Most knots cause from 40% to 50% strength reduction, which is the prime reason riggers like to terminate and connect lines with eye and end-for-end splices. A professional buried eye splice with a double braided line, for example, can retain 100% of the strength of the line and an end-for-end splice can retain 90% of the strength.

Because knotting can still serve a useful function, however, Samson recently conducted a series of tests on the knotted strength of double braided line and three-strand line.

The basic reference used was the: "Encyclopedia of Knots and Fancy Rope Work," fourth edition, Graumont and Hensel; and the rope used were 4" circumference Samson 2-and-1 braided nylon, with an average breaking strength of 54,000 lbs. and a 4" circumference

three-strand twisted nylon with an average breaking strength of 43,000 lbs.

Tests indicated that the Samson bowline-reeved loop bend was the knot that retained the highest precentage of the breaking strength in both the braided, as well as the three-strand twisted construction. Specific results were: the Samson 2-in-1 braided nylon line broke at 36,100 lbs. and the 3-strand twisted broke at 24,900 lbs. This indicates that the knotted doublebraided rope retained 67% of its average splice-breaking strength, and 80% of the

minimum splice-breaking strength of a new 3-strand twisted rope according to Military Specification MIL-R-17343D.

A important factor in strength reduction is the tendency for the loose end in most knots to slip and "walk through" the knot under heavy and cyclical loads.

Additional data developed during the test program include the facts that a bowline bend on double-braided rope is the most stable knot; it holds tight even if ends are not whipped; loops can be linked rather than reeved, although reeved is considered less abrasive; and it can be untied after loading.

Testing was done on the Samson-Young 300,000-lb. capacity tensile tester, in the Samson Research and Development Laboratory which is certified by the Cordage Institute and by U.S. Government agencies.

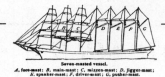

⊛ "The Deadeye: How it was made in Lunenburg, Nova Scotia'
by John M. Kochiss.

The Marine Historical Association, Mystic, Conn.
1970, 43 pp., illustrated, glossary, bibliography,
paperbound, $3.95.

When you first have a look at this book on
the shelf, your first reaction is: "Aw, come on.
Who in the world is going to want to read that?"
You chuckle to yourself and smugly pick it up,
thinking all the while that some nitpicking
professor probably forced some poor master's
degree candidate to write this as his thesis.

But you pick it up and find yourself reading
it, and liking it. The illustrations alone tell the
story, and the glossary and bibliography for this
43-page book put to shame most 200-pagers. In
a short time, you learn more about deadeyes
than you ever knew before and you're glad you
have. The detail is fine but not excruciating, and
by page 43 you're ready to replace all those
turnbuckles in your rigging with nice, salty,
practical, lignum vitae deadeyes.

The price, incidentally, is steep. The only
consolation in this regard is that the publisher
uses good paper and two colors. When you
consider all the money you'll save making your
own deadeyes (there's enough information here
to do just that), though, it's probably a small
price to pay.

—PHS

"Working in Canvas" by P.W. Blandford.
Brown, Son & Ferguson, 52 Darnley St.
Glasgow, Scotland.
1965, 72 pp., illustrated, paperbound, glossary-index, 7/6.

Not how to make sails, but how to work in
canvas, which means that it is a book on
stitching, trimming, grommet-fastening, folding,
etc. There is good material on tools, instructions
for making a canvas sea bag, and quite a bit on
miscellaneous fastenings, such as eyelets, snaps
and other attachments. Something unique is a
combination glossary and index — you look up a
word or term, read its definition and get a page
number to turn to for amplifying information.

—PHS

From "Working in Canvas"

Mark an outline around the damage parallel
with the stitches on the edge of the patch. Cut
this out and make short cuts at each corner so
that the edges may be turned under (Fig. 18*c*).
Sew these edges to the patch in the same way as
the outer lines of stitching.

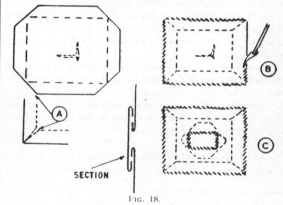

SECTION

FIG. 18.

159

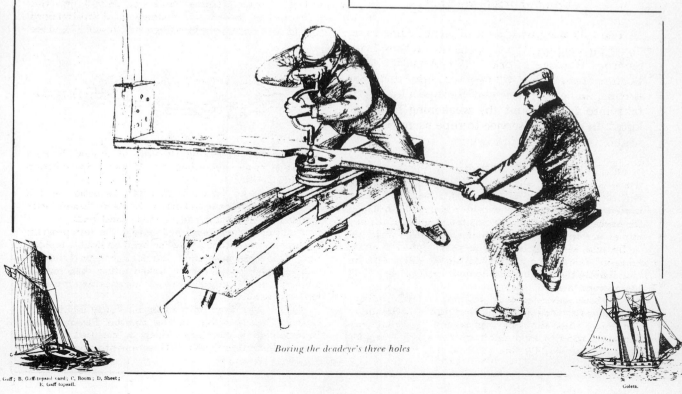

*Boring the deadeye's three holes*

a. Bowsprit; b. Bobstays.

# Rigging

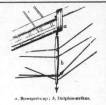

a. Bowsprit-cap; b. Dolphin-striker.

✪ "Splicing Wire and Fiber Rope" by Raoul Graumont and John Hensel.
Cornell Maritime Press, Cambridge, Md.
1945, 112 pp., paperbound, illustrated glossary, index, $3.

As it was published in 1945, this book doesn't cover the new synthetic ropes, but that doesn't matter too much, since the principles are still the same. There are 259 examples here, so it is difficult to imagine anyone's questions going unanswered. In addition to the splicing material, there is information on fiber rope sizes and characteristics (same for wire), blocks and tackles and terminology. The index is divided into two parts, one on wire rope and the other on fiber rope, which makes it easy on the practical user.

—PHS

### Quotes, diagram from "Splicing. . ."

*Standard Types of Wire Rope* are made up of 7, 12, 19, 24, and 37 wires each. Such a rope consisting of six strands of 12 wires each is commercially known as 6 by 12 rope, which is obtainable in varying degrees of flexibility, as previously explained, as are the other sizes.

When rope is used for ship's rigging, derrick guys, or under similar conditions involving continued exposure to the elements, the wires should be galvanized. Rope subjected to constant bending around drums and sheaves is not usually so treated.

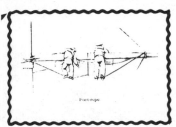

Foot-rope

*Lubricating Wire Rope.* Wire rope should be protected by a suitable lubricant both internally and externally, to prevent rust and to keep it pliable. The lubricant used should not only cover the outer surface of the rope but it should also penetrate into the hemp center, to prevent it from absorbing moisture, and at the same time lubricate the inner surfaces of the wires and strands. Best results cannot be obtained from thick, heavy grease and oils and the sticky compounds frequently used for this purpose.

★ "Wire Splicing" by R. Scot Skirving.
Brown, Son & Ferguson, Glasgow, Scotland.
1968, 49 pp., paperbound, illustrated, $1.

A bargain at the price. The book is divided into five parts on general points concerning wire rope, the eye splice, the short splice, wire grommets and the stropping of blocks and the long splice. Though certainly writing for the pro, Skirving also has the amateur who lacks the necessary tools in mind: for instance, he recommends a long screwdriver, ground fairly sharp and narrow at the end, as a makeshift marlinespike.

—PHS

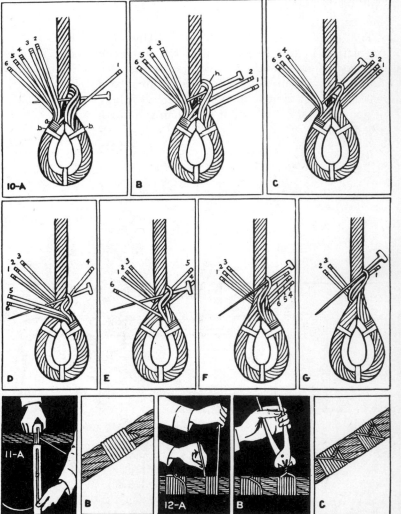

PLATE 8—DIAGRAMMATIC STEPS IN SPLICING AND SEIZING

● "Handbook for Riggers" by W.G. (Bill) Newberry.
Newberry, Box 2999, Calgary, Alberta, Canada.
1967, 118 pp., illustrated, glossary, $2.95.

When you pick up a book by an author who lists his nickname in parentheses, you **know** it's going to be good and practical. This one is. It's a little shirtpocket handbook loaded with practical details, tables, diagrams, step-by-step instructions and advice.

There are three basic sections: wire rope information, synthetic ropes and general rigging information. Some of the specialized categories are winch line and choker specs, uncoiling and spooling wire rope, reeving wire rope, splicing synthetic ropes, knot efficiency, safe working loads for rope and tackle blocks, timber and plank strengths, chain strengths, guy stresses, inclined planes, needle beam platform and bosun's chair, and weights of seamless and welded pipes. Especially useful are the numerous times that the author presents diagrams showing the right way and the wrong way of doing something.

—PHS

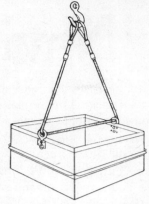

FIG. 3. Basket hitch. If the load is prevented from tilting, such as by the use of two hoists or cranes, this hitch is suitable for lifting shafts, boiler drums, tanks, etc. (*American Chain & Cable Co.*)

FIG. 4. A choker sling gets a viselike grip on the load. (*American Chain & Cable Co.*)

**From "Handbook for Riggers**

But let us look into the amount of work that he may be expected to accomplish in an 8-hour day, and then compare his effort with the cost of doing the job electrically. If electric power costs, let us say, 3 cents per kilowatt-hour, and assuming that the electrically driven apparatus is 50 per cent efficient, then the cost equivalent of the man's labor may be somewhat near the figures given below: Keep in mind that for continuous work a man may be expected to deliver about 0.10 hp, while for a very short time he may exert from 0.4 to 0.5 hp.

A strong man can lift 86 tons (say bags of cement) from the ground to a height of 4 ft in an 8-hour work day, averaging 0.045 hp. The cost of doing this electrically would be about 1.6 cents per day.

A man can carry 22.3 tons up a ramp or stair to a height of 12 ft in an 8-hour day, averaging 0.034 hp. Electrical cost 1.2 cents.

Pushing a wheelbarrow he can move 40.7 tons up a 3-ft ramp in 8 hours, and averages 0.015 hp. Power cost 0.52 cents.

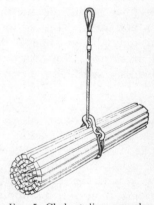

FIG. 5. Choker sling can also be used with a hook where it is more convenient. (*American Chain & Cable Co.*)

161

Section of Eddystone Light-house.

FIG. 2. Component parts for a single sling, choker sling, or basket sling. (*American Chain & Cable Co.*)

"Handbook of Rigging" by W.R. Rossnagel.
McGraw-Hill, New York.
1964, 383 pp., illustrated, index, $15.

The sub-title of this book is "for Construction and Industrial Operations," which is true enough, but the content just as applicable to boatmen. It is a textbook more than a handbook, and the range is encyclopedic.

A sampling of the 23 chapters: fiber rope, wire rope, hoisting chains and hooks, planks for scaffolds, portable ladders, strength calculations for timbers, handling loads on slings and accident prevention. The appendix is full of useful reference tables.

—PHS

# Navigation

Celestial navigation, to beginners, has an air of mystery to it. Maybe it's because of the stars, which play such a key part in the entire process. Learning to navigate by using the heavenly bodies is no more difficult than learning to repair a marine engine. But you don't find anybody choking up when he is told to examine closely a schematic drawing of an exhaust manifold; yet mention a few of celestial navigation's buzz words, like celestial triangle, Greenwich hour angle and meridian altitude, and most people will dive for cover.

There's an army of people preying on this attitude — some of them pure snake-oil salesmen. Everywhere you turn you find correspondence schools, books, pamphlets and magazine articles all chanting at the same time, over and over, "Listen to me, my method is best, don't listen to anybody else. I will sort out the mysterious convolutions that will otherwise hopelessly twist your brain." Don't you believe it.

After learning celestial navigation twice, once privately and once when I was in the Coast Guard, and after reading through most of the books in print on the subject, I have come to the conclusion that there is no easy way to learn how to navigate; however, there's nothing really difficult or mysterious about it either. You need a clear head and the willingness to study hard, that is all.

Books on celestial navigation can be divided into two camps: those that begin with theory and then methodically build up your knowledge and understanding, and those that say "forget the theory, forget everything else you might have learned, and follow me." Dutton, Bowditch, and Wright are in the first camp; Kittredge and Blewitt are in the second. I, for one, can't see how anyone can learn how to navigate without understanding the theory behind the practice, but then again, I'm one of those people that has to be able to visualize something before he can grasp it.

Most methods of celestial navigation taught these days rely one of three sets of tables: HO 214, HO 229 or HO 249. The first two are used in conjunction with the "Nautical Almanac"; the last uses the "Air Almanac." The first two give you more precise positions; the last, originally intended for aircraft navigation, gives you adequate but less accurate positions.

⚫ "Celestial Navigation" by Frances W. Wright. Cornell Maritime Press, Cambridge, Md. 1969, 142 pp., illustrated, examples, bibliography, index, $7.50.

Uses HO 249 with the "Air Almanac." Has good, clear illustrations to carry you through the theory. Wright's sight reduction form is labyrinthine, but once you've got it, you're home free.

⚫ "How to Navigate Today" by M.R. Hart. Cornell Maritime Press, Cambridge, Md. 1970 (5th edition), 111 pp., illustrated, index, paperbound, $2.50

Uses HO 214, but does discuss HO 249 and other tables as well.

⚫ "Celestial Navigation for Yachtsmen" by Mary Blewitt. John de Graff, Tuckahoe, N.Y. 1964, 94 pp., index, illustrations, $4.95.

Uses HO 249 and the "Air Almanac." Blewitt cuts the subject right down to the bare bones.

"Self-Taught Navigation" by Robert Y. Kittredge. Northland Press, Flagstaff, Ariz. 1970, 81 pp., $1.95 paper.

Uses HO 249 and the "Nautical Almanac." This uses the "you-can-learn-in-10-easy-steps" technique.

The following publications used in celestial navigation are available from the U.S. Naval Oceanographic Office, Washington, D.C., or your friendly local nautical chart agent:

HO 214, Tables of Computed Azimuth and Altitude.
9 volumes, one for each 10 degrees of latitude.

HO 229, Sight Reduction Table for Marine Navigation.
6 volumes. This is the replacement for HO 214, which will be phased out in 1975.

HO 249, Sight Reduction Tables for Air Navigation.
3 volumes.

162

—PHS

✪"Celestial Navigation Step by Step" by Warren Norville. International Marine Publishing Co., Camden, Me. 1973, 157 pp., illustrated, index, $11.95.

An excellent book for the small boatman who wants a concise course in celestial navigation without the wizardry. In other words, when Warren Norville says he will guide you "step by step," he does just that. No sidetracks into jargon-ridden territory, no fancy footwork around obsolete formulas or thousand-dollar electronic equipment installations, no promises to reveal "hitherto unrevealed" shortcuts that make navigating the trackless wastes as easy as slicing butter with a hot knife. None of that pie-in-the-sky garbage.

If you begin at the beginning and go right through to the end and if you work in a little practical experience as you progress, then you should come out ok. The book has everything you need: Excerpts from the necessary tables and almanacs, sample problems with solutions, convenient sight reduction forms and a trunkload of helpful hints. And the beauty of it all is that Norville doesn't confine his discussion to one method; he describes the major ones (H.O. 214, H.O. 249, and H.O. 229) and lets you choose the one you want.

—PHS

### From "Celestial Navigation Step by Step" by Warren Norville

The paradox of navigation is that so many people think it is such a mysterious thing, and yet they do not realize how much navigation they really do on an almost professional level every time they go afloat. They may not use the most sophisticated instruments, but this really shows how good they are. For example, let us look at a rather ordinary situation that could happen to any two people we might know.

Two fellows were in a small fishing skiff. They had been having fabulous luck, but it was time to return to shore. Since they were in a new spot, they wanted to be able to find this spot again. They were wise enough to know that the technique of Boudreaux and Batiste, who marked the spot by making an X on the bottom of the boat, would not do.

One of them had a pocket compass. He sighted over it to a tall tree on a point on the river bank. He told his companion, "We can come back to where that tree bears 125° on my pocket compass."

His companion thought a moment, and he said "That won't tell us if we are over our fishing hole. Why don't you sight on that other tree over there too?" A line from this tree made a large angle when it intersected the line of bearing from the first one.

The first man replied "Good! It is 020° on my pocket compass."

What had they done? They had obtained a pair of lines of position. Anybody who has ever fished seriously has done this. It is just common sense. Maybe they didn't use a compass, but they carefully eyeballed the landmarks. This is good navigation.

In celestial navigation we also use lines of position. Technically, they are not straight lines, but arcs of circles of equal altitude.

The following publications are available from the Superintendent of Documents, Government Printing Office, Washington, D.C., or your chart agent:

Nautical Almanac, published annually.
Air Almanac, published three times a year.
American Ephemeris and Nautical Almanac, published annually (contains the same information as in the "Nautical Almanac" as well as additional information for astronomers).

—PHS

### Sight Reduction Tables

I don't think many small-boat navigators realize that there are sight reduction tables for celestial navigation that are much more compact and less expensive than the universally used H.O. 214 and H.O. 249. I am referring to H.O. 208 (Dreisonstok) and H.O. 211 (Ageton), each a small book of about 100 pp., costing $1.20 from the U.S. Government Printing Office. Either of these books has all the tables needed for quick, accurate and practical solutions of the navigational triangle, along with complete instructions and many worked-out examples. Unfortunately the government stopped printing them in 1972, so the best place to look is in used-book stores. (I understand that Carlsen and Larsen of Seattle, Wash., has a reprint edition of H.O. 211 available at $2.95).✪

The only disadvantage of 208 or 211, compared with 214 and 249, is that the solution requires a little more figuring — for example, with 208, three more additions and two more table entries — perhaps one minute's extra work per sight. This is a small price to pay for the joy of having tables for the whole world and every celestial body within one thin volume that takes up only 3/8" of your bookshelf.

—John Letcher

**"American Practical Navigator"**
**by Nathaniel Bowditch.**
**U.S. Government Printing Office.**
**Available from the Superintendent**
**of Documents,**
**Washington, D.C., and authorized sales agents**
**of the U.S. Naval Oceanographic Office.**
1966, illustrated, $7

Bowditch, above all else, is a reference work. Beginners should rely on less complete texts to learn navigation, and turn to Bowditch for more information, or amplifying information. I've never "read" my copy — only used it to clarify details left unanswered elsewhere.

—PHS

Anybody who has studied navigation has probably heard: "You can find more about that in Bowditch," a statement that has much truth to it. Since the first edition (1802), this book has come to symbolize the last word in navigation. The main difficulty with it if you could call it that, is that it is so complete. It's easy to get lost in the pages of Bowditch unless you know what you are looking for.

**From "American Practical Navigation"**

**2611. Importance of dead reckoning.**—Of the various kinds of navigation, dead reckoning alone is always available in some form. It should never be neglected, but in a lifeboat it is of more than average importance. A close check should be kept on the direction and distance made good, and all disturbing elements such as wind and current should be carefully evaluated. Long voyages have been successfully completed by this method alone, and landfalls have been made with surprising accuracy. This is not meant to minimize the importance of other methods of determining position, but with the methods generally available in a lifeboat, one may well find that, during the first few days, his dead reckoning positions are more accurate than those determined by other methods. If the means of determining direction and distance—the elements of dead reckoning—are accurate, it might be well to make an adjustment to the dead reckoning only after consistent indication of the magnitude and direction of its error. The dropping of the dead reckoning at each uncertain "fix" is at best a questionable procedure. The conflicting information likely to be available calls for careful analysis and good judgment on the part of the navigator.

**2616. Position by dead reckoning.**—Plotting can be done directly on a pilot chart or plotting sheet. If this proves too difficult, or if an independent check is desired, some form of mathematical reckoning may be useful. Table 2616, a simplified traverse table, can be used for this purpose. This is a critical-type table, various factors being given for limiting values of certain angles. To find the difference or change of latitude, in minutes, enter the table with course angle, reckoned from north or south toward the east or west. Multiply the distance run, in miles, by the factor. To find the departure, in miles, enter the table with the *complement* of the course angle. Multiply the distance run, in miles, by the factor. To convert departure to difference of longitude, in minutes, enter the table with mid latitude. Divide the departure by the factor.

| Angle | Factor |
|---|---|
| ° | |
| 0 | 1.0 |
| 18 | 0.9 |
| 31 | 0.8 |
| 41 | 0.7 |
| 49 | 0.6 |
| 56 | 0.5 |
| 63 | 0.4 |
| 69 | 0.3 |
| 75 | 0.2 |
| 81 | 0.1 |
| 87 | 0.0 |
| 90 | |

TABLE 2616.—Simplified traverse table.

*Example.*—A lifeboat travels 26 miles on course 205°, from L 41°44' N, λ 56°21' W.

*Required.*—Latitude and longitude of the point of arrival.

*Solution.*—The course angle is 205°−180°=S 25° W, and the complement is 90°−25°=65°. The factors corresponding to these angles are 0.9 and 0.4, respectively. The difference of latitude is 26×0.9=23' (to the nearest minute) and the departure is 26×0.4=10 mi. Since the course is in the southwestern quadrant, in the northern hemisphere, the latitude of the point of arrival is 41°44' N −23'=41°21' N. The factor corresponding to the mid latitude 41°32' N is 0.7. The difference of longitude is 10÷0.7=14'. The longitude of the point of arrival is 56°21' W+14'=56°35' W.

*Answer.*—L 41°21' N, λ 56°35' W.

Sting Ray (*Trygon pastinaca*).

"United States Coast Pilot"
National Ocean Survey, Rockville, Md.
Published in 8 volumes, indexed.
No. 1  Eastport, Me., to Cape Cod, Mass., $2.
No. 2  Cape Cod, Mass., to Sandy Hook, N.J., $2.50.
No. 3  Sandy Hook, N.J., to Cape Henry, Va., $2.
No. 4  Cape Henry, Va., to Key West, Fla., $2.
No. 5  Puerto Rico and Virgin Islands, Gulf of
      Mexico, $2.50
No. 6  (There is no number 6!)
No. 7  California, Oregon, Washington, and Hawaii, $2.50
No. 8  Dixon Entrance to Cape Spencer, $2.50.
No. 9  Cape Spencer to Beaufort Sea, $2.50.

Homelyn (*Raia maculata*).

In my opinion, the "Coast Pilot" has it all over any of the commercial cruising guides, mainly because it provides unadorned information that is essential for safe navigation. There are no ringing descriptions of glorious sunsets, or cliches about "quaint" villages at the end of a day's run, or trite exclamations over coastal scenery. Just the facts, and enough of them to get you from here to there with the least amount of fuss.

The "Coast Pilot" is intended for use in conjunction with your charts: the details amplify the skeletal charted information to give you a three-dimensional picture of what is ahead. The writing is so objective and tight that you can learn all you need to know about an upcoming landfall with a quick glance at your chart and the appropriate section of the narrative. This might not be necessary when you are planning a voyage in your easy chair at home, but it is an obvious asset when at sea.

Besides the coastal descriptions, there is additional material of real worth: Distress signals and procedures, radio warnings and weather, aids to navigation, navigation regulations, addresses of key government agencies, climatological tables, tables of distances and all sorts of vital information.

The "Coast Pilot" is available from the National Ocean Survey or your nautical chart agent. "Coast Pilots" Nos. 1, 3 and 4 are published annually and are produced on a computerized format. "Coast Pilot" No. 2 and No. 6 through No. 9, are also revised annually by means of supplements — after the individual purchases the initial "Coast Pilot" the supplements are provided free-of-charge on an automatic mailing.

—PHS

165

"Sea Signalling Simplified" by Captain P.J. Russell.
Adlard Coles, London, England.
1969 (3rd edition), 86 pp., illustrated, index. $3.

The trouble with using signals at sea these days is that you might know the signals, but the guy you're signalling to might not. Or vice-versa.

In some cases for some people, only the spoken word will do, but you can imagine the difficulties in that — distance and language, to mention only two. The least thing you can do (must do) is learn the international distress signals. The most you can do is learn them all.

A compromise is to get a copy of this handbook, study it, and keep it on hand in your boat. In it you'll find the International Code, the Morse Code, semaphore, flashing light, Morse signalling by hand-flags or arms, sound signalling, radiotelephony, loud hailer and coding and de-coding. When it comes time to use them, pray like hell the other fellow had as much foresight.

—PHS

Watering-pot (*Asper gillium vaginiferum*), one half natural size. *a*, the pair of small valves.

Butter Island, 186 feet high and 0.5 mile northwest of Eagle Island, is wooded. The passage between Butter Island and the northeast island of the Barred Islands, 300 yards westward, is reported to uncover at low water. Oak Island, 1.5 miles west-southwestward of Eagle Island, is grassy and uninhabited. Burnt Island, just south of Oak Island, is wooded except for its northeast end which is grass covered.

There is a passage northward of North Haven Island which is used in winter when Fox Islands Thorofare is closed by ice. To go through this passage, pass about 300 yards southward of Eagle Island steer for Spoon Ledge, 15 feet high with grass on top, about 0.5 mile northwest of Oak Island. On this course pass 400 yards northward of Grass Ledge, 15 feet high and grass covered, 0.9 mile east of Oak Island, to a position about 400 yards northward of Oak Island. Then pass midway between Oak Island and Spoon Ledge and steer for Rockland Breakwater Light (44°06.2' N., 69°04.7' W.). The least charted depth in this passage is 25 feet.

The preceding paragraphs give the simplest directions for Isle au Haut Bay and East Penobscot Bay by pointing out the difficulties and the dangers, and especially, when necessary, the need for local knowledge. By close attention to the chart and following the aids, no difficulty should be experienced in navigating the area in daylight and in clear weather.

⭐ "The Book of the Sextant" by
Dunlap and Shufeldt.
Weems & Plath, Annapolis, Md.
1971, 43 pp., illustrated, $1.50.

Solid facts on sextants, adjustment, sextant altitude corrections, observations, star identification, reducing the sight, sextant care. This booklet is for those who already know how to navigate; the authors are not teaching celestial navigation to beginners here.

If you have Dutton's "Navigation and Piloting," revised by Dunlap and Shufeldt, it wouldn't do you much good to buy this book. The information is basically all there. But if you rely on, say, "Celestial Navigation for Yachtsmen" by Blewitt, you'll want to get this book, since there is nothing on the mechanics of the sextant in Blewitt.

From "The Book of the Sextant"                    —PHS

To eliminate or reduce excessive index error, the <u>horizon</u> glass must be adjusted so that its lack of parallelism to the index mirror is reduced.

With the Plath and several other commercial sextants the horizon glass is adjusted within the mirror frame.

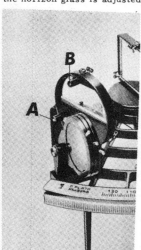

When holding the sextant vertical only the upper screw is (A in Figure 301) used. The one adjusting screw is tightened or loosened slightly, using a key supplied with the sextant. This moves the mirror against the mounting springs. When the sextant is properly adjusted the horizon will appear as in Fig. 302 with the sextant reading zero. When index error is present the horizon will appear as in Fig. 303.

Fig. 302

Sextant.

Fig. 303

166

# SEXTANTS

"Choosing a Marine Sextant"
by Robert E. Kleid
Robert E. Kleid Nautical Instruments.
Fairfield, Conn.
1972, 12 pp. illustrated, papercovered, $1.

I highly recommend this booklet if you are in the market for a sextant. The author analyzes, in detail, the Standard Plath, Plath Yachtsman, Simex, Hughes Mate and Heath. He tells you, in non-salesman language, the differences among them. In the process, he comes down heavily on Japanese sextants, and on the last page he says he doesn't recommend them and therefore will not sell them.

And there is where your judgment must come into play. Does Kleid not recommend Japanese sextants because he doesn't carry them, or does he not carry them because he doesn't recommend them?

—PHS

From "Chosing a Marine Sextant"

Now let's talk numbers. I think the average person would find magnifying powers above four to be too difficult to use on a yacht under forty feet, and above 2½ too difficult on a yacht under thirty feet. Actually, I see no necessity for powers higher than four, even on very large vessels.

For sighting stars and planets the relative brightness of the image (both celestial body and horizon) is more important than the magnifying power. The theoretical* relative brightness is the square of the exit pupil diameter, which is the diameter of the objective lens in millimeters divided by the magnifying power. But exit pupil diameter in excess of 7mm is not usable, since the maximum diameter of the pupil of the human eye is about 7mm. This limits the theoretical relative brightness to about 50. The table below gives the theoretical relative brightness for various sextant telescopes and monoculars.

| Sextant | Scope or Monocular | Theoretical* Rel. Bright. |
|---|---|---|
| Plath, Standard | 4x40 | 50 |
|  | 6x30 | 25 |
| Plath Yachtsman | 3x30 | 50 |
| Simex | 4x40 | 50 |
|  | 7x35 | 25 |
| Hughes Mate | 2.5x30 | 50 |
| Heath 130M | 3x28.5 | 50 |
| MC1 | 4x40 | 50 |

Before deciding that a 4x40 scope is the one to get if you're buying a Plath or a Simex, please read the section on Shade Glasses. It discusses the relationships between the size of the scope objective lens and the sizes of the shade glasses and mirrors, for the various sextants.

* Discounting internal light losses.

# COMPASSES

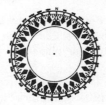

● "Compasses in Small Craft" by C.A. Lund.
Brown, Son & Ferguson, 52 Darnley St.
Glasgow, Scotland.
1969 (3rd edition), 64 pp., illustrated, paperbound, 9 s.

This is a good little book on compasses and
compass correction. The author describes
deviation, how it is determined and how it is
corrected. He goes into the earth's magnetism,
permanent magnetism and describes swinging
ship.

From "Compasses in Small Craft"          —PHS

The bearing of the sun may
be taken by means of a
"shadow pin," which is a piece
of brass wire fixed vertically in
a little socket in the centre of
the glass of the bowl. As its
shadow falls across the compass
card the bearing may be noted,
and the *reverse* of this is the
compass bearing of the sun.

The shadow pin may also be
used for taking bearings of
other objects by noting the
graduation on the card, which
is directly in line with the
object, the pin and the
observer's eye. (Fig. 3).

If the compass is not fitted
with a shadow pin it is quite
easy to make one. Obtain a
round rubber suction washer,
such as is used to stick a
cigarette ash container on a car
wind screen, bore a hole partly
down the centre of it, insert a
straight piece of brass wire
about four inches long and
press the washer firmly on the
centre of the glass of the bowl.

"Magnetic Compasses and Magnetometers" by Alfred Hine.
University of Toronto Press, Toronto, Canada.
1968, 385 pp., illustrated, bibliography, index, $30.

Maybe I'm wrong, but compass adjusting
appears to be a wide-open field; not wide open
in the sense that any old jack can do it, but in
the sense that there are very few practitioners of
the art. How one goes about becoming a
compass adjuster is hard to determine, but
judging from the number of craft with
un-adjusted or poorly adjusted compasses, there
is a vacuum waiting to be filled.

For those serious enough to become a serious
adjuster, this appears to be the book. It is an
anthology of previously published and original
material on the magnetic compass, with reams of
technical diagrams, formulas and practical
information on how the various types work.
There is a separate chapter just on adjusting.

This book is not for the casual reader; it's for
the professional who knows advanced
mathematics.

—PHS

From "Magnetic Compasses. . ."

*Liquid damping*

A more familiar method of damping is provided in the liquid-filled compass.
The liquid is used for two reasons. Firstly, it enables a large proportion of the
weight of the magnet system to be taken off the pivot by the incorporation of a float in
the system. By this means much larger and stronger magnets may be used without
damaging the pivot and introducing friction. Secondly, the liquid, by virtue of its
viscosity, provides a convenient method of damping. This is not quite so exact a
method as that provided by eddy currents, since surface tension and other effects
tend to produce restraining forces and to introduce 'drag' on the magnet system
independently of its rate of movement; consequently the damping term is not pro-
portional to $dx/dt$.

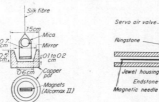

FIG. 3.11. Detail of the Sucksmith
magnetometer

FIG. 3.12. A double-pivoted needle with
eddy-current damping

This is the Askania compass that was used
in the VI flying bombs during the 1939-45
war.

The effect of swirl can be much more pronounced than with-eddy current damping since rotation of the whole compass imparts an angular momentum to the liquid
which does not cease when the compass bowl comes to rest. There is then relative
movement between the liquid and the bowl, and between the liquid and the magnet
system, with the result that the latter may be displaced by a large angle for an
appreciable period of time. To reduce the effects of swirl, the magnet system is
made as free as possible from unnecessary projections and a large annular gap is
allowed between the magnet system and card and the bowl.

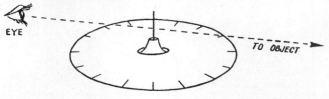

EYE

TO OBJECT

# Weather

"Weather for the Mariner" by William J. Kotsch.
United States Naval Institute, Annapolis, Md.
1970, 164 pp. illustrated, bibliography, index,
flexible binding, $6.50.

⊛ "Weather, Water and Boating" by Donald A. Whelpley.
Cornell Maritime Press, Cambridge, Md.
1961, 151 pp., glossary, index, $4.00.

Two books that are attempting the same thing — simplified meteorology for small-boat sailors. Each has its good points, depending on what you are looking for.

Kotsch takes the textbook approach by leading off with theory and building on this to bring the reader to the practical end: simple weather forecasting. Whelpley follows a looser structure, with a more informal approach. Kotsch is loaded with good, clear diagrams and illustrations; Whelpley is illustrated, but not as well.

For instance, Kotsch shows some excellent cloud photographs and with them he provides descriptions and summations of what they mean. Whelpley has a few cloud pictures, but not enough to make any comparisons worthwhile. I guess what I am saying here is that if you want a more detailed discussion of the weather, pay more money and get Kotsch; if you are interested in the weather in a more general way and don't want to wade through the more technical details, pay less money and get Whelpley. Either way, you won't be cheated.

—PHS

From "Weather, Water and Boating"

From "Weather for the Mariner"

168

"Meteorology" by William L. Donn.
McGraw-Hill, New York.
1965 (3rd edition), 484 pp., illustrated,
   bibliography, index, $9.95.

If you really want to learn about the weather, this is the book for you. It's truly comprehensive, while at the same time having a marine slant. Too many advanced weather books take the landsman's point of view; too many seamen are victimized by marine weather books that are too simplistic.

If you plan to spend more time at sea and less time plugged into a dock, you should, you must, give the study of weather more than just a quick once-over. After all, weather is the greatest single influence over small craft at sea. Though the marine aspects of this book are directed at large ships rather than small boats, the weather confronted by both is, after all, the same. You might not have the latest meteorological instruments aboard your boat, but you at least have a head on your shoulders. This book teaches you how to put it to good use.

Besides chapters on weather in general, with plenty of marine principles sandwiched in, there are separate chapters on weather at sea and the oceans. For instance, the chapter on weather at sea contains: Weather bulletins and data broadcasts, use of radar, ship routing, trip analyses, average weather for the North Atlantic Ocean and average weather for the North Pacific Ocean. At the end of each chapter are study questions.

The illustrations, graphs and charts are excellent. The bibliography is first class. To top it off, there is a fantastic appendix that has in table form the average monthly weather summaries for principal ports and islands of the world.

From "Meteorology"                    —PHS

(a) Jet stream begins to undulate    (b) Rossby waves begin to form

(c) Waves strongly developed    (d) Cells of cold and warm air bodies are formed

_Fig. 10·5 Waves in the upper westerlies. (A. Strahler, The Earth Sciences, after G. T. Trewartha)_

⭐ "Instant Weather Forecasting" by Alan Watts.
Dodd, Mead and Co., New York
1968, 64 pp., illustrated, $3.75.

This is a very simplified guide to weather prediction. It presupposes that you have limited knowledge of meteorological theory; what theory there is in the book is introductory in nature and makes no attempt to explain the "why" of the weather, only the "how." Definitions are brief and to the point and handled in table form wherever possible.

The weather forecasting system used by Watts is based on the condition of the sky. He provides 24 color photographs of the sky, each photo accompanied by a description of what that sky portends. The assumption is that you can look at the clouds and tell, within certain limitations, what future weather conditions will be. Watts divides sky conditions into eight broad categories: skies that (1) mean deterioration, (2) are associated with bad weather, (3) are associated with sudden change, (4) are associated with no immediate change, (5) are associated with sudden local change, (6) are associated with temporary deterioration, (7) are associated with improvement, and (8) are associated with change.

I tried this out on the clouds outside my window. Though I've had difficulty matching up my sky with one of those in the book, once I have settled on what I have been looking at, my results aren't too bad. Watts in his introduction suggests that maybe 75% of the time your predictions will be correct when matched against his 24 sky photographs. Not bad when you consider what your local TV weatherman's percentage must be.

—PHS

**WEATHER INSTRUMENTS**

**If-You-Don't-Own-One,
You've-Always-Wanted-One Dept.**

A very good professor of history quoted his wise mother as once telling him, "Whether you're rich or whether you're poor, it's always better to have money." A reasonable argument against this escapes me just now, but the truth of an analogous remark is etched indelibly on my mind; "Whether you're a something-for-everybody mail-order house or whether you're a specialist, it's always better to do the best job in the world."

Take weather instruments, for example. How many stores and mail order houses in the world sell <u>one</u> model of a baragraph or barometer, one

169

_Contd. on next page_

_Contd. form preceding page_

anemometer, one thermometer even. How do we know just how good the one offered model is? We don't.

Every house looks over what is available to it. Perhaps not every model of this or that product is considered, but a lot of them are. It then looks at its "target group," its intended market, and decides what model of what product, of what quality, at what price best yields optimum sales to this target group. But this is not the way the product is sold. We are not told, "Hey there, upper-middle class, two-car, newly-nautically-oriented citizen whose name just came to us on a mailing list sold to us by the Sink 'r Swim Boat Corp., Inc., here is the product in this category our computer tells us you are most likely to buy . . . " We're simply offered the product to do this or that job, take it or leave it, thank you. Certainly this is not a totally fair statement to make of the whole industry. Many houses are conscientiously and responsibly operated and, indeed, the one model offered really is a good buy. But anyone on those mailing lists knows what I mean, that the retail nautical supply industry has much room for improvement.

You know something about anything along the lines described above, tell us. Meanwhile, in weather instruments we are approaching the heart of the matter.

SCIENCE ASSOCIATES, INC., had the following remarks in the introduction to their catalog:

> There have been four guiding principles in Science Associates' development:
>
> 1.  To present in a single catalog quality instruments, covering a broad range of specifications, in varying price classifications.
> 2.  To serve as a consulting agency for all who desire assistance in selecting the proper instrumentation in accordance with requirements and budgets.
> 3.  To expedite delivery of equipment, regardless of source, in a single shipment by carrying a large stock in our Princeton warehouse.
> 4.  To assure satisfactory performance of equipment in accordance with guaranties and warranties and to continue to assist the customer in the operation of his equipment.

It sends a thrill down your spine. The table of contents lists the following categories: Temperature, Humidity, Pressure, Wind, Precipitation, Solar Radiation, Wind, Ceiling, Visibility, Stations and Equipment. Every category offers a full range of tolerance and price, literally page after page of them. When writing them, ask for folder "H". An item from their catalog is shown below.
—GP

Science Associates
Box 230, Nassau St.
Princeton, N.J. 08540

# <sup>170</sup> Barographs

350

**No. 350. ELECTRO BAROGRAPH.** A compact recording barometer for the amateur meteorologist, with some innovations that make maintenance and operation easy. The chart drum is activated by a readily available 1.5v. battery, easily installed in the base; the three aneroid cells, linkage, and pen arm rotate as a unit in order to change the pen position and the flow of ink to the 2¾ x 9½" chart, printed for 28/31" Hg. Complete with instructions, battery, 1 year supply of weekly charts, and ink. Wt. 3/shpg. 5 lbs. $94.00

## Fouling And Pesticides

Will the addition of a potent pesticide to your anti-fouling bottom paint help keep off borers and barnacles? Probably not, warns the Virginia Institute of Marine Science, and in any event, its use will probably be worse than the hoped-for cure. DDT and other hard pesticides are deadly to most fish life in extremely small quantities while the chemicals in the bug-killer may change the characteristics in your bottom paint, causing it to flake off and expose the bottom to direct attack.

Best advice: If your paint isn't doing the job, try another brand or a better grade of copper, or try one of the stronger coatings formulated for tropical waters.

# clothing and comfort

## FOUL-WEATHER GEAR

### By Frank Daignault

The threat of rain or snow is an obvious daily danger to sportsmen afield. Were this the only consideration in our efforts to stay dry there would be little complication. But the fact that we are either preparing to stand in, or be otherwise washed down by an unpredictable sea, adds another dimension to our problems. For even under blue skies coastal work may call for a good set of "oilskins."

When buying foul-weather gear you'll notice that two distinct groups of imports dominate the market: Japanese along with other free-Asian nations and those that come from the Scandinavian countries — Norway and Sweden.

The Asian suits can be had for ten bucks (you'll blow ten more feeding coins in some dryer). Material is weak, thin and easily torn. Many sets have rivets, snaps and buckles that rust and stain your other garments. Finally, when the snaps stiffen, you'll pull them apart some night only to find them separating from the material. If you don't catch on, two sets per season is about right. Another thing, you can get involved with the semantics of "waterproof" and "water-repellent"; they say that there is a difference — why bother.

Suits made in Europe go for around $30. Here you get the feeling that they must have sent some poor guy fiord-ing out into their equivalent of our northeaster in a dingy for field testing. Who but they would design an outfit with drawstrings, stainless hardware, waterproof pockets, flaps that have cross openings and stretch suspenders on the pants — it's all there. Most important, the material holds up. The Norwegian suits I've seen have

High-fitting pants.

the pants that guy high on the back and chest — another important feature.

For the head, a lot of boat skippers prefer the sou'wester type hat — which is a pie shaped thing that laces under the chin similar to those you see in famous old paintings. Their argument is that you can turn the head without looking into a hood. I'll give up the vision, for I prefer the covering the hood affords on the back of the neck. Surfcasters should insist on the hood, which is better for turning their backs on a green one.

A couple of kinks:

—Fit yourself on the big side for those cold days or nights when you'll be wearing thick undergarments — the best "oilskins" can be torn when you struggle.

—Don't discard foul-weather gear that has torn snaps. Auto upholstery shops have the tools to replace them in a minute and are usually willing to oblige nice guys.

My suit comes from Norway — "Helly—Hansen" (Provincetown dragger crews are all wearing them).

*Helly-Hansen*
—of Norway

| | | |
|---|---|---|
| **CP** | **SOLE IMPORTERS USA AND CANADA:** | **CANOR PLAREX INC.,** 6, WESTCHESTER PLAZA, ELMSFORD, NEW YORK 10523. |
| | **CANOR PLAREX INC.,** 4200 — 23RD AVE. W., SEATTLE, WASH. 98199. | **CANOR PLAREX IND. LTD.,** 41 ALEXANDER STREET, VANCOUVER, B. C. CANADA |

Oriental stuff is available in any discount house and some garbage cans. Many come through with a listing of all-night laundromats for both coasts. Handy.

Surfcasters often break up their foul-weather gear using the two pieces separately. The top supplements waders and is usually sealed down over them with a belt or rope. Many surfmen never use bottoms, permitting waders to fill that gap.

On the other hand most overlook the old-fashioned hip-boot which, when supported with oilskin trousers for splash protection, is really all you need on some beaches or rockbound spots like Narragansett or Newport. Or, if you are working a jetty or plan to fish from a beach vehicle or auto, stopping often to cast here or there, these can be a more comfortable combination than the waders for driving and getting in and out of your vehicle. Far less cumbersome than waders, hip boots and "splash pants" will permit you to literally do a dance — something you can't do in waders. Save the waders for wading.

## WADERS

The boat that I could have bought gets two feet longer every season when I think about the money over the years that I have spent on waders. Whether you buy the $50 jobs, or burn up four pairs of Japanese imports at $12 a copy, you inevitably come to the conclusion that waders can be a drag on your plug money.

Gone are the old reliable higher-priced "Ball-Bands" that used to sustain stream-wading trout fishermen and surfcasters alike. This domestic product line — as we know it — has been discontinued along with the black, industrial-grade waders that U.S. Royal once put out. In the long-haul, both of these formerly were the best choice for serious sportsmen. Along with good workmanship and quality material, both had a wrap-around section running vertically from waist to waist. This minimized failure at the critical crotch, a spot where wader failure is most common. No more.

For a while the remaining alternative was the low-priced Jap waders, which were prone to failure only a few short weeks after you bought them. However, many

171

_Contd. from preceding page_

regulars stuck with them reasoning that at such a low price ($10 to $12) the things were expendable and they kept an extra pair around. The added luggage, along with the wet nights and the occasional pair that leaked **sooner** than expected has driven this school underground. Believe me, I've gone down both trails — it's a paradox, or was.

About two years ago a lightweight nylon creation hit the market that was very slow in gaining acceptance. I tried a pair last spring out of desperation. (Remember, my only alternative was the ten-dollar jobs.) Readers should be reminded that I fish before work days and full time for three months. After one season, the nylons are still part of my tackle and have not yet seen a patch. At last, the utility I've been looking for!

I bought a second pair for my wife, that didn't see as much service, but they still held up beyond what I had at first expected. No question, these are the lightest boot-foot waders ever put on the market and both of us can feel a difference after a night of walking a beach. On the minus side, and there is usually a tag attached that warns of this: Nylons "sweat" — condensation forms between a warm body and the cold sea. A friend of mine says wet is wet and that he doesn't care how it gets there, he doesn't like it. On the other hand, I feel that this dampness is negligible and well worth the other advantages of low price (in the low twenties), lightness and reliable service.

Sears has a pair; I bought mine from a "Gob-shops" store the first time. Next time around for the wife — a discount house. All make the grade.

The only remaining "top-shelf" wader is put out by Gra-Lite; these are of a space-age material that is guaranteed for five years. Waders come through with a registration number. (It's like having your bottom bonded.) They sell them through the mail for $60 a copy and will custom make a pair for big guys at $10 more. I've never owned a pair but there are a half dozen regular hard fishermen out on Cape Cod that showed up this season on their second year — not bad.

172

Because of the crouching and bending in normal activity, and considering all the seams that come together there, the crotch is the most likely place to let go on waders. If you find it necessary to patch here, depending on individual makes, an oversize patch sometimes does the trick. For rubber surfaces routine punctures from fish hooks, gaffs or the dorsal fins of gamefish can be easily repaired with cold patches used for the repair of inner-tubes. These you can pick up at any highway service station. Don't forget the glue. Also, never burn cement before applying a patch — why destroy ingredients? Nylon, vinyl or canvas can be patched with a swimming pool repair kit under a dollar.

When buying, watch for old stock or that which has been stored improperly. I've seen dealers keep waders too near the ceiling for a long time, or put product on display by removing it from its package, triggering a count-down on the shelf life of waders. Try to buy the ones in a package. Many come through packed in a white, talcum-like powder which is often a sign of care and freshness.

Another thing a lot of guys overlook is the choice of suspenders. Cheap ones tend not to stretch and that can be tough on the buttons. Besides, the whole garment takes a beating without the give and s-t-r-e-t-c-h of suspenders. You can usually get the right suspenders from a shop that sells work clothes; ask for the kind firemen wear. Also, it's a chance to buy an American product.

—Frank Daignault

### French-Made Parka

After sharing Frank D.'s experience with the cheapie stuff, we decided to go first class for once. We chose a standard parka jacket with hood from Moby Dick (Imperex), a French-made item that is basically nylon coated with PVC both sides, with electronic welds at the seams. We're now in our third season with this jacket with no indications of wear (the jacket, not us). It's great stuff. Jacket was $18.95; other items in the teens and twenties.

—DRG

### Glasses for Glasses

A Nova Scotia neighbor who had spent many years at sea once confided in me that a contributing factor to his coming ashore was the problem of eyeglasses. His always seemed to be coated by salt spray or befogged by condensation.

Mine too.

Preparing for a 1972 cruise to Newfoundland I came across a pair of $1.98 ski goggles, the kind that can be worn over eyeglasses, and I suddenly remembered all those WW II movies that had their heroes (usually British) out on the bridges of their

_Contd. on next page_

*Contd. from preceding page*

ships (usually destroyers), bundled up against the North Atlantic and wearing (usually around their necks) goggles. And while going to Newfoundland wasn't quite like going to war, or even to Murmansk, $1.98 was little enough — and besides, there was no one to see me.

They worked. Mine, vented top and bottom, coped with spray far better than my eyeglasses and I ever had. Perhaps it's the larger expanse of glass or plastic, perhaps it's the shape. For whatever reason, spray seems to affect that large single lens far less than it used to affect my eyeglasses, and a swipe of the thumb serves to clear the lens adequately. Too, fog forms less readily on them, and — the clincher for me — forms only on the **outside** of the lens. In consequence, I saw more of Newfoundland than I had expected.

—Steve Rubin

Apparently Steve wasn't the only man with a foggy outlook on the world. Along comes a product called Foggles (beautiful!) for the glassed-in skipper. The frames are surgical grade, non-allergic vinyl in a smoke tint, fasteners are non-corrosive and the elastic strap is nylon. The Foggles come with interchangeable clear and amber lenses. Price is $4.70 from:

West Products
161 Prescott St.
East Boston, Mass. 02128

—DRG

## SUNGLASSES
## A MUST IN EYE PROTECTION

I doubt if there is one of us that hasn't, at one time or another, suffered from a little too much sun. Depending upon the extent of exposure, symptoms can be as severe as bounding back and forth from chills and fever to violent nausea. At that level of severity a hat could have made the difference. On the other hand if the common price for you is only a headache, you could be suffering from a frequent cause of eyestrain related to excessive sunlight.

I've always been amazed by the number of outdoorsmen who can, or are willing to, withstand a day of bright, often heavily water-reflected, sunlight. Some of us pay the above price, some don't. So much for prevention.

One of the least appreciated reasons for caring for your eyes during the day is that you will see better at night. I don't know whether there is scientific evidence to support this, but it is commonly believed that exposure to bright sunlight during the day compromises night vision — a temporary form of night blindness. I'm sure you can envision (no pun intended) after a long day afloat, the advantages of seeing channel markers and familar horizons after sundown with every possible protection from the temporary effects of a day in the bright sun. Day or night, the advantage of sunglasses is that you end up seeing better, but it doesn't end there.

If you choose "Polaroid" type sunglasses, your eyes penetrate the surface glare and you can be cut in on the little visual extras. It might be a small pod of baitfish that twinkles above the surface in only an instant, but the sight betrays the presence of feeding gamefish. At times — if you wear the right glasses — the dim shadows of gamefish can be seen spreading outward from both beams. Or, when a fish is ready for the gaff, it helps to see him below the surface — call it an edge.

&ast; Stick with the inventor — Polaroid.

&ast; Get the kind that bend around toward the temples.

&ast; Around five dollars.

—Frank Daignault

### If the Shoe Fits . . .

I have extremely wide feet (size 7½, EEEEE width), and while I can stretch a pair of Topsider canvas sneakers to fit over the course of an agonizing week, I cannot wear the Topsider moccasin. It's just too narrow. Hitchcock Shoes, Inc., 165 Beal St., Hingham, Mass. 02043, is a mail order firm which supplies wide-sized boots and shoes for people like me. As I understand it, they send wide lasts to footwear manufacturers, who make wide shoes with them and return them to Hitchcock. The latter does not manufacture the shoes. The firm carries two models of boating shoes with non-skid rubber soles, one of which is of the moccasin style. I have had two pairs of these, and cannot say enough good about them. They are made of rugged water-repellent leather, have a rawhide lacing, come in one extra-wide width for sizes 5-13, and they cost only $20, which is cheap if you've ever had to wear shoes which are too narrow for your foot. Once you have purchased a pair of shoes from Hitchcock, your name and shoe size will always be on record at their plant. Hence, in the future, all you have to do is order from their catalog, which is sent periodically once you are on their mailing list.

—Nim Marsh

Nim's shoe.

173

# AT SEA

Cephalopoda Loligopsis.

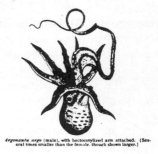

*Argonauta argo* (male), with hectocotylized arm attached. (Several times smaller than the female, though shown larger.)

**"The Craft of Sail" by Jan Adkins.**
1973, Walker and Co., N.Y., 64 pp., $5.95.

This is a primer of sailing and to my way of thinking, it surpasses all the other basic books that promise "to have you out on the water and sailing after reading this book." Adkins makes no rash guarantees like this, but if you don't understand what sailing is all about after reading this book, you probably never will.

He uses illustrations primarily to prove his points, and it is his imagination that makes the theory real: for instance peanuts being pulled by ants going in different directions replace the vector diagrams you see in other books. The best thing is that Adkins' illustrations are not sterile; they give you a feel for being on the water in a sailboat. A real gem of a book.

—PHS

**"The Development of the Boat: Select Bibliography."**
National Maritime Museum, Greenwich, London
**SE109NF, England**
1971, 120 pp., index, 80 pence.

This does for small boats what Albion has done for maritime history in general. It is divided into two parts: Studies of Contemporary Boats, and Ancient Boats. There are over 1400 listings, including magazine and journal articles and books. A substantial number of the listings are American publications.

If you do decide to order this bibliography, ask the museum to send its free catalog, which contains a listing of its guides, catalogs, monographs, picture booklets, books, color prints, posters, medals, souvenirs and color transparencies.

—PHS

174

**⊕"Books of the Sea" by Charles Lee Lewis.**
Greenwood Press, Westport, Conn.
1972 (reprint of 1943 edition), 318 pp.,
    sketches, $14.

This is a valuable book for anyone's reference library. It is in reality an annotated bibliography, but not dry like the ones normally encountered. Lewis writes about sea literature in a narrative style, leading you from one book to another. He covers novels, short stories, accounts of voyages, poetry, biography, plays, history, and more.

The principal value of this book is the way it guides you from one book to another. For instance, if you are turned on by a book you picked up on the merchant marine, Lewis will help you choose more like it to read, with solid information on their strengths and weaknesses.
—PHS

*Pristiophorus cirratus.*

**From "Books of the Sea"**

In a similar setting among the islands of the French coast is placed the episode of the corvette *Claymore* in Hugo's *Ninety-Three,* which narrates the famous struggle between the gunner and the runaway cannon that was on the point of wrecking the ship. Still, as far as verisimilitude is concerned, this novel only further exemplifies its author's remoteness from reality. Moreover, when he leaves the Channel Islands and the coast of Normandy, he seems to be depending more on books than on observation and experience for his portrayal of the phenomena of the sea. But that he loved the sea and was moved deeply by its varied moods is evident, and it was doubtless as a sea-lover that he appealed so strongly to the English poet Swinburne, who has written some excellent sea verse. Hugo's *Han d'Islande* is almost a romance of the sea—the sea of Ossian, dark, mysterious, horrible, and destructive. *Les Miserables,* though in no sense a sea novel, has some unforgettable passages relating to Jean Valjean as a galley slave.

**"The Classic Boat Monthly"**
108 Germonts Road, New City, N.Y. 10956
One year (12 issues) $5.

This delightful publication is in the tradition of Day, Atkins and all the nautical journals and journalists who have acted the role of advocate for traditional marine design and skills. It is a difficult role because of the stereotypes cast for it, "crank" and "reactionary" being two of the more common ones. This stereotyping is a ridiculous phenomenon arising in large part out of arrogance, that great and expensive synonym for ignorance. To call a traditional craft a "character boat" is much like calling a Renaissance painting "very good for its time." It is a form of temporal racial prejudice, and is an insidious one because of its propaganda value for a largely decadent industry.

People who say that a gaff rig is as good or better as an all round sailing rig as a marconi are not just a bunch of foolish rustics; they are at least as right as those who pout the contrary. This can of worms being opened, we'll put it on ice and say that the "Classic Boat Monthly" is a serious, well run and nicely constructed journal about boats in the older traditions of hull form and rig; not nostalgia, but solid copy of immediate value to owners and admirers of these craft, whether new, old or yet-to-be-built.

—GP

**"The Telltale Compass"**
18418 South Old River Dr.
Lake Oswego, Ore. 97034
One year (12 issues)/$20.

A unique, interesting, and extremely useful publication for the yachtsman, or any boatman for that matter, is a monthly folder called "The Telltale Compass." The publication is a four-paged newsletter containing important boating information, opinions from nautical experts and worthwhile evaluations of boats and marine products. Although coverage may be not quite as broad as that of a typical consumer's report, evaluations of individual products are generally detailed, thorough and based on first-hand knowledge. Furthermore, opinions are completely candid and unbiased, for "The Telltale Compass" carries no advertisements, and therefore it has no fear of offending advertisers. In short, it is beholden to no one.

Articles appearing in the newsletter are written by its staff and members of a Board of Advisors, who are knowledgeable and experienced boatmen. Many of the advisors are actively affiliated with the boating industry and prefer to be anonymous in order that they can feel free to be completely frank. Subjects covered, other than boat and gear evaluation, range from boating legislation and regulations to trends in design, construction, workmanship, problem reports, purchasing tips and caveats, seamanship, accident analysis and various aspects of safety afloat. Evaluations in "The Telltale Compass" are not the usual dry facts and statistics found in a typical consumer's report, but more often than not, boats and gear are described in a lively, interesting manner. Not all product reports are critical, for the writers are quick to point out the plaudits as well as the deficiencies. In fact, the publication's policy seems to place great emphasis on fairness and objectivity.

"The Telltale Compass" is edited and published by Victor Jorgensen who, for 14 years, was managing editor of "The Skipper," an unusual and highly regarded nautical magazine. The associate editor is Hugh D. Whall, a well-known boating writer, formerly an editorial assistant on "The Skipper" and now the yachting editor of "Sports Illustrated."

About the only drawback of "The Telltale Compass" is its subscription cost of $20 per year, which is necessary because of its lack of advertisers. Actually, such a price should not scare away many yachtsmen, who often pay as much for one small boat fitting. As a matter of fact, when one considers the value he gets from the newsletter, the cost seems very reasonable indeed. The reader could easily save the subscription cost many times over when he is heedful of the warnings about marine products that are faulty, of poor quality or overpriced. Furthermore, subscribers are offered what might be called a limited consultation service, whereby certain readily answerable questions about specific gear, techniques or trends will be answered without charge. If the reader is willing to pay a reasonable charge, complicated or involved questions requiring research might be answered also by the staff or an advisor.

—Richard Henderson

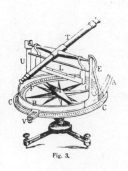

Fig. 3.

175

# Eric Hiscock

⊘ "Cruising Under Sail" by Eric C.
  Hiscock.
Oxford University Press, New York.
1965 (second edition), 468 pp., index, illustrated,
  bibliography. $15.95.

⊘ "Voyaging Under Sail" by Eric C. Hiscock.
Oxford University Press, New York.
1970 (second edition), 315 pp., index, bibliography,
  illustrated. $14.95.

These two books are classics in their field.
"Voyaging" is more or less a sequel to
"Cruising," though the former concentrates on
offshore sailing and the latter covers coastwise
sailing. There is so much information packed
into these two volumes that you can get sucked
in and lost for days. Questions you never
thought of asking are answered, and details
usually forgotten in most books are dragged out
into the open and examined. You would
probably have to read scores of books to extract
the information found in these two.

"Cruising" is divided into three parts — The
Yacht and Her Gear, Seamanship and
Navigation, Miscellanea — and is followed up
with three appendixes. It's impossible to list
everything in the book, but some of the subjects
covered are: hulls, construction, rigs, rigging,
ropework, ground tackle, cruising yachts,
maneuvering, sail handling, weather, tides, heavy
weather handling, engines, dinghys and ship's
business. Worthy of note is Hiscock's
bibliography (in this volume and in "Voyaging")
which is annotated. Too many books leave out
this essential detail, an extremely useful one for
those who want to read on.

"Voyaging" is divided into two parts — The
Ocean-going Yacht and Her Gear, and Voyaging
— and has three appendixes. Subjects include
hulls, construction, rigs, sails, self steering,
equipment, examples of notable ocean-going
yachts, planning the voyage, seamanship,
navigation and port details. Hiscock is an expert
photographer and processes and prints his own
film. As a result, he has included a chapter on
photography afloat that should interest
photography buffs. "Voyaging" repeats quite a
bit of the information found in "Cruising,"
which cannot be avoided, but essentially it is a
different book.

Since these books are British, there might be
a little confusion in terminology, but not as
much as in most British books not intended for
overseas audiences. For instance, Hiscock refers
to British navigational publications when he
talks about piloting and navigation, which will
be a problem for American readers. But on the
other side of the coin, sail handling, boat
management, fitting out, etc., all use a universal
language.

—PHS

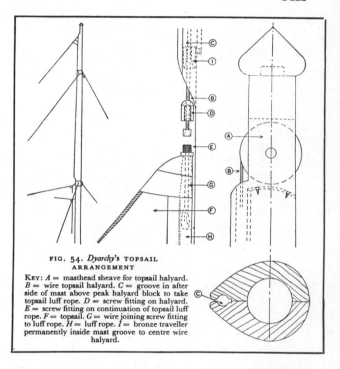

FIG. 54. _Dyarchy's_ TOPSAIL
ARRANGEMENT

KEY: _A_ = masthead sheave for topsail halyard.
_B_ = wire topsail halyard. _C_ = groove in after
side of mast above peak halyard block to take
topsail luff rope. _D_ = screw fitting on halyard.
_E_ = screw fitting on continuation of topsail luff
rope. _F_ = topsail. _G_ = wire joining screw fitting
to luff rope. _H_ = luff rope. _I_ = bronze traveller
permanently inside mast groove to centre wire
halyard.

**Sketch and quote from
"Cruising Under Sail"**

In the past many abortive attempts have been made to get yachts
to lie head to wind and sea by streaming sea-anchors from their bows—
I have made such an attempt myself—and even today, when there has
been some clearer thinking on this subject, that is still sometimes
thought to be the best means of survival in a great gale.

This is largely due to the writings of Voss, who used a sea-anchor
successfully in that manner during his long voyages in the canoe
_Tilikum_; but she, like a ship's lifeboat, with which a sea-anchor is
equally effective, had about the same windage and the same draught
forward as aft, and could therefore be made to lie bows on to wind and
sea with the help of a small riding sail set aft. But a normal yacht,
drawing more water aft than she does forward, and having greater
windage forward than she has aft, will not lie like that. No matter how
large the sea-anchor, she is bound to make sternway; her bow, having
less grip than her stern on the still, deep water, is more affected by the
wind, breaking crests and surface drift, so that it falls off to leeward;
the hull pivots on its heel, and eventually takes up a position more or
less beam on to wind and sea (Fig. 48A), just as it will when lying a-hull.
If a riding sail is set aft and sheeted flat, the position may be improved
(Fig. 48B), but even then the yacht will not lie head to wind, though
she may come up occasionally and fall off on the other tack, the sail
flogging dreadfully at times, and the strain on the rudder caused by
sternway being great. By attempting to make the yacht lie bows-on
one is fighting against her natural inclinations and against the elements,
and achieving no good result. It is therefore much better to work with
her in her natural desire to head down wind, and to stream the sea-
anchor—if it must be streamed

*Photo and quote from "Voyaging Under Sail"*

*Buoying the anchor*

The bottoms of many rivers and harbours are foul with the anchors and chains of moorings, some of them long since abandoned, and if his anchor should chance to hook on to one of these the owner may be put to considerable trouble or expense in recovering it, or the anchor and a length of chain may even be lost. If the chain on which the anchor has hooked is a light one, it may be possible to heave it up within reach by means of the yacht's windlass so that a line can be passed beneath it to hold it up while the anchor is lowered away and cleared. But if it is too heavy, or is tightly stretched between two anchors, assistance may have to be sought from the local yacht yard which will probably have a barge capable of lifting the mooring. First, however, it may be worth while to try the following expedient if the anchor is a fisherman. Get two dinghies to row a few yards apart from the yacht's bow towards her anchor, dragging between them a length of light chain with plenty of slack in it; with perseverance the bight of chain may be induced to slide down the cable and to catch on the upstanding fluke of the anchor; when that has been achieved twist the two parts of chain together to minimize the chance of them slipping off the fluke, and by hauling on them it should be possible to lift the anchor clear of the obstruction. This method cannot, of course, be used with a Danforth or C.Q.R. anchor, but it may be possible to get either clear by sailing or

## Cruising Staples

Two fine home-packed staples for the working or pleasure mariner are the following whose preparation was supplied by "National Fisherman" Food Editor Carolyn Kelley.
—DRG

### HOME CURED CORNED BEEF

Use fatter cuts like flank, chuck and rump. Remove bones. Cut in 6" squares uniformly thick. Cool and use quickly as fresh as can be. Don't use frozen meat. For each 50 lbs. of meat use 4 lbs. granulated salt (not iodized). A layer of salt ¼" deep is put in a stone jar or barrel. Pack meat closely in 6"-thick layer. Alternate layers of salt and meat. Put a lot of salt at the top. Let set overnight. In the morning make this brine: For 50-lbs. of meat use 2-lbs. of sugar, 1-oz. of baking soda and 2-oz. of saltpeter. Dissolve in ½-gal. lukewarm water. Add 1½-gals. of cold water. Weigh meat down with a clean stone and make sure that all of the meat is covered with the brine so there will be no spoilage. Keep in a cool place so that sugar won't ferment the brine. (If it should start spoiling take meat out and start all over again after washing off old brine.) Between 28 to 40 days is the length of time for a good cure. Keep meat in brine until used or you can remove it and smoke or can it.

### SALTING PORK

Cut slabs of pork 6" x 4" and about 2" thick. Make a brine of salt (not iodized) and water thick enough to float a potato. Make a layer of the pork in the brine and salt about ¼" thick. Make alternating layers of salt and pork. Salt the top heavily and weight down. (Weight with a plate with a large stone on top.) This should be made in a barrel or stone crock. Keeps indefinitely.

## Freeze Dried Food

I remember the childish amazement I felt upon discovering that air was something, not nothing. A few years later I discovered that food was mostly water, usually 80% or more, and again I was amazed. Amazement has turned to satisfaction about the air and to frustration over the food. The experience of a hundred-mile hike with a 75-lb. pack, a dumped canoe in fast deep channel or a small tender sailboat with a two-week supply of food that is 90% water aboard becomes a supremely dumb situation. Using freeze dried food may not be the cheapest way to eat, but it is a very tasty one and comfortable all out of proportion to its extra cost.

Stow-a-way sells several brand-name freeze dried foods, including their own, and the nine pages of small print listing what is available will have you consulting "Larousse Gastronomique" as readily as the more humble trail and galley guides. They offer not only the foods, but a line of quality equipment, expedition services and packing as well.

—GP

Stow-A-Way Sports Industries
166 Cushing Highway (Rte. 3A)
Cohasset, Mass. 02025

● **"Sailing Alone Around the World"** by Joshua Slocum.
**Sheridan House, New York.**
**1899 (repr. 1972), 294 pp., illustrated, $7.50.**

This is the book, and the man, that really began it all. The number of people influenced by Slocum is legion; the number of words written on the man, his boat (the Spray) and his book is fantastic. If Helen's was the face that launched a thousand ships, then Slocum's tale of his cruise sired a thousand voyages. His boat has been copied scores of times, his writing style is at the root of many books that followed and his name can be found everywhere.

Just recently, I noticed a new company with the name Josh Slocum Productions, and I even have a friend who named his dog after the good Captain. For myself, I can remember the day, the location and the weather when I bought the book, facts which I couldn't tell you about any other book I own.

Slocum was the first man to sail around the world alone, doing it from 1895 to 1898 in a derelict oyster sloop that he rebuilt himself. The voyage was unparalleled at the time, and the book he wrote about the exploit is considered a classic, not only as a sea story, but also as a piece of literature. If you are going to read only one small-boat adventure story, I recommend that it be this.

A few words about editions: The edition listed here is a reprint of the original 1899 edition, including the wonderful illustrations by Thomas Fogarty and George Varian. A

**178**

paperback version of the original edition, including the illustrations, is available from Dover Publications, New York, at $2.00. Another paperback edition that includes Slocum's "Voyage of the Liberdade" is published by Collier, New York, at $1.25. In addition, the complete text can be found in "The Voyages of Joshua Slocum," edited by Walter Magnes Teller and published by Rutgers University Press, N.J., at $10.

After you've read "Sailing Alone Around the World," you'll probably want to read more about Slocum:

**"Joshua Slocum"** by Walter Teller
**Rutgers University Press, N.J.**
**1971, 253 pp., illustrated, index, sources, $9.**

This biography was originally published in 1956 as "The Search for Captain Slocum" and has been revised as a result of the discovery of more biographical details by the author.

**"Captain Joshua Slocum"** by Victor Slocum.
**Sheridan House, New York.**
**1950, 384 pp., illustrated, index, $10.**

A biography by Slocum's son.

● **"In the Wake of the Spray"** by Kenneth E. Slack.
**Rutgers University Press, N.J.**
**1966, 274 pp., illustrated, index, notes, $7.50.**

An analysis of the design and performance of the Spray and descriptions of the many copies of that boat.

—PHS

● **"Deep Sea Sailing"** by Erroll Bruce.
**John de Graff, Tuckahoe, N.Y.**
**1967, (rev. ed.), 248 pp., index, illustrated, $10.**

● **"Heavy Weather Sailing"** by K. Adlard Coles.
**John de Graff, Tuckahoe, N.Y.**
**1967, 304 pp., index, illustrated, $12.50.**

Two books on the same subject: going to sea in small boats, with the emphasis on the more hair-raising aspects. The way the authors talk matter-of-factly about the "ultimate" wave merely adds more horror to the tale. Bruce and Coles are both highly experienced ocean passage-makers, and what they have to say is not tainted by armchair sailoring. Both men are British and, as the British are notorious for exhausting a subject, they do just that. The difference between the two books is in approach. Coles relies on the case-history method of getting his points across, while Bruce's style is more textbookish. Both men are excellent writers.

"Heavy Weather Sailing" is a collection of descriptions of storms weathered by Coles, though other sailors' experiences are described as well if they have the learning value. Coles' technique is simple: he describes the boat involved, the people involved, the development of the weather, the results of the storm and then draws conclusions from the experience. The last two chapters sum it all up with a discussion of "The Meteorology of Depressions" by Alan Watts, an experienced yachtsman who is also a meteorologist, and "Heavy Weather Conclusions" by Coles. The excellent appendixes cover wave theory, freak waves, yacht design and construction and rigs.

"Deep Sea Sailing" is more of a practical book, with the emphasis on offshore boat design, rigs, emergency repairs, safety precautions, crews, provisions, keeping watch, etc. Bruce has distilled his years of experience into a guide to sailing offshore. He differs from Coles in that he doesn't dwell solely on foul weather, though every piece of knowledge he

_Contd. on next page_

_Contd. from preceding page_

imparts is aimed at safety and survival offshore in the worst weather possible.

I especially like the way he puts his finger on a problem, as when he talks about monomania: "It is a common failing among skippers in small craft . . . to try to fight the battle single-handed, whether it is a battle against the elements or some racing rival." Out of the dozen or so small boats I have crewed at one time or another, 12 of them were skippered by such a character.

It is interesting that both authors treat in detail a storm in the Gulf Stream during May 1950. Both were participants — Coles in Cohoe and Bruce in Samuel Pepys. Other yachts in on the action were Mokoia and Vertue XXXV, skippered by the renowned Humphrey Barton. It is rare that two accounts of the same storm in the same location by two able observers can be found. (Actually, there are three. Barton describes his experience in the book, Vertue XXXV.)

—PHS

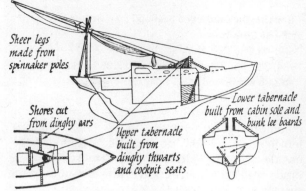

Fig. V, 7. Preparation for rigging jury mast at sea

_Individual idiosyncrasies._

Different people vary greatly in the foods they like, their habits of eating and the quantity they need to consume. Dislikes may be due to some ridiculous chance like being slapped by a nanny at the age of two while eating porridge, for throwing a cup of milk at the cat, since when the distaste for porridge has persisted; eating faster or slower than the normal may be due to well-established habit and the variety of quantity needed may be due to some minor metabolism. Whatever the causes, this variety in human need exists and must be allowed for when planning the food requirements, particularly in a long race when it is the caterer's problem to ensure that all the crew eat enough to sustain them for the powerful effort required.

**Above from "Deep Sea Sailing"**
**Below from "Heavy Weather Sailing"**

179

26. Bernard Moitessier describes the seas which _Joshua_ encountered in the South Pacific as 'breaking without interruption from 650 to nearly 1,000 ft.' He ran under bare pole taking them 15° to 20° on the quarter to avoid being pitchpoled. The yacht was of steel construction, steered from within a steel cupola. _Photo: de Lange._

A Periwinkle
(*Littorina littorea*).

●"Stalking the Blue-Eyed Scallop" by
 Euell Gibbons.
David McKay Co., N.Y.
1964, 332 pp., illustrated, index, $7.95 hardbound,
 $2.95 softbound.

All of the following have something in common: coon oyster, razor clam, mussel, left-handed whelk, dog whelk, digger wedge, cockle, rough piddock, lancelet, sea lettuce, orach and sour sorrel. Give up? They're edible sea life.

This book will astound you. Hundreds of living things you've seen around the sea that you've never eaten are, it turns out, not only edible but delicious. Gibbons knows his way around the subject so well I'll lay you odds that, if you follow his advice, you can live on seafood, seaweed and shellfish alone for weeks at a time without spending a dime. Not only can it be done, but you'll love it, because Gibbons has a way of making the most distasteful-looking stuff (try goose barnacles) sound like ambrosia from the gods.

He does what the writer of good pornography tries desperately to get you to do: slaver over a juicy morsel. But don't take my word for it. Read pages 92-97 in chapter 9 (Transcendental Seafood Combination) on how to have a clambake, and then try not to do it. My wife read that section at 10 p.m. one August evening and had to be physically restrained from rushing down to the beach to dig a steaming pit.

180

Other books by Gibbons and the same publisher, of the same quality and the same approach, are "Stalking the Wild Asparagus" ($7.95 hardbound, $2.95 softbound), "Stalking the Healthful Herbs" ($8.95 hardbound, $2.95 softbound), and "Beachcomber's Handbook" ($5.50). The latter is the author's description of his successful effort to live for three years in Hawaii on wild food he harvested himself.

—PHS

Wing-shell (*Strombus gigas*), one seventh natural size.

Abalone, or Ear-shell.

**From "Stalking the Blue-Eyed Scallop"**

AMERICA is blessed with many kinds of large edible gastropods that are easily available to the beachcomber. The fact that many Americans reject these perfectly delicious seafoods, because of an entirely illogical and unreasonable prejudice, should not bother us, indeed we should be glad such prejudice exists, for when everyone discovers what a good thing he has been missing, these creatures will become rare and expensive instead of being available in their present abundance. These seafoods are eagerly sought and highly appreciated in many countries, and immigrants from those countries long ago discovered that our American gastropods were just as delicious as the ones they had left behind. Whelks sometimes appear on big city markets in this country, but they are sold only to those discriminating immigrants from countries where the large, snail-like creatures are eaten.

It is hard to understand this American prejudice against eating snail-like mollusks, for this prejudice did not exist in any of the countries from which the majority of Americans came. Nor did the early settlers find it among the Indians over here, for these aborigines freely ate all these creatures and in some instances seemed to prefer them to other kinds, as the great shell mounds or "kitchen middens" they left behind show. Even in modern America this prejudice is inconsistent, for the conch is widely eaten in the South, while on the West Coast the Abalone is considered a delicacy and sold at luxury prices, and both these creatures have single, coiled shells and are definitely within the snail-like division of gastropods. If you are infected with this prejudice, the easiest way to cure it is to sample a well-cooked dish made of the flesh of one of these creatures.

The Common Whelk (*Buccinum undatum*). 1/3

"Smoked Fish" by Johnie H. Crance.
Fact Sheet L-1043
Texas A&M University
Agricultural Extension Service
College Station, Tex.

"How to Freeze and Store
Seafoods at Home,"
by Johnnie H. Crance and Sally E. Springer.
Texas A&M University
Agricultural Extension Service
College Station, Tex.

These two excellent pamphlets are aimed at Texas consumers, but readers beyond the Lone Star State still find valuable information here. "Smoked Fish" goes into the technical details for preparing and smoking fish but does not provide mechanical details for building smokers. However, there is an excellent bibliography which includes several sources of this information. "How to Freeze, Etc." Uses drawings, tables and text to provide the consumer with the basic skills needed to assure one's getting the best from any seafood. Emphasis is on careful handling, good sanitation and proper storage. Its theme is what we've always believed: Seafood is a delicacy, and should thus be treated delicately. Here's how.

—DRG

Chub, p. 229.　Smelt, p. 1247.

**"Fishes of the Gulf of Maine"**
by Henry B. Bigelow and William C. Schroeder.
USGPO 1953, 577 pp., $13 from
Museum of Comparative Zoology,
Harvard University.
Oxford Street, Cambridge, Mass. 02139

Over the years we've had a copy of this book, we've enjoyed it as much as any we've owned. That's saying a lot for a book that is (a) written by a couple of fisheries scientists, (b) deals in commercial statistics, biology and other normally dry facts about various species of fish, and (c) is published by the U.S. Government Printing Office. Fortunately, a, b and c are overwhelmed by d, which stands for "delightful."

If you can imagine a thorough scientific work couched in the language of almost casual conversation, you'll get the first insight as to why "Fishes of the Gulf of Maine" is something special. Started in 1912 as a joint U.S. Bureau of Fisheries/Harvard University survey, carried on for several years with much of the fisheries material prepared by W.W. Welsh and completed and published by H.B. Bigelow in 1925, the work was revised and greatly added to by Bigelow and Schroeder after World War II and reissued in its present form. However, the relatively small printing was gone by 1961, so the Woods Hole Oceanographic Institution and the Museum of Comparative Zoology contracted for a photo-offset printing of the book in 1965 and it is this version which is now available for $13 (a bit above the $4.25 hardcover book sold by the government in 1953).

But "Fishes" is still well worth it. If you want to know about underwater livestock in that huge bight between Nova Scotia and Cape Cod, this is the book to turn to first. It's all there: Fact and theory, reports by commercial and sport fishermen, basic biology of the many fishes both common and unusual, how they are caught, their value to man and to other fishes and their migrations and availability. Excellent line drawings of each species are a great assist in making identifications. A 16-page bibliography as well as a Common Index and an Index to Scientific Names add to the ease of using the book and extending one's studies beyond its own meaty pages.

Any commercial fisherman working the waters of the Northeast is lacking an important tool if he does not have this book. Sport fishermen will find in it a tackle-box's worth of information about their quarry. As for the casual reader; well, let's just say this is **the** best scientific work we've ever read. And read. And read.

—DRG

Drawings on this page from "Fishes . . . "

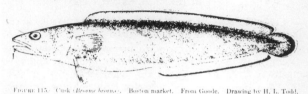

FIGURE 115.— Cusk (_Brosme brosme_). Boston market. From Goode. Drawing by H. L. Todd.

**"Readings in Marine Ecology"**
by James W. Nybakken.
Harper and Row, 1971, $9.

There is an abundance of general works on general ecology for the general reader; that is, myths about myths for myths. Those who are truly concerned about ecology should become knowledgeable about the actual specific processes that make Nature what it is. To continue to understand ecology in terms of generalities and conclusions sooner or later makes us victims of the obscurantists that are flying about; religio-eco mystics, industrial apologists and tsk-tskers. It is better to **know** what it's about.

This book of readings is a technical potpourri of papers on planktonic, benthic, demersal, intertidal and tropical ecology. There is a lot of tabular and statistically derived data. No question, a lot of it dull. But if you take the various data and chew on it a bit, it takes on an intellectual flavor that by and by becomes a solid taste that instantly identifies the fraud, the shoddy and half-thought. If you can figure out what's wrong with the lawn mower, you can figure out what most of these papers are about.

There is a collection of conceptual papers at the end of this book which provides the basic concepts of the field around which specific information can be placed; the principles of selection, diversity, stability, complexity, productivity, etc. We would not think of allowing our education system to "produce" a graduate who could not understand the basics of our cultural life. How is it that we daily "produce" graduates who know absolutely nothing about how the physical and natural world works?

—GP

181

FISHERY BULLETIN OF THE FISH AND WILDLIFE SERVICE

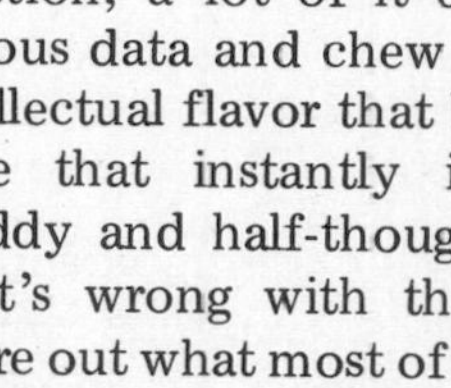

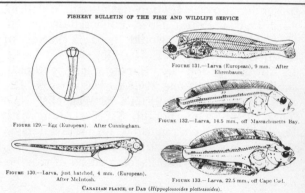

FIGURE 129.— Egg (European). After Cunningham.

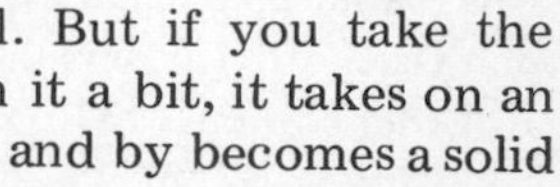

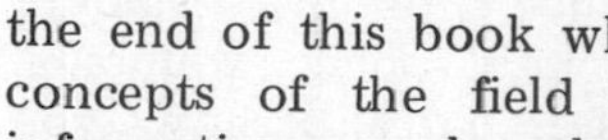

FIGURE 130.— Larva, just hatched, 4 mm. (European). After McIntosh.

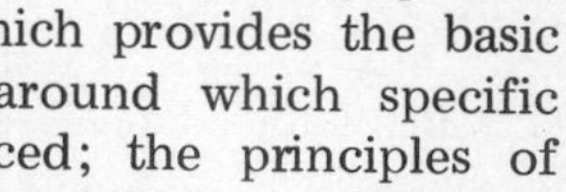

FIGURE 131.— Larva (European), 9 mm. After Ehrenbaum.

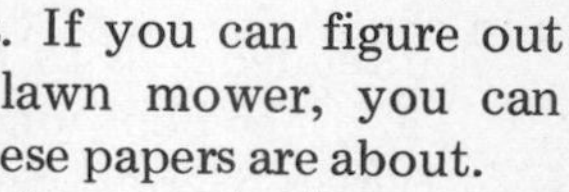

FIGURE 132.— Larva, 14.5 mm., off Massachusetts Bay.

FIGURE 133.— Larva, 22.5 mm., off Cape Cod.

CANADIAN PLAICE, or DAB (_Hippoglossoides platessoides_).

### Marine Articles On Tap

Mystic Seaport publishes "A Bibliography of Periodical Articles on Maritime and Naval History." Each bibliography is in the form of an annual volume containing a compilation of articles pertaining to maritime and naval history. Volumes exist for the years 1970, '71 and '72.

Inaugurated by Dr. Charles Roy Schultz, former librarian at the G. W. Blunt White Library, these bibliographies were begun to complement Dr. Robert Greenhalgh Albion's "Naval & Maritime History, An Annotated Bibliography" (published by the Seaport in 1972) which is limited principally to books. Few of the periodicals which carry articles on maritime history are included in standard indices, making it difficult for a researcher to determine whether or not anything has been written on a given subject. It is the aim of these volumes to fill that important need.

Articles are listed by subject. All people and most places which appeared in either titles or annotations have been included in the subject index. All periodicals and authors have been listed in seperate indices.

Copies of this 88-page document are available at Mystic Seaport Stores at $3 per copy plus 30¢ postage and handling. This is a paperback edition.

**Mystic Seaport**
**Mystic, Conn.**

○ **"The Marlinspike Sailor" by Hervey Garrett Smith.**
**John De Graff, Tuckahoe, N.Y.**
**1971 (3rd edition), 131 pp.,**
     **illustrated, $7.95**

The tendency is to look at this book and say "Aw, another book on knots." Anyone familiar with Hervey Garrett Smith's work would realize right away that this is not entirely true. Smith not only shows you a knot, splice, whipping, lanyard and what-all else, but also shows you what to do with it. On top of that, he shows you how to make a pump, a fascinating anemometer, sail stop bag, canvas deck bucket, deadeye, rope handles, and much more.

There are notes on the make-up and composition of rope, both synthetic and natural fiber, and an excellent section on splicing Samson braided ropes. The diagrams drawn by Smith are of a quality seldom achieved in books of similar subject. If you went out and outfitted your boat with the finer touches described in this book, you would have a vessel of distinction.

Another book by Hervey Garrett Smith, similar in content and style to this one, is "The Arts of the Sailor" (Funk & Wagnalls, New York, 1968, paperbound, $1.75). Along with the marlinespike seamanship, he has chapters on the sailor's vernacular, the technique of reefing, towing procedures and keeping ahead of trouble.

—PHS

**"Naval and Maritime History: An Annotated**
   **Bibliography" by Robert G. Albion.**
**The Marine Historical Association, Mystic, Conn.**
**1972 (4th edition), 370 pp., author index, subject index,**
   **$15 cloth, $5.95 paper.**

A complete bibliography of maritime history that gets bigger and better with each edition; over 5000 entries in this edition. This is for the serious student of nautical literature, since Albion includes a minimum of "atmosphere" books and adventure stories. Books only are covered (including PhD theses), but there is a short section describing maritime journals.

The annotation consists of short statements about selected books; those of particular significance are indentified with an asterisk. Not all books are annotated, however. The major sections of the bibliography are: reference works, merchantmen and warships, captains and crews, maritime science, exploration and expansion, commerce and shipping, navies, special topics. Each section is sub-categorized.

The only shortcoming of this valuable book is that publishers of individual books are omitted. This doesn't matter too much for books out of print, but you will have to look in "Books in Print" to find publishers of those books you might want to buy.

—PHS

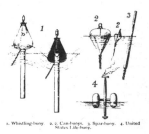

1. Whistling-buoy.  2. 2. Can-buoys.  3. Spar-buoy.  4. United States Life-buoy.

### U.S. Government Publications
### Of Interest To Boatmen And Mariners

Several agencies of the U. S. Government distribute excellent, and cheap, pamphlets, brochures, graphs, charts, even books of information interesting and often vital to an intelligent maritime life. One of the most interesting arrays of available literature comes from a division of the U. S. Department of Commerce. Their pamphlet, "Publications from the NOAA Office of Public Affairs," lists what they have available.

**Office of Public Affairs**
**NOAA**
**Rockville, Md 20852**

**Superintendent of Documents**
**U.S. Government Printing Office**
**Washington, D.C. 20402**

## A Good Place
## To Purchase Marine Gear

We took the catalogs of 11 major marine suppliers and chose 21 items that would typically appear on a boatman's buying list. Only one organization regularly beat the others for price. This is Defender Industries Inc. Not only are their prices better than most, but their service is excellent. Response is fast, they don't backorder you to death and their line is complete, not only for running your boat, but building it as well.

The reason begins with their catalog. It's printed on pulp paper and the pages are jammed. No class, no frills, no nonsense. If you want it, they have it and will sell it to you at a good price.

Defender Industries, Inc.
255 Main St.
New Rochelle, N.Y. 10801

Items from Defender catalog.

# SPRAY URETHANE FOAM
### RIGID - SELF ADHESIVE
### SELF EXTINGUISHING-INSULATING

Two Part System — 1 can of Urethane Lock into 1 can of Activator. Shake until warm, then use. Provides 5 minutes of spraying. Can be used for Floatation. Stop leaks on Hot Pipe. When poured into void it gently expands to fill all crevices. Has density of 1.5 and "K" factor of 1.2.

**Spray Foam makes it easy to get at hard to reach areas.** (N28-4)

12 oz. can = ¾ Cu. Ft. $4.25

Excellent as a noise deadener

## FLOATATION FOAM IN PLACE

A new, highly useful pour-in-place rigid poly-urethane safety foam. A two-part, pre-polymer system, wherein components are mixed together to start a chemical reaction producing uniform light weight foam. It has low water permeability and thermo conductivity, and offers sound-deadening and structural qualities useful in all craft. It will adhere to any surface clean of oil or grease. After adhesion it is resistant to solvents, oil and grease. May be painted or covered with polyester and epoxy resins.

MIXING IS QUITE SIMPLE, MIX EQUAL PARTS OF A & B AT ROOM TEMPERATURE (65-70 DEGREES), STIR VIGOROUSLY FOR APPROXIMATELY 30 SECONDS UNTIL LIQUID TURNS MILKY, AND RAPIDLY POUR INTO VOID. USE SMALL BATCHES UNTIL FAMILIAR WITH PROCEDURE. HARDENS IN ONE MINUTE, FINAL CURE IN TWENTY MINUTES. IMMEDIATE OR LATER POURING OF NEXT BATCH PERMITTED. ONE QUART WEIGHS 2½ POUNDS, AND SHOULD YIELD 1.2 CUBIC FEET, WITH A BUOYANCY FACTOR OF 70 TO 80 POUNDS. THE GALLON IS 10 POUNDS.

BETWEEN FRAMES — AGAINST TRANSOM — UNDER SEATS — UNDER FLOOR BOARDS — IN THE BOW

| | | |
|---|---|---|
| 2 1/2 lbs. (1qt.) $4.90 | 5 lbs. (1/2 GAL.) $8.95 | MIX AND POUR IN WELL VENTILATED AREA. AVOID PROLONGED INHALATION IF SKIN IS SENSITIVE USE GLOVES. |
| 10 lbs. (1 GAL.) $15.50 | 50 lbs. (5 GALS) $69.95 | |

100 lbs. - 10 gals. $125.00 (N28-2)

## RIGID EXPANDED POLYSTYRENE FLOATATION AND INSULATION FOAM

| SHEET SIZES | THICKNESS | PRICE | |
|---|---|---|---|
| 24" x 96" | 1" | $4.95 | |
| 24" x 96" | 2" | 8.75 | (N28-3) |
| 48" x 96" | 1" | 8.75 | |
| 48" x 96" | 2" | 16.50 | |

Self Extinguishing — Marine Groth Resistant — Cannot Rust, Rot or Deteriorate in Fresh or Salt water. Will not take on water when damaged or punctured. Extremely Low "K" Factor — Joined with Epoxy Putty or Epoxy Resin — Stock Sizes indicated below — Other sizes from 3/8" Thick to 48" Width by 144" L. On order.

(This material is somewhat softer than Styrofoam by Dow) (and somewhat tenderer)

**ALL PRICES ARE FOR N.Y. WAREHOUSE — SPECIAL SIZES F.O.B. FACTORY — EXTRA PACKING CHARGE OF 10% PACKED FOR SHIPPING — OTHERWISE WILL BE SHIPPED UNPACKED AT NO EXTRA CHARGE — SOME POSSIBILITY OF DAMAGE IN SHIPPING**

SAME MATERIAL AVAILABLE IN LOG FORM, SIMILAR TO DOW STYROFOAM, AT LOWER COST THAN STYROFOAM, BUT ONLY QUANTITY ORDERS ACCEPTED. PLEASE WRITE FOR QUOTES.

# Stoves
## and
## Heaters

_Good ship's stove,_
_How do I love thee?_
_Let me count the ways._
_Bad ship's stove,_
_How I do hate you!_
_Let me scream and shout,_
_Dry mine eyes and_
_Add you to the mooring cable._

_(Old Viking saying)_

### By George Putz

There is something in the ship's stove that can be profound. Whether for heating or cooking, or both, the ship's stove is a technical, existential, aesthetic and sometimes spiritual focus aboard a boat. Do you know what I mean? Other areas in this category are the wheel (right?), the knightheads and forward winches (right?), the ship's clock and so on; all those things aboard a boat that command your direct, regular engagement. Boatmen in northern waters become especially attached to their stoves and there is real pride in owning and becoming competent with a fine one.

I suppose that alcohol and gas stoves now vastly outnumber those using wood, coal and kerosene and this is understandable; though the understanding comes from psychology and market-economics more than reasoning. Please do not misunderstand me. Alcohol and gas stoves are now **very** good, most of the poorly designed and constructed ones having eliminated themselves. But both do tie you to the marine supplier and the alcohol "required for marine use" is a fantastic rip-off; indeed, it is an outrageous scandal!

All stoves have drawbacks and it is a matter of choosing which you care to live with. We'll readily admit to a bias. But it seems to us that the main reason why coal/wood is today the least common cooking fuel on board boats is that people somehow associate these stoves with primitiveness, harder times ("the bad old days"), poverty and, therefore, being dirty. This is nonsense.

Seasoned hardwood pieces, hard coal or charcoal can be pre-packaged into starter, medium and full-heat bags before placing them aboard and a fiberglassed bunker is easy to keep clean

and tidy. In any case, the heat of a coal/wood stove is incomparable, not only for general heat but all cooking, especially baking. To be sure, such stoves are most practical north of Massachusetts Bay on the East Coast and San Francisco Bay on The West Coast. From these areas northward, however, there is no better ship's companion. Here are some we really like:

**Shipmate Stove Div.**
**Richman Ring Co.**
**Souderton, Pa.**

Other quality marine stove manufacturers must wince when they hear the name Shipmate. It is a standard in the field and everyone in this part of Maine who doesn't have one, wants one. It's one of those cases where a trade name has become the generic name for the product. Even though you're drinking "UN—," you're still on a "Coke*-date." Shipmates are made for all purposes, in all sizes and finishes for all fuels. They are excellent.

The SHIPMATE Skippy will burn any solid fuel. It is also available equipped with a simple natural draft oil burner for use with kerosene or fuel oil. It is heavy cast iron with a wrought iron pot rail. The flat top with two removeable covers will hold a coffee pot and a skillet. It weighs 38 pounds.

184

**Fatsco Stoves**
251 N. Fair Ave.
Benton Harbor, Mich. 49022

Fatsco stoves put out an enormous amount of good comfortable heat for their diminutive size. They are handy, easy-to-install, attractive, efficient and very inexpensive. They are ideal as a back-up heat stove for persons with liquid or gas cookstoves, especially for the northern boatman who commissions early and hauls late. For that little empty place on your bulkhead...

## FATSCO STOVES - PRICE LIST

|                  | No.     | Wt.      | Price   |
|------------------|---------|----------|---------|
| Trail Blazer Kit | 50      | 24 lbs.  | $19.00  |
| Woodsman         | 25      | 27 lbs.  | 22.20   |
| Heart of the Camp| 100     | 68 lbs.  | 39.00   |
| Buddy            | 200     | 31 lbs.  | 23.95   |
| Chummy           | 300     | 23 lbs.  | 21.50   |
| Midget           | 300-M   | 14 lbs.  | 12.95   |
| Tiny-Tot         | 400     | 15 lbs.  | 15.00   |
| Pet              | 450     | 13 lbs.  | 13.50   |
| Little Pal       | 600     | 85 lbs.  | 44.85   |
| Pet 2-Lid        | 450-2L  | 21 lbs.  | 22.75   |
| Tiny Tot 2-Lid   | 400-2L  | 22 lbs.  | 23.40   |

Note: 400-2L and 450-2L are combination heating and cooking stoves. Top size 9" x 14½" O. A.  (Stove pipe round, exactly 3")

Fits the much used 100-lb. grease and oil drums. Most all filling stations dispose of them. Drum diameter: 13⅞" x 23¼" long (approx.) Door is almost as large as drum and will take large chunks of wood.

Kit contains: Door, frame, legs, hinge, draft-regulator, handle, braces, and 6" smoke collar. All parts except drum and elbow furnished. Weight packed, 24 lbs. approx. The Kit $19.00

For a larger Drum Stove get our WOODSMAN. Fits both 30 or 50 gallon drum. (6" smoke pipe) Wt. packed 27 lbs. The Kit $22.20. The finest barrel stove made.

**All items from Fatsco catalog.**

185

## LITTLE BEAUTIES

To fill those small spaces with comfort and utility

Efficient - Dependable

| No. 450 | No. 450-2L | No. 400 | No. 400-2L |
|---------|-----------|---------|-----------|
| **The PET** | **2-Lid PET** | **The TINY TOT** | **2-Lid TINY TOT** |
| With Stainless Steel Shield and S-S Body. See S-S price list. | Cooking Top 9" x 14½" Made with S-S or regular body | Stainless or regular body Carrying bail optional both models | WITH SEA RAIL: Now made with round bars; not shown Cooking Top 9" x 14½" |
| Ht. 11½" Shield 10½" dia. Wt. 10½ lb. | Ht. 13" Wt. 20½ lb. | Ht. 14" Shield 10½" dia. Wt. 10½ lb. | Ht. 15½" Wt. 21½ lb. |

Portland Stove Foundry Co.
57 Kennebec St.
Portland, Me. 04104

This grand old New England firm makes two models of small ship's cookstoves and they are absolute gems! In fact, if your requirements call for a really small unit burning wood/coal, one of these units should be seriously considered. They are built well and are the most attractive stoves you can buy.

Items from Portland Stove catalog.

# 212 "HOLIDAY" SHIP STOVE

### DIMENSIONS

| | |
|---|---|
| Weight (uncrated) | 188 lbs. |
| Weight (crated) | 206 lbs. |
| Overall Height (including legs and rail) | 21¾" |
| Height floor to top of smoke collar | 19¼" |
| Height of top rail from covers | 3¾" |
| Height of legs | 5" |
| Width (front to back) | 19½" |
| Length (overall) | 23½" |
| OVEN: Width | 11" |
|     Height | 8½" |
|     Depth | 11" |
| FIREBOX: Size Length | 9½" |
|     Width | 5½" |
|     Depth to covers | 8" |

Smoke collars straps — 14" for 4½" pipe
16" for 5" pipe
PIPE may be reduced to 4" both models.
— ALL Cast Iron Construction —
Samples on request.
Stove Black or Porcelain Finish — Red, Green,
Blue, Yellow, Coppertone, Avocado.

186

# 210 "HOLIDAY" SHIP STOVE

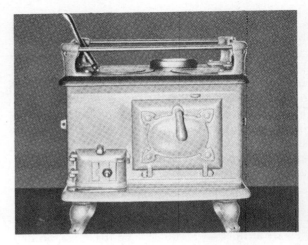

### DIMENSIONS

| | |
|---|---|
| Weight (uncrated) | 119 lbs. |
| Weight (crated) | 134 lbs. |
| Overall Height (including legs and rail) | 20¼" |
| Height floor to top of smoke collar | 18" |
| Height of top rail from covers | 3" |
| Height of legs | 5" |
| Width (front to back) | 13" |
| Length (overall) | 19" |
|     Height | 6½" |
| OVEN: Width | 8⅝" |
|     Depth | 9" |
| FIREBOX: Size Length | 10 3/16" |
|     Width | 5⅜" |
|     Depth to covers | 7½" |

Smoke collars straps — 14" for 4½" pipe
16" for 5" pipe
PIPE may be reduced to 4" both models.
— ALL Cast Iron Construction —
Samples on request.
Stove Black or Porcelain Finish — Red, Green,
Blue, Yellow, Coppertone, Avocado.

**PORTLAND STOVE FOUNDRY CO.**
57 Kennebec Street, Portland, Maine 04104
207-773-3864

Dagon of the Assyrians.—Bas-re-
lief from Khorsabad.

## Vent That Cooker

When charcoal burns, it produces deadly carbon monoxide. This is no problem in a properly vented stove, but if you've just used the hibachi on the fantail to cook supper steaks and are now thinking that it might be a good idea to use the softly glowing coals to heat the cabin — don't. It's not a good idea and can, in fact, be deadly. Well-burning charcoal gives off little in the way of fumes you can smell, but carbon monoxide is odorless and is a major product of charcoal combustion. In the close quarters of a small-boat cabin those few coals that did such a good job on your steak could do an equally good job cooking your goose. Leave the hibachi topside and heat your cabin only with a properly vented heating device.

—DRG

**Washington Stove Works**
P.O. Box 687
Everett, Wash. 98201

The Washington Stove line is a beautifully built, tough, no-nonsense line of stoves that has earned the respect and gratitude of serious professional mariners. They have more models for more galley requirements than any other manufacturer in the business. Indeed, they are in the business not only of supplying galleys, but planning and building custom equipment for them as well. Their line of marine electrical stoves is especially notable.

—GP

All items from Washington Stove catalog.

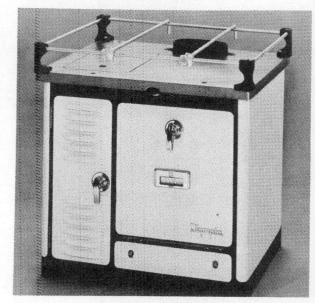

THE OLYMPIC L-10 MARINE ENGINE. A lightweight economy porcelain enameled model with polished iron top. Equipped with a 7" natural draft burner and carburetor (float valve). Operates on kerosene or light stove oil only. Porcelain enameled oven controlled by slide draft control. Thermometer on oven door. Cleanout located under the oven.

### MIDGET II

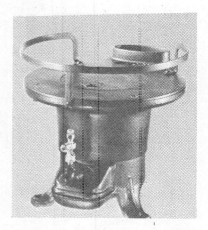

| | NEPTUNE† | | | MIDGET | |
|---|---|---|---|---|---|
| MODEL NO. | IA | 2A | 15A | I | II |
| TOP SIZE | 20¾"x15" | 24½"x17" | 24½"x22" | 12½" x 16½" | |
| HEIGHT O.A. | 22" | 23" | | 11¼" | |
| BODY | 14" | 15" | | 9¾" | |
| HEIGHT LEGS | | 3½" | | | |
| OVEN SIZE | 9" x 9½" x 7" | 11" x 11½" x 8" | 11" x 15½" x 8" | | |
| FLUE SIZE | | 5" | | 4" | |
| WEIGHT | 116 lbs | 160 lbs | 197 lbs | 31 lbs | 34 lbs |
| SHIP. WT. | 143 lbs | 188 lbs | 237 lbs | 35 lbs | 38 lbs |
| WOOD/COAL | YES | YES | | YES | |
| STOVE OIL | YES | YES | | | YES |
| KEROSENE | YES | YES | | | YES |
| DIESEL | | YES | | | |

### NEPTUNE†

# CUSTOM

Washington Stove Works has been building special marine ranges for nearly a century. Shipowners, builders and designers rely on our ability to solve difficult space, weight and food handling problems. Our experience, our reputation for craftsmanship, our knowledge of the sea uniquely qualify us to design and build marine ranges that get special jobs done in a special way. And, equally important is the fact that our experience and facilities enable us to turn out the finest custom marine ranges at a reasonable price. After all, anybody can build a good custom range if you don't care how much it costs. ■ Sailboats, tugboats, fishing boats and pleasure boats, tankers and cruisers—even if your galley happens to be on an ocean liner, Washington Stove Works' experience and know-how can help you. Whatever your choice of heat (wood or coal, gas or oil, electricity or even micro wave elements) we use the best materials available to handle the job. Only the products and careful craftsmanship which have been tested against the corrisive elements of the sea are used on all of our marine products. Contact one of our local dealers for a quotation or write direct to our Marine Products Division outlining your plans.* Chances are that we have already built similar units, and, the experience is burning a hole in our pocket.

*Please include as much information as possible, dimensions, voltage, AC or DC, etc.

187

## Stove Parts

Those with liquid-fueled stoves will on occasion want to replace parts. In cases where the manufacturers do not want to engage consumers directly, the consumer can get rather badly hungdown with peanut butter and jelly. A firm which offers a complete line of stove parts, as well as blowers, ports, sundry marine odds and ends, is the E.J. Willis Co.

The E.J. Willis Co.  —GP
Middleville, N.Y.

From Willis catalog.

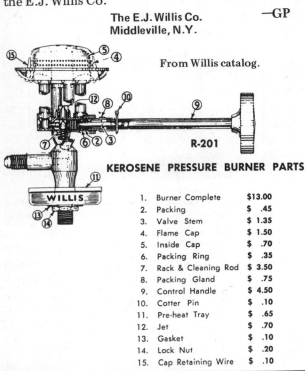

R-201

**KEROSENE PRESSURE BURNER PARTS**

| | | |
|---|---|---|
| 1. | Burner Complete | $13.00 |
| 2. | Packing | $ .45 |
| 3. | Valve Stem | $ 1.35 |
| 4. | Flame Cap | $ 1.50 |
| 5. | Inside Cap | $ .70 |
| 6. | Packing Ring | $ .35 |
| 7. | Rack & Cleaning Rod | $ 3.50 |
| 8. | Packing Gland | $ .75 |
| 9. | Control Handle | $ 4.50 |
| 10. | Cotter Pin | $ .10 |
| 11. | Pre-heat Tray | $ .65 |
| 12. | Jet | $ .70 |
| 13. | Gasket | $ .10 |
| 14. | Lock Nut | $ .20 |
| 15. | Cap Retaining Wire | $ .10 |

188

## Alcohol Conversion

If you prefer the less volatile alcohol stove to your present gasoline model, a low-cost device is now being offered that appears to convert your stove with little difficulty. The manufacturer claims the following:

Coleman and Sears gasoline camp stoves can now be operated on alcohol with a new conversion kit by Nashcraft. With this kit and one of the popular low-cost camp stoves, boat and camper owners can enjoy the safety and cleanliness of alcohol cooking at a fraction of the cost of conventional alcohol stoves. The kit is designed for new and used two-burner Coleman models 425E and 413G and Sears models 476.72301 and 476.72302. The kit consists of two stainless steel snap-on parts that modify the vapor generator and carburetor of the stove for alcohol operation.

Also in the kit is an asbestos pre-heating wick, a polyethylene priming bottle, a self-adhesive decal indicating conversion to alcohol and a complete instruction booklet. The kit can be installed in seconds without tools. The converted stove uses the original fuel tank and operates on both burners with ethyl alcohol, marine alcohol stove fuel or shellac thinner. The stove can be changed back to gasoline operation in seconds. Kit price is $4.95 and is available at hardware and accessory dealers or postpaid from Nashcraft Marine Products, 32906 Avenida Descanso, San Juan Capistrano, Calif. 92675.

## Cheap Heat

All that waste oil that is drained from the crankcase of your car or marine engine has to go somewhere. It may go into a tank for disposal in a dump, may end up on a gravel road, may eventually find its way to the sea — or may produce heat and hot water in the Clean Air Waste Oil Burner and Water Heater, Model PB-10.

"According to the manufacturer, this model is capable of burning a broad range of waste oils at a rate of up to two gallons per hour (10 litres per hour). Since atomization is not employed in this new process, this unit can consume any residue which can be pumped with positive displacement gear pump. Wastes with up to 10% of water or a high BS&W content can also be handled without interfering with proper operation of the unit. The unit helps eliminate oily wastes which might otherwise contribute to water pollution.

The PB-10 Clean Air Waste Oil Burner provides heat recoveries of 80,000 to 140,000 BTU/hr. (20,000 to 35,000 k cal/hr.). The hot water may be employed for industrial or domestic uses or to provide space heat. These units are being used to provide hot water for commercial buildings, metal processing, plating, chemical

Model PB-10, the oil eater.

processing, textiles, forest products, paper and pulp and mining. They may be readily connected to new or existing central hot water heating tanks, reducing the fuel drawn by existing burners or boilers.

"Space heating uses include all of the conventional requirements plus special applications such as factories, warehouses and numerous other applications requiring an inexpensive source of heat."

**Industrial Products Division**
**Barclay and Company, Inc.**
**500 Sansome St.**
**San Francisco, Ca. 94111**

**⊕ "The Strange Last Voyage of Donald Crowhurst"**
by Nicholas Tomalin and Ron Hall.
Stein and Day, New York.
1970, 317 pp., illustrations, index, $7.95.

This book is a real chiller, especially when you consider that it is a true story. Donald Crowhurst was an entrant in the 1968 non-stop singlehander's race around the world. His craft was a trimaran, Teignmouth Electron, that theoretically was to have been one of the most advanced of its type. But because of the rush to get to sea and into the race, most of the innovations intended by Crowhurst to help him win the race were untested and did not work.

Eight months after he set sail, Teignmouth Electron was found drifting in the South Atlantic, Crowhurst nowhere in sight. His logbooks, diaries, tapes and movies were still aboard, and Tomalin and Hall used them to reconstruct Crowhurst's strange voyage.

I'm not going to tell you what happened. Suffice to say that Alfred Hitchcock would have a difficult time inventing a story like this one. But the thrilling side of this tale is not all. There are lessons to be learned here, not the least one is that planning and attention to detail for a deepwater voyage can mean the difference between success and tragedy. After you get sea fever from "Sailing Alone Around the World," you might temper your enthusiasm with "The Strange Last Voyage of Donald Crowhurst."

—PHS

**"Boats and Harbors"**
Crossville, Tenn. 38555
One year (36 issues)/$2 third class mail/$6 first class.

**"Equipment Advertiser"**
P.O. Box 35287
Minneapolis, Minn. 55435
One year, $4 3rd class (12 issues), $9 1st class (24 issues)

Good buys in boats, work vessels, tools and other marine equipment are to be found in these two unpretentious yellow-sheeted advertising flyers.

"Boats & Harbors" published three times a month, usually runs 16-24 tabolid-sized pages of solid maritime advertising, covering everything from used boats to Navy surplus. For the working mariner, the paper is a virtual "must" as a source of gear at reasonable prices. For the pleasure mariner, there are many great boat buys for the man looking for something special in hull or rig. Winches, generators, hydraulic motors, blocks, turnbuckles, coils of rope and wire, tarps and crankshafts. Man, this is marine commerce in the raw — and readable in itself.

"Equipment Advertiser" leans more toward the land contractor and industrial equipment user, but there is a lot here too for the boatman, yard operator or shipbuilder. Tools of all kinds, light and heavy hauling equipment, engines and parts, surplus specials, chain-rope-cable, they're all here.

One has to be somewhat of a knowledgeable buyer to really take advantage of advertising papers such as these. Shipping costs, shoddy goods, too-great quantities and similar factors can knock the pins from under your apparant "bargains." But awareness of comparative prices, familiarity with items being considered, knowing how to ship at the lowest costs possible and, hopefully, some information on the outfit with whom you are dealing, should put you in the black — by dozens, hundreds or even thousands of dollars.

189

**⊕ "How to Build Boat Trailers"** by Glen L. Witt.
Glen L Marine Designs, Bellflower, Calif.
1971, 92 pp., illustrated, paperbound, $4.

Exactly what the title says it is. The book covers building trailers from the beginning to the end, including how to handle them, and launch and retrieve boats with them. Some of the esoteric subjects discussed (in all the detail you could want) are: axles, springs, wheels, hubs, tires, bearings, brakes, frames, couplers, tongue stands, forms, winches, lights and hitches.

—PHS

# Index

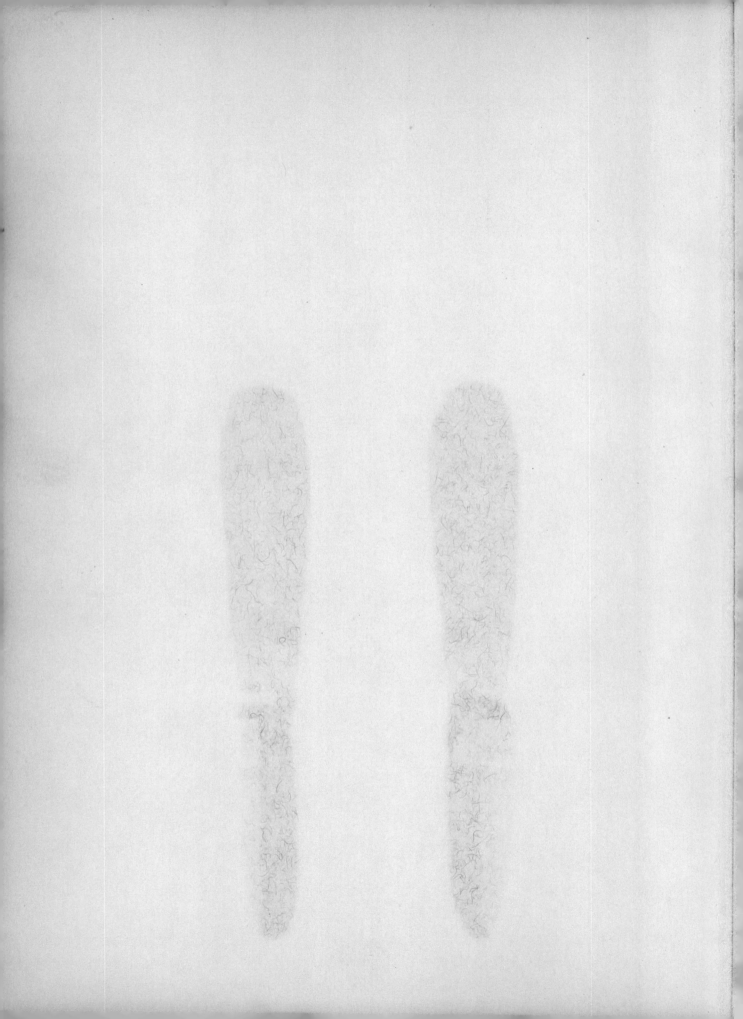

9-2977-1

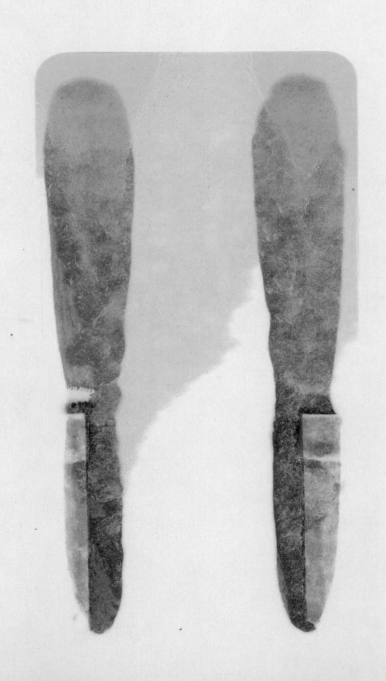

9-2977-1